ANTHROPOLOGY'S GLOBAL HISTORIES

Perspectives on the Global Past

Jerry H. Bentley and Anand A. Yang
SERIES EDITORS

Interactions: Transregional Perspectives on World History
Edited by Jerry H. Bentley, Renate Bridenthal, and Anand A. Yang

Contact and Exchange in the Ancient World
Edited by Victor H. Mair

Seascapes: Maritime Histories, Littoral Cultures, and Transoceanic Exchanges
Edited by Jerry H. Bentley, Renate Bridenthal, and Kären Wigen

Anthropology's Global Histories

The Ethnographic Frontier in German New Guinea, 1870–1935

Rainer F. Buschmann

University of Hawai'i Press
Honolulu

© 2009 University of Hawai'i Press
All rights reserved
Printed in the United States of America

14 13 12 11 10 09   6 5 4 3 2 1

Library of Congress Cataloging-in-Publication Data
Buschmann, Rainer F.
  Anthropology's global histories : the ethnographic frontier in
German New Guinea, 1870–1935 / by Rainer F. Buschmann.
      p.   cm—(Perspectives on the global past)
  Includes bibliographical references and index.
  ISBN 978-0-8248-3184-4 (hard cover : alk. paper)
  1. Anthropology—Papua New Guinea—History.
  2. Anthropology—Research—Papua New Guinea—History.
  I. Title.
  GN671.N5B87 2009
  301.023'953—dc22
                                    2008029221

University of Hawai'i Press books are printed on acid-free
paper and meet the guidelines for permanence and durability
of the Council on Library Resources.

Composed by Santos Barbasa Jr. of the University of Hawai'i Press

Printed by The Maple-Vail Book Manufacturing Group

For my parents

Contents

Acknowledgments

This work originated in the early 1990s, while I was finishing my master's degree in anthropology. The discipline of anthropology was deeply in the throes of the so-called literary turn. In the midst of this intellectual confusion, I enrolled in a fascinating seminar about the Trust Territory of the Pacific Islands taught by Karen Peacock, the librarian of the Pacific Collection at Hamilton Library at the University of Hawai'i. She made the bold suggestion to situate anthropology in a historical context. She further encouraged me to contact David Hanlon at the History department, who quickly introduced me to the field of Pacific Islands history and highlighted its potential to illuminate anthropological studies. He also pointed at the close relationship of my study to world history and encouraged me to work closely with Jerry Bentley. Drs. Bentley and Hanlon provided much-needed guidance as I used a historical perspective to explore important issues in German anthropology. Two other historians were also tremendously important in shaping the work at hand: Herbert Ziegler, who assisted with his expertise in German history, and David Chappell, whose input on Pacific imperial history was of prime importance. This book also greatly benefited from Alan Howard, who instructed me in my first approaches to ethnography.

Financial support for research and writing came from many sources. I received a generous dissertation grant from the Dai Ho Chun Foundation as well as two Trustees' Scholarly Endeavors Program Grants at Hawai'i Pacific University and several faculty development grants at the California State University Channel Islands (CSUCI), including a Martin V. Smith Grant for Scholarly Excellence. A sabbatical leave (2006–2007) from CSU-CI paved the way to bring the manuscript to conclusion.

Numerous individuals aided in the production of this book by supporting my quest for archival sources. Robert Welsch at the Field Museum of Natural History in Chicago provided me with initial insights into the nature of ethnographic collecting in New Guinea and continued to advise me as the project moved further along. In Germany, it was the friendly staff at the Linden Museum in Stuttgart that assisted me in my mission, especially Ingrid Heermann, Ulrich Menter, and Dietrich Schleip. At the Berlin Ethnological Museum Markus Schindlbeck assisted with sources and publications. In Obergünzburg, Ingrid Weiß provided me with information from her personal collection of letters and photographs. The staff at the museums of Bremen, Cologne, Dresden, Hamburg, Leipzig, and Munich as well as the official state and national archives contributed greatly to this endeavor.

I am grateful to my peers who assisted in the development of the work, read the manuscript or parts of it, and made helpful suggestions: Pierre Asselin, Izabela Betlinska, Matti Bunzl, Bill Cummings, Celine Dauverd, Amy Denton, Andrew Evans, Jerry Feldman, Shannon Farley, Christoph Giebel, Marta González-Lloret, Chris Gosden, Anne Hatori, Nian-Sheng Huang, Mimi Kahn, "Jun" Montemayor, Michael O. Hanlon, H. Glenn Penny, Glenn Petersen, Joakim Peter, Dave Robyak, Ed Slack, John David Smith, Richard Sperber, Peter Wilcox, Lora Wildenthal, Sabine Wilke, and Andrew Zimmerman.

My deepest thanks are reserved for my family, who made this work possible. My parents Jürgen and Irmgard Buschmann were most unwavering in their support of this book, and my dedication of this book cannot fully illustrate my debt to them. Further gratitude is owed to close relatives and friends who opened their doors to me during my yearlong research in German archives.

Toward a Global History of Anthropology

T he last decades of the twentieth century saw an increasing reconcili-
ation between the disciplines of anthropology and history. Moving
beyond the synchronic method of participant observation, anthropologists began to infuse a temporal dimension into the societies they studied. Conversely, historians realized that the temporal divide separating them
from their sources was similar to the cultural division separating anthropologists from their subjects of study.[1] But even as historians and anthropologists
reached across this methodological divide, they realized that certain types of
studies could not be bridged. The interplay between anthropology and history bore fruits in the local understanding of a particular society's historical
development. When this historical approach was placed within a global context, however, anthropologists balked at the resulting loss of methodological
applicability.

Despite these conflicts, world historians have embraced anthropology with open arms, as Jerry Bentley suggests: "Anthropological and eth-
nohistorical inspiration has been most important for scholars examining the
results of encounters between peoples of different civilizations or cultural
regions. . . . Even when anthropologists and ethnohistorians have not specifically intended their works as contributions to world history, they have often
thrown useful light on the dynamics of cross-cultural encounters."[2] Bentley's
caution that anthropologists may not have intended their work to service
world historians is an understatement. Anthropologists are, on the whole,
less than enthusiastic about global approaches. Generally specializing in a
single society, anthropologists fear the work of world historians may eclipse
the significance of their localized studies. Practitioners argue instead that
global events (such as imperialism) have and continue to experience local
negotiations. Such negotiations may lessen or augment the impact of global
occurrences. While expressing concern that global historical approaches may
obscure local agency, anthropologists also argue that one should understand
history not "in abstract, but in terms of moments of cultural entanglement
[involving different social players]."[3] This approach favors a "particulariz-

ing anthropology," which understands historical events locally rather than globally.[4]

Anthropology's shift from globalism to localism has been gradual. Eric Wolf, a noted anthropologist critical of his own discipline, commented on its origins: "Anthropology, ambitiously entitled The Science of Man, did lay special claim to the study of non-Western and 'primitive' peoples. Indeed, cultural anthropology began as world anthropology."[5] In the nineteenth and early twentieth centuries, for example, anthropologists traced the psychological underpinnings of humans or mapped shifting cultural areas in their comparative studies. Shortly before the Great War, however, anthropology's global consciousness dissipated. Practitioners became dissatisfied with the grand narratives of their predecessors and preferred small inquiries within clearly delineated areas. These anthropologists limited their studies to a single non-Western society, and comparative studies generally materialized as a consequence of theoretical comparison. The chief advantage of this method was the establishment of anthropology as a university discipline. When funding agencies eventually shifted their emphasis to local inquiries, subsequent generations of anthropologists conformed accordingly.[6] Generally, anthropology's resort to localism and its neglect of global contexts fell victim to what some have labeled a collective "disciplinary amnesia."[7]

In recent years historians of anthropology have returned some of the global flavor to the discipline. Up until a few decades ago such approaches were plagued by celebratory accounts extolling theoretical directions at the expense of alternative approaches.[8] Over the last three decades, however, historians of anthropology led by George Stocking have developed a distinctive subfield of anthropological inquiry.[9] A cornerstone of this inquiry lies in Stocking's notion of "multiple contextualization," an approach that locates a particular national tradition's development in numerous social and cultural contexts affecting anthropology.[10] Laudably, such contexts include extra-European arenas, in particular the all-encompassing Euro-American imperial reach.[11] Even so, historians following Stocking's lead frequently adhere to a particular "national" anthropology, be it British or American, or, more recently, French and German. Such histories are at odds with world history's agenda, which seeks to transcend the nation state so as to delve into global accounts.

Delineating Anthropology's Global Histories

World historians propose to transcend national boundaries for a more global historical analysis. Within this system, two approaches are worthy of note. The first is an inversion of analytical categories. Proponents of this approach have traditionally been world historians whose work centers on comparisons between Europe and East Asia. England, for instance, set the norm for industrialization, prompting researchers to ask why similar events were rare outside of the European continent. Questioning China's inability to emulate England led historians to speculate on cultural, demographic, and even racial impediments. However, once historians reversed the question and asked why England was not like China, they revealed few inherent European advantages. Thus, world historians now regard Western superiority as a brief event in world historical chronologies and propose alternative conceptualizations to analyze the course of human history.[12]

The inversion of categories also benefits the history of anthropology, which owes its existence to the dynamic interplay between metropole and periphery. The metropole provides much of the theoretical framework for the early development of anthropology, while the colonial periphery supplies vital data for the study of "non-Western" societies. Steering clear of their seemingly "natural" point of departure, historians of anthropology now scrutinize new subjects of analysis previously considered outside of the discipline's boundaries. In this view, merchants, colonial officials, and even indigenous peoples become collectors of anthropological information. Their agendas take into account boundless "colonial projects" that may or may not agree with metropolitan concerns in anthropology.[13] The accentuation of the peripheral regions also provides vital points for comparative analyses of existing national traditions. Such comparative analyses not only constitute the world historian's playground, they also further our understanding of anthropology's global histories.

Another notable contribution of world history is the identification of novel units of analysis. Eager to transcend the nation state, world historians have, for instance, emphasized the importance of ocean and sea basins in their studies. While such bodies of water cover more than 70 percent of the earth's surface, scholars have traditionally favored firm continents rather than liquid surfaces. In tandem with geographers, world historians are currently rethinking some of the geographical configurations of global space, converting oceans into valid units of analysis. Partially inspired by the pioneering work of maritime historians, world historians understand oceans less as obstacles and more as engaging avenues for cultural and economic exchange.[14]

Significantly, the Pacific Ocean covers 30 percent of the earth's surface and thus figures as an important "peripheral" region for the development of anthropology as an academic discipline. Milestones of that development include Bronislaw Malinowski's sanctioning and refinement of participant observation (better known as fieldwork) among the Trobriand Islanders. Similarly, Margaret Mead's extensive study among young women in Samoa yielded enough information to fuel the nature-nurture debate for years to come.[15] In addition, the value of the cultural area generally designated as Melanesia for the study of anthropology is well documented. The area harbors more than a quarter of the world's languages (1,450 out of approximately 4,000). Its diversity has always preoccupied anthropologists. For example, according to Bruce M. Knauff, the area "was at the cutting edge of most of the principal theories of society and culture developed in anthropology over the twentieth century."[16]

Historians of the Pacific have long realized that early anthropological attention to this location derived from a misconstruction of the cultures residing in the region. Western observers maintained that the vast distances between islands located in the Pacific Ocean had prevented the same cultural diffusion presumed in the Atlantic and Indian counterparts.[17] From the earliest occupation this has not been the case. By the first millennium CE, Austronesian settlers originating from Asia explored the liquid spaces of the Pacific Ocean and occupied the most distant corners of Hawai'i, New Zealand, and Easter Island. Oceanic mariners, with little interference from either the American or Asian continents, developed prominent regional exchange systems. Cemented by marriage alliances and ongoing material and symbolic exchanges, Pacific societies displayed a high degree of fluidity that could not easily be mapped against nascent European concepts of race.[18] The arrival of Europeans incorporated static classifications of physical and cultural boundaries. Unwilling to acknowledge indigenous maritime abilities, Dutch, English, French, and Spanish observers theorized Pacific waters as barriers preserving Oceanic cultural and racial unity. In short, the Pacific Ocean presented static timeless societies, antithetical to the hybridity of polities in the Atlantic and Indian oceans.

GLOBAL ANTHROPOLOGY IN THE PACIFIC: FROM ETHNIC BOUNDARIES
TO ETHNOGRAPHIC FRONTIERS

The Pacific Ocean was an important field for European explorers of the sixteenth and seventeenth centuries. Despite its popularity, its vastness frustrated any thorough charting. Not until the second half of the eighteenth century did important intellectual and technological changes occur in European exploration. The introduction of reliable maritime chronometers, for example, enabled accurate determination of longitude and greatly facilitated the mapping of the Pacific Ocean. Ships and crews transformed not only into floating laboratories, but also into vital instruments for detailed charting tasks.[19] Furthering geographical knowledge was but one aim of the enlightened naturalists traveling on these vessels. Under the rubric of "natural history," learned individuals devoted themselves to botany, zoology, and, most important, ethnography. The official literature resulting from these voyages gave birth to a public increasingly fascinated by the indigenous inhabitants of Oceania. Their interest had a tremendous impact on the history of anthropology.[20]

During the last decades of the eighteenth and the early decades of the nineteenth centuries, such inquiries crystallized into two leading concerns: ethnic boundaries and ethnographic frontiers. Their origin stemmed from the assumption that Pacific waters separated rather than unified Oceanic polities. From the 1800s forward, learned individuals looked to the Pacific Ocean for answers to cultural and racial puzzles.[21] The delineation of ethnic boundaries became a primary concern in the local delineation of Oceania's vast liquid spaces. For the remainder of the nineteenth century, budding anthropologists attempted to locate physical evidence for the problematic categories of Melanesia, Micronesia, and Polynesia.[22] Dumont d'Urville, who led several expeditions to the Pacific Ocean between 1826 and 1840, is the alleged author of this tripartite division. Recent studies, however, suggest that such divisions were already present and d'Urville simply borrowed from already existing descriptions to supplement his own insights.[23]

Over the course of the nineteenth century, the attempt to identify local ethnic boundaries gave way to a different concern. The watery divide of the Pacific Ocean provided opportunities to study pristine cultures seemingly unmolested by the increasing Euro-American presence in the region. With the diluting contacts of the Atlantic and Indian Ocean worlds absent in the Pacific Ocean, Western observers pried the region for new insights into human history. A new intellectual trend popular throughout the second half of the nineteenth and the first decades of the twentieth century clamored for the uncovering of pristine "natives" for a universal history of humankind. These decades, characterized by a search for new societies, pushed the imaginary ethnographic frontier into the Pacific Ocean. The hope was that by expanding one ethnographic frontier researchers could provide universal answers to pressing global ethnographic puzzles.

The term "ethnographic frontier" has been greatly inspired by world historical inquiries. Frontiers have always occupied an important status in the historical profession. Initially outlined by American historian Frederick Jackson Turner, the term expanded in meaning to indicate a process of progressive settlement that promised insights into the unique American character of the early twentieth century. More recent less celebratory studies suggest the term "borderland" to account for the agency of the indigenous peoples involved in Turner's frontier of expansive settlement.[24] Similarly, for historians operating outside the American field, frontiers are significant for the study of the Roman Empire as well as Chinese dynasties following Qin unification. Specifically the division between "civilized" settled societies and "barbarian" nomads gave the frontier a physical and permanent form.[25] Outside the Chinese and Roman context, historians now regard such frontiers as vital to the process of ethnic formation.[26] The term is now considered a fluid construct that involves constant negotiations, whether peaceful or violent. Mary Louise Pratt, for instance, speaks of a contact zone between European scientists and indigenous peoples, and explores how the latter manipulated and influenced the encounter.[27] In the Pacific Ocean, Greg Dening employs the metaphor of a "beach" to designate a neutral space within which the cultural categories of Oceanic peoples are negotiated with Euro-American arrivals.[28]

In the pages to come, I will follow such intellectual leads in my exploration of ethnographic frontiers in the Pacific Ocean, which I regard as vital for a global understanding of anthropology. The almost unrelenting pursuit of societies theorized as frozen in time remained pivotal for comparative studies of anthropology up until the onset of the Great War. Comparative ethnological studies required collection of primary data along the frontier as anthropologists increasingly came to believe that the Pacific Ocean offered a final frontier of sorts, a world that time forgot, untainted by European influence.

The Pacific Ocean gains additional significance as an ethnographic frontier from another concept: salvage anthropology.[29] Western anthropologists shared the belief that global cultural diversity would ultimately fade with the arrival of Euro-American civilization. While they regarded this process as an unavoidable fact, anthropologists also advocated an urgent salvage operation for the remaining cultural heritage around the world. In the late 1800s this translated into a rush for the few postulated "unexplored" spots around the globe. The seemingly isolated societies of the Pacific Ocean became a hotbed for anthropological exploration of the expanding ethnographic frontier. Although nagging anxieties about the disappearance of contacted societies accompanied the learned individuals on their eighteenth-century voyages, it was half a century later before they took on prominent dimensions. Renato Rosaldo proclaimed salvage projects to be an outgrowth of an "imperialist nostalgia," a concern about preserving what one had endeavored to destroy.[30] More recently, H. Glenn Penny has argued for a "doctrine of scarcity" that views indigenous peoples and their material culture as precious rapidly disappearing commodities.[31] The project of salvaging the cultural heritage of newly contacted people became the primary driving force behind the ethnographic frontier's shift further into the Pacific Ocean. Even as it provoked intellectual changes in the metropole, this ethnographic frontier remained tied to the metropole while interacting with related colonial projects during the arrival of the new imperialism in Oceania.

Exploring such ethnographic frontiers transcends mere anthropological endeavors. Indeed many researchers operating within the framework of postcolonial studies have argued that anthropology was merely one among many "colonial projects" that frequently intersected with, for instance, commercial and evangelical concerns along the colonial periphery.[32] The importance of such enterprises lies in their ability to dismantle the colonial juggernaut and to reveal inconsistencies and competing agendas that were ultimately exploited by indigenous peoples. Yet they remain on the whole tied to local rather than global explorations, effectively arguing that colonialism or better colonialisms were locally defrayed and negotiated. The tensions between localism and globalism here resemble those outlined earlier in the case of anthropology and world history. A comparative examination of ethnographic frontiers in the Pacific Ocean does not, however, preclude local examinations of colonial projects. Indeed a comparative dimension provides the global elements frequently missing from anthropology's histories.

Initiating such a study is no easy task. On the whole, the Pacific Ocean is too broad a category in which to conduct a thorough investigation of such

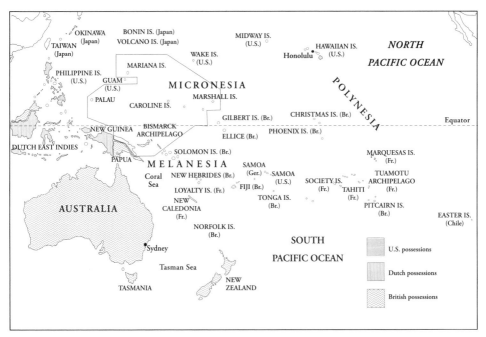

Map 1: German New Guinea (boxed area)

ethnographic frontiers. There is, however, one area that warrants specific investigation: German New Guinea. This colonial territory was a bit of an aberration, since the creation of this administrative unit was a combination of increasing German commercial interests in the Pacific, fortuitous (from a German perspective) colonial conflicts, and negotiations with other imperial powers. Although imperial conquest began in 1884, it was not until 1906 that the territory encompassed the northern Solomon Islands, the northeastern corner of New Guinea, the Bismarck Archipelago, as well as the Marshall, Caroline, and Northern Mariana islands. German tenure in the Pacific came to an abrupt halt during World War I, when all of Germany's colonies were occupied by Allied forces. German New Guinea had incorporated most of the territory designated as Micronesia (notable exceptions were the Gilbert Islands and Guam), a significant portion of Melanesia, and some Polynesian outlier societies. In short, it presented the possibility of investigating solid ethnic boundaries delineating Melanesia, Micronesia, and Polynesia. Moreover, the territory cemented Germany's status as the second largest Pacific colonial power with holdings that, although clearly dwarfed by Britain's presence in New Guinea, New Zealand, and Australia, by far surpassed France's Pacific holdings.[33]

Besides its connotations for anthropological research on ethnographic frontiers, German New Guinea presents intriguing interchanges between the ethnographic frontier and other colonial projects. Recent studies have underscored the unique status of German colonialism. In a fascinating analysis, Susanne Zantop posits that Germans throughout the eighteenth and nineteenth centuries developed "colonial imaginations" that fed the eventual drive toward colonial annexation.[34] In the Pacific Ocean, however, such colonial imaginations were few and far between. To be sure, Germans were frequent travelers in the early expeditions to the region.[35] Yet, on the whole their interest in the Pacific remained lukewarm, fueled mostly by commercial interest in the region.[36] The German public showed more interest in the African colonies that were closer to the metropole.

Such moderate public interest also figured as an important aspect of a recent historiographical controversy over New Guinea. The most complete assessment of German rule in this region continues to be Stewart Firth's monograph, which has drawn controversy ever since its publication in the early 1980s.[37] While Firth asserts that the Germans generally archived much more than other colonial powers in Melanesia, he believes that "[s]uch developments came at a price. The Germans were much more callous than the British and Australians. . . . They were stricter disciplinarians. . . . They tolerated greater loss of life. . . . By various methods they alienated more land from villagers' control."[38] German historians soon took offense to such interpretations. Firth's main detractor is German historian Hermann Hiery, who recently launched a wide-ranging revisionist campaign. "To be sure . . .", Hiery maintains, "Germany was not the extended arm of the Salvation Army."[39] Yet, Hiery continues, "[t]o compare the German approach and the Melanesian response to the well-known colonial wars fought in German South West and East Africa . . . is absurd."[40] While Germany's African colonies experienced frequent indigenous insurrections, German New Guinea and Samoa had, comparatively speaking, few revolts. According to Hiery, this state of affairs had a number of implications for the German Pacific colonies. In economic terms, it meant that most German possessions in the Pacific operated on a shoestring budget since the majority of government support went to Africa. By the same token, however, this situation lessened the German metropole's hold on its Pacific colonies, allowing greater latitude for colonial officials in New Guinea, for example, than was available to their counterparts in Africa. In turn, this relative liberty permitted the incorporation of "Melanesian principles" in German colonial rule. Hiery is somewhat vague as to what such principles entailed, particularly since his description of administrative measures, involving hostage taking and communal responsibility for individual criminal behavior, better fit general, global patterns than local "Melanesian" ones. Hiery's rosy depiction of German colonial practices has experienced considerable critique in the last few years.[41]

Despite the portrayal of Germans as "better" colonizers, Hiery's argument provides an important point of departure for investigations of ethnographic frontiers in the Pacific Ocean. Far removed from public scrutiny and eager metropolitan administrators, colonial officials and other German residents had a considerable degree of freedom in their actions. This facilitated an increasing engagement with anthropological concerns that speaks to anthropology's global histories. One would be hard pressed to find a better test case than German New Guinea to investigate the interaction between the ethnographic frontier and its interplay with the multitude of colonial projects existing in the Pacific Ocean.

Before advancing further, a brief summary of subsequent chapters is required to underscore the explicit goals of this project. Chapter 1 traces and contextualizes the emergence of the "ethnographic frontier" at the largest German ethnological museum in Berlin, founded in 1886. Director Adolf Bastian's theoretical visions of the ethnographic frontier inverted negative connotations commonly associated with New Guinea and the region known as Melanesia. Through the creation of an African and Oceanic division in the museum, Bastian hoped to monopolize Germany's colonial agents operating along the imperial periphery. Felix von Luschan, future director of this division, was left to work out the practicalities of such a monopoly, a task that was fraught with difficulty from the very beginning.

Luschan's task to reach out to New Guinea is addressed in the second chapter. His attempt to secure the prominent German commercial presence in German New Guinea soon clashed with the traders' "colonial project" of securing profits from the exchange. The opening section to this chapter illustrates that the conceptual clashes over indigenous artifacts separating science from commercialism predated Luschan's predicament by a century. The disagreement over the conceptualization soon became a widening gap, as Luschan demanded artifacts to be accompanied by exact descriptions. Such qualitative demands on artifact collection clearly contradicted the quantitative German merchant commercial project. In his attempt to gain independence from colonial agents, Luschan now searched for new alternatives, pushing the anthropological field into new directions.

These alternatives are explored in the subsequent chapters and return the analytical focus to the German metropole. Chapter 3 explores how Luschan's African and Oceanic division met with resentment among other German anthropological institutions. Shortly after the turn of the century, Bastian's theoretical visions came under attack for their impracticalities. Similarly, Luschan's division within the Berlin Ethnological Museum was blamed for maintaining a monopoly position among German institutions. Combining theoretical argument with an increasing ability to solicit local civic support for their efforts, museum officials in Hamburg, Stuttgart, and Leipzig soon outflanked Luschan in Berlin. Increasingly isolated, Luschan built upon the methodological innovations developed through his disagreements with commercial agents in German New Guinea.

Novel anthropological ideas were welcomed by a restructured German colonial administration; these developments are explored in Chapter 4. As German colonialism came under close scrutiny following massive indigenous uprisings in Africa, newly appointed colonial directors were drawn to solutions that were at least partially inspired by anthropology. In return, anthropologists exploited such colonial interest to prepare expeditions to German New Guinea. Facing an increasingly divided anthropological community, German colonial officials decided to intervene in the distribution of colonial artifacts. Solutions including mounting all-German expeditions to New Guinea and "nationalizing" indigenous artifacts met with resistance from the anthropological community, and negotiations continued until the outbreak of the Great War.

The massive anthropological interest in German New Guinea coupled with transforming methodologies deeply affected the Pacific periphery. Chapter 5 explores Governor Albert Hahl's reaction to this interest, chronicling his attempts to convince the anthropological community to move beyond artifacts and to consider the mental cultures of the indigenous peoples living in German New Guinea. In essence, Hahl sought to incorporate the ethnographic frontier to solve colonial predicaments affecting his colonial administration. The ongoing methodological dialogue between Hahl as colonial administrator and anthropologists arriving in New Guinea solidified some of the methodological changes.

Chapter 6 assesses the impact of the ethnographic frontier on the indigenous peoples of German New Guinea. Arguing for a dual conceptualization of the anthropological scheme, that is, a Western and Pacific one, this chapter traces selected incidents of indigenous counterethnography in the western isles of the Bismarck Archipelago and on the island of New Ireland. These indigenous attempts at resistance are an important counterpoint to the "colonial projects" descending on German New Guinea.

The loss of Germany's colonial empire following the Treaty of Versailles might seem like a logical conclusion to the present work. Yet German anthropologists did not cease their intellectual endeavors. Chapter 7 analyzes how the tremendous backlog in material culture and ethnographic information gathered during the expedition age in German New Guinea maintained the discipline following the colonial loss. Similarly, Germany's sudden entry into a "postcolonial" age provided an additional stimulus for anthropologists. When practitioners turned to crafting their monographs, their salvaging attempts along the ethnographic frontier were influenced by postcolonial demands to exonerate the German administration from potential abuses against the indigenous populations in German New Guinea.

Finally, a concluding chapter reads the development of the ethnographic frontier in German New Guinea against similar anthropological efforts in the Pacific Ocean. Understanding German anthropological investigations in comparison with American, English, and French ventures in the Pacific not only provides a comparative framework for anthropology's history, but also provides new venues for exploring the global history of the Pacific Ocean between 1760 and 1945.

CHAPTER 1

Berlin's Monopoly

G erman imperial expansion to Africa and Oceania increased the possibilities for anthropological research. Although the founder of the Berlin Ethnological Museum, Adolf Bastian, openly opposed colonial expansion and annexation, he did not fail to see the possibilities for research emerging from German imperial ventures. Bastian and his assistants at the museum saw the import of Oceania and New Guinea for anthropological endeavors. Supposedly isolated for centuries, Oceanic regions promised unspoiled cultures that were fit to salvage and display in museum hallways. This "salvage" project, however, also required Bastian and Berlin's future director of the African and Oceanic division, Felix von Luschan, to engage the very agents who threatened the cultural continuity of Oceanic cultures. In short, the ethnographic frontier needed to interact with the colonial periphery. Such interaction could hardly avoid an intersection with German colonial projects. This engagement brought about a split between theory and practice of ethnographic collecting that would ultimately inform the development of the anthropological discipline in Germany. This chapter chronicles how Bastian and his caretaker Luschan attempted to control German colonial agents' collecting practices. This practice did not fail to trigger resentment among other museum officials not affiliated with the Berlin institution.

THE ADMINISTRATIVE CONTEXT IN BERLIN

In 1886, on a cold mid-December morning, the Berlin Ethnological Museum (Völkerkundemuseum) held its opening ceremony. This event occurred almost directly because of an increase in spending by the Prussian Ministry for Cultural Affairs. The opening of a new museum was a rare event in Berlin during the first half of the nineteenth century, although this state of affairs would soon change. The Old Museum (Altes Museum) opened its doors in 1830; its expansion, the New Museum (Neues Museum), opened in 1855 to accommodate among other things a large Egyptian collection. The

New Museum also housed until 1885 the ethnographic collections. After the German unification of 1871, the construction of new museums accelerated. Construction of the National Gallery (Nationalgalerie) was completed in 1876, and in 1881 the Museum of Art (Kunstgewerbemuseum) was ready for occupancy. Other museological projects, especially the large museum complex located on an island in the river Spree, were under way before the end of the century. Given the ever expanding museological landscape in Berlin, the opening of the ethnological museum must have seemed a rather unremarkable event for the notables attending the ceremony. Indeed, the unification of Germany following 1871 triggered a wealth of administrative changes that placed Berlin's museums on a par with those of other European capitals. Wilhelm I, king of Prussia and German emperor, appointed his son, Crown Prince Friedrich Wilhelm, as protector of the royal museums in Berlin. By this move, Wilhelm I hoped to direct the political aspirations of his son.[1]

Partially inspired by his more artistically inclined wife, Friedrich Wilhelm put much energy into this project. Unfortunately for him, he could not draw on broad German national resources to restructure Berlin's cultural landscape: the German constitution granted the pursuit of the arts and sciences to the empire's individual states. Although the amount of money appropriated to support the creation of museums in Prussia was rather small in comparison to other endeavors, Prussia, with almost two-thirds of the German population as well as over half of the empire's land surface, was able to command larger financial resources than its smaller counterparts.[2]

The establishment of a number of different museums in Berlin led to an ever increasing administrative jungle. Museum administration was an inherent part of the Prussian Cultural Ministry, headed by the general museum director (*Generaldirektor*), who was normally appointed by the German kaiser. He in turn oversaw the work of the individual museum directors, while approving and disapproving their individual acquisitions. Prevailing individual attitudes in such leading positions could thus greatly influence the cultural policies of the Berlin museums. Guido von Usedom, the general director of the Berlin museums between 1872 and 1880, serves as a prominent example. Usedom was not a trained art historian but a close associate of the Prussian court. Nicknamed "gypsum-pope" by the museum directors under his department, Usedom followed an outdated mid-nineteenth-century museum practice. Instead of purchasing originals to increase the collection of sculptures of the German capital, he argued that a good gypsum copy could serve as an adequate replacement. With the ascendancy of Friedrich Wilhelm as protector of the different museums in Berlin, this policy underwent a drastic change. In 1880 Richard Schöne succeeded Usedom as the new general director. Trained in archaeology, a discipline he taught at the

University of Halle until his appointment, Schöne was instrumental in the creation of a new statute for the Berlin museums in 1878 that reduced the power over individual acquisitions wielded by the general museum director. The most central activity of museum work, the acquisition of individual artifacts, became the task of the trained curators and directors within the individual museum divisions. They thus welcomed the arrival of Richard Schöne on the Berlin scene and expected to see Berlin turn into a renowned art metropole.[3]

This wider administrative context also had implications for the Ethnological Museum. Although Usedom was open to the idea of establishing an independent museum of ethnology, it was under Schöne's tenure that this project became a reality. His archaeological training made Schöne sympathetic to the concerns of the ethnological curator, as he realized that Berlin's ethnological division housed objects that differed radically from those exhibited in the museums dedicated to sculpture and painting. Over the course of the nineteenth century, ethnologists tried to abandon the arrangement of ethnographic objects according to complicated aesthetic schemes developed by mostly Western art historians and advocated instead a recognition of these "foreign" objects as scientific objects in their own right.[4] This led to the appointment of different commissions, sharply separating art objects from "ethnographica." For the Berlin ethnological collection, this development translated into the establishment of a Commission of Learned Gentlemen (Sachverständigen Kommission) that was to decide on purchasing objects exceeding the sum of 1,000 marks (roughly U.S. $250 at that time). To qualify for inclusion, members of the commission had to profess at least a partial understanding of ethnology.[5]

Other ethnological collections existed throughout Germany, particularly in Dresden, Hamburg, Leipzig, and Munich, but none of them had a building exclusively reserved for ethnology. The Berlin museum, dedicated to the exploration of all branches of ethnology, therefore stands as an important milestone in the history of ethnological thought in Germany.[6] The special status of the Berlin Ethnological Museum was accentuated in a speech delivered by von Goessler, Prussian minister for cultural affairs, for the opening ceremony on 18 December 1886. Goessler claimed that establishing this museum would contribute to bridging the gap between museums dedicated to art and art history and those dedicated to the natural sciences. While Goessler pointed out the placement of ethnology between the humanities and the natural sciences, he failed to specify how he envisioned its accomplishments. Still, his speech hinted at the scientific potential of the ethnological discipline. German travelers and explorers, he told his audience that morning, had provided ample evidence of the alterity of humankind. The parallels between the material culture of the newly contacted societies and that of the prehistoric record in Europe permitted the ranking of societies along an evolutionary scale. "As such the Royal Museum of Ethnology shall guide our gaze into the humble foundations of our own past."[7] Goessler also highlighted the collecting efforts of Germans traveling overseas, whose important supply line figured as the central theme of Crown Prince Friedrich Wilhelm's speech.

Dressed for the occasion in the uniform of his very own Silesian Eighth Dragoneer Regiment, the crown prince stood in as substitute for his father. To excuse his absence, Wilhelm I cited health problems for what was most likely a lack of interest in ethnology.[8] Friederich Wilhelm seemed equally disinterested in the ceremony, as he reportedly took little notice of the newly constructed museum. He delighted instead in entertaining and being entertained by the many invited dignitaries assembled in the atrium and seemed particularly impressed by a well-traveled individual from Cologne (presumably Wilhelm Joest). The multitude of decorations garnishing his chest made Friedrich Wilhelm comment: "I'll be . . . , if only I could muster similar accomplishments."[9] The crown prince's own speech was a far cry from Goessler's imperfect argument for a positioning of ethnology between the sciences and the humanities. Friedrich Wilhelm preferred to highlight something more familiar to him. Rather than a scientific institution, the crown prince preferred to understand the museum as a "monument to the spirit of cooperation and sacrifice of our compatriots in distant continents."[10]

As different as these speeches may have appeared to the audience in attendance that day, together they underscored two principal meanings associated with material culture and its collection. In Goessler's speech, on the one hand, one encounters scientific curiosity regarding other cultures, especially their ranking relative to European society characteristic of evolutionary thinking of that time period. The crown prince's speech, on the other hand, highlighted an alternative understanding where material culture was tantamount to a celebration of recent German overseas expansion and its ensuing colonial mission. The tension surrounding multifarious interpretations of material culture will be an important one throughout this work.

The crown prince's speech also highlighted the possibility of understanding material culture as a potential source of obtaining badly needed funds from private benefactors.[11] Prices for ethnographica could not rival those of the art masterpieces starting to be accumulated in the Berlin museums, but such objects too developed their own market. Even gradually rising acquisition budgets could not match the needs of the newly established ethnological museum. In order to survive in a competitive market, museums became increasingly dependent on specialized societies composed of wealthy patrons as permanent members.[12] The Ethnological Assistance Committee (Ethnologisches Hilfscomité), established in 1881, provided an important addition to the ethnological collections in Berlin. The committee's purpose was to provide financial assistance to travelers collecting in distant lands. Membership was theoretically open to anybody, yet only those investing a minimum amount of 3,000 marks were considered full-fledged members of the committee. Membership was never large, but it did provide the ethnological museum with the necessary cash funds when the Prussian General Museum Administration's financial resources were insufficient or faced cash shortage owing to other obligations.[13]

Museum officials created such assistance committees to coordinate the financial efforts of their individual patrons (Mäzene). The patrons of the ethnological museum had two important roles. They could support the museum's financial efforts through actual monetary contributions, or they could donate ethnographic collections to augment the objects housed in the museum. Patrons belonging to the assistance committee fell mostly into the first category, but generous contributions were the exception rather than the rule. By and large the greatest number of museum patrons were casual donors whose contribution varied from a few dozen to only a handful of artifacts. Many patrons were affiliated with two important imperial agencies active in supporting the museum's collection ventures. First, the German Imperial Navy office advised its officers to gather artifacts during their tour of duty on the world's oceans; and second, the German Foreign Office encouraged its diplomatic representatives to do the same in distant territories. Many representatives of both the German Imperial Navy and the German Foreign Office were among the guests of honor attending the opening ceremony on 18 December 1886.[14]

LINKING SCIENCE AND MUSEOLOGY: ADOLF BASTIAN'S
"THESAURUS OF MANKIND"

The driving force behind the establishment of the ethnographic museum was Adolf Bastian (1826–1905). At sixty years of age, Bastian was the second oldest museum director in Berlin. In energy and eccentricity, however, he may have surpassed them all. Even close friends and associates characterized him as a "loner," spending much time laboring over books while eschewing large gatherings. His life stood in almost complete contradiction to his theoretical postulates. Although heavily influenced by Aristotle's dictum that "man" was by his very nature a zoon politikon (social being), Bastian kept human interaction to a minimum. As the son of a wealthy Bremen merchant family, Bastian embarked first on a medical career. On the completion of his studies, Bastian sailed around the world on numerous ships as a ship surgeon, awaking his slumbering interest in the alterity of different peoples he encountered. In 1868 he was able to pursue his interest professionally when he became curator of the Berlin ethnological collection, then housed in the New Museum. That same year he became president of the Berlin Society for Geography, a post that he used to promote ethnographic contributions. In the following years, Bastian cofounded two important societies devoted exclusively to anthropological pursuits. The German Anthropological Society as well as the Berlin Society for Ethnology, Anthropology, and Prehistory emerged from cooperative efforts between Bastian and his close friend and associate the German pathologist Rudolf Virchow. His actions won him much acclaim in and around Germany. In the 1870s Bastian's name became associated with the incipient discipline of ethnology, but his organizational work in Germany was frequently interrupted by extensive journeys that took him to all corners of the world. The tendency to leave his post for years provoked much speculation among his colleagues. Some argued that it was his wish to escape the cold Berlin winters; others proposed he was pursuing his native Bremen's motto *navigare necesse est* (which argued that one had to be in perpetual motion to keep business from faltering). Whatever his motives may have been, his incessant traveling led to the accumulation of important ethnographic collections.

Bastian's collection activity is best characterized as extensive rather than intensive, owing to his wish to visit as many places as possible in the available time.[15] Moreover, Bastian's informants were rarely indigenous people but usually local European residents who professed an expertise in the local culture. Despite these shortcomings, Bastian published a wealth of books and articles reflecting his wide-ranging interest in journalism, travel literature, geography, descriptive ethnography, and comparative ethnology. Some of his many writings were less accessible than others, leading his contemporaries to argue that his style was intentionally cryptic.[16] This did not deter him from continuing to write, collect, and compile until his death in February 1905 in Trinidad during one of his journeys.

On 18 December 1886 Bastian was at the height of his career. Yet for him the ethnographic museum hardly represented the ideal way to enshrine ethnology in the German intellectual landscape. In fact, his main ambition had been to create a number of ethnological chairs at different German universities as a final step toward the academic acceptance of this discipline. Bastian did obtain an honorary instructor position at the Berlin University in 1868, but university chairs in ethnology did not become a reality in Germany until the second decade of the twentieth century. The museum thus remained the only viable institution to ground and establish ethnological interest within the German empire. Still, it took Bastian thirteen years to establish an independent ethnological museum in Berlin (1873–1886).[17] Bastian was by no means idle during these years. He did much to develop a coherent framework within which to place and operate the ethnological endeavor.

For Bastian, ethnology was above all a psychological endeavor. Unlike academic psychology, which focused on the individual alone, Bastian wanted ethnology to be about larger social units. Ethnology became, in his view, an ethnopsychology (*Völkerpsychologie*). Bastian's extensive travel experiences increased his greater awareness of the commonalities and antagonisms among the many societies he encountered. His ultimate goal was to discern human universals lurking below the seemingly endless variations characterizing human societies around the world. Bastian based his framework on two central cornerstones, which he termed folk ideas (*Völkergedanken*) and elementary ideas (*Elementargedanken*). He referred to the entire interpretive realm of a society as folk ideas. Such ideas resulted from the interaction of a set of innate and finite elementary ideas with historical or geographical stimuli. Generally speaking, Bastian's writings sought to investigate two related issues. First, he attempted to chart "mankind's" psychic unity, that is, to identify the set of finite and common elementary ideas. Second, departing from the elementary ideas, Bastian sought to identify the mechanisms by which different societies arrived at their contemporary state. Superficially then, Bastian had much in common with other leading evolutionists, particularly in England. However, he differed from them by vehemently rejecting Charles Darwin's evolutionism. Bastian argued that Darwin had come to his conclusions by way of deduction rather than inductive data gathering. Moreover, Bastian envisioned the evolutionary process as a spiral rather than a number of set stages. Taking the universal elementary ideas as a starting point, Bastian postulated that interaction with a particular geographical environment, which he called a "geographical province," containing similar folk ideas would set in motion an evolutionary process that would come to a halt once the outside stimuli had exhausted themselves. Subsequent development remained circular until a new stimulus (such as migration or sudden climate changes) propelled the society onto another evolutionary spiral, only to repeat the entire process.

Despite his rather fluid scale, Bastian maintained the division between peoples of nature and peoples of culture. This scale postulated that peoples of nature were characterized by less sophisticated cultural overlay. Simpler than the peoples of culture, they figured as important case studies in Bastian's scheme, since their lack of cultural overlay encompassed an access to elementary ideas lurking below. Although peoples of nature lacked a writing system,

Bastian emphasized the importance of material culture to study their mental activity and its developments. Ultimately he created a statistical tabulation of ideas (*Gedankenstatistik*) to provide a comparative (inductive) framework for his theoretical outlook. The ideal site for his inductive folk psychology was the ethnological museum, which then became a "thesaurus of mankind."

Bastian had his own ideas connected to the collection of ethnographic objects. He firmly believed in the imminence of cultural extinction, because Western encroachment into even the remotest corners of the globe endangered the cultural universe of the very peoples of nature he sought to investigate. Advocating a project known as "salvage anthropology," Bastian asked his associates to gather all possible information before the impending demise of the peoples of nature became a reality. Like his British evolutionist counterparts, he feared that the fading of the peoples of nature would result in a loss of insight into one's own past. Bastian's research, however, involved not just the past. Rather than identifying past stages of development, he sought to identify evolutionary processes that were still operational in his own contemporary European society. Ultimately, Bastian envisioned extending his project from the simpler peoples of nature to the more sophisticated peoples of culture. Hence, the painful loss of comparative material among nature peoples suggested not just a loss of insights into the past, but also into the present and the future of Western society.[18] The institution that opened on 18 December 1886 advanced his theoretical outlook, serving both as a central ethnological institution for comparative purposes as well as a storage facility for rapidly disappearing non-Western cultural heritage.

SALVAGE ANTHROPOLOGY AND THE ETHNOGRAPHIC FRONTIER IN THE PACIFIC OCEAN

Bastian had a sense of urgency about the disappearing cultural heritage of indigenous peoples around the world.[19] Clearly, Bastian was not alone in his assumption that Western contact had a tainting influence on indigenous material culture. While material culture continued to be produced even after contact, there were many concerns about the "authenticity" of the collected artifacts. To be classified as "authentic," the artifacts were not supposed to be tainted by Western production methods, involving, for instance, industrially manufactured coloring or iron tools. Even if Bastian did not specify this in his instructions, in the closing decades of the nineteenth century it was already clear that collectors preferred artifacts that had been involved, before their acquisition by the collector, in ritual activity or the general social life of the society of their producers. Artifacts produced for Western collectors were frowned upon and deemed "inauthentic."[20] Bastian sought to employ the services of the German colonial institutions for his general salvage agenda. This agenda exhibited what Renato Rosaldo has called "imperialist nostalgia," which delineates the contradiction between the cultural destruction following European expansion and the desire to preserve threatened cultural heritage.[21] To put it bluntly, in his efforts to salvage the material culture of peoples of nature, Bastian engaged the very agencies that he implicitly condemned because they brought about the perceived demise of culture.[22]

The urgent need to collect the last remnants of material culture in the world also compelled Bastian to take a closer look at the Pacific Ocean and at times to turn the commonly accepted intellectual division between Melanesia and Polynesia on its head. Historically this conceptual rift takes its origin from James Cook's voyages of exploration, where a superficial rendering of local languages, indigenous reception of Europeans, and assumed treatment of women provided initial ground for classification. Naturalists accompanying James Cook noticed that the inhabitants of the area that was to become known as Polynesia, on the one hand, professed mutually intelligible languages, were generally more hospitable toward Europeans, and were relatively respectful toward women. Societies in Melanesia, on the other hand, posed serious linguistic puzzles, were generally deemed xenophobic, and were prone to domestic violence. The French geographer Dumont d'Urville cemented this division by arguing for the higher standing of the more "natural" hierarchical societies of Polynesia, which shared little in common with the "lower" confusing, egalitarian societies of Melanesia.[23]

Such ideas influenced Bastian, but in his evolutionary scheme of things, the societies of Melanesia held equal if not greater importance. In Bastian's ethnophysiological investigations, the "less developed" societies of Melanesia were of tremendous importance in the uncovering of elementary thought processes. Likewise, the inhospitable nature of its climate and its supposed xenophobic population made the area a primary "ethnographic frontier" of investigation. While Bastian had never visited Melanesia, he had ample experience in Polynesia to venture such judgment. Between 1879 and 1880 he had spent several months in Polynesia, from which he returned with a number of artifacts as well as a grim outlook on the ethnographic future of the area. While staying in Hawai'i for a few weeks, Bastian was confronted with the breathtaking beauty of the island, which he contrasted with the massive changes affecting its native peoples in the less than one hundred years from the emergence of the Hawaiian kingdom to Bastian's ethnographic present. Bastian felt a deep concern over the decline of the indigenous population. He maintained that knowledge of the traditional *kapu* system was fading with the passing of each Hawaiian individual. He thus felt an immediate need for a large-scale salvage operation in order to record what he regarded as the last vestiges of Hawaiian culture. Bastian himself led the way when he convinced King Kalakaua to allow him to write down the *Kumulipo*, the story of the genesis of the Hawaiian Islands and its people. Similarities between the *Kumulipo* and ancient Greek mythology deepened Bastian's convictions of a common, universally shared humanity.[24]

Although Bastian called for an immediate salvage operation in Hawai'i, he saw little hope for any in-depth ethnographic exploration of the islands of the Polynesian triangle. Hawai'i was not an isolated case in Polynesia, Bastian maintained, since similar disrupting processes were also at work in Tahiti, New Zealand, Tonga, and Samoa. Few, if any, untainted folk ideas could emerge out of the area. Therefore, he advocated a shift in the ethnographic gaze to Melanesia, where the unsettling trade and mission frontiers had done limited damage. Melanesia was to become the premier region for a German mission of salvage. Evoking the American, British, and French initiatives to sponsor ethnographic research, Bastian forcefully reminded his superiors: "The time has come for Germany to take its deserved place among other nations. . . . Most importantly we have to focus on the *terra incognita* of the Melanesian isles: specifically on New Guinea, New Britain, the Solomon Islands, and the New Hebrides."[25] Bastian's choice of words is noteworthy. Similar to British and French explorers who had pursued an elusive Terra Australis Incognita (unknown southern continent) throughout the eighteenth century, Bastian postulated a new frontier for exploration. This time it was not for cartographic but for ethnographic purposes, and instead of insisting on the delineation of ethnic divisions among Melanesians and Polynesians, he proposed charting the unknown dimensions of human *Elementargedanken*. While the cartographic carving up of Oceania had ceased by the mid-nineteenth century, with the German contribution shamefully subsumed under the glory of other European nations, on this new ethnographic frontier Bastian advocated a leading role for German efforts.[26]

MONOPOLIZING THE ETHNOGRAPHIC FRONTIER: THE CASE OF THE GERMAN NAVY

Delineating the ethnographic frontier was one thing; ensuring collection activity along the same was quite another. That German colonial agents could have a prominent role in collection activity became obvious to Bastian when the German naval agents returned with important artifacts from Melanesia. In 1874 the German navy commissioned one of its newest vessels, the *Gazelle*, to journey around the world. The primary objective of the expedition was to undertake astronomical and oceanographic observations at different intervals. Bastian, on hearing about this mission, approached his superior, Usedom, to assist him with contacting the German navy. After a successful round of negotiations between Prussian authorities and the German Admiralty, naval authorities agreed to include ethnographic collecting among the scientific tasks of the ship's crew. Officers of the *Gazelle* were to pay special attention to the unexplored areas of New Ireland and New Britain lying to the north of New Guinea. Expenses for the collecting effort amounted to about 500 marks, a small sum considering the rich ethnographic treasures returned to Berlin by the ship's crew.[27]

The artifacts from the northern half of New Ireland raised considerable attention among the German ethnological community. The masks, statues, and friezes, characteristic of the mortuary ceremonies known as *malaggan* on New Ireland, granted Bastian what he had hoped to find.[28] The quasi-surreal expressions of these objects convinced Bastian that the scientific world had underestimated, once again, Melanesian cultural accomplishments. "It seems obvious," Bastian wrote in one of his many publications, "that from this last of the untouched areas we have extracted authentic sources . . . which will ultimately redefine many of our theories surrounding human Weltanschauung in it, primitive state."[29] The Melanesian folk ideas embodied in the *Gazelle* collection confirmed Bastian's hypothesis that New Guinea and its surrounding islands were indeed a final ethnographic frontier that merited exploration through the precious collaborative help of the imperial navy. A comparison of the New Ireland artifacts with similar cultural phenomena elsewhere in the world represented an additional step in Bastian's near endless task of disentangling the differences between elementary and folk ideas.[30]

Bastian was not alone in his attempts to benefit from collection activity by the German navy. In the files of the Saxony state archives, an interesting competition between Dresden and Berlin museums emerges. The idea of influencing the German navy to launch a salvage operation to the remote but ethnographically interesting island of Rapa Nui (better known as Easter Island) originated with Albert Bernard Meyer and not Bastian. As director of the Dresden Ethnological Institution, Meyer approached Bastian with his proposal. Through Bastian's intervention, the ship *Hyäne* was dispatched to Easter Island. The ship's purser, Jakob Weissner, had only limited time to assemble roughly one hundred artifacts. The collection, which for lack of space did not include the majestic carved stone heads, was nevertheless remarkable.[31] Although Bastian and Meyer had tacitly agreed to share the collection, Bastian decided to keep almost 75 percent of the artifacts, at which Meyer protested by involving Saxon state authorities on his behalf. The bureaucratic negotiations between Saxon and Prussian officials ended by increasing Meyer's share to about 56 of 113 artifacts. Meyer was, however, highly displeased with the outcome, believing that Bastian had kept the better objects.[32]

Realizing that cooperation between his institution and that of Berlin would always be to Dresden's detriment, Meyer appealed directly to naval authorities. He compiled a booklet listing all the desired objects from East Asia and the Pacific Islands, which he hoped to circulate among the naval officers. Meyer forwarded several hundred of these booklets to the Naval Office in order to engage potential donors for his museum but with limited results.[33] While the conflict between Bastian and Meyer was minor, the struggle over Easter Island artifacts nevertheless illustrates that Berlin's ethnographic collection policies were geared to exclude rather than include other German institutions.

MONOPOLIZING COLONIAL COLLECTIONS: THE CASE OF THE
GERMAN COLONIAL OFFICE

Bastian pursued his colonial connections even further as German flags went up in Africa and the Pacific Islands between the years 1884 and 1885. In the Pacific Ocean, the German government carried out large-scale annexations in Melanesia (New Guinea) and Micronesia (Marshall Islands).[34] Bastian skillfully pursued his plan by emphasizing other nations' ethnographic successes. He regarded French endeavors in Africa as well as the American governmental policies among different Native American tribes as something to be emulated by the German authorities. Bastian appealed to his superiors' national pride, arguing that surely Germany did not want to be inferior in the ethnographic pursuit and study of the societies in its African and Oceanic colonial realm.[35]

In essence, Bastian shared much with German chancellor Otto von Bismarck. Bismarck was no colonial enthusiast but was propelled into the direction of colonial annexation for diplomatic, economic, and social reasons. Bismarck's social imperialism, his attempt to use overseas expansion to detract from domestic woes in Germany, caused much controversy in the German literature.[36] Yet ultimately, whatever his reasons for colonial annexation, he was above all an opportunist who recognized how much he stood to gain from the German colonial adventure. Bastian's reasons for his support of the German colonial adventure were more transparent. Much like Bismarck, Bastian was no colonial agitator. His liberal political position propelled him to oppose outright colonial annexation on a political level, a view he shared with his close associate Rudolf Virchow. Neither civilizing mission, nor arguments for large-scale German overseas settlements, nor downright racist statements following social Darwinistic dogma sat well with Bastian's personal outlook. In agreement with Virchow, he advocated a free trade policy governing the exchange between different countries.[37] In his role of museum director, however, Bastian could hardly ignore the advantages deriving from Germany's colonial venture and the agencies connected with the colonial expansion (the Admiralty, the Foreign Office, and a number of commercial companies operating in the German colonies), which figured among the most important patrons of the Berlin Ethnological Museum. Many of the representative agencies were important invitees to the opening ceremony on 18 December 1886, and Bastian naturally sought to pursue further contact with them.[38]

Bastian could hardly ignore the apparent benefits of colonial acquisition. Most important, when Otto von Bismarck convinced the Berlin Conference from November 1884 to February 1885 to alleviate colonial tensions in Africa, one of the most important outcomes was the doctrine of effective occupation. This doctrine underscored the belief that the settlement of nationals in a particular colonial territory would precede international recognition of that territory. In Bastian's view, such effective occupation translated into the availability of ethnographic collectors in Africa and the Pacific Islands. German settlers and colonial administrators were potential agents on the ethnographic frontier, especially in the interior of Africa and New Guinea. Moreover, in his urgent appeals to his superiors, he never failed to underscore the potential for creating a central institution for ethnographic investigation of the German colonies. Bastian further enshrined the close connections between ethnography and colonialism in the Berlin museum by merging the African and Oceanic collections into one single division. The main connection among these continents in the mind of the Berlin museum director was the German colonial investment in the region. The merging of the two regions, which was later often criticized by leading anthropologists, derived from Bastian's political collection agenda rather than any abstract theoretical concerns.[39]

Although Bastian's actions were approved by his superiors, authorities in the newly established German Colonial Division showed little interest. While German colonial authorities vowed to urge colonial officials to support the museum's collection efforts in the colonies, Bastian also was informed that administrative duties would prevent colonial officials from becoming active collectors for the Berlin institution. Monopolizing valuable administrative time for ethnographic collection was out of the question for the German Colonial Division.[40] This flat refusal illustrates two important issues. Neither was Germany's nascent colonial administration prepared to recognize the potential benefit of ethnographic activity, nor was Bastian able to package the colonial utility of the collection activity properly. That was left for the next generation of German anthropologists.

That Bastian still obtained a virtual monopoly over artifacts from the German colonies owes as much to luck as to any of his diplomatic actions. On 24 June 1888 Deputy Chancellor von Boetticher introduced a well-intended resolution at the German Federal Council that asked for centralization in the museums of the German capital of Berlin of all ethnographic and natural scientific specimens hailing from official expeditions to the German colonies. This proposal would have far-reaching consequences for the museological landscape in Germany. The council, meeting with little resistance from non-Prussian German states, approved Boetticher's course of action on 21 February 1889. It has often been asserted that this resolution emerged from a series of coincidences rather than from a clear plan by Berlin museum officials.[41] There is some truth to such statements, as the expeditions to the German African colonies (especially to Cameroon and Togo), following in the wake of colonial acquisitions in the mid-1880s, led to an accumulation of large scientific collections in the German Foreign Office. Foreign Office officials did not have adequate storage facilities to cope with the arrival of both natural scientific and ethnographic artifacts, so they turned to the Prussian Museum Administration for help. Museum Administration officials in turn approached Bastian about the possibility of housing some of the colonial collections in the newly erected Ethnological Museum.[42]

There was never any intention to centralize the artifacts in Berlin permanently. However, the close proximity between the museums in Berlin and the German Foreign Office, in comfortable walking distance, made such a proposal feasible. Though initially few German officials considered the deposit of colonial collections in the Ethnological Museum in Berlin permanent, once the proposal landed on Bastian's desk, the request by the German Foreign Office was infused with a different purpose.[43]

For Bastian to include even the ethnographic specimens among his permanent collection required some tactical maneuvering. The size of his museum, the level of training of its employees, and its location made the Berlin museum the logical choice for centralization. Bastian thus argued that his museum should become the central collecting institution for the German colonies. Furthermore, his museum employees could relieve the Colonial Department of the burden of deciding on a distribution of the artifacts among German institutions. Colonial officials found this proposal acceptable but decided to consult the rest of the German states represented in the German Federal Council. The Federal Council Resolution of 1889 thus provided the legal groundwork for Bastian's ambitious plan. A number of circulars published in the *Deutsches Kolonialblatt,* the official organ of the

German Colonial Department, communicated the nature of this decision to the colonial civil servants in the colonies.[44] Similar provisions also affected the centralization of botanical and zoological specimens.

THE DISTRIBUTION COMMISSION AND THE ISSUE OF DUPLICATES

The wealth of artifacts arriving at the Berlin Ethnological Museum in response to the resolution of 1889 also increased the responsibilities of this institution.[45] A commission was especially established to oversee the distribution. The commission included representatives of those museums located in the capital of Berlin benefiting the most from the resolution: the botanical, ethnological, and zoological institutions each appointed one official. The original membership of the commission involved curator Adolf Engler of the botanical museum, Karl Möbius of the zoological museum, and Felix von Luschan of the ethnological museum. Luschan was a natural choice owing to his role as curator of the African and Oceanic division within the Berlin Ethnological Museum. The main task of the commission was to publish lists of duplicates, which were sent to participating non-Prussian museums at regular intervals. Prussian museums besides those located in Berlin received the worst deal; they could only acquire those objects not claimed by other museums within six months after the circulation of the publication lists.[46] Initially the committee moved quickly, issuing the first collection register in the summer of 1889. As collection activity increased and collections started to accumulate in Berlin, however, the printing of the collection registers became more sporadic. A total of six registers were issued between 1889 and 1903, with the last three registers listing only the duplicates to be passed on to other institutions.[47]

The Colonial Division assisted the museum committee's efforts by issuing a circular in its central organ, *Deutsches Kolonialblatt,* promoting the resolution of 1889. From 1892 onward, the resolution was further extended to individual colonial officials, requiring them to relinquish their collections to the museums located in Berlin. By 1896 the Colonial Division extended similar provisions to the German colonial troops (*Schutztruppen*) and their colonial officers in Africa.[48] It was in light of such successes that Bastian once again opted to introduce collection provisions into the contracts of colonial civil servants. Much like his earlier attempts, however, his request was politely refused by colonial authorities.[49]

On paper, the commission seemed to have been efficiently staffed and supported. However, the burden of deciding on duplicates from the colonial collections detracted from the original work of museum officials assigned to serve on the commission. Besides the additional work for the commission members, another more conceptual problem soon emerged: what was to be considered a true duplicate? In the realm of the natural sciences, practices governing the study and collection of botanical and zoological specimens were agreed upon by the end of the nineteenth century. Botanical specimen collections, for instance, required close documentation by the collector in the field, with a trained botanist operating in a museum or herbarium providing a name and a clear taxonomy for every newly encountered specimen. An original was constituted when the botanist published, in print, a clear-cut description and classification of a particular specimen. All other specimens of the same plant were designated duplicates and could be either stored or traded with other institutions. Similar deliberations governed the acquisition of zoological material.[50] Such deliberations allowed for a division into a scientific collection (*wissenschaftliche Sammlung*) and a display collection (*Schausammlung*); the former was accessible only to the interested practitioner, while the latter, consisting mostly of duplicates, became an integral part of the museum and was accessible to the public. Problems emerged, however, when the whole system found itself translated into the realm of ethnology and ethnography.[51] Most museum officials working in this realm agreed that duplicates among human-made objects, or ethnographica, were the exception rather than the rule. The duplicate issue would only cloud the distribution of ethnographic objects among other German museums.

It seemed as if the Berlin museums had assumed a hegemonic position in Germany's museological landscape. This translated into a prominent position for Felix von Luschan, who supervised the monopoly in the German colonies. However, there are indications that by the time the museum committee issued its third register of colonial artifacts in 1897, there was mounting dissatisfaction with the distribution system. The introduction to this register included an apologetic note by the committee's chairman, Karl Möbius:

> The number of duplicates may not satisfy some of the museum directors. They should consider, however, that the Berlin museums have to account for all the costs accompanying the acquisition, preservation, transportation, and storage of the collections. Moreover, the same institutions issue free-of-charge instruction about collection and preservation. . . . If one adds to this the vast correspondence maintained with the colonial authorities within and outside Germany, it is understandable why the Berlin museums should be entitled to keep the majority of the specimens. [In Berlin] they are readily available to all researchers for their specialized studies.[52]

Möbius' statement illustrated a growing discontent among other German museums with the Berlin monopoly. In the realm of ethnography, such a monopoly could only be rationalized in the light of scientific output of the Berlin Ethnological Museum's African and Oceanic division, but from the onset there were doubts. By the time of the museum opening ceremony, the African and Oceanic division was under the leadership of Luschan, an Austrian native who was a physical anthropologist by training.[53] Luschan had accepted the post at the Berlin museum because he had hoped to establish a physical anthropological division at this institution. Not only did such a division not emerge under Bastian's tenure, but Bastian added insult to injury when he declined any further purchase of anthropometric material.[54] Conceptual differences explained Bastian's actions, as he felt that the study of physical anthropology differed from that of ethnology. The former was a branch of anatomy, the latter a developing discipline focusing on ethnopsychology.[55]

Luschan made the best of what he had, especially since academic jobs in anthropology were few and far between in the late nineteenth century. Meanwhile, there was a growing recognition among ethnographers in Germany that Luschan may not have been the right man for the job.[56] Luschan, for his part, often found himself on the defensive, forced to legitimize the African and Oceanic division as well as his job, something that he found difficult to do in the wake of the rising criticism. Subsequent chapters explore the development of the division and Luschan's thought on ethnography and ethnographic collecting. Although ideologically more nationalistic than Bastian, Luschan shared the salvage concerns of his erstwhile superior. Convinced of the superiority of his museum over similar institutions in Germany, Bastian had theorized the need to monopolize the German colonies within his salvage construction. It fell on Luschan's shoulders to administer Bastian's idea. Luschan approached what turned out to be a thankless job with unrelenting zeal. The waning years of the nineteenth century find Luschan negotiating agreements with the German Naval Office, sending collection instructions to colonial officials in the German territories, and enlisting travelers for his museum.[57] Collectors enlisted in the German colonies could only intersect with existing projects on the colonial periphery. Consequently, Luschan had to contend with a powerful and troublesome force in German New Guinea: resident merchants. The following chapter relates Luschan's painful experiences with commercial agents and his attempts to venture beyond the bureaucratic administration of the African and Oceanic division's monopoly to embrace fruitful methodological innovation.

CHAPTER 2

Commercializing the Ethnographic Frontier

F elix von Luschan's attempt to engage the commercial frontier in German New Guinea for the purposes of his African and Oceanic division at the Berlin Ethnological Museum had ample precedent. Luschan was not alone in realizing that, along with the evangelical sector, commercial agents had penetrated the very regions deemed interesting by German anthropologists. Yet enlisting such agents was not without its problems. While on the surface commercialism and ethnography were not mutually exclusive, commercial agents sought to capitalize on the renewed interest in indigenous artifacts.

CONCEPTUAL TENSIONS IN MATERIAL CULTURE: ETHNOGRAPHICA AND COMMODITIES

There has been a close historical relationship between commerce and ethnography. In recent years estimated values for artifacts from Hawai'i, New Guinea, or Tonga, especially if produced before European contact, have rivaled those for works of Western artists. This was hardly the case during the nineteenth century, but even at that time the conceptual tensions between scientific and commercial understandings of material cultural had had a long history. Indeed, a concern with "things foreign," Mary Helms argues, was not an exclusively European phenomenon. In her survey of world cultures, Helms asserts that travelers returning with "precious" materials from abroad have enjoyed increased admiration and status.[1] For Europeans, the introduction of objects from other cultures increased scientific curiosity and ultimately commercial possibilities.

While foreign artifacts intrigued Europeans before the age of expansion, the number of cross-cultural encounters increased markedly after the fifteenth century. These contacts filled the curiosity cabinets of European monarchs and noblemen with objects from exotic places. The influx of foreign materials coincided with shifting European values. The Renaissance "episteme," Michel Foucault argues, recognized similarities among things formerly regarded as particular or remarkable.[2] While the European engagement in classifying foreign objects started early in the metropole, on the periphery the notion of "oddity" or "curiosity" lingered well into the nineteenth century. Labeling an artifact a curiosity, Bernard Smith contends, expressed "an interest without passing aesthetic judgment."[3] I would add that besides a lack of aesthetic judgment, "curiosity" also connotes the absence of classification. Yet the interest, amazement, or wonder that led to the collecting of objects was not as innocent as one might initially assume. Stephen Greenblatt, for instance, argues that wonder and amazement were central components of the European discourse of discovery; cognitive processes deeply intertwined with emerging systems of representation along edges of constantly expanding overseas horizons. Wonder, according to Greenblatt, became the very conceptual tool through which Europeans filtered their perceptions, linking an expanding Western metropole with an ever-shrinking non-Western periphery. During the late Middle Ages "wonder" shook the reigning intellectual paradigms, but during the Renaissance "wonder" became an essential element of Europeans' physical and intellectual appropriation of the world, a discursive instrument of possession.[4]

"Curiosities," the physical evidence of wonder, troubled Europe's intellectual landscape.[5] Three new approaches emerged to assign meaning to exotic artifacts. The first, labeled "narrative perspective," allowed objects to stand for memories of particular experiences, events, or people. "Curiosities," in a narrow sense, fell under this category, marking specific encounters during voyages of discovery and exploration. The second, more utilitarian perspective, evaluated objects in terms of their expected economic return. "Commodities" fit into this category. The third, more systematic approach placed collected objects within a classification taxonomy and among other things created the category "ethnographica."[6] These three approaches were not clear-cut, and tensions existed among them, as illustrated by James Cook's voyages to the Pacific Ocean in the second half of the eighteenth century.

Although shaped by the Enlightenment, the conceptual tools available to the late-eighteenth-century naturalists who sailed with Cook had changed little since the Renaissance. Distinguishing indigenous cultural artifacts from flora and fauna still followed the rigid separation of *artificialia* and *naturalia* prescribed by Renaissance humanists.[7] *Naturalia* referred to new specimens of plant and animal life that did not fit readily available European categories, while *artificialia,* as the name indicated, denoted "artificial" or human-made objects. The gap between "artificial" and "natural" further widened in 1735 with the publication of Swedish naturalist Carl Linne's (a.k.a. Linnaeus) *Systema Naturae.* Linnaeus' system classified plants by reproductive apparatus and created a taxonomy that accommodated the new plant types encountered during Cook's voyages. With regard to plants, the Linnean system was a major step in Europe's development of global concepts, what Mary Louise Pratt calls a "planetary consciousness."[8] While Linnean categories functioned well in the realm of *naturalia,* one could not extend them to artificial curiosities. Lacking a viable conceptual apparatus to classify indigenous artifacts, the gentlemen scholars who served as naturalists therefore concentrated largely on natural specimens.[9]

To compound the problem, the acquisition of artificial curiosities, absent a clear system of classification, challenged collection activity itself. The naturalists accompanying Cook went to great pains to demonstrate that their endeavors were indeed licensed rather than licentious. Depicting artifacts in engravings without regard for their indigenous context became the preferred mode of representation. Naturalists chose engravings because "the abstraction of artifacts into a scientific enclave was a double operation that recursively authorized the natural philosopher's travel and collecting by making the particular claim that a curiosity was a specimen, something in a scientific enclave, rather than an object of fashion or mere commodity that those lacking scientific authorization might traffic in and profit from."[10]

Unlike Cook's gentlemen, the less-educated crew collected indigenous items for profit, often in competition with naturalists. Artificial curiosities required less effort to collect, preserve, and store than natural specimens. Cook's sailors lacked scientific training, and the cramped conditions aboard his vessels made proper storage of natural curiosities difficult. Their motivation to collect stemmed from the continuing existence of curiosity cabinets in Europe. These cabinets remained popular despite late-eighteenth-century attempts at better classification. In England itself, Cook's voyages fueled interest among many private individuals in collecting South Sea "curios." The best known, Sir Aston Lever, established a significant personal collection. Tensions between the naturalists' nascent interest in "ethnographica" and the sailors' interest in potential "commodities" generated increasing competition for artificial curiosities. Indigenous peoples in the Pacific often mocked this charged atmosphere. In Tonga, for instance, the scramble for artifacts between naturalists and crew was so intense that a Tongan boy decided to stick a piece of human excrement on a stick. He then offered his "artifact" to every European he encountered.[11]

Ironically, natural philosophers also benefited from the demand for Pacific artifacts. Georg Forster, a naturalist on Cook's second voyage, collected objects initially as "curios," but financial troubles forced him to sell them. Financial need and the commercial possibilities of the collected "commodities" overpowered whatever initial interest Forster may have had in "ethnographica."[12] Forster's experience was far from unique: the many items collected during Cook's expeditions fueled an expanding European market for artificial curiosities. Concepts of indigenous material culture as "commodity" and "ethnographica" thus emerged at virtually the same time.

Increased scientific interest in artifacts over the next century did not displace the commodity value of such objects. If anything, potential profit from material culture increased with the many ethnological museums opening in the second half of the nineteenth century. Specialized companies, for instance, emerged by capitalizing on the increasing demand for "ethnographica." The Umlauff family in Hamburg is a well-known example of such a venture. By 1868 Johann Friedrich Gustav Umlauff had established a business specializing in the sale of natural and artificial curiosities, which he expanded greatly by 1884. His sons continued the business, known under the ominous name of Umlauff's World Museum, and traded in zoological, ethnographic, and anthropological specimens. Their customers included private collectors as well as museums and scientific institutions around the world. Although financial difficulties were frequent, the Umlauff venture continued until 1943, when Allied bombs destroyed their entire inventory.[13]

When Germany's commercial frontier reached the Pacific in the latter half of the nineteenth century, Adolf Bastian's salvage ethnography project offered a wealth of commercial opportunities. In addition to commodities traditionally exported from the Pacific, such as copra (dried coconut meat employed for oil production), managers of commercial companies considered trade in indigenous material culture a viable option to increase profit margins. Bastian closely monitored German commercial ventures in the Pacific during the second half of the nineteenth century.[14] His interest had good cause, as several companies' commercial agents promised to explore the ethnographic frontier on behalf of the Berlin Ethnological Museum. Enlisting commercial agents as collectors, however, was ethically ambiguous. Above all, the operations of commercial companies in the Pacific, according to Bastian, threatened to disrupt the fragile social fabric of indigenous cultures. Bastian often expressed his ambivalence in published and unpublished ethnographic literature and correspondence. His correspondence files reveal many attempts to secure commercial agents' patronage.[15] The person Bastian designated to pursue commercial connections in the Pacific was Felix von Luschan, who was soon over his head in dealing with the German companies.

From "Firewood" to "Commodities": The Godeffroy Company's Ethnographic Ventures

Accepting commercial agents as ethnographic collectors was not easy, since most had little regard for ethnography and seldom shared Bastian's urgency. Nicholas Thomas, for instance, suggests that European settlers in Fiji had a vested interest in denying the worth of indigenous cultures and emphasizing the "barbaric" aspects of Fijian society. In particular objects deemed as "cannibal forks" allegedly represented Fijian primitivism—an idea that settlers perpetuated through their display of indigenous material culture.[16] German disregard for indigenous material culture was equally commonplace in the Pacific, although it was less aggressive. Germans assigned the generic label *Feuerholz* (firewood) to indigenous objects, a term that suggests how little value they attached to Pacific artifacts. How this term originated is unclear, but German ethnologists frequently cited the term in their complaints about the attitude of colonial residents toward ethnography.[17] "Among one hundred colonial residents," ethnographer Emil Stephan reported, "you will find ninety-nine opportunists, and when they actually have additional interest in making money, it is usually not in the exploration of the life of the 'dirty Kanak.'"[18] Yet Stephan also mentions settlers' opportunism, which alerted them to the commercial possibilities inherent in ethnographic objects. This was the case with the employees of Johann Caesar Godeffroy und Sohn in the Pacific.

The Godeffroy venture established a secure base in the Samoan Islands by 1857, later expanding into the northern and southern corners of the Pacific. Exporting copra, instead of extracting coconut oil in the islands, the Godeffroy Company established a trading empire that dominated Pacific commerce for two decades from 1860 to 1880.[19] Along with the seemingly endless supplies of copra arriving in Hamburg flowed a steady stream of indigenous objects, attracting the inquisitive spirit of the company's owner, Johann Caesar Godeffroy. Initially, Godeffroy set aside a company building as a museum for the artifacts. Next he hired a trained curator, Johann Dietrich Eduard Schmeltz, who oversaw the preservation, storage, and organization of the collection. Under Schmeltz' supervision, the museum's holdings steadily expanded and its renown grew, fostered in part by a scholarly publication series titled *Journal des Museum Godeffroy* dedicated to exploring the natural science and ethnology of the Pacific. Cooperation between Schmeltz as scientific curator and Godeffroy as enterprising company leader did not stop there. Rather than leave the acquisition of artifacts to chance, Godeffroy directed his employees to collect items in support of his museum's efforts. Soon thereafter, Schmeltz and Godeffroy sent a selected group of trained collectors to the Pacific. This group, which included Johann Kubary, Theodor Kleinschmidt, and Amalie Dietrich, had few trading responsibilities: their task was to acquire, store, and ship specimens for the company's museum in Hamburg. This effort amounted to one of the first documented cases of active support for science by a commercial company.[20] The collectors' exploits provided rich sources for natural science and ethnology in the Pacific, and illustrate how commercial interest intersected with ethnographic research after 1860.

The German scientific community, having much to gain from such activity, showered Godeffroy with praise.[21] Their appraisal casts Caesar Godeffroy as a disinterested patron of ethnographic research, yet recent scholarship suggests otherwise. His Hamburg-based private museum was more than a research institution; it was a long-term investment.[22] Godeffroy appreciated the demand for ethnographic objects generated by Adolf Bastian's call for a "salvage anthropology." While other trading companies also specialized in the purchase, handling, and sale of ethnographic objects, few invested much time in proper arrangement and publication of their acquisitions.[23] Here, Godeffroy's venture differed. In systematically documenting, storing, and, above all, publishing its acquisitions, Godeffroy's museum was far more advanced than its rivals. Godeffroy speculated that his artifacts were worth a great deal more than those hastily assembled by other companies. As supposedly healthy investments, the holdings of the Godeffroy Museum highlight the complexities of the commercialization of material culture. Godeffroy's valued attempt at collection placed quality over quantity as exact determination of an artifact's point of origin, indigenous name, and cultural use was increasingly important in nineteenth-century museology.

The intense trade in ethnographica and natural specimens stimulated by the Godeffroy Museum tested the market for ethnographic objects in Germany. Between 1864 and 1881 Schmeltz issued no fewer than eight directories of ethnographic duplicate objects for sale to interested institutions, but the profits were not sufficient to save the institution from eventual closure and disintegration.[24] Bad investments after German unification bankrupted the company, and it fell to Schmeltz to liquidate Godeffroy's ethnographic investments. In 1879 Godeffroy ordered Schmeltz to write a comprehensive review of the museum's holdings to expedite the collection's sale. This was no easy task, since it required the sorting of three thousand objects, accompanying collectors' correspondence, and relevant secondary literature. The result was the most successful publication of Godeffroy's private museum.[25] In conjunction with the physician Rudolf Krause, responsible for the physical anthropology section of the volume, Schmeltz issued a 700-page ethnological and anthropological survey of the Pacific. Although largely descriptive in nature, the volume received positive reviews.[26] Its scientific reception notwithstanding, Schmeltz' first comprehensive survey of Pacific artifacts amounts to little more than an annotated sales catalogue.[27] Despite aggressive marketing by Godeffroy, his collections failed to fetch high prices. In part this reflected the fact that the sale of the artifacts was no longer dictated by Godeffroy but rather by the growing demands of his creditors.[28] The struggle over Godeffroy's ethnographic treasures pitted the most prominent German museums against each other.[29] Although ultimately the Berlin Ethnological Museum failed to acquire the collection, Bastian's efforts to secure it alerted him to the possibilities of employing commercial companies as collectors.[30] Despite the collapse of Godeffroy's for-profit ethnography, other companies saw potential. Encouraged by Bastian's continued call for salvage ethnology, both the New Guinea Company and the Hernsheim Company engaged in the commercialization of indigenous material culture.

FROM "COMMODITIES" TO "DECORATIVE FIREWOOD":
THE ETHNOGRAPHIC VENTURES OF THE NEW GUINEA COMPANY

In 1884 the New Guinea Company, a consortium representing powerful German business and financial interests, dispatched an expedition to New Guinea to found a German colony in the region. Organized by company director Adolf von Hansemann, the expedition was led by naturalist/ethnographer Otto Finsch. Hansemann's engagement with ethnography started when he offered the Berlin Ethnological Museum a rich collection of 2,128 artifacts returned by Finsch from the coastal areas of northern New Guinea.[31]

Originally, Hansemann did not plan to sell this collection for profit; rather his aim was propaganda. Hansemann asked the Prussian administration to provide a separate hall in the new ethnological museum bearing the inscription "Property of the New Guinea Company" over the entrance. Hansemann envisaged a display merging material culture and natural scientific specimens from the island. Thus displayed as colonial curiosities, Hansemann thought the artifacts would contribute to company efforts to attract prospective German settlers to northeastern New Guinea, now christened "Kaiser Wilhelmsland" by company officials.[32]

Bastian vehemently rejected such an abuse of "his" institution. After prolonged negotiations, the Prussian Museum Administration agreed to purchase, with some help from the German kaiser, the whole lot for 23,000 marks. The agreement further stipulated that the Berlin museum had right of first refusal on all artifacts subsequently gathered by the New Guinea Company.[33] This unexpected income stimulated Hansemann to invest in ethnographic collecting. Finsch himself remarked that company accountants entered the collection's sale as income in the books. All in all, the collection defrayed 10 percent of the estimated expedition costs of 300,000 marks. Even as small as this transaction was, it alerted Hansemann to the commercial potential of ethnography.[34]

Superficially the New Guinea Company and Godeffroy Company endeavors were similar. The New Guinea Company supported a journal, *Nachrichten aus Kaiser Wilhelmsland*, that published articles on the exploration, ethnography, and natural science of northeastern New Guinea, although it was less scientific than the *Journal des Museum Godeffroy*. Hansemann also hired two former Godeffroy Company collectors: Richard Parkinson and Johann Kubary.[35] They quickly left the company, however, suggesting major differences between the New Guinea Company and Godeffroy. Richard Parkinson, for instance, joined the New Guinea Company expecting to broaden his ethnographic horizons traveling through the new German colony, but by 1892 he had left the company in disgust as personal differences with high-ranking company officials and a sea of restrictions made his life miserable: "It is a pity that the [New Guinea] company has no interest in ethnographic research. If only von Hansemann could have the same [ethnographic] interest as the late Godeffroy, then my whole venture would have had a purpose. The [company], however, is solely guided by practical interests and is out to pull hard-earned money out of the poor settlers' purses. Moreover, [company officials] make our lives unbearable with their milelong edicts while they refuse to contribute their share."[36]

There was much truth in what Parkinson said of his tour with the New Guinea Company. The company restricted the movement of its employees and their consumption of alcoholic beverages, regulated the treatment of indigenous people, and micromanaged the collection of natural and ethnographic artifacts. It added long supplements to its employees' contracts. One paragraph stipulated that all objects obtained, specifically those with ethnographic value, were the property of the New Guinea Company. The company promised reimbursement for collection expenses, but employees had no say in the final disposition of their collections.[37] Such restrictions generally enjoyed little popularity among those stationed in New Guinea: "Rest assured that we could have secured dedicated people interested enough in the pursuit of natural science. Unfortunately their efforts were hindered by many ill-devised armchair decisions according to which each employee had to surrender his collection to the company. Taking this into account, who would waste his free time establishing collections? . . . Eventually the decree was dropped, but by then the young men's enthusiasm and efforts were all but gone."[38]

One employee went so far as to play a practical joke on the "ignorant and careless" company officials in Berlin. Amateur entomologist Stephan von Kotze found that collecting insects provided a welcome opportunity to transcend the boredom of daily administration in New Guinea. Fearing official confiscation of his collection, he devised an elaborate hoax, using his free time and ingenuity to fabricate a unique insect collection to satisfy the company's demand. Among von Kotze's "remarkable" collection were thirteen-legged and multicolored specimens and beetles sporting shiny shells composed of tiny glass fragments. Company officials, deeply impressed with his collection, rushed it to the Museum for Natural History in Berlin. However, Kotze's hoax was soon discovered. Kotze later claimed his action led to the abolition of the hated policy governing New Guinea Company collection activity.[39]

Contentious company officials also reduced the efficacy of the few large-scale expeditions to Kaiser Wilhelmsland. In 1895 the German Foreign Office organized a number of scientific ventures to Kaiser Wilhelmsland in conjunction with the New Guinea Company. They brought together naturalist Carl Lauterbach with part-time traveler and ethnographer Ernst Tappenbeck. Tappenbeck, the official chronicler, soon clashed with company officials over the extensive control they intended to exercise over the expeditions. Hansemann, objecting to Tappenbeck's attacks on the company in official reports, withheld the reports from the German Foreign Office and relieved Tappenbeck of his duties. Naturally such episodes negatively affected the expeditions.[40] Although they contributed to a survey of the Ramu River, Governor Hahl later commented that the expeditions were ultimately of little significance to Germany's exploration of New Guinea.[41]

Felix von Luschan at the Berlin Ethnological Museum, deeply dissatisfied with both the quality and the price of New Guinea Company artifacts, also questioned company ethnographic practices. While the original Finsch collection was valuable and groundbreaking, those arriving over the next decade contained no fresh categories of artifacts.[42] Moreover, company officials had no qualms about overcharging the Berlin museum. Each artifact sent to Berlin carried an average price of about 25 to 30 marks, which Luschan thought excessive. "The New Guinea Company remains above all a commercial enterprise," Luschan complained, "so we can hardly reproach [their officials] for exploiting their monopoly in the most brutal manner."[43]

As cooperation between the Berlin museum and the New Guinea Company ground to a standstill, Hansemann found another use for the artifacts collected by his firm. At the German Commercial Exposition of 1896 (also known as the German Colonial Exhibition), Hansemann and other New Guinea Company officials returned to using artifacts to promote the colonization of New Guinea. From its beginning, the exhibition straddled a fine line between scienctific inquiry and commerce. The way the exhibitors displayed their ethnographic objects illustrates this ambiguity. The exposition's scientific section aligned artifacts according to the latest insights of ethnological comparison, while exhibitors in the "colonial hall" used ethnographic objects merely as a decorative backdrop to settlement and commerce. Ethnographic collections on display in the scientific section included those of important traders in ethnographica, such as J. F. G. Umlauff, who sought an air of scientific legitimacy. The colonial exhibit, chiefly organized by the New Guinea Company, included ethnographic collections from Kaiser Wilhelmsland. Company officials made no attempt to organize the artifacts in a scientific manner, arranging them as curiosities, "decorative" pieces underscoring the colonial landscape of German New Guinea.[44]

With the popular success of the exhibition, New Guinea Company officials considered establishing a museum to showcase the commercial and ethnographic resources of the German colonies. A group of colonial enthusiasts, including C. von Beck, New Guinea Company deputy director, launched a massive campaign to find a permanent home for the colonial exhibit's products. Their efforts culminated in a joint-stock company that founded such a museum in Berlin in 1896. Its self-proclaimed purpose was educational as well as promotional: informing visitors not just about agricultural and mineral products from the German colonies, but also about opportunities for emigration and investment. The museum represented the indigenous population as a labor pool for developing German colonial interests. An arrangement of artifacts, house models, and an artificial landscape communicated a false sense of harmony to visitors. It erased colonial tensions, presenting an image of an unspoiled paradise begging for development and settlers.[45] The colonial museum displaying indigenous artifacts as trophies and curiosities troubled Berlin Ethnological Museum employees.

Felix von Luschan attacked the misuse of valuable scientific specimens at what he called a museum in name only. He decried the union of colonial fantasy and shallow ethnography on display at the colonial museum and vehemently criticized the arrangement of the artifacts as colonial curiosities without order or taxonomy. "[B]ehind the pompous name of 'German Colonial Museum,'" Luschan wrote to one of his staunchest supporters, "some people attempt to establish a sort of panopticon for black odds-and-ends."[46] In a review of the German Colonial Exhibition, Luschan wrote, "How could ethnographic collections of high value arrive at the colonial hall rather than the [more comparative] scientific exhibition? Their sole purpose here seems to be empty wall decoration. They carry no labels, lack appropriate protection against dust and insects, and are rendered scientifically unimportant."[47]

Luschan hoped to put an end to what he regarded a ludicrous venture by involving many important people within colonial circles.[48] Popular opinion, however, supported the colonial museum, and Luschan fought an uphill battle, which he ultimately lost.

Luschan suffered a similar defeat when he clashed with New Guinea Company officials over their attempts to change established place names in the Pacific Ocean. Following the annexation of German New Guinea, company officials were eager to stamp a particularly "German" identity on the territory. The German part of New Guinea thus became Kaiser Wilhelmsland. New names also emerged in the Bismarck Archipelago; the former Duke of York Islands became Neu Lauenburg; New Britain turned into Neu Pommern, and New Ireland changed to Neu Mecklenburg. German nationalists regarded this as a natural process of "liberating" the territory from its former British presence. Furthermore, the English names suggested the possibility of Britain reclaiming these territories based on the right of "first European discovery," a common practice during the sixteenth and seventeenth centuries.[49]

Nationalists criticized those who refused to use the new names in publication. Prominent editors targeted Luschan for his retention of the dreaded English names for German Pacific colonies. No one questioned Luschan's ethnological authority, but his loyalty to Germany's colonial agenda was clearly in doubt. Luschan replied in several short publications, professing loyalty to the German cause in the Pacific. His concern was not with colonial policies, Luschan simply regarded rechristening place names as counterproductive to an organized scientific agenda. The work of scholars, Luschan argued, required a clear-cut designation of place names; changes to accepted names only led to confusion. The rechristening policy of the New Guinea Company was superfluous and burdensome to scholarly literature. Luschan proposed an alternate naming system for international recognition: wherever possible, indigenous names should be retained; where a satisfactory indigenous name could not be found, names given by the first European discoverers should be used. Luschan found agreement from ethnologists and geographers worldwide, even gaining unanimous approval from the Seventh International Geographical Congress in Berlin in 1899.[50] But international resolutions had little impact on the German Foreign Office or the New Guinea Company, whose officials adhered to the new names. Luschan persistently retained the old names in his publications, one of the few within Germany to do so.

Conceptual clashes in Germany over the nature of indigenous material culture as well as restrictions on the ethnographic collecting in New Guinea prevented the New Guinea Company from reproducing Godeffroy's early success. Squabbles with Luschan over place names and the nature of collecting did not help matters. By 1899, the New Guinea Company no longer considered "investment" in ethnography a viable option and largely abandoned this venture.

THE HERNSHEIM COMPANY: ENVISIONING A LARGE-SCALE COMMERCIALIZATION OF ETHNOGRAPHY

After the demise of the Godeffroy Company, a third venture, Hernsheim & Company, emerged as a strong player in the ethnographica trade. Initially its main export item was copra, but soon commercial interest in indigenous objects emerged.[51] However, few ethnographic enthusiasts who toured the German colonies had good things to say about the company's acquisition of ethnographica: "I acquired a complete collection from a young man on Matupi. He had traveled extensively in the territory, and he was willing to surrender the whole lot after he and I had endured a horrible night of heavy drinking. When we finally brought our activity to an end in the early morning hours, the owner of the collection was so loaded that he was unable to provide me with concrete information about the artifacts. There was no time to wait around, because I had to leave on the next steamer. This is how one collects in this area!"[52]

The young man who gave Max Buchner his collection was probably none other than Max Thiel, nephew of company founder Eduard Hernsheim and later manager of Pacific operations. Max Thiel, realizing that such collections would fetch more than a few pints of beer, soon started to peddle ethnographica to German travelers in New Guinea. He accumulated such objects at his station on Matupi, a small island off the coast of New Britain's Gazelle Peninsula. Thiel's collecting lacked ethnographic direction, but the acquired artifacts soon found buyers.[53] In 1899 an expert ethnographer inspected one of Thiel's collections assembled in the far-flung stations of the Admiralty Islands and found it lacking. Although the collection contained old pieces, the expert remarked on its hasty assembly and general poor labeling. The reasons for the poor state of Thiel's collection were obvious:

> Those places visited by government steamers are entirely depleted of artifacts. The only white person in close contact with the natives is the hopelessly isolated trader, who is visited at the most once or twice [a year] by a company schooner. Hailing from a rather low educational background, this poor soul has understandably very little interest in local "curiosities," unless they are somewhat connected to commerce. Those occasional ethnographic acquisitions are usually sent as commodities to the main station from where

they are eventually forwarded to a museum; sometimes interested visitors intercept them before leaving the territory. One can thus hardly expect [these artifacts to bear] proper categorization, places of origin, native names, etc.[54]

One cannot establish from the written record whether Thiel took such criticism to heart. By 1902, however, Thiel had hired Franz Hellwig, a former employee of the Deutsche Handels-und Plantagengesellschaft to assist him in his collecting.[55] A veteran of several years of residence in the Bismarck Archipelago, Hellwig had accumulated a large collection, which he advertised for sale in Germany in 1899.[56] Although clearly an amateur in the eyes of museum ethnologists, Hellwig's expertise landed him employment as an ethnographic collector on his return to German New Guinea. Ironically, Hellwig began collecting not for one of the many German ethnological museums, but for Max Thiel's Hernsheim Company. Thiel's large-scale for-profit ethnography was related to what is commonly known as the "Matty mystery" in the German ethnographic literature.

THE "MATTY MYSTERY" AND THE FAILURE OF COMMERCIAL "FIELDWORK"

Among Franz Hellwig's main destinations was a set of islands in the western corner of the Bismarck Archipelago that had recently come to the attention of the ethnological community. The islands of Wuvulu and Aua entered European consciousness through eighteenth-century maps, named "Matty" and "Durour," respectively.[57] Their remoteness from major shipping lanes left them largely undisturbed until the New Guinea Company steamer *Ysabel* visited "Matty" in 1893. Always in need of plantation laborers, New Guinea Company officials sent their employee Ludwig Kärnbach on a recruitment mission. While he failed in his primary task at the islands, Kärnbach did return with thirty-seven artifacts from Matty. Because of the aforementioned agreement between Berlin museum officials and the New Guinea Company, the collection ended up in Berlin's Ethnological Museum, where it came to Luschan's attention. Luschan recognized that the artifacts forwarded by the New Guinea Company barely resembled those from the New Guinea mainland.[58] Nonetheless, based on the scarce evidence of thirty-seven artifacts and Kärnbach's brief notes and recollections, Luschan proclaimed the importance of "Matty" island. What initially dazzled Luschan was that the island, located roughly 150 kilometers from the mainland, displayed a previously unknown material culture. Similarly, according to Kärnbach's sketchy firsthand observations, its inhabitants were of lighter skin color than their Melanesian neighbors. Their weapons, some spiked with shark's teeth (see Figure 1),[59] suggested an affinity with some neighboring islands, especially

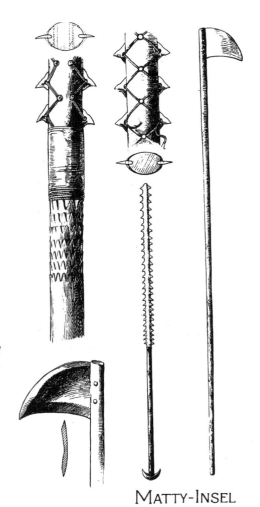

Figure 1. Artifacts from "Matty" island (From Internationales Archiv für Ethographie 8 [1895])

MATTY-INSEL

the Ninigo group, as well as some superficial connections to the area known as Micronesia.

Luschan was too careful a scholar to jump to conclusions with insufficient data, yet he understandably drew attention to the curiously non-Melanesian nature of the physical traits and material culture of "Matty's" inhabitants. Citing Kärnbach's assertion that they knew neither iron nor tobacco, Luschan maintained that people living on "Matty" had been isolated from other areas for perhaps ten generations (approximately three hundred years). Luschan thought the encounter with "Matty" to be of tremendous scientific importance. In Bastian's scheme, Melanesia was significant because of the supposedly elementary thought patterns of its societies. Far from interested in wide-sweeping theoretical generalizations, Luschan was more concerned with delineating cultural boundaries within his African and Oceanic division. The "fuzzy" boundaries of Melanesia, Micronesia, and Polynesia bred conceptual headaches for Luschan and his contemporaries. Today, the old European tripartite categorization is recognized as problematic at best and racist at worst, but late-nineteenth-century scholars craved clear demarcations, finding physical differences equivalent to cultural divisions.[60] German New Guinea, and the Pacific in general, bustled with linguistic and cultural puzzles; Luschan hoped "Matty" would provide the key to solving them.[61] Along this vein, Luschan's articles also called for careful analysis of the island's material culture. Ideally, Luschan argued for long-term stationary study among "Matty's" people. The candidates best suited for this venture were New Guinea Company officials, who had a duty (*Ehrenpflicht*), as colonial administrators of this territory, to investigate the island's heritage.[62]

To press his call for systematic exploration of "Matty," Luschan forwarded several copies of his articles to prominent residents in German New Guinea. One article found its way, via Richard Parkinson, into the enterprising hands of Max Thiel.[63] Luschan's article prompted Thiel to undertake what he had been considering all along: opening a trading station in the western islands of the Bismarck Archipelago. In early 1896 Thiel dispatched the schooner *Welcome,* under Captain A. F. V. Andersen, to Wuvulu along with a Mr. Schielkopf, designated as the island's resident Hernsheim trader. Several laborers recruited from the island of Buka accompanied Schielkopf. Thiel expected Schielkopf and his indentured laborers to establish a thriving business on "Matty," including among the usual agricultural crops a fair share of indigenous artifacts.

On arrival, Captain Andersen approached Wuvulu with a small cutter flying both the German and Hernsheim colors. On the beach the captain encountered a crowd of some three hundred indigenes to welcome him. After elaborate greeting ceremonies, Andersen selected about two hundred square meters in the neighborhood of his landfall for the future Hernsheim station. His attempts to purchase the land were initially unsuccessful. Yet he soon devised a solution by inviting a number of those he regarded as "chiefs" to his schooner, where he convinced them to sign a deed. It is doubtful whether the "chiefs" did indeed fully understand the gravity of this transaction. To provide further incentives, Andersen gave each "chief" an iron hatchet and obtained the legal land title. The relationship between the inhabitants of "Matty" and the Hernsheim party remained peaceful until Andersen's departure.[64]

Problems soon arose. Andersen left behind Schielkopf with three young laborers from Buka and a quickly constructed shack with a corrugated tin roof. When a ship called on the island in March of 1896, only several weeks after the initial landfall, it found the station destroyed and Schielkopf and his Buka employees missing. The German colonial authorities immediately dispatched the naval survey vessel *Möwe* to Wuvulu. The crew first located the laborers from Buka, who claimed that the indigenes had murdered Schielkopf, forcing them to flee into the interior of the island. The *Möwe*'s crew, however, gauged no hostility among the locals, who freely traded in "curiosities" with the German sailors. Doubting the Bukans' version, the crew of the naval vessel took the laborers to Matupi for further investigation. Colonial authorities also distrusted the Buka witnesses and decided to shelve the case.[65]

While colonial authorities considered the matter closed, Max Thiel sought to profit from the ethnographic material returned from the island. Arriving in Germany with Luschan's article under his arm and a hull filled with artifacts from Wuvulu, Thiel arranged an exhibit at the Hamburg Museum of Natural History. Many prominent visitors inspected the two thousand or so artifacts on display. One was Luschan, author of the article that inspired the rush to the island. Thiel was sure he could get at least 20,000 marks for the lot and consequently rejected Luschan's attempts to lower the price.[66] Although interested in acquiring the collection, Luschan had reservations about its quality, which on first inspection seemed to duplicate the original thirty-seven artifacts that had served as the centerpiece of his article. Furthermore, Luschan disapproved of what he witnessed in Hamburg. He claimed Thiel's traders "had collected in the most abominable fashion. They deprived the poor [Matty] people of thousands of weapons . . . enough to supply all museums in the world."[67] Because of such criticism, Luschan ultimately failed to secure Thiel's artifacts, which were mainly purchased by Karl Hagen, interim director of the Hamburg Ethnological Museum, and a Mr. Ohlendorf of Schwerin.[68]

Ironically, Luschan had fallen prey to his own article. As much as Luschan highlighted the need for careful collecting activity in New Guinea, his writing increased the value of ethnographic commodities from "Matty." Luschan, upset about this turn of events, voiced his discontent once again in writing:

> My publication [on "Matty"] has influenced the representative of the [Hernsheim] company in Matupi, Mr. M. Thiel, to instruct one of his captains to establish an ethnographic collection. Unfortunately this man did not fully understand his mission and has collected tremendous numbers of spears and clubs, all closely related to those appearing in my publication. Yet he has collected nothing that could in any way get us closer to the scientific questions surrounding the origin of the Matty islanders. In fact we still know

very little about them; not a single hair of theirs has been analyzed nor a single syllable of their language. The whole exercise amounts to a plundering action unique in the history of ethnography that has failed to yield any significant scientific results.[69]

Luschan reiterated something Caesar Godeffroy had identified several decades earlier—an object lacking indigenous context was a mere "curiosity." Luschan maintained that extensive documentation of artifacts was central to all collection activity. Thiel agreed but took great offense at Luschan's characterization of his collection as "plunder." For several years their relationship was anything but cordial. Thiel thought Luschan was out of touch with commercial realities in the German territory. "Do you honestly think," Thiel asked one of Luschan's close associates, "that I can lecture my ship captains about the ethics of international law?"[70] Thiel did not expect an answer to this rhetorical question. He did, however, hire professional collectors to improve the quality of his ethnographica. This hiring practice allowed Thiel to return, for a short while at least, to Godeffroy's extensive collection agenda. Consequently, Thiel retained F. E. Hellwig for the Hernsheim Company.

True connoisseurs of ethnology were rare among the European residents of German New Guinea. Hellwig proved to be an exception, and the German ethnological community generally approved of his collection.[71] For Thiel, more than money was at stake. He intended to restore his reputation, tarnished by Luschan's comments on the "plunder" of Wuvulu. Thiel had not forgotten the ethnographic interest in the western islands of the Bismarck Archipelago, especially Wuvulu and Aua. Although Hellwig's task was primarily to gather material culture, his duties exceeded mere acquisition. Guided by Luschan's criticism, Hellwig spent considerable time on both Wuvulu and Aua—almost a year combined, which was one of the first long-term ethnographic studies in German New Guinea.[72] Hellwig's stay in the Bismarck Archipelago was primarily a commercial enterprise. Its scientific mission was secondary, inspired only by the need to provide greater value and legitimacy to the ethnography.

Historians of anthropology tell us that fieldwork has a long history and tradition. The concept of the "field" was born of the natural sciences. "Practitioners determined that naturalists must break with their long habit of relying on theories articulated by armchair scholars, that scientists could not do credible analysis unless they had themselves gathered their data on which their generalizations rested."[73] This shift in knowledge gave way to what James Clifford calls "fieldwork habitus," which allowed for the institutionalization of anthropology during the early twentieth century when other forms of knowledge deriving from missionaries and colonial officials were no longer deemed sufficient.[74] Long-term residence determined a new type of inquiry, supposedly superior and less politically charged than that of the colonial pioneers.[75] Ultimately a swing in funding policies, from museum collecting to long-term studies of indigenous societies, confirmed fieldwork as the predominant methodology for university-based anthropologists.[76] But in many ways, Hellwig's time on Wuvulu and Aua suggests other neglected influences in the history of anthropology. While ideas behind the commercialization of artifacts were still very much grounded in "salvage" projects advocated by Adolf Bastian, a successful ethnographic collection had to transcend mere accumulation of seemingly unrelated objects. As museum officials, Luschan in particular, demanded inquiries into the manufacture and purpose of such artifacts and the meaning of indigenous material culture, collectors embarked on investigations that resembled the later activity of fieldworkers, who pushed anthropology into new directions. The Hellwig study indicates that the often postulated radical break between collectors and fieldworkers in anthropology was in fact much more fluid. Hellwig's responsibilities and freedom clearly exceeded what Godeffroy offered to his official collectors. Hellwig enjoyed the complete support of the Hernsheim trading empire throughout the Bismarck Archipelago. Where Hernsheim's commercial influence did not reach, Thiel negotiated deals with other trading companies. This was particularly the case with Wuvulu and Aua, which by 1902 had become part of the domain of Heinrich Richard Wahlen, whose agents dominated commerce in the western Bismarck Archipelago.[77]

To be sure, Hellwig was not a trained ethnographer. In his reports, including those to the German governor, Hellwig recognized the scientific potential of the mission but made it clear he had no intention of solving the "Matty mystery": "Until now I was unable to ascertain the degree of linguistic and ethnographic relationship between the inhabitants of Wuvula [*sic*] and Aua and those of the Eastern Caroline Islands, so I have refrained from any speculations. This is not important after all, since I am only collecting material for later investigations. As far as the inhabitants of Wuvula and Aua are concerned, I would like to say that they require our increased attention."[78] Hellwig's reluctance to provide clear-cut answers to Luschan's "Matty mystery" served Thiel well. The commercialization of the islands depended, among other things, on its potential for shedding light on the scientific puzzle. A solution, however, would likely lower the collection's price tag. The next step was marketing the collection to potentially interested parties in Germany. Thiel used German travelers to the territory to spread the word to the German museological community. Rumor had it that Hellwig's collection was to be the last complete assemblage of artifacts from the Bismarck

Archipelago.[79] The collection could have had no better advertisement, and many German museums impatiently awaited its arrival.

When Hellwig's much anticipated collection arrived in Germany, a short struggle over its acquisition ensued between major ethnological institutions of Berlin, Cologne, Hamburg, and Stuttgart.[80] Eventually, Hamburg acquired this collection for its ethnological museum. Georg Thilenius, recently appointed director of the museum, used his influence with the Hernsheim Company to keep the collection in Hamburg. The cost of the collection, which numbered some 3,300 artifacts, totaled 20,000 marks, although some expense was defrayed by selling duplicate artifacts to Berlin and Cologne.[81] Compared to the Godeffroy collection, which held a similar number of artifacts, the sale price was rather low. Moreover, contemporary sources estimated Thiel's expenditure on Hellwig's expedition at 20,000 marks, the price fetched for the collection.[82] Thiel's investment was a losing proposition, and large-scale commercial ethnography consequently waned. Thiel's ethnographic effort is perhaps better understood as an attempt to reestablish his reputation, which had been tarnished by Luschan, since Thiel did not want to be remembered in the history of ethnography for his "plunder" of Wuvulu and Aua. While individual colonial agents continued to collect in the Bismarck Archipelago and elsewhere in German New Guinea, no company again invested in commodifying its ethnography.

FELIX VON LUSCHAN'S GERMAN SOUTH SEA EXPEDITION

German museum officials drew their own hard lessons from the "Matty mystery." With commercial concerns, especially Thiel's Hernsheim Company, attempting to push ethnography into more profitable realms, museum specialists tried to regain their position on the ethnographic frontier by sending experts to the Pacific. The failed combination of commerce and ethnography is at least partially responsible for the opening of the "expedition age" in German New Guinea after 1904. Felix von Luschan's disagreements with Thiel triggered a call for an expedition to the Pacific equipped with its own steamer. Starting in 1903, Luschan proposed a broad sweep of the majority of the islands located in Melanesia, Micronesia, and Polynesia. Hawai'i figured as a noticeable exception, since Luschan located these islands within the "sphere of influence" of the Bishop Museum in Honolulu. Luschan decided, however, to go beyond the German colonies to arrive at cultural rather than political divisions in the Pacific. While his survey was to include botanical, geographical, and geological studies, its main objective was the collection of ethnographic data, material culture, and anthropometric measurements. Among other things, Luschan expected this endeavor would generate several monographs highlighting his and the Berlin Ethnological Museum's contributions to the ethnology of the Pacific. Given the nature of the expedition, Luschan proposed to draw the majority of its members from the discipline of ethnology and physical anthropology. Luschan planned to send two trained ethnologists (one as expedition leader), a physical anthropologist, a linguist, and a photographer. Two others would represent the disciplines of zoology and either geography or geology. Luschan estimated roughly four years for the entire project.

Much of Luschan's proposal reads as a strategy to regain some sort of control over ethnographic collecting. He was obsessed with procuring exact information about collected artifacts, with ensuring that objects returned to Berlin would be qualitatively better than those acquired by others. By "others" he meant both other museum officials and commercial companies. The procuring of a steamer for the expedition was imperative, Luschan argued, as he envisioned operating as much as possible outside of the reach of colonial residents, including colonial administrators, missionaries, and traders.[83]

Luschan's urgent call to his administration for such an independent expedition derived partially from his negative experiences with the German resident traders in the Pacific. His need for independence, however, also doomed the proposal. The chief obstacles to his venture were his astronomical financial estimates. The construction of the expedition's steamer alone he estimated to be 250,000 marks, to which he added several hundred thousand more for the purchase of ethnographic objects, provisions, and scientific equipment. In all, Luschan needed to raise no less than one million marks for the project, yet such sums were well beyond the means of local Prussian administrators. Only the German government had that kind of money. To invite such funds, however, Luschan required practical applicability of his proposal. Yet in light of his urge for "independence," the proposal teemed with attempts to monopolize the prospective information for Berlin's museum. In sum, it was not what a budding Pacific colonial power needed to hear. Moreover, the expedition was to survey the Pacific Islands generally, not just German colonies in New Guinea, Micronesia, and Samoa.[84] Any such proposal must have appeared odd, if not suspicious, to the German colonial administration, especially since Luschan presented the proposal at a critical time.

When Luschan unveiled his plan to close associates in December 1903, he could hardly have foreseen that only a few months later the German colonies in Africa would be shaken by indigenous uprisings. The impending Russo-Japanese War was also a consideration among colonial officials, who wanted to wait until its conclusion before launching an expedition.[85] Other dignitaries were less enthusiastic about the proposal. Ferdinand von

Richthofen, chairman of the Berlin Geographic Society, refused Luschan help and claimed he would prevent any expedition of such magnitude.[86] Luschan's idea of operating independently in the German Pacific proved too impractical and ultimately undermined the planned expedition.

Felix von Luschan's failed attempt at exploration emerged out of his disappointment with the ethnographic results emerging from German commercial agents residing in the Pacific. Rather than resigning himself to the fate of obtaining large quantities of "curiosities"—or ill-determined artifacts—Luschan decided to be proactive. His attempt to send trained ethnographers on a wide-sweeping Oceanic collection trip failed to materialize but provided a foundation for future endeavors. Luschan's attempt to move away from the reliance on local, nontrained, collectors became even more crucial as other German museum officials actively objected to Berlin's monopoly on colonial artifacts. The first decade of the twentieth century witnessed a reaction against artifact centralization in Luschan's division. Mirroring his experiences with commercial agents in German New Guinea, this threat ultimately forced Luschan to take the offensive. Realizing a potential quantitative loss of colonial artifacts, Luschan was gearing up to propose qualitative solutions to the collection impasse. Experiences along the colonial periphery and the defense of an inadequate monopoly played crucial roles in pushing German anthropology into new methodological directions.

CHAPTER 3

Losing the Monopoly

E ven though Felix von Luschan grew increasingly impatient with commercial agents in German New Guinea, he could expect little sympathy from fellow German museum officials. Faithful to the Federal Council Resolution achieved by Bastian, Luschan defended the monopoly position of his African and Oceanic division on scientific grounds. Only the Berlin Ethnological Museum, Luschan maintained, had the qualified personnel to sift through artifacts from the German colonies of Africa and the Pacific leading to informed publication. Yet actions spoke louder than Luschan's esteemed words. As accumulated colonial artifacts turned Luschan's division into a fire hazard rather than a temple of learning, other German museum officials quickly geared up to attack Berlin's monopoly. Their efforts took a two-pronged approach. On one hand, kind words and an increasing flow of state decorations to residents of the German colonies lured collectors away from the Berlin museum. On the other hand, Luschan's lack of ethnographic dissemination provided a firm intellectual platform for calls for decentralization. Under increasing critique, including, much to his chagrin, criticism from his own superiors, Luschan decided to reevaluate his line of thinking. Partially inspired by his experiences with commercial collectors in German New Guinea, Luschan argued for a collecting activity that emphasized qualitative rather than quantitative criteria. This way the Berlin Ethnological Museum might lose the quantitative edge over other museums in Germany, yet he maintained that sharply delineated collections, backed by concise monographs, would maintain the museum's lead in the scientific exploitation of the German colonies. Where other museums displayed mere curiosities, Berlin's hallways and storage areas would be filled with ethnographica, whose indigenous meanings had been determined by trained anthropologists in the field. In short, the competitive atmosphere among German museums set in motion prominent methodological steps that would in turn influence the colonial periphery in German New Guinea.

Felix von Luschan saw the Berlin Ethnological Museum as the premier German institution. Only in this fashion could Luschan justify continued centralization of colonial artifacts in his division. He argued that centralizing ethnographic specimens enabled the Berlin museum to provide a unified picture of the German colonies. For him, the main threat to scientific investigation lay in the fragmentation of colonial ethnography, which he attempted to prevent at all cost. Lifting the resolution of 1889, he argued, would intensify such fragmentation. Several regrettable instances of fragmentation already existed. Luschan cited the dispersal of the collections resulting from James Cook's famed eighteenth-century expeditions as well as those following Britain's punitive expedition to Benin in 1897 to underscore his point.[1] Fragmentation was counterproductive, especially since the centralization effort in Berlin aided not only the German ethnological community but also colonial administration. Luschan was less explicit on how ethnology and empire interacted, but he emphasized that knowledge was indeed power. Luschan hoped to make the centralization not a Prussian but rather a universal German agenda. Science became a patriotric enterprise.[2]

In this sense, Luschan believed in more focused collection activity, and he issued detailed collecting instructions for the German colonies.[3] In 1897 Luschan prepared a short list of collecting instructions for the German colony of Togo, which he forwarded to colonial officials in other German colonies as well.[4] By 1899 his efforts coalesced into a more general collection guide.[5] While Luschan's directives for collecting were loose and flexible, he encouraged local collectors to refrain from mere accumulation of artifacts without proper documentation: "[S]imply collecting . . . objects is not enough. In the end one can collect spears and shields just like beetles and butterflies; information on place and time is sufficient. Not so with things connected with religious ideas: in these cases it is paramount to know all the possible meanings of each single piece."[6]

While Luschan professed to do more than the mere hoarding of artifacts, conditions in his division told a different tale. By the turn of the century, it was painfully obvious that the facilities in Berlin were inadequate to accommodate the growing number of ethnological collections reaching the institution. Luschan's own African and Oceanic division illustrated this quite well. Over a twenty-year period (1886–1906), the number of artifacts increased tenfold and left Luschan scrambling for alternatives.[7] Moreover, overcrowding at the museum forced intervention by local authorities, who deemed it a fire and safety hazard. The closure of the museum was imminent unless stairs and passageways were cleared of ethnographic objects. The museum administration responded by establishing a storage facility on the outskirts of Berlin large enough to house some of the collections. This in turn created problems with conservation, as humidity and insects threatened to damage the objects.[8] Luschan was not alone in his predicament. Other divisions of the museum were bursting under the acquired artifact volume, which limited the institution's scientific output.[9]

To the untrained, Luschan's division indeed seemed well equipped to handle the flow of artifacts from the German colonies. In terms of trained personnel, Berlin towered over similar institutions within Germany. Following Bastian's policy that the whole of human cultures be preserved in the museum, increased specialization characterized the different divisions of the institution. By 1904 Bastian's five assistants presided over independent departments spanning Africa and Oceania, the Americas, East Asia, South Asia, and prehistory. For the African and Oceanic division alone, director Felix von Luschan supervised numerous assistants engaged in cataloging and organizing incoming collections.[10] The output of the museum on the whole, however, was rather low. While geographical journals and the *Zeitschrift für Ethnologie* (the journal affiliated with the Berlin Society for Anthropology, Ethnology, and Prehistory) published researchers affiliated with the Berlin museum, the museum itself never established a regular publication series. The *Original-Mittheilungen aus der Ethnologischen Abteilung der Königlichen Museen zu Berlin* appeared in 1885–1886, immediately before and after the opening of the independent museum building. The transformation of this journal into the *Veröffentlichungen aus dem Königlichen Museum für Völkerkunde* brought additional publication space, but in the thirty years between 1889 and 1919 only eight volumes appeared. To augment this meager scholarship, Bastian commissioned the *Notizblatt* for shorter ethnographic pieces, but it ceased publication by 1904. It was only in 1911, through a large endowment from world traveler Arthur Baessler, that the museum could finally support a regular journal.[11]

Nonetheless, the Berlin museum was, comparatively speaking, the only game in town. If one discounts internal memoranda and occasional visitors' guides, museums in other German states generated few museum publications. Even Luschan's most vociferous critic, Stuttgart's Karl von Linden, had little time or money to publish reports of his ethnographic treasures in academic journals. Much less was he able to produce a regular journal devoted exclusively to ethnology. Only Dresden, whose museum published the *Publicationen aus dem königlich-ethnographischen Museum zu Dresden* under A. B. Meyer's tutelage, stood out. Meyer, however, was above all a zoologist, and much of his energy was spent on sorting, cataloging, and describing acquired objects.[12]

The Berlin museum sorely missed a journal devoted to the classification of the artifacts it acquired under the Federal Council Resolution of 1889. Colonial collections received some attention in other publications, but by and large Luschan could not maintain his claim to an adequate dissemination of ethnographic knowledge. This became obvious when Luschan, in a paper presented to the First German Colonial Congress in 1902, attempted to highlight the importance of ethnology in the colonial endeavor but was rather unclear about the intents and purposes of the discipline.[13] Furthermore, Luschan's cautious policy governing the distribution of ethnographic duplicates did not allay accusations of mismanagement; the decreasing quality and quantity of artifacts listed in the duplicate catalogues seem to prove his critics right.

LEARNING CIVILITY: STUTTGART AND THE GERMAN COLONIES

Disgruntled museum officials protested when the system that distributed "duplicates" to other institutions faltered. The most vociferous protests emerged from the southern state of Württemberg. In 1882 a group of Swabian citizens established the Württemberg Society for Ethnology and Commercial Geography in Stuttgart. The society's regional identity increased once the charismatic Count Karl von Linden assumed the society's helm in 1889, coincidentally in the same year the Federal Council passed the resolution establishing Berlin's monopoly.

Like many ethnologists, Linden heeded Adolf Bastian's urgent call for ethnographic salvage operations before the expected disappearance of non-Western societies. Linden gradually increased his society's small ethnographic collection located in a commercial hall in Stuttgart.[14] From the perspective of the salvage agenda, Linden regarded the centralization of colonial artifacts in Berlin as counterproductive. Involving more museums in the storage and preservation of indigenous artifacts, Linden argued, would ultimately increase the salvage impetus. In private, however, Linden's position was politically motivated. Acquiring artifacts was not only an attempt to spread the ethnographic harvest, but also to assert regional autonomy.

Linden accelerated his collection activity as a consequence of Luschan's unyielding determination to uphold the Federal Council Resolution of 1889. In fact, Luschan, while visiting Linden's collections in Stuttgart, ridiculed the count's efforts and failed to endear himself in southern Germany.[15] Linden warned Luschan of the emerging divide between Prussian and non-Prussian institutions: "What are you doing with all your duplicates? You must be literally drowning in them.... Your administrative norms seem inspired by a generosity and a patriotic spirit that reminds me of the north-south divide

Table 1. Decoration Bestowal on Resident Collectors in German New Guinea

Resident Collectors	Berlin (Prussia)	Dresden (Saxony)	Leipzig (Saxony)	Munich (Bavaria)	Stuttgart (Württemberg)
Rudolf von Bennigsen[1]					OWK (1902)
Franz Boluminski[2]	KO IV (1904) RAO IV (1909)		AO RK I (1910)		FO RK II (1904) FO RK I (1909)
Albert Hahl[3]					FO KK II (1912)
Emil Loessner[4]					FO RK II (1906)

Decorations: Prussia: KO = Kronenorden (Order of the Crown), RAO = Roter Adlerorden (Order of the Red Eagle); Saxony: AO = Albrechtsorden (Order of Albert); Bavaria: MO = Orden vom Heiligen Michael (Order of St. Michael); Württemberg: OWK = Orden der Württembergischen Krone (Order of the Crown of Württemberg), FO = Friedrichsorden (Order of Frederick). *General decoration designations:* RK = Ritterkreuz (Knight's Cross), KK = Komturekreuz (Commander's Cross). Roman numerals indicate the class of the decoration (the higher the numeral, the lower the class).

1. First governor of German New Guinea; Hauptstaatsarchiv Stuttgart, E 46, Bü 1009.
2. Colonial Official, Nusa/Kaveing Station—Northern New Ireland; Hauptstaatsarchiv Stuttgart, E 46, Bü 1009; Staatliche Museen zu Berlin—Preussischer Kulturbesitz, Museum für Volkerkunde, IB Astralien/E 815/08; Museum für Völkerkunde, Leipzig, KB 1910. See Rainer Buschmann, "Franz Boluminski and the Wonderland of Carvings: Towards an Ethnography of Collection Activity," *Baessler Archiv* n.f. 44 (1996): 185–210.
3. Second governor of German New Guinea; Hauptstaatsarchiv Stuttgart, E 46, Bü 1009. See Rainer Buschmann, "Colonizing Anthropology: Albert Hahl and the Ethnographic Frontier in German New Guinea," in *Worldly Provincialism: German Anthropology in the Age of Empire,* ed. H. Glenn Penny and Matti Bunzl (Ann Arbor: University of Michigan Press, 2003), 230–255.
4. Employee of the Jaluit Company on Pohnpei; Hauptstaatsarchiv Stuttgart, E 46, Bü 1009.

(*Mainlinie*)—even more, [it reminds me] of the good old times when, while traveling, one encountered a different border control every two hours."[16] Linden soon contested Luschan's monopoly with a shrewd plan. "Obviously my blue eyes alone," Linden later revealed to one of his colleagues, "won't induce any potential patron to relinquish his collection to our museum; alas I soon discovered the proper cure for buttonhole ailment, and even if I cannot provide . . . a guarantee for my cure, it is safe to say that as far as I can remember most of the patients have left my clinic in good health."[17] "Buttonhole ailment" in the correspondence refers to a metaphoric disease. Social status in Wilhelmine Germany often derived from overtly displayed symbols. Orders or decorations, for instance, illustrated a high honor bestowed on an individual for excellence in civic or military service. These orders were usually fixed in a buttonhole on the left side of the overcoat—hence the

Table 1. *(continued)*

Resident Collectors	Berlin (Prussia)	Dresden (Saxony)	Leipzig (Saxony)	Munich (Bavaria)	Stuttgart (Württemberg)
Karl Nauer[5]				MO IV (1914)	
Richard Parkinson[6]		AO RK I (1897)			FO RK I (1904)
Max Thiel[7]	RAO IV (1908)	AO RK I (1910)			FO RK I (1908)
Arno Senfft[8]	RAO IV (1899)				FO RK I (1901)
Wilhelm Wostrack[9]	KO IV (?)[10]				FO RK II (1909)

5. Captain of the *Sumatra,* employee of the Norddeutscher Lloyd; Bayrisches Hauptstaatsarchiv, Munich, Kultusministerium, 19455. See Rainer Buschmann, "Karl Nauer and the Politics of Collecting Ethnographic Objects in German New Guinea," *Pacific Arts* 21/22 (2000): 93–102; see also Andrea Müller, "Der Lloyd-Kapitän Karl Nauer als Sammler in der Südsee für das Überseemuseum," *Arbeiterbewegung und Sozialgeschichte* 10 (2002): 32–56.

6. Collector/ethnographer, employee of the Forsayth Company, collected throughout the Bismarck Archipelago; Sächsisches Hauptstaatsarchiv, Dresden, Ministerium für Volksbildung, 19307; Hauptstaatsarchiv Stuttgart, E 46, Bü 1009.

7. Head manager of Hernsheim & Company, resided on Matupi ; Sächsisches Hauptstaatsarchiv, Dresden, Ministerium für Volksbildung, 18819; Hauptstaatsarchiv Stuttgart, E 46, Bü 1009; Geheimes Staatsarchiv—Preussischer Kulturbesitz, Berlin, I HA, rep. 89 Geheimes Zivilkabinett, 20489.

8. Colonial official, Western Caroline Island station, Yap; Hauptstaatsarchiv Stuttgart, E 46, Bü 1009.

9. Colonial official, Central New Ireland station, Namatanai; Hauptstaatsarchiv Stuttgart, E 46, Bü 1009.

10. Emil Stephan and Albert Hahl proposed Wostrack for the Kronenorden, but museum files do not reflect whether he received the decoration.

name "buttonhole ailment" to characterize a craving for decoration and recognition. This longing intensified among German residents in the colonies. Many potential ethnographic collectors reported to Linden that decorations conferred status in the German colonies as well as at home.[18]

Between 1800 and 1945 the German states established no less than 3,500 decorations of all categories and classes. After 1871 there were twenty-five states within the German union; they divided themselves into four kingdoms (Bavaria, Prussia, Saxony, and Württemberg); seven grand duchies; four duchies; six principalities; three free cities (Bremen, Hamburg, and Lübeck); and the imperial province of Alsace-Lorraine. Only the three free cities did not possess a decoration system, giving Germany a unique concentration of state orders. This potential flood of decorations became even more pronounced in the absence of a common national decoration.[19]

Linden's efforts to reward collectors with Württemberg state decorations gave him a clear edge over Berlin and other German institutions in the German colonies. Between the turn of the century and Linden's death in 1910, the Stuttgart collections increased by about two thousand artifacts from German New Guinea alone. Table 1 lists the flow of state decorations to German New Guinea. The table underscores Linden's lead over his closest German competitors. Luschan had to grudgingly accept Linden's emerging investment in the German territories.

In terms of orders and decorations, Linden had an unfair advantage and, as Table 1 illustrates, he was not afraid of using it. Since King Wilhelm II of Württemberg was a major protector of Linden's ethnographic collection efforts, the Stuttgart count evidently had access to such state decoration. Furthermore, Linden's close affiliation with the royal family facilitated the process of bestowal. He made ample use of these decorations, at times to raise funds for the society's museum in Stuttgart and to gain additional collections for the future museum. Much like the initial purpose of monarchic "house orders," Linden hoped to tie the services of colonial collectors to the Württemberg state. The order became almost an official contract between an individual collector of ethnographic objects and Linden's emerging institution.[20] Luschan in Berlin had also a decoration system at his disposal, but the bestowal of Prussian orders was a great deal more complex than in Württemberg. Unlike Linden's connection to Württemberg royalty, Luschan did not enjoy close attention from the Prussian monarchs. Only Adolf Bastian, the director of the Berlin museum, had the necessary title (privy councilor) to initiate a formal nomination for a decoration. This nomination set in motion a complex Prussian bureaucratic machinery that made a quick decoration bestowal next to impossible.[21]

Orders were an important incentive along the colonial periphery; accompanied by Linden's kind words and genuine interest, they made all the difference in driving collectors into Stuttgart's arms. One of Luschan's associates writing from German New Guinea is worth quoting:

[Max] Thiel complains about receiving only official letters from the Berlin museum. Count Linden meanwhile sends personalized attentive letters. I told him that the large number of collectors for the Berlin museum prevented us from addressing each collector individually, to which he retorted: That may be possible, but such letters (he cited many examples) make a greater impact and were spiritually uplifting. . . . "Linden says," he read me passages, "that acquiring the objects was primary, while ethnographic determination could be left for a later date; Berlin, on the other hand, lets us have an earful if we don't provide clear instructions with the artifacts."[22]

Civility, in short, was just as important as the decoration. Luschan's "cold-hearted" scientific approach made no friends on the colonial periphery, while Linden's personalized attention endeared himself to the collectors. Luschan had much to learn in this regard.

Initially Luschan refused to give in and had bitter exchanges with Linden. "I would like to point out once again," Luschan wrote to Linden, "that the Berlin museum should have a priority in [colonial collections] and you should, for your own scientific interest, regard Berlin as a central institution, at least as long as we possess a larger staff of trained personnel than any other institution in Germany."[23] "Naturally," Linden added, "from its Olympic heights Berlin will not appreciate the activities of Stuttgart's insignificant earthworm." "Your ridicule," Luschan sourly countered, "about the 'Olympic heights' of the Berlin museum is undeserved. I am well aware that you have outstripped us in terms of many private and official collectors, but there is nothing we can do about this. We will do what we can with our current budget. We too would like to make use of orders and titles, but we have to do without them."[24] To Luschan, Linden's work was unscientific, and the "dangerous dilettante" threatened to undermine the ethnological endeavor.[25]

Luschan soon discovered, however, that Linden's abilities to harness collectors in the German colonies were to be more than a nuisance. Indeed, once civility and order bestowal were combined with sound scientific practices, they provided a powerful critique. Luschan stood at the center of attention as his administration of the African and Oceanic division came under increasing attack.

HAMBURG AND THE ESTABLISHMENT OF SCIENTIFIC JOURNALS

The first major challenge to Berlin's monopoly was dissemination of scientific knowledge in specialized journals. The Berlin Ethnological Museum's own publication series was sporadic and could hardly keep pace with ethnographic acquisition.

Realizing this predicament, an enterprising Georg Thilenius, who assumed the helm of the Hamburg Ethnological Museum in 1904, made the creation of specialized journals central to his agenda. Before assuming his job in Hamburg, Thilenius had traveled extensively through the Pacific Ocean and had gained considerable ethnographic experience.[26] Several high-ranking officials in the Hamburg Senate appreciated Thilenius' efforts. One senator, Werner von Melle, was keen on transforming Hamburg into a German center for higher learning and became Thilenius' main supporter. When Thilenius unveiled his plan of establishing a new, independent building for the museum, Melle lent his support. Planning started shortly after

Thilenius' appointment, although the building did not open its doors until 1911.[27] Melle's expression of civic pride for the museum converted the Hanseatic city of Hamburg into one of the most powerful ethnological centers in Germany.

Thilenius was not unknown in ethnological circles. Shortly before assuming his post in Hamburg, he became editor of the *Archiv für Anthropologie*, an influential organ of the German Society for Anthropology, Ethnology, and Prehistory. Before his appointment, the journal had stressed physical anthropology over ethnology, but Thilenius slowly reversed this emphasis. He soon added a second, smaller journal, *Zentralblatt* (Central Papers), which aired debate on ethnological museums in a national arena.[28] This publication detracted from the Berlin-centered *Zeitschrift für Ethnologie*. In Hamburg, Thilenius also established the journal *Mitteilungen* [Communications] *des Hamburger Museum für Völkerkunde*. He recognized the need to publish recent ethnographic acquisitions, especially since the central institution in Berlin was falling behind in this regard. "Against the habit of some museums to leave new acquisitions unpublished," he wrote to his superiors, "we have decided to publish our collections as soon as possible."[29] Chapter 2 discussed the background of the important Hellwig collection on Wuvulu and Aua. Thilenius underscored its significance by devoting the entire second volume of the *Mitteilungen* to its preliminary evaluation.[30] Congratulating his colleague Willi Foy in Cologne on the launch of Cologne's journal *Ethnologica,* Thilenius wrote: "The number of journals in Germany is increasing rapidly, and I would welcome any new additions in this regard. This would at least undermine the need for a centralization [in Berlin], and should be replaced with the option for each museum to maintain control over its collections and duplicates. Moreover, such an option would greatly reduce any of the involved costs. I am well under way in developing a project encompassing all German museums."[31]

Ethnology, Thilenius argued, was a discipline in theoretical flux. Bastian had done much to explore the discipline's psychological components, but new notions were quickly appearing. The main problem facing ethnology's theoretical constructs was the sheer wealth of information stored in collected indigenous artifacts. Many objects, however, lacked proper description and cultural context, making suspect many theoretical comments. Thilenius called on museum officials to determine artifacts' contexts. Collectors should not only concern themselves with new artifacts, but also investigate objects already housed in museums, he advised. It was only then, Thilenius argued, that a broad theoretical construct might emerge. Converting mere curiosities into scholarship was the main scientific task of museums and their trained personnel. Publication of the result was key to this endeavor.[32]

With this outlook, Thilenius felt secure enough to comment on Berlin's hegemony. In a private exchange with Luschan, Thilenius sought to appease the worried director of the African and Oceanic division. Hamburg, Thilenius informed Luschan, did not intend to assume Berlin's central status. But, he added, Luschan needed to realize that secondary institutions had much to offer the advancement of ethnology.[33] Thilenius publicly engaged the situation in Berlin in an article for his *Zentralblatt*, advocating a gradual decentralization of the colonial artifacts. He even suggested that Berlin surrender some of its own collections to fuel the scholarly output of other German museums.[34] At times he adopted a harsher tone: "The study of Germany's colonial peoples did not progress very much for good reason. Based on a dubious resolution the Berlin Ethnological Museum seeks to centralize all collections deriving from federally funded expeditions. Massive material crowds the museum's hallways and will never see the light of publication. The available personnel simply cannot cope with the requirements."[35] To convince museum administrators that his words were not idle talk, Thilenius took immediate action. His efforts focused on Hellwig's collection from German New Guinea (see Chapter 2). In just three years Thilenius and his assistants sifted through the roughly four thousand artifacts, shared duplicates with the museums in Berlin and Cologne, and published the results in a coherent monograph that shed light on debates surrounding Para-Micronesia.[36] Although Thilenius shied away from open conflict with Berlin, he was not afraid to suggest reducing Berlin's dominance. Thilenius also opened channels of communication with Wilhelm Bode, newly appointed general director of the Prussian museums. The Hamburg director thus initiated dialogues that went well over Luschan's head, effectively isolating the Berlin director of the African and Oceanic division.[37] Journals did much to undermine Luschan's claim at scientific dissemination. Yet it was a major theoretical shift that endangered the very nature of his division.

NOVEL THEORETICAL CONSTRUCTS: COLOGNE AND THE PRIMACY OF THE DIFFUSIONIST METHOD

Shortly before Adolf Bastian's death in 1905, a group of young scholars, ironically based at the Berlin Ethnological Museum, issued programmatic statements that are collectively known as the "diffusionist revolt."[38] These scholars took the lead from German geographer Friedrich Ratzel, who had outlined its features in a number of influential works. Ratzel was not an ethnologist by training, but his interest in writing a general human geography following the lead of Alexander von Humboldt led him to consider some of the insights developed by ethnology. Ratzel briefly studied under Bastian in the early 1870s and seemed attracted to Bastian's idea of "cultural provinces." The notion that similar geographical environs produced similarities in material culture was never central to Bastian's early writings, but it became paramount in Ratzel's postulates. Ratzel's approach—which he labeled anthropogeography—concentrated on the interaction of human groups with physical environment and geography. Ethnology, according to Ratzel, became instrumental not so much in the identification of common underlying psychological foundations, but in tracing the movements of peoples, artifacts, and ideas across the earth's surface.[39]

In 1904 two of Luschan's assistants in the African and Oceanic division, Bernard Ankermann and Fritz Graebner, presented two influential papers to the Berlin Society for Anthropology, Ethnology, and Prehistory. Published in the society's main organ, *Zeitschrift für Ethnologie,* the work of Graebner and Ankermann gained popularity throughout Germany.[40] Elaborating on earlier work by Leo Frobenius, Graebner and Ankermann set out to explain cultural similarity in Oceania and Africa.[41] They aimed to develop a systematic methodology for comparing material culture, employing the term *Kulturkreis* (culture circle) for a geographical area within which certain cultural forms prevailed. Although they restricted their work to Africa and Oceania, their hope was to extend this framework across the globe. Their methodology would soon become known as diffusionism or cultural history. Ankermann and Graebner initially abstained from direct attacks on Bastian's theories of human psychology, but their model offered an alternative that reinvigorated the study of material culture.[42]

Ironically this novel outlook challenged many of the divisions created by Bastian in the last decades of the nineteenth century. Most notable was Luschan's African and Oceanic division, which served as an incubator for Ankermann and Graebner's theoretical visions. The division's main purpose was administration of artifacts arriving from the German colonies—clearly nonsensical from a diffusionist perspective. Fritz Graebner took serious issue with Luschan: "Uniting Africa with Oceania cannot be supported by their cultural relationship alone. These areas are more closely connected to Asia than to each other, and their connection can only be explained through the intervention of the Asian continent. In short, without Asia any relationships among African and Oceanic societies are impossible to explain." Graebner continued his attack by chastising Luschan's division for failing to put results into print.[43] On the defensive, Luschan retorted:

> Dr. Graebner's letter is filled with outrageous judgments concerning my administrative work and scientific capabilities. . . . Any long-term fruitful cooperation with him is clearly out of the question, and I will not support

his employment here. . . . [As far as publications are concerned] it is imperative for my division—during the period of colonial penetration of Africa
and Oceania—to salvage the fragile material for posterity. Our main mission remains to salvage in the last hour those artifacts that will soon forever
fade. . . . The cataloging of artifacts thus takes priority over publication of
the results.[44]

By evoking Bastian's by now outdated salvage agenda, Luschan was able to
keep Germany's leading diffusionist out of his division and to preserve its
existence.

Banned from the Berlin Ethnological Museum, Graebner found refuge
in Cologne, where like-minded intellectuals were involved in the creation of
a new ethnological museum. Until the opening of the new museum building
in November of 1906, William (Willi) Foy succeeded in creating a society of patrons (*Förderverein*) that supported further acquisition of artifacts.
Since Foy had to be content with an acquisition budget of 2,000 marks, local
Cologne dignitaries continued to play a prominent role in the museum's expansion. Through the combination of local resources and the inclusion of a
decidedly diffusionist component in the museum, Foy hoped to find acclaim
in the German ethnological community. Hiring Fritz Graebner greatly aided
Foy's project.[45]

As a relative latecomer to the museological scene, Foy was greatly influenced by the visions of other museums around Germany. He rejected the
idea of a combined ethnological and natural scientific agenda. Ethnology
had developed into its own field of inquiry, focusing on the study of mostly
non-Western societies. He argued that there was a need for a comparative-
evolutionist section in the museums, because it was only then that museums
could make the transition from mere descriptive (ethnographic) to comparative (ethnological) institutions. Foy warned, however, of the dangers that
emerged from a superficial rendering of artifacts in evolutionary schemes.
He cited the evolutionary displays of prominent British museums (for instance the Pitt-Rivers museum in Oxford) as examples of clearly failed experiments.[46] Careful historical study of cultural areas had to predate any
studies of evolutionary principles. "To understand the cultural history of different geographical areas," Foy wrote, "is the primary concern of the ethnological museum; only following such analyses can one gain insights into the
temporal development of diverse cultural elements and their different forms.
The most crucial mission is thus geographically informed research and collection. At this point it is fair to say that a comparative-developmental section can only be an addition to the ethnographic-geographical divisions."[47]
While geographical arrangements became paramount to Foy's cultural his-

torical concerns, the Cologne museum still maintained evolutionist "survivals." Visitors to the museum, for instance, were encouraged to start their tour of the museum at the bottom floor, which contained the more "primitive" societies of Australia and the Pacific Ocean. Visitors were then guided to the exhibits of the pre-Columbian Americas, followed by the iron-smelting societies of Africa and Southeast Asia, before concluding their tour with the "high" cultures of East Asia.[48]

Since Cologne figured as an integral part of the Prussian state, its ethnological museum was in a disadvantaged position with regard to the distribution of colonial duplicates from the Berlin museum. Following the duplicate distribution procedures, Foy could only obtain those objects not claimed by any other non-Prussian institution. In short, there were few to no artifacts available to him. Yet, Foy refused to challenge this system openly. Indeed, Berlin's rich ethnographic treasures should have destined that museum to perform the type of cultural historical analysis envisioned by Foy. Implicitly, Foy criticized authorities in Berlin for not engaging in this type of research.[49] To allay similar accusations, Foy launched his own publication series—*Ethnologica*—which was to support the methodological and theoretical efforts of the diffusionist school.

Any overt critique of Berlin's activity Foy deferred to Graebner, who had an axe to grind. While Graebner had previously communicated his discontent with Luschan division via official channels, he now opted for a more public expression. In an article published in the journal *Globus,* Graebner aimed at nothing short of reforming the mission statement governing the Berlin museum:

> The original arrangement [of the Berlin museum] was driven by more or less superficial motives, linked through the weak bond of folk ideas [*Völkergedanken*]. The great religious cultures of Asia, with the methods developed in their own respective disciplines, were arranged almost randomly with the primitive cultures of Africa and Australia with hitherto undeveloped methods. Now we have learned how to operate in a cultural historical manner. We see that it is not only the mere existence of human beings but intensive cultural connections that unite the individual continents, and it is now that we are gaining our first insights into a general cultural history of mankind.[50]

Ethnological studies based on the diffusion of cultural elements, Graebner argued, could only be performed in an ethnological museum that encompassed all global regions. The absence of a publication series further jeopardized the central status of the Berlin Ethnological Museum for the performance of such studies. Berlin's collection activity, Graebner claimed, followed the random preferences of division directors rather than cultural historical imperatives and should be recalibrated to reflect the new mission statement.[51]

KARL WEULE AND LEIPZIG'S CRUSADE

Another institution took the attack on Luschan's African and Oceanic division a step further by involving state authorities. Karl Weule, like Graebner a former assistant in Luschan's division, started his employment with the Leipzig Ethnological Museum in 1898. Shortly before assuming the helm of this institution in 1906, Weule took serious issue with Berlin's monopoly. Weule proved to be a skilled learner who consulted and visited many ethnological collections around Germany. Karl von Linden in Stuttgart, for instance, taught him the importance of cultivating collectors with polite, personalized letters and state decorations.[52] In this regard, Weule was able to draw on the yeoman's work of Leipzig's first director, Hermann Obst. Yet Weule and Obst soon collided over the museum's scientific purpose—a conflict sadly resolved by Obst's passing in 1906. To prompt the museum's scientific output, Weule increased publications. Two publication series served to underscore this point. The *Jahrbuch,* the annual reports of the museum, allowed for the inclusion of smaller articles illustrating the active museological work of Leipzig museum officials, while the *Veröffentlichungen* (publications) were geared toward greater monographic treatment of particular societies. Weule, like his Hamburg counterpart Thilenius and unlike Foy in Cologne, was a careful theorist. Although he had engaged Ratzel's diffusionist ideas in his dissertation, Weule had also entertained Bastian's evolutionist outlooks while learning his trade at the Berlin museum. Toying with the idea of combining both approaches, Weule opted to postpone lengthy theoretical treatises for scientific evaluation and publication of collected artifacts.[53]

The German colonies played an important part in Weule's endeavor, and he felt Leipzig had to exploit "our ethnological gold mines," as he called them on occasion. To expedite this mission, Weule sought to establish direct links between his museum and collectors in German territories.[54] His success was almost instantaneous. Over a four-year period, Weule recruited experienced collectors in Cameroon, the Caroline Islands, East Africa, the Mariana Islands, New Guinea, and Togo.[55] Then, in 1904, difficulties arose. The escalating conflict between Luschan and Linden prompted the former to appeal to colonial authorities, requesting they cut Linden's colonial supply lines. The result was a stern reminder to colonial officials to adhere to the 1889 Federal Council Resolution. Not only did the Colonial Division reprint this resolution in the *Deutsches Kolonialblatt,* but it also circulated an official letter among civil servants threatening disciplinary measures for future violations.[56] Museums enjoying close ties to the German territories immediately felt the impact of this measure. "Luschan may have placed," commented Linden laconically from Stuttgart, "a foul egg into his overly protected nest."[57] Luschan's obsession with curbing Linden triggered a visit of Oswald von Richthofen, the secretary of state for the German Foreign Office, to Stuttgart in July 1903. After a two-hour inspection of the Stuttgart collection, Richthofen concluded that Luschan had blown Linden's actions out of proportions, though he also conceded they were in violation of the 1889 resolution. Instead of reprimanding Linden, Richthofen in effect assured the count that he could continue independent ethnographic acquisition. Disarmed by this encounter, Linden opted not to involve Württemberg state authorities in his tangle with Berlin.[58]

In Leipzig Weule did not entertain high-ranking German official visitors, but he did sense reluctance to collect from colonial civil servants, who feared possible repercussions.[59] Weule acted quickly to prevent long-term damage to his carefully crafted network of colonial collectors. In February 1904 Weule circulated a confidential letter among all major German ethnological institutions, by which he hoped to garner support to counteract what he considered Luschan's draconian measures:

> L[uschan] has indeed been successful in preventing the collection activities of our officers abroad. His method was easy enough: he simply influenced the colonial director to impress the Federal Council Resolution of 1889 on the gentlemen abroad. Furthermore he certainly also influenced [the colonial director] to draconically add: "Violations will trigger disciplinary measures." This friendly reminder cannot be found in the pages of the *Kolonialblatt*, but our gentlemen abroad have certainly taken it to heart. . . . Until recently Berlin has acquired the lion's share of everything colonial, but other museums could obtain some pieces when some gentlemen decided to show this old, shortsighted resolution the cold shoulder. Now, however, when faced with disciplinary measures, they say to themselves: "I have no interest in collecting for Berlin, since I am a native of Bavaria, Württemberg, or Saxony, etc. Only through a complicated paper trail can I collect for other museums; consequently, I will cease my activity altogether." We have in fact received many letters confirming this view; in Togo, for instance, the collection activity has come to a grinding halt.
>
> In the emerging crusade against Berlin, we will have to emphasize that the current system [of distribution] is generally detrimental to the ethnographic endeavor. I cannot agree to the fact that our gentlemen should not collect for foreign countries; to oppose this we have to strive for their

complete freedom of distribution within the German Reich. [This freedom] is completely restricted under the current conditions. Moreover, the entire collection endeavor is affected at a time when we have to acquire as much as possible [before it is too late].[60]

By framing Luschan's actions as detrimental to ethnology, Weule's call for a "crusade against Berlin" went out to the German museological periphery. The response, however, was not as he had hoped, since only Linden in Stuttgart, for obvious reasons, showed interest in the proposal. Other museum directors chose not to comment on Weule's proposal. Few museum directors were willing to challenge Luschan in the open.[61]

Despite limited support by fellow German museums, Weule pushed on to enlist the support of colonial enthusiasts. His main ally in this affair was Hans Meyer, a German colonial agitator whose wealth derived from a successful publishing business.[62] Meyer was a prominent member of the German Colonial Council, an advisory body to official colonial authorities. The council adopted Meyer's motion "against the preference of Berlin museums in colonial distribution" and forwarded it to the appropriate authorities.[63] Germany's colonial authorities, however, had more serious events to cope with, including a series of uprisings in the African colonies, and chose to ignore the Colonial Council's recommendation.[64] Luschan, receiving word of Leipzig's initiative, had to be on his guard, especially since the involvement of higher authorities alarmed his superiors. Serious countermeasures were needed for Luschan to save his position at the African and Oceanic division.

LUSCHAN THE PROACTIVE BUREAUCRAT

Mounting external critique was difficult to bear, but Luschan soon was losing ground among his immediate superiors. In 1906 Wilhelm Bode assumed the post of director of the Berlin museums. Bode, a renowned art historian with little training in anthropology and associated fields, soon took Luschan's division to task. Bode's memoirs put it bluntly:

The ethnological museum exhibited the worst conditions I encountered. The senseless amassing of artifacts, especially through acquisitions from our colonies in Africa and Polynesia [sic] via the unprepared gifts from colonial civil servants, led to an unbearable overcrowding of the facilities. None of the directors could be convinced to moderate the collection activity or to surrender or store some of the collections. The director of the largest and by far the most impacted division, Professor Luschan, disputed the existence of the term "duplicate." He was insatiable in his appetite to acquire more. . . . This condition worked against the idea of constructing a new facility.[65]

Bode certainly exaggerated the situation, but when he approached Luschan about the possibilities of sharing duplicates among other German museums, an irate answer ensued. Duplicates, Luschan retorted to Bode, while commonplace in the natural sciences, did not exist in the realm of ethnology. Human-made artifacts precluded the possibility of duplication. Careless sharing of artifacts superficially rendered as duplicates could only result in inquiries detrimental to the scientific endeavor. Luschan maintained that only a new building in the suburbs of Berlin could solve overcrowding in his division. He wrote energetically: "I would rather lay down my job than spend the rest of my life on inadequate solutions."[66]

Wilhelm Bode, however, was little impressed with Luschan's ranting and included a gradual program of artifact decentralization in a proposal to alleviate the crowded conditions in the Berlin Ethnological Museum.[67] Georg Thilenius in Hamburg immediately jumped on the possibility of involving other German museums: "It is conceivable to retain in Berlin display collections for certain regions, while relinquishing scientific collections to the provinces. . . . Public interest would not be affected, but the scientific output greatly intensified. . . . [T]he ideal task of the museum should not be competition with all its ensuing disadvantages, but critical collecting and adequate handling of material, all of which only contributes to the scientific endeavor."[68] Opening lines of communication with Bode, Thilenius threatened to isolate Luschan at the heart of the German capital. In several letters, Thilenius allayed Bode's fear of competition, arguing instead for peaceful cooperation and exchange among German museums. Thilenius' compromising position endeared him to Bode, much to Luschan's chagrin.[69]

In addition to critique at home, Luschan had to contend with losing the ethnographic acquisition battle in German New Guinea. For Luschan, Karl von Linden was a real concern because of his success in incorporating colonial officials, planters, missionaries, and settlers into the ranks of collectors for Stuttgart. Luschan's claim held weight as Linden did recruit many patrons from the German colony. What Luschan ignored, however, was that Linden also received much support in German New Guinea. Most colonial officials held Luschan's centralization in complete abhorrence and appreciated Linden's flow of Württemberg decorations to the territory. But Linden in Stuttgart was not alone in making great strides over the Berlin Ethnological Museum. Institutions in Vienna and Budapest gained tremendously from collectors sent to the territory; Cologne and Leipzig had forged ample connections in New Guinea; traders hailing from the important seaport of

Hamburg patronized the local museum; and lastly officers of the steam-ship company Norddeutscher Lloyd established increasing collections for Bremen's museum.[70] Berlin was clearly losing out. "Luschan," wrote one observer of German New Guinea, "seems to antagonize everybody—whenever possible."[71]

Luschan's main ties to the territory were a few colonial officials who, despite the attraction of Saxon or Württemberg state decorations, kept respecting the restricting Federal Council Resolution of 1889. Georg Fritz, located on the island of Saipan in the Marianas, was one of them, but he was very much an exception among colonial civil servants. The other prominent ethnographic supply line for the Berlin museum was the German navy. This connection strengthened when the German Admiralty decided to dispatch a survey vessel to German New Guinea. Their choice fell to the *Möwe* (Seagull), originally based in Africa, which was sent to German New Guinea to perform meteorological and geographical observations. Moreover, the vessel had a clear political agenda, seeking "to promote the prestige of the protecting power with the natives and with nations seeking to trade with the protectorate."[72] Luschan pursued this issue further by negotiating an agreement with German naval officials that involved the training of naval personnel in the African and Oceanic division of the Berlin museum. Moreover, the Prussian Museum Administration agreed to supply a small monetary amount (roughly between 1,000 and 2,000 marks) to support the *Möwe* crew's ethnographic collection efforts.[73]

Statistics confirm that the total number of ethnographica from German New Guinea to the Berlin Ethnological Museum was on a steady decrease. Figure 2 maps this trend graphically. While the turn of the century (October 1898 to October 1900) witnessed the peak arrival of 3,189 artifacts to the museum from German Pacific territories, the volume declined over the next years.[74] Few colonial officials remained loyal to the resolution of 1889; only Georg Fritz, much to the regret of Linden, adhered to its provisions.[75] The crew of the survey ship *Möwe,* tied to the limited monetary subsidies of the Berlin museum, remained loyal suppliers as well.[76] Other colonial sources, formerly supplying the museum, dried up. German Governor Albert Hahl, for instance, ignored the Berlin museum. While he shipped a total of eighty artifacts to Berlin at the turn of the century, his supply trickled to a mere six artifacts in the first decade of the twentieth century.[77] Once Fritz and the *Möwe* crew reduced their collecting efforts, the full extent of the crisis became obvious. Between 1905 and October 1907, the number of artifacts arriving from German New Guinea plummeted to a mere 360 entries.[78] Karl von Linden in Stuttgart could then triumphantly declare that his "South Sea collection equaled that of Berlin" in sheer quantity.[79]

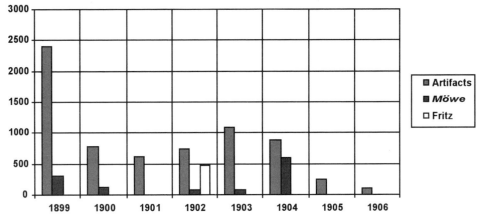

Figure 2. Luschan's fading acquisitions from New Guinea

Luschan decided to face his main competitors. In December of 1904 Luschan confronted Hans Meyer, who had recently sponsored Leipzig's crusade against Berlin's monopoly. Embarrassed by Luschan's direct confrontation, Meyer assured Luschan that Count von Linden was the main culprit behind the initiative.[80] When Luschan turned his wrath to Stuttgart, Linden feigned ignorance; he denied any involvement in Meyer's initiative, maintaining that indeed he would very much like to maintain the current conditions. Moreover, Linden, fearful of the institutions in Hamburg and Leipzig, attempted to convince Luschan that any changes in the wording of the Federal Council Resolution would ultimately be to the detriment of Berlin.[81] In order to isolate Linden in Germany's museological landscape, Luschan had to make important concessions.

LUSCHAN'S RESPONSE: "PRIMARY COLLECTING"

In April of 1905, Luschan paid a visit to Germany's most prominent museums while carefully avoiding any involvement with Linden in Stuttgart. Chief among his conversation topics was a new collecting proposal, which he called *cujus regio illius museum.* This proposal was to allow to non-Prussian colonial civil servants the donation of ethnographic artifacts to their respective state museums.[82] Director Foy proposed the opening of the Cologne Rautenstrauch-Joest Museum in late 1906 as an occasion to discuss these issues among the directors. Luschan half-heartedly agreed to this meeting but insisted on the exclusion of his nemesis Linden. Ultimately, Luschan declined the invitation to the museum opening, once again postponing any fruitful discussion on the distribution system.[83]

Indeed, Luschan never intended fully to abandon the acquisition privileges enjoyed by the Berlin Ethnological Museum and resorted to stalling tactics. In the collection battles Luschan fought in the colonies and in Germany, he learned that there were clear qualitative differences among ethnographic acquisitions. In a recent introduction to a prominent work on ethnographic collecting in Melanesia, Michael O'Hanlon differentiates ethnographic collection activity along two distinct axes. One distinguishes the gathering of artifacts as either a "mobile" (extensive) or "stationary" (limited) affair. A second axis distinguishes "primary" and "secondary" collection activity. "Primary" collections emerge from an intentional plan to gather artifacts for ethnographic study, while "secondary" collections are subordinate to other endeavors.[84] O'Hanlon's axes are also central to understanding the collection activity of Luschan's African and Oceanic division. Luschan, for instance, actively supported abolishing the provisions that prohibited colonial civil servants from collecting for museums other than Berlin. Indeed the proposal *cujus regio illius museum* he circulated among German museum officials was based on the assumption that ethnographic collection activity was of secondary importance to the colonial officers in their administrative duties. Their ethnographic output, thus, could never approach the careful work of a trained ethnographer. Secondary collections, such as the ones accumulated by Linden in Stuttgart, could thus quantitatively threaten Berlin colonial hegemony, yet poor determination of an artifact's provenience and use lessened its scientific value. The answer was qualitative rather than quantitative collecting, or what Luschan labeled "primary collections": ethnographic acquisitions assembled by trained ethnographers on specialized expeditions to the German colonies. Luschan felt other institutions, such as Leipzig and Stuttgart, might gain a quantitative edge in terms of secondary collectors, but the Berlin museum had to maintain control over the primary collectors because of their qualitative advantage.[85]

Luschan attempted to put this plan in action in German New Guinea. As Chapter 2 indicates, his plan for a large-scale expedition failed, but there was still the option to organize a smaller venue: the dispatch of a lone investigator to German New Guinea. This investigator was to have a dual purpose: to collect exclusively for the Berlin museum, using Luschan's "primary" collection methodology outlined above, and to reestablish the lost network of collectors. A financial windfall aided the project. By the summer of 1903, a well-known patron, Arthur Baessler, had agreed to donate a sum of 100,000 marks to the museum for the purpose of sponsoring collection trips to the Pacific and the subsequent publication of results.[86] Luschan thus opted to send Richard Thurnwald to German New Guinea because of his experience in the African and Oceanic division at the Berlin museum. To dispatch Thurnwald to the territory as rapidly as possible, Luschan, Baessler, and Thurnwald drew up an agreement that stipulated the conditions of Thurnwald's mission. Thurnwald was to research among few selected societies and supplement that research with the appropriate ethnographic collections. As part of his contract, Thurnwald was to contact local collectors and entice them with the possibility of working for the Berlin museum. To secure Thurnwald's ethnographic collections and observations, all ethnographica, field notes, and photographs were to remain the property of the newly formed Baessler Foundation at the Berlin Ethnological Museum.[87]

Thurnwald's dispatch to German New Guinea was to ensure Berlin's monopoly over primary ethnographic collections. Luschan knew very well that he was losing the battle over secondary collectors, that is, ethnographic collections performed by commercial and colonial residents in German New Guinea. Primary collecting served to keep Luschan's competing institutions and his own superiors at bay, but his step also had wide-reaching methodological implications. Luschan never intended to jettison the artifact as a central element of anthropological analysis. Agreeing to such a radical position would after all signify the death knell of his African and Oceanic division. Yet, at the same time, primary collecting shifted the emphasis of ethnographic study away from material culture to a careful consideration of the indigenous mentalities entering artifact production. In other words, primary collection carried with it the germ of intensive fieldwork among indigenous peoples. Thurnwald and others would take this idea to German New Guinea, where the project would coincide, as Chapter 5 will illustrate, with the goals of a maturing colonial administration. Before abandoning the German metropole for the colonial periphery of New Guinea, however, other considerations need to be taken into account. In the first decade of the twentieth century, competition among ethnological museums had ceased to be a purely anthropological affair. Leipzig's crusade against Berlin's monopoly had initiated a process involving state and national authorities. By 1910 German New Guinea became a major concern lifting anthropology, for a short time at least, to a heightened state of public awareness.

Chapter 4

Restructuring Ethnology
and Imperialism

F elix von Luschan's emphasis on "primary" collecting had resulted from an interplay between museological competition and the fact that colonial residents lacked proper collection methods. Primary collecting, however, also meant that artifacts became secondary to an understanding of the mental culture of their producers. Such concern once again resonated with existing colonial projects in the metropole and German New Guinea. It gained particular significance from a general restructuring process affecting the German colonies following 1906. Acquisition struggles among museum officials ceased to be an abstract anthropological affair and started to draw wider circles involving high-ranking state and federal officials. Under the rubric of "scientific colonialism," Bernhard Dernburg, the newly appointed secretary for colonial affairs, invited participation from all segments of German society involved in imperial ventures. German anthropologists interpreted the challenge by building "scientific colonialism" into their civil ventures. Dernburg expected his idea to have a broad effect on Germany's African colonies. However, for anthropological projects, the peripheral colony of German New Guinea reigned supreme. The outcome was a multitude of anthropological projects in New Guinea that have recently collectively been called an age of expedition.[1] Deeply embroiled in national politics, German New Guinea once again accentuated the interplay between metropole and colonial periphery in the final decade before the First World War. While museum officials conceived artifacts as a means to understand indigenous mentalities, colonial officials started to regard artifacts as national treasures and important colonial resources. Similarly, where museum officials employed the nascent restructuring process to serve local civic goals, colonial officials attempted to transcend museum squabbles in an effort to integrate anthropological work in a national platform addressing colonial administration.

In the second week of January 1904, the colony of German Southwest Africa became the center of attention as indigenous pastoral, cattle-raising Hereros took up arms against the small German community. Since the turn of the century, epidemics had decimated the cattle population of the Hereros, severely threatening their livelihood. Moreover, the Hereros also faced increasing demands by the German colonial administration in tax payments and land confiscation. In early 1904, the Herero people took advantage of the absence of the majority of the German colonial forces to launch an attack. They soon overran the meager remaining German defenses, interrupting communication in the territory, destroying railway lines, and besieging major German settlements. Within days of the uprising, more than one hundred German settlers and colonial soldiers lost their lives.

News of the rebellion spread to Germany immediately. The uprising's timing and the inability of the colonial administration to cope effectively with this conflict triggered a major crisis in German colonial politics. The full extent of the crisis became apparent when in October the indigenous Nama joined the Hereros in their rebellion. With the outbreak of the Maji-Maji rebellion in German East Africa in 1905, warfare now shook the two largest German colonies. Although German colonial troops—ironically called protective forces, or *Schutztruppen*—slowly managed to control the situation, indigenous guerrilla actions against the German colonial presence continued until 1906 in East Africa and until 1907 in Southwest Africa.[2]

This crisis exacerbated preexisting opposition to colonialism within the German empire. With the exception of smaller colonies (such as Togo and Samoa), the German territories were not economically self-sufficient. The private business sector, however, eschewed investments in the German colonies. Furthermore, there were mounting accounts of abuses against the colonial populations, and colonial tensions (such as the 1906 Morocco crisis) had created an explosive situation within Europe, pitting Germany against other established colonial powers. All of these concerns needed to be addressed by the German government, and the cry for reform turned even supporters of colonial expansion into its detractors.

Germany was a relatively young colonial power. It was only in 1884 that the German government under Otto von Bismarck had moved ahead to annex areas in Africa and the Pacific Ocean. Chancellor Bismarck was a reluctant colonialist and tried to transfer the administrative costs of these territories to a number of chartered companies. Most of these efforts, however, resulted in utter failure.[3] Eventually, the government had to assume administrative duties in the colonies. Such increasing governmental involvement in colonial affairs led to the establishment of a Colonial Division within the German Foreign Office by 1890. Four years later, this office gained more independence through the appointment of a colonial director. Few German civil servants desired this job, and many appointees were chosen not because of their colonial expertise, but for their loyalty to the German imperial court. There were some exceptions, yet even the most capable directors, such as Oswald von Richthofen, soon moved on to better and more respected positions in the German Foreign Service.[4]

Aside from the appointment of a director, few changes in the colonial administration occurred between 1894 and 1906, when the voices of opposition reached their zenith. The German Parliament (Reichstag) itself now became a hotbed of colonial criticism. Heading the opposition was the Roman Catholic–oriented German Center Party and its vociferous member Matthias Erzberger. Erzberger excelled in exposing colonial scandals and rallied many members of Parliament behind him. When, in late 1906, Chancellor Bernard von Bühlow attempted to push for further appropriations for the African colonies, a majority in the German Reichstag rejected his request. Bühlow dissolved the Reichstag and called for new elections, which became known as the "Hottentot election" because of their colonial connections. Bühlow and his associates emerged victorious from this election. Their success was partially attributable to their ability to convey the image that the anticolonial faction of the Reichstag was expounding anti-German values. Most important, however, was Bühlow's presentation of a reform program for the German voter. This program involved creating an independent Colonial Office led by a secretary of state solely responsible for colonial affairs. When Bühlow announced his choice for a future colonial secretary, he surprised many by nominating Bernhard Dernburg. Dernburg was a prominent banker who did not follow the pattern established by past colonial directors, but he did restructure the German colonial administration.[5]

Historians generally agree that the so-called Dernburg era reformed the edifice of German colonialism. Its effect on German ethnology, however, is often dismissed in literature.[6] Rhetorically speaking, Dernburg's program of "scientific colonialism" was promising; he summarized it as follows: "Colonization . . . means utilization of the soil, of its resources . . . and above all of its inhabitants for the benefit of the economy of the colonizing nation, and the latter is pledged to repay [the indigenous population] with its higher civilization, its moral concepts, its better methods."[7] Much in this definition warranted closer attention to the discipline of German ethnology.

Despite Dernburg's lack of colonial experience, he purged controversial members from the old Colonial Division and provided the newly established Colonial Office (Reichskolonialamt) with a fresh start. He undertook journeys to German East Africa and Southwest Africa to gain firsthand impressions; from these trips, he developed plans to increase the self-sufficiency of the German colonies. His vision included promoting general economic interest in the colonies, further investment in the territories, a better education for colonial civil servants, and improvement of the colonial infrastructure, especially in terms of railways.[8]

In theory, scientific colonialism, as defined by Dernburg, provided a window of opportunity for German ethnology. The exploration of such window, however, proved a difficult task. Each ethnological museum director had his own agenda and wanted Dernburg to act accordingly. Felix von Luschan in Berlin expected Dernburg to protect the interests of his museum, especially the monopoly over colonial artifacts.[9] Other museum officials expected the opposite. Karl von Linden in Stuttgart, for instance, hoped for a clear change in the distribution system from the colonial secretary.[10] Similar overtones sprang from other German institutions. Viewed from Dernburg's perspective, an anthropological agenda centered entirely on artifacts had limited applicability. Yet he was willing to entertain the idea if and only if German museum officials were willing to present proposals congruent with Dernburg's scientific colonialism. Realizing the potential emerging from Dernburg's reforms, many enterprising German museum directors clothed the civic ambitions of their respective institutions in the respectable mantle of the German colonial agenda. In so doing, the anthropological community created institutional and intellectual foundations for potentially fruitful cooperation with the Dernburg administration.

CREATING NATIONAL ORGANIZATIONS: LEIPZIG AND
THE GEOGRAPHICAL COMMISSION

The resourceful Karl Weule of the Leipzig Ethnological Museum was in a most advantageous position since he could rely on the ongoing support of Hans Meyer, a Leipzig native and leading member of the Colonial Council. Constituted in 1890 as an advisory body to the Colonial Division of the German Foreign Office, the Colonial Council was composed of important representatives of German business, shipping, and mission interests in the colonies.[11] Although its role was strictly advisory, the Colonial Council under Meyer's leadership served to coordinate scientific endeavors in the German colonies. During the First German Colonial Congress of 1902, Meyer presented a paper urging an inclusion of scientific investigation in the colonial endeavor. "In the colonizing endeavor," Meyer argued, "the purely practical individuals, the prospectors, traders, settlers, etc., were first to arrive. But only when science went along with these individuals have we witnessed great economic success."[12] Speaking mostly for the discipline of geography, Meyer suggested moving beyond mere descriptive data collection to focus on the causal connections among the individual components within a specific geographical region. Climate, quality of soil, and availability of water, for instance, all had considerable influence on plant growth. Such factors also influenced indigenous societies living in the region. This emphasis on "causal geography," as Meyer called it, was of pivotal importance for the economic future of the German colonies. He felt an urgent need for a coordinated effort to investigate the German colonies appropriately. Meyer stated that financial assistance should emerge from the "Africa Fund," the German Reichstag's monetary subsidy for the exploration of German colonies.

Meyer's initiative predated Dernburg's restructuring process and met with success. In July of 1904, Colonial Director Oskar Stübel asked the Colonial Council to create a commission under Meyer's leadership. The aim of this commission was the unified geographical exploration of German colonies paying homage to Meyer's concept of modern causal geography. The first meeting of the Commission for the Geographical Exploration of the German Protectorates (Landeskundliche Kommission zur Erforschung der deutschen Schutzgebiete), in September of 1905, illustrated an inclusive concept. Geographical exploration was extended to involve the disciplines of cartography, geology, meteorology, botany, zoology, and, most important, ethnology.[13] Over the next years, the commission funded and subsidized a number of expeditions to the German colonies.

Weule could only welcome this turn of events and quickly acclaimed Meyer's efforts at charting a clear path for a systematic exploration of the German colonies. This operational modus carried trained experts to the colonies who would publish a number of significant monographs. Weule suggested that some of the colonial newsletters, particularly *Communications from the German Protectorates* (*Mitteilungen aus den deutschen Schutzgebieten*), should dedicate themselves to publishing research outcomes. Popularizing scientific results would lead to increased funds for the commission. Moreover, Weule did not fail to point out the significance of the commission for the distribution of ethnographic collections. Weule believed that rather than centralizing the collections in Berlin's museum, the commission should be charged with finding a satisfactory alternative for all German museums.[14] He expected his close associate Meyer to assist the Leipzig museum in particular.[15] Between 1906 and 1910, the commission sponsored six expeditions, including Weule's travel to German East Africa. Meyer and the commission members also felt that German New Guinea deserved additional attention.[16] By 1907, the commission decided to send Karl Sapper, professor of geography at the University of Tübingen, on an exploratory tour to the Bismarck

Archipelago. Georg Friederici became Sapper's assistant and was responsible for undertaking ethnographic collections and observations on the trip.[17]

Under Meyer's tutelage, the Geographical Commission became a useful institution that fit Dernburg's emerging vision for German colonialism. Meyer's programmatic statements provided an ample field for ethnological applications in colonial settings. Moreover, the commission provided a "neutral" pan-German organization for future decisions concerning colonial artifacts. As might be expected, Felix von Luschan in Berlin balked at the idea of the commission's neutrality. "The Geographical Commission," he wrote, "is in the hands of self-declared enemies of Prussian interest." Luschan suggested notifying Dernburg of the commission's biases—a suggestion politely ignored by his superiors.[18] Meanwhile, similar developments were occurring in Hamburg.

NEGOTIATING CIVIC AND NATIONAL CONCERNS: HAMBURG'S COLONIAL INSTITUTE AND THE SOUTH SEA EXPEDITION

Much like Weule, Georg Thilenius jumped on the possibilities emerging from the colonial restructuring process. By the time of Dernburg's appointment as colonial secretary, Thilenius had already made great strides in Hamburg. When Thilenius assumed his post as museum director in October 1904, he soon realized that he had stepped into a hornets' nest. Under the leadership of Hamburg senator Werner von Melle, a small group of notables entertained the idea of establishing a university in the Hanseatic city. The general mood was against them, however, as many Hamburgians believed that a university would detract from the city's unique character. According to a long-standing Hamburg tradition, the sons of wealthy merchants acquired hands-on education abroad before entering their fathers' companies. Melle, not necessarily wishing to break with this tradition, nonetheless refused to relinquish his dream of establishing a center for higher learning. To further support his plan, Melle gathered benefactors through the creation of a Hamburg Scientific Foundation (Hamburger Wissenschaftliche Stiftung). The foundation's goal was to increase the awareness of scientific pursuits among Hamburg citizens. Melle's efforts raised several million marks. Two million marks alone came from Alfred Beit, a Hamburg native who made a fortune through his association with Cecil Rhodes in southern Africa. The foundation was officially chartered in April 1907. All it needed was a suitable proposal to sponsor.[19]

To that end, Thilenius developed a plan to increase the museum's holdings via a large-scale expedition. Ironically, it was Luschan himself who had given Thilenius the idea in 1903 when, as a reaction to his failure to engage commercial agents, Luschan developed a plan for a grand expedition to the South Pacific. The plan was so extensive that it met with rejection (see Chapter 2). Luschan had shared the proposal with individuals who had extensive Pacific experience, including Thilenius, who in 1903, still held a less than sterling job in Breslau. When Thilenius assumed the directorial post in Hamburg a year later, he recalled Luschan's floundering plan and revised it for his own purposes. Luschan's failure to enlist federal funds for the undertaking made Thilenius look for monies on the municipal level. Thilenius first expanded Luschan's short proposal into a pamphlet of almost thirty pages. The proposal went through two revisions between 1904 and 1907, emphasizing Thilenius' growing local and national connections.[20] The emergence of the Hamburg Scientific Foundation became the needed windfall for the expedition.

In addition to a suitable proposal for the exploration of German New Guinea, Thilenius was instrumental in creating an important colonial institution: the Colonial Institute. In April 1907 the budget commission of the German Reichstag suggested the creation of a university chair for colonial studies. This suggestion came to the attention of Werner von Melle, Thilenius' close supporter in Hamburg. Melle contacted Thilenius about the possibility of bringing this chair to Hamburg, whereupon Thilenius replied that a single professorship was hardly enough to represent the important standing of the city. Thilenius anticipated instead the creation of a colonial institute that would combine available resources in Hamburg, such as the Institute for Tropical Diseases, with the needs of the colonial administration. This represented a step toward creating a university in Hamburg.

In May of 1907 Thilenius ventured to Berlin to meet with Dernburg. The colonial secretary found the idea of a colonial institute compatible with his "scientific colonialism." The institute could combine theory and practice in terms of colonial reform, and it could be instrumental in furthering the education of civil servants leaving for the colonies. Dernburg wanted the Hamburg Scientific Foundation to fund the institution, which threatened to undermine the dialogue. Thilenius maintained that it was impossible to draw on the foundation's fund for the colonial institute. The money, Thilenius continued, came from local dignitaries who wanted to see the establishment of a university in Hamburg. Any attempts to redirect their monetary contributions to support a national institute would endanger their commitment to the foundation. Thilenius, however, assured Dernburg of the foundation's willingness to assist the efforts of the colonial institute, especially through the funding of individual expeditions. While engaging in dialogue with Dernburg, Thilenius continued to advise Melle, not to compromise the resources of the Hamburg Scientific Foundation, as this would jeopardize his future expedition. Paving the way for his expedition, Thilenius emphasized the important role of monographic production in the creation of practical scientific knowledge to support the concerns of the colonial administration. Skillfully he argued that the Berlin Ethnological Museum in particular had missed a good opportunity despite being in an advantageous position owing to the Federal Council Resolution of 1889. Again and again, he continued, the Berlin institution had proven itself unable to handle the sheer wealth of material, ethnographic as well as natural scientific specimens, arriving from the colonies. The prospective Hamburg institute was not meant to compete with the Berlin institution but to relieve some of their pressure. The conference with Dernburg ended on a positive note, and Thilenius went back to Hamburg to work on a detailed plan. The institute, he argued in a proposal, was to draw on the scientific institutions available in Hamburg. These included the museums of ethnology, zoology, and geology, among others. By emphasizing the available resources in Hamburg, Thilenius was able to allay some of the cost for a colonial institute. In June of 1907 Dernburg visited Hamburg with his assistant Heinrich Schnee. The visit was a success, and Thilenius proceeded to work closely with Schnee, whom he had met during his trip to the Pacific, on details of the plan. A number of bureaucratic tangles had to be overcome, but by October of 1908 the institute was officially opened to the public. While the city of Hamburg financed the majority of the project, the federal government assisted the institute through subsidies and scholarships for some of the civil servants in attendance. For his efforts as go-between, Georg Thilenius became the chairperson of the institute's Professorial Council.[21]

Thilenius' proposal for the South Sea Expedition reflects a careful juggling of local and national concerns. Dernburg's concerns were addressed as follows:

It is our conviction that Europeans are influencing the indigenous population in good ways and in bad ways, which lead to rapid population decline. We are aware that Europeans cannot easily communicate with the natives, because the natives possess an old and distinguished culture that differs from our own only in its development and not its temporal depth. Conversely, we cannot influence the native if we take our own culture as the point of departure. The solution of the labor question can only be reached in conjunction with exact knowledge of the population from which to extract the workers.[22]

Thilenius won the approval of Albert Hahl, governor of German New Guinea, on labor questions.[23] Indeed, Thilenius' role in the negotiations with colonial authorities in Berlin proved highly beneficial. His frequent visits to

Berlin won him Dernburg's trust and full support for the Hamburg South Sea Expedition.[24]

At the same time, Thilenius had to outline the benefits of the expedition for the city of Hamburg in order to satisfy the requirement of the Hanseatic city's Scientific Foundation. In terms of the expedition's scientific product, Thilenius expected participants to return with large artifact collections and ethnographic information. These "sources" in turn would form the basis for several monographs (Thilenius initially predicted their number to be less than twenty) that would increase Hamburg's standing in the ethnological community:

> The tangible results [of the expedition] amount to an increase of the [Hamburg] collection by about 15,000 to 20,000 pieces. To this should be added about 2,000 photographs as well as a large number of anthropometric measurements. Lastly, we have the expedition participants' notes and reports, which will culminate in a multivolume work accessible to the global scientific community. . . . I hardly need to emphasize that the position of our museum vis-à-vis those of Berlin, Vienna, Paris, London, Washington, and so on, will be greatly improved.[25]

Thilenius emphasized the fate of the Godeffroy museum (see Chapter 2), which had established Hamburg as a respected center for ethnological research. Once the majority of the Godeffroy collection was sold to Leipzig, however, Hamburg's standing in this line of research had declined. Thilenius' expedition would remedy this state of affairs. His arguments hit home, and, by December 1907, the foundation agreed to fund the "Hamburg South Sea Expedition," with an estimated price tag of roughly 600,000 marks.[26]

Methodologically too, Thilenius sought to make his mark. Although loosely structured along the lines of the Cambridge University venture to the Torres Straight Islands, his expedition was a more ambitious undertaking.[27] For the duration of several years (1908–1910), the Hamburg South Sea Expedition was to visit the whole of German New Guinea. Thilenius was intrigued by the possibility of exploring the cultural boundaries of the territory, which included societies that were generally considered to be Melanesian, Micronesian, and Polynesian. To gain independence from colonial and commercial residents in the territory, Thilenius sought to charter a steamer to carry a team of anthropologists. He hired a number of prominent researchers: Friedrich Fülleborn, the expedition's leader through Melanesian waters, was affiliated with the Hamburg Institute of Tropical Diseases; Augustin Krämer, who led the expedition's second leg through the Micronesian isles, was a naval surgeon by trade but had written extensively on Pacific ethnography and would later become scientific director of the Linden Museum in Stuttgart. Thilenius was quick to bind the participants to the Hamburg museum by contract. All of their collections, photographs, as well as private diaries became the property of Thilenius' institution.[28] This team was to perform extensive rather than intensive research; that is, they were to investigate as many places as possible in the time period available rather than spending long periods of time in a particular region, which would characterize Felix von Luschan's expedition outlined below. Thilenius was acquainted with the advantages of intensive work, but he felt this to be the job of German residents in the territory, especially missionaries.[29] For his intents and purposes, and those of his financial and political backers, extensive research was the most satisfying research.[30]

Thilenius and Weule became instrumental in the creation of two prominent colonial agencies that integrated ethnology into Dernburg's scientific colonialism. Thilenius took an additional step by providing a locally sponsored expedition that sought to establish a unique collection of ethnographic objects from Oceania while also addressing colonial predicaments in German New Guinea. In Berlin, Felix von Luschan provided the next move by integrating his "primary collecting" agenda into Germany's quickly transforming colonial landscape.

RECALIBRATING BERLIN'S NATIONAL AGENDA

Unlike Weule in Leipzig and Thilenius in Hamburg, Felix von Luschan was not actively involved in Germany's colonial restructuring process. Berlin already sported the most important colonial institutions, and Luschan had done much to antagonize principal officials. His obstructionist policies came again to the forefront when Luschan made several unsuccessful attempts to halt Thilenius' expedition. Luschan had his superior Wilhelm Bode contact Alfred Beit, Bode's close friend and financial backer of the Hamburg Scientific Foundation. Beit, however, while conceding that he had provided money for the foundation, denied any involvement in the Pacific expedition.[31] Luschan then attempted to offer Thilenius employment in Berlin. Thilenius not only turned down Luschan's offer but used the employment offer to strengthen his own position in Hamburg.[32] In a last desperate attempt, Luschan turned to colonial authorities to prevent Thilenius' success. His argument that a single German state (Hamburg) was increasing its ethnographic holdings at the expense of others must have sounded unconvincing in light of his steadfast adherence to Berlin's monopoly over colonial artifacts. Not only did Luschan alienate himself with Dernburg's new office, but now Bode was communicating with Thilenius about the distribution issue.[33]

Luschan's final option was to put his "primary collection" agenda into practice by organizing a counterexpedition, as he put it, "to erase the significant setback my division experienced due to the Hamburg expedition."[34] This was easier said than done. With eroding support within Germany and his own museum administration, Luschan could hardly expect a large budget. In desperation, Luschan turned to the one institution that had provided continuous support for his division: the German navy. Since the turn of the century, the German Naval Office had risen steadily to become a politically powerful body in Wilhelmine Germany. With Alfred von Tirpitz as naval secretary, the German navy had embarked on an escalating arms race with Britain. Important popular organizations, such as the German Naval League, assisted in popularizing the naval expansion.[35] With the acquisition of the port of Jiaozhou in China, the navy became directly involved in the administration of German colonial territory. In addition to its increasing administrative tasks, the Admiralty was responsible for patrolling colonial waters, especially those surrounding the German territories of the Pacific Islands.[36]

The navy established a constant presence in German New Guinea in the survey vessel *Möwe* (Seagull), which had provided the Berlin Ethnological Museum with several important ethnographic collections. Luschan invested considerable time and money training selected naval officers to increase collection activity.[37] By 1897 Luschan had negotiated an agreement with German naval officials under which the Berlin museum would provide the vessel's crew with a budget (varying between 1,000 and 2,000 marks) for collection purposes. The majority of the crew, however, had little interest in this activity.[38]

This all changed with the arrival of Emil Stephan. Boarding the *Möwe* as a naval surgeon, he soon discovered a passion for ethnography.[39] Stephan invested much of his free time in the investigation of the psychology of indentured laborers aboard ship. Much like Bronislaw Malinowski roughly ten years later, Stephan believed that in-depth study of indigenous populations provided insights different from those of missionaries and traders. Unlike Malinowski, however, Stephan had little time to conduct "fieldwork" in an indigenous village but had to deal with the schedule of a busy German warship. He directed his attention at six young native men from western New Britain who called themselves Barriai. Departing from German ethnological convention, Stephan mentioned the names of his informants and the ways he gathered information. His findings often contrasted sharply with the writings of prominent ethnologists. "Above all I was amazed to uncover," he wrote, "in each of these 'wild men' a clearly defined individual character. This contradicts the belief that the nature peoples are by and large a group of undifferentiated people and that differences in character emerge only through education and upbringing."[40]

Stephan's unorthodox view of ethnography contradicted ethnological dogma.[41] Diffusionists in particular took serious issue with his statements, which they attributed to his lack of training. When Stephan returned from German New Guinea, he immediately went to work on classifying the objects he had brought back. His passionate discovery of ethnography led to the publication of two important monographs.[42] One volume, coauthored with Fritz Graebner, was a traditional survey of material culture in New Ireland. The other monograph, which considered Oceanic art, broke the mold of German ethnographic outlook.[43] Stephan's coauthor Graebner argued that an ethnographic monograph was above all the product of a trained ethnologist. This scholar was to study an area carefully, appreciating the commercial and cultural relationships among neighboring indigenous communities. Graebner detested museum catalogues that described objects in isolation. Only through comparison with other objects could one situate them in historical relationships. For Graebner, such an undertaking was the epitome of meaningful museum work.[44] The mere listing of artifacts in monographs implied a deceptive closure that "prevented the recognition of important commercial and cultural relationships" among different indigenous societies.[45] Graebner, in agreeing to work with Stephan, set out to avoid common mistakes made in descriptive works that reduced their scientific utility. Graebner read the material culture of southern New Ireland against that of other societies in and around the Bismarck Archipelago. He openly complained that his task was hampered by Stephan's insistence on publishing some of the artifacts in his other work on Oceanic art. "We have intentionally opted not to omit any differences in opinion [throughout this volume]."[46] In order to sidestep Graebner's criticism, Luschan favorably reviewed Stephan's monograph, arguing that the former naval surgeon provided approaches that complemented diffusionist outlooks.[47] Graebner, however, remained unconvinced. On learning of Luschan's decision to place his former coauthor in charge of an expedition to German New Guinea, Graebner was less than kind in his assessment of Stephan. Graebner recognized that Stephan was "an energetic, goal-oriented person," but "to place a nonethnologically trained person in charge of such an expedition makes no sense whatsoever."[48] Graebner believed Stephan's expedition to be a mere salvage operation ultimately counterproductive to the development of ethnology.[49]

Luschan worried little about Graebner's concerns, as he realized how much Stephan's research mirrored his own primary collection aims. After years of disappointment with colonial collectors in German New Guinea and incessant competition from other German ethnological museums, Luschan responded by changing his own emphasis from a mere accumulation of indigenous artifacts to what he called "monographic work." Working intensively rather than extensively to understand the indigenous meanings lurking behind collected artifacts, "monographic work" would counter the general charge of the Berlin museum's lack of dissemination of ethnographic knowledge. Stephan's concern for indigenous individuality sat well with Luschan's agenda of developing a qualitative rather than quantitative edge over other German museums.[50] Furthermore, Luschan and Stephan's cooperation illustrates once again the dynamic interplay between the ethnological museums and the colonial periphery of German New Guinea in the production of novel ethnographic outlooks.

Methodological affinity was not the only reason prompting Luschan to sponsor Stephan. Indeed, Stephan was well connected to the German Naval Office, and Luschan hoped to engage the tremendous financial resources of the German Naval Office to underwrite ethnographic projects, including the publication of monographs.[51] Furthermore, Stephan developed an almost uncanny gift for selling ethnography to an audience of colonial enthusiasts. The diffusionist revolt questioned Bastian's salvage agenda, developed in the nineteenth century, on theoretical grounds.[52] Stephan, for his part, gave the salvage agenda a decidedly nationalistic twist. In his work on Oceanic art Stephan urged Germans to fulfill a "national burden of honor" (*nationale Ehrenschuld*). By acquiring colonies in the Pacific, Stephan contended, the German nation had assumed responsibility for conserving the heritage of their inhabitants.[53] His call for a *nationale Ehrenschuld* found a favorable reception in high-ranking circles in imperial Germany.[54]

The importance of Stephan's "national burden of honor" became apparent soon enough. For his upcoming expedition, Luschan sought the support of his own administration and the powerful German Naval Office, but he never revealed the plan to Dernburg's office. When Naval Secretary Tirpitz approached Dernburg for further assistance with the expedition, he received a courteous yet forceful inquiry as to whether naval authorities sought to meddle into the colonial affairs of New Guinea. Dernburg's reply illustrated his concern over a powerful naval office that could garner immediate support from the German kaiser and large segments of the German populace. A flabbergasted Tirpitz wrote a long letter in which he denied any involvement in colonial affairs. Tirpitz' centerpiece was Stephan's transformation of the salvage agenda into a "national burden of honor," which had received the highest approval of Kaiser Wilhelm II.[55] With Stephan's idea receiving the support of the kaiser, there was little Dernburg could do but to lend his support as well. Luschan's reliance on the German navy, however, completely eroded his support with the German Colonial Office.[56]

Uniting Stephan's interest in indigenous psychology and his transformation of the salvage agenda into a "national burden of honor" with Luschan's own primary collecting emphasis, Luschan set out to organize the expedition. Unlike Thilenius' extensive ethnographic survey of German New Guinea, Luschan picked a small, clearly delineated area for his expedition. The hitherto little-contacted Barrai people of western New Britain, some of whom had served as Stephan's subjects on board the *Möwe,* became the focus of the expedition. Funding, Luschan wrote, was not an issue, since he expected the Naval Office would finance Stephan's party and the resulting monograph. He estimated 60,000 marks to be sufficient to send along two ethnographers and a photographer.[57] Luschan was careful not to reveal his whole plan to Tirpitz. He especially avoided any mention of costly monographs in his correspondence with the secretary of the German navy. Tirpitz, presuming that the Prussian Museum Administration would bear the majority of the costs, gave his approval.[58] Tirpitz placed the expedition under the German navy's protection and ordered that the new naval survey vessel *Planet* support its participants.[59] By the end of the summer of 1907, with a name more portentous than the venture, the German Naval Expedition steamed toward German New Guinea. Its funding was a mere fraction of that of Thilenius' expedition, but its schedule was a full year ahead of its Hamburg competitors.

Erasing Berlin's Colonial Monopoly

Accommodating Dernburg's scientific colonialism in local visions of anthropology established institutional and intellectual foundations for the discipline's development. Moreover, such accommodation made anthropologists more visible and their internal conflicts more pertinent to the colonial administration. The distribution of colonial artifacts remained a major bone of contention. Eliminating Berlin's controversial monopoly thus became a preoccupation. By 1908 the kingdoms of Bavaria, Saxony, and Württemberg had united in an attempt to press for the following demands: first, to allow colonial civil servants to donate their ethnographic and natural scientific collections to a museum of their choice; and second, to obtain a more equal share in collections resulting from expeditions sponsored through federal funds. To avoid a national uproar over such a trivial issue as the distribution of colonial duplicates, Prussian authorities decided to involve the Colonial Office.[60] Responding to such broad-based initiatives, the German Colonial Office proposed a meeting of representatives of all major German states to discuss the issue. Originally scheduled for 8 October 1909, the meeting was later moved to 21 March 1910 with Deputy Colonial Secretary Friedrich von Lindequist as chair.[61] In attendance were important personalities of German ethnography and natural science, as botanical and zoological specimens were also affected by the 1889 resolution. The only notable absence was Stuttgart's Karl von Linden, who had passed away two months before the meeting.[62]

In terms of ethnographic objects, the meeting resulted in a clash between Luschan and Thilenius. Both had arrived with extensive proposals regarding the distribution issue. They agreed that restrictions on secondary collection, that is, collection performed by colonial officials, should be lifted. They vehemently disagreed, however, on how to handle primary collection. Thilenius argued that distribution should consider an ethnological museum's scientific worth and dissemination of ethnographic knowledge. A museum's artifact holdings and journal publications should determine which institutions were worthy of receiving colonial artifacts. Lesser museums, generally those without a publication series, were to obtain leftover artifacts.[63] Given the prominent role played by Prussian institutions, Thilenius was willing to concede almost 50 percent of all artifacts to their museums. His move was clearly political, hoping the Berlin museum administration would meet him halfway.[64]

Luschan's proposal was a great deal simpler. He was less concerned with a museum's perceived scientific standing. Assured of Prussia's prominent role, he proposed a distribution according to seats in the German Federal Council. There was good reason for this. Out of fifty-eight delegates to this council, Prussia had seventeen seats. The state of Bavaria was a distant second with six delegates; Saxony and Württemberg followed with three seats each. Most of the other states had merely a single representative—this included Thilenius' employer, the city-state of Hamburg. Luschan was willing to retain only 30 percent of all of the primary ethnographic collections returned from the colonies, but he insisted on his right of first choice.[65] Luschan's proposal received support from Lucius Scherman, director of the Bavarian state museum in Munich. With six representatives in the Federal Council, Scherman had much to gain from Luschan's initiative. Combining their efforts, Luschan and Scherman hoped to derail Thilenius' proposal.[66]

The meeting settled the first issue raised—colonial civil servants were now at liberty to donate ethnographic collections to the museum of their choice—but fell short of achieving its second purpose. Despite uniting Germany's most prominent anthropological, botanical, and zoological authorities, no consensus emerged on how to divide collections deriving from federally sponsored expeditions. Lindequist proposed to support the abolition of the Federal Council Resolution of 1889 by establishing a commission to determine the fate of colonial collections.[67] In addition to abolishing by decree the restrictions on secondary collections, the Colonial Office announced the future appointment of a commission for artifact distribution primarily from federally sponsored expeditions.[68] The ethnographic frontier in New Guinea provided an opportunity to enact such new proposals.

GERMAN NEW GUINEA'S ETHNOGRAPHIC FRONTIER AS AN ISSUE OF NATIONAL SECURITY

Dernburg's scientific colonialism program focused almost exclusively on Africa, where natural resources and railway construction beckoned investments. The German colonies in the Pacific, in contrast, received little support. From an anthropological perspective Oceania, however, had just as much clout as the African territories. One might even venture that, with regard to the distribution issue, German New Guinea reigned supreme. Propelled by collecting, Bastian's stipulated ethnographic frontier made inroads in the Bismarck Archipelago (especially New Britain and New Ireland), the coastal regions of New Guinea, and then, following the Sepik River, quickly moved inland. While the turn of the century witnessed increasing collection activity on New Britain and New Ireland as well as the coastal regions of New Guinea, the ethnographic frontier soon shifted to other islands and New Guinea's interior following 1906. The Sepik River, named Kaiserin-Augusta Fluß during German times, was New Guinea's second largest stream and the largest waterway of the German Oceanic possessions, measuring almost seven hundred miles. It soon was to gain fame in ethnographic circles for its exuberant indigenous artistic styles. So many collectors, professional and otherwise, visited the Sepik that one leading anthropologist, Augustin Krämer, compared, tongue-in-cheek, the region to Berlin's Friedrichstrasse, a favorite shopping destination.[69] Maps 2 and 3 below visualize the ethnographic frontier's expansion.

By and large, the exploration of this ethnographic frontier was a German affair, pitting Luschan's African and Oceanic division against competitors within Germany. While other foreigners did arrive in German New Guinea, they did so briefly and with limited financial resources. The arrival of American collectors from the Field Museum of Natural History would change this state of affairs in 1908. A relative latecomer to the American ethnographic collection scene, the Field Museum nevertheless soon made a name for itself through the unconventional collecting methods of George Amos Dorsey, director of the Field Museum's ethnographic division since

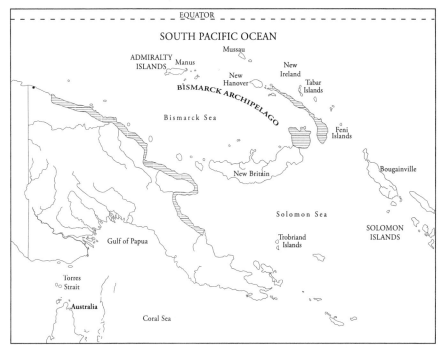

Map 2: The ethnographic frontier to 1890

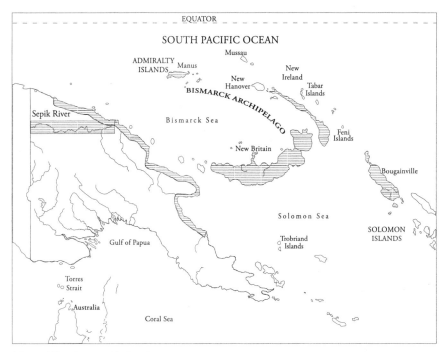

Map 3: The ethnographic frontier to 1914

1897. Although Dorsey was initially reluctant to extend the museum's collection activity beyond America's boundaries, America's conflict with Spain in 1898 alerted him to the nation's growing geopolitical involvement.[70] Dorsey undertook extensive tours through European museums and was particularly impressed with German institutions.[71] Berlin's museum in particular caught his attention, and he decided to establish exchange programs to enrich the Field Museum's holdings of African and Oceanic artifacts. Dorsey also represented unparalleled financial power, which he demonstrated when he purchased a vast Oceania collection from the ethnographica collector J. F. G. Umlauff—something German museum directors were reluctant to do.[72] The collection, with a price tag of 65,000 marks, had been available for quite some time before Dorsey purchased it in 1905. Numbering almost 13,000 artifacts, it included pieces from German New Guinea. Important places along the ethnographic frontier in German New Guinea, such as Matty Island (see Chapters 2 and 6) and New Ireland (see Chapter 6), were well represented. To highlight the significance of this collection, Dorsey also emphasized the need to extend the museum's boundaries to the Pacific:

> With the addition of the collection . . . we at once take a position among the museums of the world as the possessor of Pacific Island collections. It need not call your attention to the fact that the logical extension of our ethnographic section is towards the Pacific and South America. . . . If we are ever to extend the limits of our department beyond the contours of North America, this is certainly the most favorable opportunity we shall ever have for making a beginning in this direction.[73]

With this programmatic statement, Dorsey placed an American anthropological claim on the Pacific, with special attention to German New Guinea. By the summer of 1908, Dorsey was ready to pay a visit to this territory. Dorsey immediately readied himself to perform large-scale collections in the coastal areas of New Guinea, the islands of New Britain, New Ireland, and Bougainville. During his trip, he assembled two thousand artifacts, many of them purchased from local colonial residents. His speedy collection methods left little time to collect detailed information about the objects.[74]

Dorsey's main impact was his participation in the opening of the Sepik River for ethnographic collectors.[75] German governor Albert Hahl proposed such a journey to increase labor recruiting for German plantations.[76] As was so often the case, Hahl's practical colonial concerns paralleled vivid ethnographic interests in the area. By 1908 the Sepik was regularly visited by different steamers, and their crews started to collect artifacts in great num-

Figure 3. Inhabitant of the Sepik region offering artifacts for exchange (Courtesy Linden Museum Stuttgart)

bers. Dorsey participated in the exploratory journey to the Sepik on board the New Guinea Company steamer *Siar,* captained by Heinrich Voogdt, a veteran of many years of service with the company during which he had developed a keen interest in ethnographica. Since the *Siar*'s holds did not, as expected, overflow with labor recruits, both Dorsey and Voogdt used the empty space for ethnographic treasures, thus turning the ship into a floating museum. The objects returned from the Sepik created a stir in the territory, and Dorsey felt he could ill afford to ignore the area in the future.[77] "We should," Dorsey suggested to the Field Museum's director, "expend within the next three years in the region between central Australia and the Philippines, and between Singapore and Fiji the sum of one hundred and fifty thousand dollars—at least."[78]

The ethnographic frontier in German New Guinea with the Sepik River at the center caused a great stir. Dorsey's "shopping spree" through German New Guinea and the alliances forged with prominent collectors gave rise to a number of rumors. The news reaching the German ethnological museums was that Dorsey was to get his own ship to empty entire regions (particularly the Sepik River) of ethnographica. There was little agreement over when and how this expedition was to reach the German territory, but most colonial residents agreed that it was imminent.[79] Fear of Dorsey resulted again and again in calls for a unified German ethnographic initiative. Hamburg expedition member Wilhelm Müller best addressed these fears in an anonymous letter to the Berlin Ethnological Museum: "Which German museum will take the initiative? Fire, fire, fire everywhere!!! Why do we fight over a few lousy duplicates when the Americans take everything! The museums should put aside their differences, pool their resources, and agree on a fair exchange of artifacts. Only in this way can we save some of the ethnographic types in our territory."[80]

Warnings were not sufficient, and some researchers even suggested closing German New Guinea to foreign researchers. Richard Neuhauss, a prominent traveler and collector for the Berlin museum, urged German authorities to act as soon as possible. He cautioned that a large-scale American expedition could "empty" the region of its ethnographic treasures. "You would be best advised," Neuhauss wrote to Felix von Luschan, "to urge the Foreign Office to forbid [the American ship] to travel upriver."[81] This was indeed a radical solution to the imagined crisis. Luschan considered the option for a while, but his cautious inquiries met with "uncomfortable answers."[82] On the whole, colonial officials were not supportive of an idea that would trigger protests from foreign governments allowing free access to German researchers in their colonies. Albert Hahl, for instance, reminded Luschan that Richard Thurnwald had enjoyed free access to the British Solomon Islands during his stay in Oceania.[83]

THE ARTIFACT'S RISING SIGNIFICANCE: MOUNTING AN
ALL-GERMAN SEPIK EXPEDITION

Dorsey's impact on German New Guinea was greatly overestimated, but a lingering fear remained that outsiders might exploit a disunited ethnological community. Similarly, German anthropologists, in their attempts to displace Berlin's monopoly, were repositioning the artifact as a vital colonial resource as stipulated by Dernburg's "scientific colonialism."[84] The idea of protecting such resources for ethnological interests found an agreeable audience at the German Colonial Office.

Personnel changes facilitated this task. Felix von Luschan's dream of attaining a full-time teaching position at Berlin University became a reality toward the end of 1910. This appointment was only partially based on his merit. It seems that Wilhelm Bode, whose differences with Luschan were all too apparent, was instrumental in pushing Luschan out of the museum business.[85] Luschan's departure from the African and Oceanic division had crippling effects. After his long twenty-five-year "reign," Luschan's former division threatened to descend into mediocrity. Luschan's "primary collecting" emphasis fell by the wayside as the African and Oceanic division was placed under the control of Albert Grünwedel, a South Asian specialist and stout opponent of universalizing theories in ethnology. Grünwedel's lack of expertise in either African or Oceanic ethnography forced him to defer the administration of Luschan's division to Bernard Ankermann, a diffusionist with little concern for indigenous mentalities. Ankermann himself was an Africanist by training who soon neglected the Oceanic division.[86] Emil Stephan, the leader of the German Naval Expedition to New Guinea who shared Luschan's methodological concerns, would have been a worthy candidate. Yet, as the next chapter chronicles, he failed to return from German New Guinea, losing his life to tropical disease. The Oceanic collections were left to August Eichhorn, who had no field experience. Eichhorn complained bitterly that Ankermann was neglecting this region of the world, with the only collection arriving from the Pacific originating from Luschan's expeditions planned before his departure.[87]

Wilhelm Bode, however, stood to benefit from this state of affairs. With Luschan gone, Bode calculated that his successors in the African and Oceanic division would be more willing to part with artifacts considered duplicates. He wanted to employ such duplicate objects to create wide-sweeping alliances with essentially smaller museums; this would keep the larger institutions in Germany in check. Concerned that such larger institutions might outstrip Berlin, Bode even considered a position on Hans Meyer's Geographical Commission. In order to keep informed about the distribution of artifacts, Bode sought close connections with the German Colonial Office.[88] He found a congenial spirit in Friedrich von Lindequist, who had replaced Bernhard Dernburg in June of 1910. As former undersecretary in Dernburg's office, Lindequist was intimately familiar with the distribution issue since he presided over the meeting to abolish Berlin's monopoly. Lindequist was more conservative than Dernburg, as he drew his support from the National Conservatives in the German Reichstag. He also had ample colonial experience, especially as governor of Southwest Africa during the troubled years of 1905 to 1907.[89] Bode and Lindequist established an exchange that centered on preserving crucial ethnographic frontiers, especially the Sepik, from American "poachers" destined to empty German colonies of indigenous artifacts. "[W]e have to arrive there before the Americans," Lindequist wrote to Bode, "perhaps even exclude them from the area."[90] Deemed an area of ethnographic national interest, the Sepik River basin became an opportunity to mount an all-German expedition designed at the same time to protect the region from foreign intervention and to solve the distribution issue that troubled German ethnology. The stage was set to fulfill Emil Stephan's idea of a pan-German "national debt of honor." Lindequist thus labored on a proposal to bring ethnology into line with German colonial interests.

Lindequist expressed his hopes in a long letter that he circulated among all major German states in the union. The point of departure for this circular was the meeting on 21 March 1910. While the meeting had failed to provide a clear distribution mode, the Sepik expedition now invited large-scale, national participation. The expedition's estimated costs, Lindequist told the individual state governments, amounted to 350,000 to 400,000 marks. Lindequist was willing to provide 150,000 marks from his administration, inviting individual state governments, in the spirit of German unity, to contribute to the venture. Lindequist vowed that artifact distribution was to follow the individual contributions of each state at the conclusion of the expedition.[91]

Lindequist's expectations were soon disappointed, as most state officials politely declined the offer. The response from Bavarian and Saxon state officials was particularly disappointing. The second and third largest states in the German union not only refused to contribute to the Sepik venture but argued that their contributions to the German Federal Council were sufficiently large that they should secure a fair share of artifacts from the expedition.[92] Lindequist's proposal was equally rejected by smaller German states. When Bremen state officials asked local museum director Hugo Schauinsland to comment on the proposal, he had few nice things to say. "Those objects [obtained from the colonial administration]," Schauinsland commented, "were of no importance for our museum. Despite last March's conference on the nature of colonial distribution, I expect few changes in this state of affairs." Schauinsland continued that only locally funded museum endeavors had the potential to succeed. He shared his distrust at large-scale pan-German expeditions, such as the one proposed by Lindequist, with many other museum directors.[93] An initial positive response emerged from Georg Thilenius in Hamburg. Thilenius argued that the Hamburg expedition had surveyed the Sepik River in an extensive manner, focusing on regional interconnections. Now it was time to launch an intensive exploration of the river's basin. He considered a contribution of about 10,000 marks to the expedition but wanted to see his money well invested. Thilenius' assistant and Hamburg expedition participant, Otto Reche, thus contacted Richard Thurnwald, one of the two designated ethnographers of the expedition. Reche offered to advise Thurnwald on the ethnographic intricacies of the Sepik region. In return, Thurnwald was to fill ethnographic gaps in the Hamburg collection.

Since the talks between the two men provided Hamburg with an "unfair advantage" over other ethnological institutions, colonial authorities intervened. Fearing his money would vanish without trace in a general expedition pool, Thilenius decided to withdraw his financial support for the expedition.[94]

These were not necessarily encouraging responses from the German state periphery, but ultimately Lindequist was able to gather one non-Prussian supporter. Director Karutz of the small Lübeck museum advised his city authorities to invest the largely symbolic amount of 1,000 marks in the expedition. Instead of an all-German expedition, the venture acquired a decisively Prussian character. The total expenditure of the expedition, roughly 530,000 marks, was borne mostly by the Colonial Office (about 304,000 marks); Prussia contributed about 160,000 marks in both private and public funds.[95] Ultimately, 85 percent of the 4,200 artifacts collected went to the Berlin museum, with the rest going to Lübeck, Dresden, Munich, and Stuttgart.[96] The expedition succeeded in safeguarding Sepik ethnographic collecting from foreign intervention. Its mission to unite German ethnologists failed miserably.

"NATIONALIZING" COLONIAL ARTIFACTS

Lindequist's Sepik initiative elevated ethnographic distribution to a major concern for colonial officials and ethnologists alike. Finding a lasting solution to this issue became one of Lindequist's major legacies. When Lindequist resigned his office, mainly out of protest over Germany's stance in the last Morocco Crisis, he was succeeded by Wilhelm Solf, the former governor of Samoa in 1911. Solf, less conservative than Lindequist, prided himself on his skill in arbitration among different groups whose interests were considered difficult to reconcile.[97] Being rather heavy handed, Solf decided to get the issue off the table sooner rather than later. After assuming his job in Berlin, Solf worked closely with Prussian officials, especially Bode, to arrive at a solution.

Hans Meyer's Geographical Commission became a natural institution to tackle the distribution problem. Much to Solf's annoyance, however, the southern German states of Bavaria and Württemberg could not agree on the appointment of a member to this commission.[98] The principal bone of contention between the kingdoms of Württemberg and Bavaria was the nature of the scientist appointed to the Geographical Commission. Württemberg was pushing for an ethnologist to represent its interests, while Bavaria sought to appoint a natural scientist (either a biologist or a zoologist) to the commission.[99] It took these parties almost one year to agree on an appointment. State authorities finally agreed on Augustin Krämer, well experienced through his travels through the Pacific. Similarly, Krämer, a former naval surgeon, had also assumed the job of scientific director at the newly created Linden Museum in Stuttgart.[100]

With the appointment of Krämer to Meyer's Geographical Commission, the first representative of an ethnology museum entered into a position of power within the German colonial administration. Krämer's role became even more accentuated when he created a new organization known as the Society of German Ethnological Museums (Verein Deutscher Museen für Völkerkunde), which was chartered in 1912. Through this organization Krämer had hoped to solve the distribution issue without the intervention of colonial authorities.[101] Karl Weule in Leipzig and Georg Thilenius in Hamburg distrusted Krämer's abilities to lead the organization effectively. Operating in conjunction with other German museums, they maneuvered the society's leadership into the hands of Weule.[102]

As museum officials busied themselves deciding on the society's leadership, Colonial Secretary Solf charged ahead on the distribution issue. Now that an agreeable member representing the southern German states had been found, Solf decided to appoint selected members of Meyer's Geographical Commission to a distribution council. Instead of involving all German states, Solf decreed the formation of a small council with only three members: one northern German representative, one southern German representative, and one representative of the German Colonial Office. A simple majority was to decide where each artifact was to be sent; in case of a disagreement, Solf reserved his right to intervene. The proposal met with immediate resistance from virtually all major ethnological institutions.[103]

Sensing opposition to his ideas, Solf reconsidered. His idea was simple. As civic pride among ethnological museum directors prevented sensible solutions to the distribution issue, he designated colonial artifacts as "national property." Paradoxically, Solf's action resulted from prior ethnological arguments. Assailing Berlin's monopoly, museum directors such as Thilenius argued for a conceptualization of colonial artifacts as valuable resources. Likewise, Lindequist's actions to preserve the Sepik from foreign intervention elevated ethnographic frontiers to national security issues. Yet at the same time, artifact display and categorization furthered civic pride, bickering, and general ethnological disunity. If colonial artifacts became the property of the Colonial Office, however, a principal disagreement would simply fade.

Armed with the logical conclusion of colonial artifacts as "national property," Solf addressed Weule as the chairperson of the Society for German Ethnological Museums in April of 1914. He maintained his initial idea of creating a three-member distribution council to decide on the fate of colonial artifacts. Solf, nevertheless, added that all artifacts distributed among the museums in Germany constituted loans to be recalled in the event of a future colonial museum construction.[104] An alarmed Weule immediately contacted Thilenius for assistance. Thilenius concurred that Solf's idea of "loaning" colonial artifacts was simply unacceptable. They agreed that immediate action had to be taken to prevent Solf from enacting his proposal.[105] The upcoming anthropological congress in Hildesheim was to provide the setting to discuss the issue in depth. Weule urged the members of the museum society to attend so a united front could be maintained. "Nobody, not even myself, would have come," Weule wrote to Foy, "to listen to a few insignificant talks that I was able to put together for our [museum] session in Hildesheim. But we should take to heart the distribution question, and we should talk about the best way to combat Mr. Solf."[106]

There was a sense of urgency in Weule's exchanges building up to the session in Hildesheim. Perhaps Solf's proposal could once again provide unity among the museum directors, but as the ethnologists were gearing up to discuss possible actions against the German Colonial Office, dark clouds appeared on the political sky of Europe. The congress in Hildesheim, set to begin on 2 August 1914, never took place. With political events snowballing in the summer of 1914, more pressing issues came to the forefront. By late July 1914, telegrams started to pour into German museums canceling the meeting in Hildesheim. "On Friday," Krämer wrote to Luschan, "the last day of July, we decided to cancel the congress. We decided to have it in Hildesheim in 1915 if our enemies will grant us peace."[107] Needless to say, there was no congress in 1915, nor would there be one in the years after that. The Great War had erupted. In 1919 the disputes surrounding the distribution of colonial artifacts were finally settled not at Hildesheim but at Versailles, where the German colonial empire ceased to exist.[108]

The restructuring process engulfing the German colonies following Dernburg's appointment was aimed primarily at the African continent. From an anthropological vantage point, however, German New Guinea was most affected. Anthropologists based in Hamburg and Leipzig labored hard in developing institutions supporting Dernburg's agenda and were instrumental in the emergence of the Geographical Commission and the Colonial Institute. Luschan's African and Oceanic division, which predated Leipzig's and Hamburg's initiatives, was equally affected. Sensing increasing isolation in the newly emerging colonial configurations, Luschan responded by honing his "primary collecting" principle to fit the newly established political configuration. Willing to surrender Berlin's monopoly on ethnographic collections established by colonial officials, Luschan's collection agenda now sought to validate the indigenous cultural institutions lurking behind the collected object. Enshrined in the programmatic statement of the German

Naval Expedition, Luschan ensured his intensive research contrasted sharply with that of Thilenius' Hamburg South Sea Expedition. In this sense, Luschan sought to maintain a qualitative edge in artifact collection, leaving quantitative collecting to Hamburg or other competing institutions.

Dernburg was little impressed by anthropology's competitive ventures, but by the first decade of the twentieth century, Berlin's monopoly drew widespread diplomatic attention. Compounding the issue were American collectors' encroachment on German New Guinea. While their impact was clearly exaggerated by German residents and anthropologists, it made New Guinea's ethnographic frontier a matter affecting national security that required immediate attention. Lindequist's call for an all-German expedition to the Sepik River and Solf's attempt to "nationalize" colonial artifacts sought to address the issue of foreign encroachment. But there was more in their proposals than an attempt to safeguard a colonial territory for German anthropological purposes. Inherent in the colonial secretaries' suggestions was the belief that such projects might consolidate the German anthropological community. A successfully unified anthropological community could only be beneficial to a restructured imperial agenda. Unfortunately, the distribution issue remained unresolved until the outbreak of the First World War. Rather than stirring German anthropologists into an investigation of colonial predicaments, the unresolved matter preserved the centrality of material culture in the anthropological consciousness of the German metropole. Along the colonial periphery in German New Guinea, however, German governor Albert Hahl had eagerly followed innovative anthropological inquiries. While a concern with indigenous mentalities faded in the German metropole, in German New Guinea, they once again intersected with Hahl's colonial anthropology project.

CHAPTER 5

Albert Hahl and the Colonization
of the Ethnographic Frontier

T he interplay between the colonial periphery and the metropole had become a crucial component in the development of the anthropological discipline. Felix von Luschan's attempt to monopolize collectors' efforts on the periphery of German New Guinea failed to bring about the results he desired. Much to Luschan's chagrin, merchants incorporated their own colonial project, the establishment of ethnographic collections for profit, into the ethnographic frontier. Likewise, competing museum officials successfully challenged Luschan's monopoly on scientific grounds. Luschan's reaction, to pursue qualitatively superior collections, led him to consider the mentalities of the societies lurking behind the ethnographic objects. Such ideas, however, became increasingly muddled with the seemingly endless squabbles over the acquisition of artifacts. Shortly before the outbreak of the First World War, the competition involved several secretaries of colonial affairs and brought German New Guinea into sharp focus. While intensive collecting agendas failed to materialize in the German metropole, they became guiding principles for departing expeditions. As anthropological practitioners steamed to their destinations in New Guinea, their concepts collided once again with existing colonial projects. German New Guinea counted little in Dernburg's initial reform of the German colonial edifice. In terms of anthropology, however, the territory easily eclipsed its African counterparts.

The growing interest in German New Guinea's expansive ethnographic frontier became a welcome windfall for Albert Hahl, the colony's second governor. Hahl witnessed with distress the growing investments in the African colonies following Dernburg's reform, reducing German New Guinea even more than before to a stepchild of the German imperial venture. Scrambling for alternatives, Hahl considered the anthropological ventures to his territory as a godsend. His colonial project, however, differed greatly from earlier commercial enterprises. Where commercial officials sought to transform, with mixed success, indigenous material culture into marketable commodities, Hahl became instrumental in propelling anthropological interests into more useful directions. Deeply concerned with the demographic decline of his indigenous subjects, Hahl sought to connect anthropology with pressing colonial predicaments. Luschan's emphasis on "primary collecting" fit well into Hahl's agenda that sought to persuade anthropologists operating along the ethnographic frontier to consider indigenous mentalities. Hahl actively argued that the "salvage operation" of indigenous artifacts had exhausted itself, and practitioners needed to engage themselves in the salvaging of indigenous producers of objects. Set on methodological innovation, the German governor attempted to co-opt a restructured ethnographic frontier into addressing colonial predicaments affecting German New Guinea. The combination of "primary collecting" and Hahl's "colonial" ethnography triggered a brief yet significant Malinowskian moment in German anthropology. Much like in the colonial metropole, the ethnographic frontier in German New Guinea became a crucial component in the development of anthropological ideas and methodologies.

THE ARRIVAL OF STATE COLONIALISM

Changes in German New Guinea's colonial administration encouraged a new perception of ethnographic studies. Until the turn of the century, the New Guinea Company had administrated the territory. Company officials' interest in ethnography was merely commercial, as they hoped to profit from the marketing and sale of material culture. Chapter 2 illustrated how this plan failed when museum ethnologists placed too many demands on indigenous objects. While German ethnologists asked for qualitative improvements in collection activities, officials approached ethnography with a quantitative mind-set. The solution was to use material culture from New Guinea as decorative pieces in a "colonial museum" showcasing the German colonies. Ethnography aside, New Guinea never became the economic paradise expected by company officials. Shattered economic dreams in Kaiser Wilhelmsland initiated a series of lengthy negotiations between the New Guinea Company and the Colonial Department of the Foreign Office. By 1899 the company had transformed itself into a strictly commercial endeavor and surrendered its administrative chores to the German Reich, which compensated the company with a number of economic advantages. The company received control over large acreage in Kaiser Wilhelmsland and 4 million marks (paid in ten yearly installments) for its prior expenditures as a chartered and governing company before 1899.[1]

The territory under German control changed considerably. Indeed, after the so-called Splendid Little War in 1898, the German Reich was able to acquire for 1.8 million marks the Mariana Islands (excluding Guam), the Caroline Islands, and the islands of Palau from a defeated Spanish nation. The gains in Micronesia were complemented by the German Protectorate of the Marshall Islands, which in 1906 fell under the administration of German New Guinea.[2] The territories gained to the north of the equator were offset, however, by the loss of real estate in the Solomon Islands. During the negotiations preceding the partition of the Samoan Islands, the German government surrendered Ysabel, Ontong Java, Choiseul, and the Shortlands in the Solomon Island chain to Great Britain in order to secure the western isles of the Samoan archipelago.[3]

A new administrative system replaced New Guinea Company rule in New Guinea. The arrival of state colonialism encouraged the opening of new stations throughout the newly acquired Micronesian island realm and in strategic locations in New Guinea and the Bismarck Archipelago. Rudolf von Bennigsen became the first governor of German New Guinea. However, his tenure lasted only a few years, after which he was forced to retire for health reasons. In 1902 Albert Hahl became the second governor. Unlike Bennigsen, who had earned his distinction in German Southwest Africa, Hahl had been an imperial judge in the colony since 1896. His experience taught him to consider alternatives, especially since his administration was operating on a shoestring, even after Dernburg's reform.

Hahl regarded the ethnographic frontier as a problematic entity. The preceding chapter illustrated how this frontier closely followed the commercial and colonial opening of territories. Initially centered on the Bismarck Archipelago, especially the Gazelle Peninsula, the frontier slowly reached the mainland of New Guinea. By 1908 it was marching inland with the opening of the Sepik River for recruiting purposes. The shifting ethnographic frontier caused multiple problems. The stipulation of a possible boundary in Para-Micronesia had started a commercial boom in artifacts that endangered the lives of the arriving traders (see Chapter 2) and, as the next chapter will illustrate, the indigenous inhabitants of Wuvulu and Aua. Likewise, overzealous ethnographic collectors caused disruptions through their selfish actions. Bruno Mencke, for instance, was one such self-declared ethnographic collector who, equipped with his own steamer, had pushed beyond the settled areas of the Bismarck Archipelago in 1901. His feat resulted in armed conflict that caused his death and numerous casualties among the indigenous peoples residing on St. Matthias.[4] Similarly the rush to the Sepik, which Augustin Krämer sarcastically linked to Berlin's famous Friedrichsstraße, a place known to attract hordes of shoppers on busy weekends, caused major disruptions from which the ripples could be felt in the highest echelons of the German Colonial Office.[5] Policing a cautious expansion of the ethnographic frontier while reaping the associated benefits was thus of utmost importance for Hahl's colonial administration of German New Guinea.

IMPERIAL ORDERS AND THE ORDER OF EMPIRE: HAHL AND THE "CHEST PAIN" EPIDEMIC

The first opportunity recognized by Hahl was the intense flow of state decorations or orders for ethnographic collection efforts. Karl von Linden in Stuttgart, among others, had exploited "chest pains" (a metaphorical disease linked to decoration cravings) to gain patrons for his growing ethnographic collections, much to the chagrin of Felix von Luschan in Berlin. Strictly speaking, the augmentation of colonial officials in German New Guinea after 1899 contributed to Luschan's attempts to centralize colonial artifacts in the Berlin Ethnological Museum. The governor, individual colonial station officials, and medical officers were all bound to the terms of the 1889 Federal Council Resolution stipulating the mandatory dispatch of artifacts to the Berlin museum. The de facto situation, however, was different, as few of their collections ended up in the Berlin museum owing to the general dissatisfaction with the distribution system and the flow of state decorations to the colonies.

Hahl resented the centralization policy enacted by the Berlin museum, but aware of political intricacies, he chose not to confront Luschan directly. Karl von Linden kept Hahl well informed about what he regarded as an excessive centralization policy.[6] Through Linden's correspondence, Hahl had a better awareness of the growing displeasure with the Berlin museum. While removed from the developments in Germany, Hahl still held a better vantage point than even Luschan in Berlin. Although Luschan knew about the growing discontent against his museum emerging from the German colonies, he never suspected that even colonial governors shared the discontent. Hahl yearned to portray his ethnographic collection activity as liberal by patronizing many different German museums, and he initially trusted the Berlin distribution system to disseminate his collections within Germany. But when he dared to provide the Leipzig Ethnological Museum with some artifacts via Berlin, he was embarrassed to learn that only a fraction of the intended objects had even reached the Saxon city. To prevent further abasement, Hahl opted to bypass the Berlin museum altogether and deal with the German institutions directly. "The Berlin museum desired *omnia* [everything]," Hahl would later complain to a close associate of Luschan, "and got *nihil* [nothing]. While my generous policy would have provided the museum with many treasures, [the objects] ultimately went elsewhere."[7] This explains the presence of artifacts collected by Hahl in virtually all German museums, although Stuttgart received the lion's share.[8]

Hahl's self-proclaimed liberal policy for distributing ethnographic objects only increased the number of museum directors appealing to his patronage. "Did you release my good name?" Hahl asked Linden. "From all sides I have museum directors accosting me with a vengeance. Even in my Bavarian home they have recently rediscovered their passion for [ethnographic] collection and are seeking to get in contact with me."[9] Karl Weule in Leipzig, for instance, sought to monopolize Hahl's patronage. Weule promised him a Saxon state decoration in return for his collection efforts. Hahl, however, opposed the absorption of his ethnographic favors; he did not object to the decoration principle, but he did "not want to be tied to [Weule's] museum in any other way than giving of [his own] free will."[10] For Hahl, informal contact through state decorations was one thing, and attachment to a single German ethnological museum quite another.

Hahl realized that the flood of decorations could have both disruptive and beneficial results for the colonial administration. On the one hand, excessive decoration could disrupt the burgeoning activities of colonial officials, instilling them with the need to take additional risks in their desire to quell their "chest pains." On the other hand, Hahl also saw that decorations could serve his colonial officials well. Operating on his territory's limited budget, which included deductions for the yearly appropriations to the New Guinea Company, Hahl found it difficult to reward his officers in any financial way.[11] Moreover, the officials themselves were often a source of distress for Hahl. For instance, colonial official Franz Boluminski had made progress in the pacification of northern New Ireland, yet Hahl was appalled at his pecuniary situation. According to Hahl, only a heavy hand directing Boluminski's spending in northern New Ireland could curb financial abuses.[12] However, Boluminski ensured his position in the administration by maintaining New Ireland's high number of plantation recruits for the German territory. Hahl had no direct control over New Ireland, since there was only one governmental steamer available to him. State orders and decorations then became an alternative incentive to keep Hahl's colonial officials in check or to reward them for their work. Yet decorations took a long time to acquire. The standard procedure for Hahl was to nominate his officials for a decoration through the Colonial Division of the German Foreign Office, a lengthy procedure since colonial officers stationed in Africa had priority over those in the Pacific. Moreover, this proceeding limited the availability of state decorations, since the Colonial Division considered only the bestowal of Prussian orders.[13]

In search of other options, Hahl appealed to German museum directors, thus avoiding the bureaucratic entanglements in Berlin; he also secured access to non-Prussian state decorations by this strategy. Hahl stressed his colonial officials' active role in supplying ethnographic objects in return for state decorations. "I can communicate to you," Hahl wrote to Linden, "that Franz Boluminski in Nusa [northern New Ireland] notified me about a collection that he will soon send to your address. A monetary compensation is not expected, but he will gladly wait for a decoration."[14] Hahl also brought Wilhelm Wostrack, of the colonial station located in central New Ireland, to the attention of Linden in Stuttgart.[15]

Official expeditions also proved helpful in this regard. One of the official aims of the German Naval Expedition was to help the Berlin Ethnological Museum regain the trust of colonial residents. To this end, the expedition's leader, Emil Stephan, sternly advised Luschan to come forward with a number of Prussian state decorations. This, he argued, would not only ensure their goodwill and support for the expedition, but would also draw colonial residents into the service of Berlin's ethnographic collectors.[16] Another participant of the naval expedition, Edgar Walden, confirmed the general low opinion of the Berlin museum in the German territory. A name frequently mentioned in his discussions with colonial residents was Karl von Linden, for his highly personal letters had strengthened the ties between German New Guinea and Stuttgart. Colonial residents showed Walden many samples of such correspondence. Indeed, it seemed Linden was about to gain the upper hand in the collection effort.[17]

Stephan's proposal to increase the number of Prussian decorations in the territory clearly played into Hahl's hands. The German Naval Expedition participants stepped into Hahl's office in September 1907, marking the beginning of many rounds of talks between newcomers and the governor. Hahl's first function was to move the expedition's field site from New Britain to New Ireland, for reasons delineated below. Second, he urged Stephan to secure decoration for Boluminski and Wostrack, the two colonial officials stationed on New Ireland. When Stephan agreed to intervene on behalf of Luschan, Hahl immediately wrote to Linden in Stuttgart. With Stephan promising Prussian state decorations, Hahl hoped to obtain the equivalent from Württemberg. "Now that you know about my situation here," Hahl wrote to Karl von Linden, "perhaps you can do your part in procuring [Württemberg] decorations for these individuals."[18] Hahl's game paid off, since Linden soon promised to do what he could to secure decorations for Boluminski and Wostrack.[19] "I may be able," Linden wrote to the governor, "to fulfill my promise earlier than Stephan."[20] This was exactly what Hahl expected to hear from Stuttgart. By capitalizing on the competition between

Stuttgart and Berlin, Hahl was able to obtain a number of decorations to reward some deserving and hard-working colonial officials in his administration without having them take any unnecessary risks.[21]

HAHL'S ATTEMPT TO RECONFIGURE GERMAN ETHNOGRAPHY

For Albert Hahl decorations were battles easily won by appealing to the increasing competition among German ethnological museums. A much more difficult task, however, would be to steer German anthropologists toward directions useful to Hahl's administration. Anthropology was not new to Hahl; indeed, the governor was a bit of a budding ethnographer. He had been in German New Guinea for more than six years acquiring experience as an imperial judge and deputy governor. Having earned a doctorate in law in 1893, he also had extensive legal training, and his insights into the legal aspects of colonial rule brought him into contact with ethnography.[22]

During Hahl's tenure as an imperial judge, he began to address legal concerns in an ethnographic context—a consequence of his interaction with indigenous peoples on the Gazelle Peninsula in New Britain. Having realized that German legal concepts did not translate well into the numerous indigenous languages of the territory, Hahl immersed himself in linguistic studies of the local groups.[23] Such studies inspired his appointment of chiefly representatives and indigenous elites to the posts of *luluai* and *tultul*, a form of indirect rule through local authorities. The two terms were borrowed from the vocabulary of the Tolai people with whom Hahl was in close contact. *Luluai* originally designated local leaders whose skills were sufficiently tested in warfare to warrant leadership positions; *tultul* was a more recent term applied to a new elite group who had extensive contacts with the European community. The *tultul* emerged as important middlemen since they had an understanding of indigenous as well as European customs, while the *luluai* became colonial authority figures equipped with cap and staff to underline their position.[24] Hahl tried to apply the model elsewhere in the territory with mixed success.[25]

Hahl repeated his studies of local customs during his term as deputy governor in the Caroline Islands, and to convince others to follow his example, he published two articles with the Berlin-based *Ethnologisches Notizblatt*.[26] There, he discussed the situation in Pohnpei, where the Germans had assumed control following several wars between the indigenous population and the Spanish colonizers who had ravaged the island. Hahl tried to avoid the same problems by gaining a thorough understanding of individual customs, which were described in his articles. Hahl also read the ethnographic accounts of German New Guinea but generally found them lacking. Most of the ethnography undertaken in the late nineteenth century was rushed and yielded few insights for administrative purposes. In particular, Hahl was critical of the "colorful and imaginative" renditions of German anthropologists, which had little in common with the type of research he envisaged. Despite the disappointing quality of the ethnographic work conducted in the colony, Hahl had high hopes for the German anthropological community.[27] Indeed, the remoteness of New Guinea from German affairs allowed for a number of experiments, and Hahl was willing to pursue them.[28] Similarly, the growing ethnographic interest in German New Guinea more than made up for the political neglect.

Interestingly enough, Hahl's dialogues with ethnological museums focused less on collection practices than on new ways of performing ethnographic research. Well versed in the intellectual discourse of German anthropology, Hahl openly conversed with museum officials about the "salvage paradigm." While the great majority of German anthropologists still believed material culture to be the central text governing their discipline, Hahl attempted to convince the practitioners that a salvage action focusing entirely on material culture had come to an end.[29] His correspondence abounded with assertions that entire island chains "[were] no longer a field for the collector";[30] and he even suggested that it would be necessary to import ethnographic objects into German New Guinea in order to find any in the territory.[31] Such statements hardly expressed nostalgia for a bygone era of ethnographic collection. Quite the contrary, Hahl's correspondence with museum officials revealed an interesting dichotomy that thoroughly deprivileged a salvage paradigm centered on material artifacts. In his letters, Hahl often contrasted earlier collectors (*Sammler*) with contemporary scientists (*Wissenschaftler*). To Karl Weule, for instance, Hahl wrote that the territory was now almost entirely depleted of artifacts. But "for scientific inquiry," he continued, "the field was wide open."[32]

Beyond his invocation of a new, "scientific" anthropology, Hahl also deployed the term "field" in conjunction with ethnographic work. Historians of anthropology have identified the period before and after the Great War as the moment that gave rise to a new anthropological methodology commonly designated as "fieldwork." This method centered on the close investigation of a single indigenous society over a long stretch of time, a mode that replaced broad ethnographic surveys of large geographical areas.[33] Bronislaw Malinowski may not have invented this new methodology, but he certainly enshrined it. "The time when we could tolerate accounts presenting us the native as a distorted, childish caricature of a human being is gone. This picture is false, and like many other falsehoods, it has been killed by Science."[34]

Malinowski's words resembled the sentiments expressed by Hahl, but there were differences to be found as well.

Hahl's emphasis on fieldwork was not dictated by Malinowski's scientific concerns but instead was a function of colonial Realpolitik in the administration of German New Guinea. Hahl's main concern was to create a category of "native" as a useful abstraction for colonial administration. In general, the term "native" included all non-Europeans within the colony and was usually applied to the men.[35] Hahl hoped to illuminate native culture through intensive research into "native" cosmologies—an investigative modality that would develop common legal denominators and statistical evidence for Hahl's subjects.[36]

Understanding the "native" mind through ethnography, however, was only one of Hahl's concerns. By the first decade of the twentieth century, it had become apparent that the indigenous population was declining, at least in some parts of the territory, which had ramifications for the labor market.[37] During the New Guinea Company's tenure, officials had placed much emphasis on attracting German settlers to New Guinea. Such hopes were dashed, however, as climate, disease, and company regulations severely limited the number of migrants. What was left was the main staple of the colonial economy: coconut plantations providing copra for European markets. A steady supply of servile, low-paid labor remained the most pressing need for the German administration. During the tenure of the New Guinea Company, there had already been a labor shortage, and it continued well after the German state took over the colony in 1899. The steady increase in plantations in New Guinea, the Bismarck Archipelago, and, to a lesser extent, Micronesia made the labor issue even more central to the colonial administration.[38]

Much like the New Guinea Company, Hahl attempted to import laborers from East Asia, but their numbers fell well short of expectations. Consequently, German planters and settlers applied increasing pressure on the administration to open up new recruiting grounds and to step up the process of indenture in those areas already contacted. The effort, however, was further complicated by the privileges granted to specific companies. The New Guinea Company, for instance, had exclusive recruiting privileges on Kaiser Wilhelmsland, while the Deutsche Handels-und Plantagengesellschaft received several hundred recruits each year from New Guinea for its plantation operations in German Samoa. In light of the rising demands for labor power, Hahl turned his attention to the urgent problem of depopulation. Anthropological research could provide vital information in this regard, and soon Hahl called on museums to provide more information on the "native" producers of material culture than on material culture itself. "If science,"

Hahl wrote to a museum director, "can ultimately tell us what we have to do in order not only to save the native from extinction, but also to increase his numbers, [your research] will have contributed more than any discovery of large gold deposits."[39]

COLONIAL ETHNOGRAPHY GAINED: RICHARD THURNWALD'S VENTURES IN GERMAN NEW GUINEA

The first trained German ethnographer to set foot in German New Guinea was Richard Thurnwald, whom Luschan dispatched to German New Guinea to remedy the decline of collection activity (see Chapter 3). Thurnwald was ill informed about the expeditions descending on the colonial territory. In fact, he was upset when he found out that Luschan had launched the German Naval Expedition without his knowing.[40] Hahl's attention to the young researcher, however, provided a new opportunity through which Thurnwald was able to reconfigure his research.

Luschan could have sent no better researcher than Thurnwald to further the dialogue between colonialism and anthropology in German New Guinea. Like Hahl, Thurnwald held a doctorate in law, and he had undertaken population studies for the Austro-Hungarian government in the protectorate of Bosnia-Herzogovina.[41] He was therefore well equipped to discuss administrative concerns over indigenous law and population decline. Hahl took Thurnwald on several trips on the governmental steamer *Seestern* (Starfish) to familiarize him with different social and natural environments in the German colony. He also had extensive talks with Thurnwald about his experiences in the Balkans.[42] While aware that Thurnwald was on a collection trip for Berlin's museum, Hahl used Thurnwald's dependency on the colonial administration as well as his interest in population studies to steer the research into useful directions for his administration. Thurnwald still collected for Luschan in Berlin, but under Hahl's supervision, he also performed stationary research in northern New Britain and southern Bougainville.[43] There, Thurnwald even opened up new territory for colonial administration by facilitating a peace agreement between coastal and inland populations.[44] "It seems to dawn in our dark part of the world," Hahl enthusiastically reported to Luschan in Berlin. "May the commercial frontier keep pace with the ethnographic one."[45]

As Thurnwald's ethnographic outlook came to correspond with Hahl's, he departed from Luschan's original designs for his research. Indeed, Thurnwald's collections of material culture were slow in reaching Berlin, and Luschan quickly saw that his mission was in jeopardy.[46] When Thurnwald and Luschan clashed over the issue of ethnographic research, it was Hahl who shielded the young ethnographer. Hahl argued that Thurnwald's research into indigenous law and population statistics was not only vital to the colonial administration, but could also invigorate anthropology in Germany.[47] Thurnwald made an analogous point when he claimed that his fieldwork in German New Guinea redefined ethnographic research. Anthropologists and colonial officials had much in common, Thurnwald argued, yet they rarely connected on an intellectual level. Anthropologists relied too much on indigenous culture and not enough on the social universe of the indigenous producers. Colonial officials, in contrast, focused almost exclusively on economics. Economics and ethnographic knowledge were not mutually exclusive, however, and in the tropics, only a merger of these two aspects guaranteed both viable ethnography and a successful colonial economy.[48] Thurnwald advanced the marriage of anthropology and colonialism in a number of publications. In these essays he stressed the importance of understanding indigenous law and originated the concept of a "gendered" native. While Thurnwald neglected to acknowledge the German governor prominently, Hahl's ideas were clearly present in these writings, which enunciated the possibility of a colonial ethnography.

In terms of indigenous law, Thurnwald's long-term study of German New Guinea's peoples allowed him to support the important point made by Hahl ten years earlier that colonial law had to emerge out of a compromise between indigenous and German concepts of legality.[49] Such a syncretic vision would be aided if common denominators were found among the different legal concepts of the indigenous groups. Given German New Guinea's many languages and societies, this was a daunting undertaking, especially since Thurnwald eschewed the ethnographic use of contact languages. Much like Hahl, he derided "Pidgin English," since the lingua franca lacked the elaborate vocabulary necessary to investigate the deeper intellectual understandings of indigenous people.[50] Only local studies carried out in the vernacular, Thurnwald contended with Hahl's approval, could contribute to the formation of a common legal language that was applicable throughout the colony. For Thurnwald, the colonial advantages of such an endeavor were obvious: "As the native psyche offers the key for native justice, so the application of these insights form the prerequisite for a successful manipulation of the natives for the aims of the Europeans in a tropical colony."[51]

Thurnwald's second contribution to colonial ethnography was the concept of a "gendered native." Building on Hahl's call to focus on the "native" producers of artifacts rather than on material culture, Thurnwald developed the problematic category of the "native mother." In the British colonial realm, measures were already under way to intervene in the nurturing processes of the "native mother"—a colonial subject who was viewed in decisive opposition to the "normal" European woman. Indigenous women, the argument went, had few of the moral constraints of their European counterparts. Their open sexuality introduced venereal diseases, and their careless behavior led to a decline in childbearing as well as an increase in prostitution.[52] Thurnwald observed similar processes at work in New Ireland, where the indigenous population had experienced the greatest decline. "Native" women, Thurnwald argued, should not only be barred from the labor recruiting process, but also be kept under close surveillance for venereal diseases. "There is no question in my mind that through drastic methods introduced both to restrict the recruiting process on Neu Mecklenburg [the German colonial name for New Ireland] and to cleanse the whole area of venereal disease, we will be able to manage the dangers of native depopulation. This should be in the interest of each planter, especially when similar surveillance is put in place in other recruiting areas as well."[53]

Hahl was actively involved in writing the article, and he assisted Thurnwald with the page proofs. "Finally science and exploration are coming together even here in New Guinea," he wrote to Thurnwald with evident satisfaction;[54] and in due time he ordered three hundred offprints to be distributed in the German Reichstag.[55] With Thurnwald's help, Hahl had taken a giant step closer to a colonial ethnography, and Thurnwald supported him throughout the rest of his career.[56] But the question remained whether the initial steps taken by Thurnwald would be sustained and nurtured by the German anthropological community.

COLONIAL ETHNOGRAPHY LOST: NEW IRELAND AS A "COLONIAL" FIELD SITE

Hahl was presented with the opportunity to coordinate large-scale German ethnographic efforts in New Ireland. There he attempted to put into practice his own ethnographic designs, drawing on the insights generated during Thurnwald's visit to the German territory. A number of German ethnographic ventures in New Guinea proved helpful in Hahl's grand scheme of colonial ethnography. In chronological order, these expeditions were the German Naval Expedition (1907–1909), the Geographical Commission Expedition (1908), the Hamburg South Sea Expedition (1908–1910), and later, the Sepik Expedition (1913–1914). Several smaller endeavors and privately sponsored travelers should be added to the list.[57]

New Ireland is the second largest island in the Bismarck Archipelago. Long and relatively narrow, it stretches from northwest to southeast, covering roughly three thousand square miles. European settlements did not appear there until about 1880, when violent confrontations with the indigenous population became commonplace. By the turn of the century, the German administration had established a colonial outpost in northern New Ireland, followed a few years later by a second government station in the island's central region. Both stations increased the speed of the German pacification process. By the end of the first decade of the twentieth century, a rapid transformation of the island had occurred, bringing its population into the plantation economy. Beyond the local estates, New Ireland also supplied a large share of the indentured laborers for plantations all over German New Guinea.[58]

The transformation and incorporation of New Ireland into the German colonial economy was accompanied by numerous problems. By the time Thurnwald arrived in the territory, it had become obvious that the population was showing signs of decline. Initial surveys, including Thurnwald's, suggested that this decline was partially the result of Western contact and the related disruption of traditional societies. In Hahl's view, the ethnographic expeditions steaming to New Guinea could be put to good use in investigating this problem.

The value of ethnography for Hahl was clear. Aside from the collection of artifacts, the expeditions were to provide careful census data for the area. This was to include the ratio of males to females among the indigenous population, which he regarded as vital to any investigation concerned with population decline.[59] Hahl also desired a closer understanding of local languages in order to replace "Pidgin English" with the more "meaningful" vernaculars. In Hahl's view, which was greatly informed by Thurnwald's initial research, language was an entrepôt into indigenous cognition, yielding insights into local societies. At the same time, linguistic studies would provide a new administrative language in which both indigenous and German legal concepts would be intelligible.[60] Since New Ireland was home to close to twenty language groups, this kind of linguistic and ethnographic work was crucial. As questions of population control and investigations into local languages emerged as the priorities of Hahl's colonial ethnography, New Ireland became the test case for its implementation.

Hahl sought ethnographers similar to Richard Thurnwald in the various German expeditions. However, driven by the collection frenzy of Germany's ethnological museums, the members of the various expeditions were disinclined to engage in Hahl's prolonged colonial ethnography, hoping instead to emerge from German New Guinea as victors in the ongoing competition for artifacts.

The Hamburg South Sea Expedition was by far the best-sponsored endeavor. With a budget of 600,000 marks and equipped with its own steamer, the expedition was to conduct an extensive ethnographic survey of German

New Guinea in the tradition of earlier salvage operations.[61] Although the expedition's organizer, Georg Thilenius, went to great lengths to explain how his venture differed from earlier collection activities, Hahl failed to see its usefulness. The expedition was diametrically opposed to Hahl's agenda for the colonial ethnography of a limited area since the crew was to survey almost all of German New Guinea. Given that the expedition was to spend only a few weeks in any given place, Hahl deemed it a waste of time. The only tangible result of the venture, he thought, would be a steep increase in the territory's ethnographica prices. There was simply no room for such an extensive expedition in Hahl's colonial program.[62]

The German Naval Expedition, organized by Luschan in Berlin, was more agreeable to Hahl. Operating on a mere fraction of the Hamburg expedition's budget, the naval expedition was not a particularly mobile affair. Rather, they remained in one particular location for extended periods of time. Similarly, as discussed in the last chapter, Emil Stephan took to New Guinea an anthropological methodology, which Luschan labeled "monographic work," that rang true to Hahl's project for a colonial ethnography. Stephan was clearly a prolific writer whose two monographs, despite Fritz Graebner's diffusionist concerns, circulated widely among the German anthropological community. Hahl, however, was not impressed. When Stephan delivered the published monographs to the governor for inspection, Hahl returned the books with extensive criticism:

> I had trouble keeping awake reading your booklet [Südseekunst], since I have no intention to interrogate the latest art theories. In the book about [New Ireland], I have underlined many questionable passages where the Pidgin English has fooled you in your translation process. Beware of this main enemy of research that prevents clear communication with the natives. . . . The numbers of misunderstandings in my field are legion. For instance, how can we establish a language of legality if we are lacking even the most basic concepts?[63]

The same letter documented how Hahl sought to influence the research agendas of expeditions to New Guinea. Promoting his personal agenda of colonial ethnography, Hahl not only told Stephan to record indigenous languages and guard against "Pidgin English," but he also used the metaphor of the field (*Feld*) to talk about his stationary research mode.

Besides intervening in the expeditions' research agendas, Hahl also determined their research sites. Stephan's naval expedition was originally set to explore the lesser-known areas of New Britain (Neu Pommern) in the Bismarck Archipelago.[64] Hahl, however, invested considerable energy in redirecting it to New Ireland, arguing that the harsh climate and difficult access to the originally targeted area would threaten the expedition's safety. It was in New Ireland, of course, where Hahl saw the urgent need for linguistic study and research into population developments; and to maximize the results, he suggested that the expedition focus on the northern and southern portions of the island.[65] Stephan, resigned to the fact that there was little he could do, wrote to Luschan that a limiting of the area of ethnographic study would ultimately produce a better-determined collection and consequently better ethnographic monographs.[66]

Besides advancing his own agenda, Hahl sought to limit the naval expedition's survey area for another reason. He had reserved the central portion of New Ireland for a different expedition, the one organized by the Geographical Commission (Landeskundliche Kommission), a colonial organization created to further geographical knowledge of the German colonies. The original destination of that expedition had also been New Britain.[67] Hahl, however, saw an opportunity to combine the two expeditions' efforts on New Ireland, thereby advancing his own colonial goals. Specifically, the governor sought to complement Stephan's long-term stay (the naval expedition was scheduled to remain two years) with the insights of the more limited Geographical Commission expedition. Its members, among them geographer Karl Sapper and ethnographer Georg Friederici, were particularly agreeable to Hahl, since their interests extended beyond a concern for the rising and falling commodity prices in the world market.[68]

But while Hahl was pleased with the division of New Ireland between the naval and geographical expeditions, his broader designs were hardly shared by their participants.[69] Naval expedition member Edgar Walden wondered why he had to compete with local colonial officials over acquiring ethnographica, while Georg Friederici of the Geographical Commission expedition complained bitterly about sending two expeditions into an area that was essentially pacified and thus had little to offer in terms of anthropological research.[70] Similar concerns were expressed in the pages of prominent periodicals. Hermann Singer, the editor of the important geographic-anthropological journal *Globus,* went so far as to use the example of the two expeditions to criticize the spending policies of the entire German colonial administration.[71]

Hahl withstood such criticisms, however, because their research was producing some interesting results. Stephan heeded Hahl's warning regarding "Pidgin English," undertaking extensive research into the vernaculars of southern New Ireland, while Friederici investigated the uses and limitations of "Pidgin English."[72] Most important for Hahl's colonial ethnography was Stephan's handwritten exposé in early 1908 on the causes of population decline in southern New Ireland. Based on the empirical evidence of long-term research, the report also presented suggestions for ending the decline.[73]

The governor, though heartened by such promising results, always had to contend with the competitive ethos of the individual expeditions. Most of the ventures to German New Guinea were nominally pan-national, though the initial impetus for their efforts always came from specific museums. The German Naval Expedition, for instance, was a thinly disguised attempt by Berlin's Felix von Luschan to counter the Hamburg South Sea Expedition. Likewise, the Geographical Commission's expedition was inspired by chairman Hans Meyer's opposition to the Berlin museum's monopoly over colonial artifacts.[74]

Much to Hahl's dismay, the vigorous competition among the expeditions ultimately undermined the usefulness of their findings. While competitive forces threatened to disrupt the expeditions from their outset, the problem became acute when Stephan, leader of the naval expedition, took ill. Suffering from blackwater fever, he passed away in late May 1908. Hans Meyer was quick to exploit the resulting instability and confusion. Operating behind the scenes, he sought to fuse the naval expedition with the Geographical Commission's venture in order to "right," as he put it, "wrongs committed in the past."[75] Hurrying to prevent such a hostile takeover, Luschan quickly negotiated for a new leader. The person designated for the job was Augustin Krämer, who, together with his wife, rushed to New Ireland to join the expedition.[76] Rather than bringing stability, however, Krämer's arrival triggered a wave of protests by the other expedition members, who wished to operate independently.[77] Despite personal and institutional conflicts, Krämer kept the naval venture together. But under increasing time pressure, he could do little more than "prevent the ship from sinking (*die Karre aus dem Dreck zu ziehen*)."[78] As he embarked on a final ethnographic romp through New Ireland, Hahl's colonial agenda fell by the wayside.

Hahl was greatly disappointed with the outcome of the German Naval Expedition. The grand experiment in colonial ethnography had failed, and resignation took hold:

> I had expected [from the naval expedition] an encompassing detailed picture of the peoples in northern and central [New Ireland] in addition to the coastal populations in the southern regions. I do believe this work will never be completed; the change in personnel was detrimental to the execution of the expedition. I also believe that the young researchers were not able to cope with the practical realities of their field of inquiry. They did not have enough time to engage intensively in their respective areas.[79]

Hahl ultimately believed that most of the members of the naval expedition, especially Otto Schlaginhaufen and Edgar Walden, were simply not up to the task: "Your gentlemen," Hahl reproached Luschan, "are lacking even the most basic notions of the tropics, tropical medicine, adaptation, etc. Please make sure that such novices receive the proper instruction prior to departure. The struggle with the wilderness is hard. Capable people, such as Dr. Thurnwald, seem to be rare among your staff."[80]

The restructuring of the naval expedition put an abrupt end to Hahl's vision of the "colonial field." His grand project for New Ireland had disintegrated not for the lack of an appropriate theoretical framework, but because competition and personal issues made cooperation difficult. Even though the New Guinea expeditions safely returned to Germany, their results would not advance Hahl's agenda for colonial ethnography. Hahl's correspondence with German ethnological museums, quite extensive following his arrival in New Guinea, began to decline after 1910. Only during the planning stages of the Sepik Expedition did Hahl involve himself once again to recommend Thurnwald as a much needed expedition participant.[81]

German "Malinowskian" Moments and Counterfactual Histories

Even if Hahl failed in his grand designs for colonial ethnography, his stern interventions into anthropological research agendas triggered methodologies resembling "fieldwork" among the various expeditions' participants. Richard Thurnwald was one of the first anthropologists to experience the Malinowskian immersion of modern fieldwork, having undertaken Hahl's design of ethnographic research.[82] Emil Stephan, initially inspired by Luschan's intensive collecting, also took some of Hahl's considerations into account when he set up his base camp in southern New Ireland. And while Edgar Walden did not enjoy Hahl's esteem, his research into the mortuary rituals of northern New Ireland focused on the deeper meanings of the artifacts associated with them.[83] In doing so, he criticized the endeavors of local resident ethnographers, such as Richard Parkinson, who collected objects without comprehending their meanings. Walden felt that Parkinson's work was riddled with mistakes reflecting superficial study and utter linguistic ignorance.[84]

Walden discovered the advantages of fieldwork after Hahl assigned him to northern New Ireland, and he also was willing to share his methodological insights. In October 1908 the steamer of the Hamburg South Sea Expedition came upon Walden's area of research. Walden was allowed to board the competition's ship, and in a conversation with Wilhelm Müller, he discussed the advantages of long-term stationary research. Criticizing the Hamburg expedition for its superficial surveying of all of German New Guinea, Walden explained that the "validity of his earlier notes" had become doubtful in the course of his ten-month stay in the region.[85] Apparently, Müller took the criticism to heart, and he subsequently complained to expedition organizer Georg Thilenius that "we are trying to write publications after a mere few weeks of observation."[86] Both Walden and Müller had come to realize the advantages of long-term studies of indigenous societies.

Considering these advances toward a "Malinowskian" moment in German anthropology along the colonial periphery, why did the new methodology not become entrenched? There is an easy answer to this query: death. While it is generally accepted that the First World War caused a severe disruption in anthropological museum work, clearing the path for different methodological approaches in this discipline, the German case suggests the opposite.[87] Stephan's death in 1908 precluded any positive outcome of his research. His two monographs illustrate that he was a prolific writer, but his passing prevented the publication of his research. In fact, the results of the German Naval Expedition remained, by and large, unpublished.[88] Edgar Walden, whose results in northern New Ireland were promising, died on the Western Front during the First World War.[89] Wilhelm Müller, the gadfly in Thilenius' expedition, did publish the results of his stationary research in Yap, but they appeared posthumously after he perished from a typhoid infection in Dutch Indonesia, where he had been interned during the war.[90] The lone survivor of the war, Richard Thurnwald, spent much time in internment after being captured by Australian troops during the New Guinea campaign. His laborious return to Germany was greeted with anything but a hero's welcome, and he spent the next decades trying to gain a teaching post in Germany.[91] Even successful publication series, such as Thilenius' thirty monographs on his expedition, suffered from the impact of the war and the ensuing depression, which wiped out the funds of the Hamburg Scientific Foundations. In fact, the last monograph of this series, on New Britain, did not see the light until 1954, more than four decades after the conclusion of the expedition.[92] Moreover, the monographs reflect orthodox concerns with listing ethnographic collections, ranging from artifacts, superficial ethnographic observations, and equally shallow linguistic observations. The Hamburg monographs also ensured employment for a number of anthropologists, including ones who never set foot in German New Guinea. Orthodox concerns about description and classification took the place of pathbreaking methodological innovation.

A full evaluation of the brief, ill-fated German Malinowskian moment suggests engaging counterfactual history.[93] The potential for an imaginary "Stephanian" moment emerges for an analysis of the negotiations surrounding the German Naval Expedition's results. To be sure, this exercise remains speculative, because Emil Stephan's death of blackwater fever set in motion a process that ultimately prevented the publication of those results. The plan to have the German Naval Office pay for the expedition stalled when expedition member Otto Schlaginhaufen revealed the matter to Alfred von Tirpitz. Tirpitz immediately objected to the plan, arguing that the ethnographic nature of the endeavor conflicted with the interests of his office.[94] Looking at the project counterfactually, however, provokes a different picture. Envisioning a negative response from Tirpitz, Stephan had urged Luschan not to reveal the plan until his return from German New Guinea. Stephan advised a carefully orchestrated action to gain the Naval Office's final approval, especially since the publication costs of the expedition exceeded that of the actual undertaking. In 1911 preliminary publication estimates ran 68,000 marks (including 50,000 for actual publication costs and 18,000 for honoraria and miscellaneous expenses), or 8,000 marks above the expedition costs.[95] With the anticipated backing of the German Naval Office, Stephan envisioned the publication of six volumes equally shared by the expedition's participants.[96] Otto Schlaginhaufen was to cover material culture and physical anthropology, thus removing more orthodox anthropological concerns from the rest of the publications. The remaining four volumes allowed room for significant ethnographic experimentation. Expedition leader Stephan, for instance, proposed to write a general introduction to the expedition and a potentially rich volume on language and mental culture. If one were to extrapolate on Stephan's ethnographic agenda (chronicled in this and the preceding chapter), it is easy to envision a potentially radical break in the methods of ethnographic research. Stephan's earlier work revealed a concern for indigenous individuality and a keen interest in long-term study, and his two volumes could easily have enshrined his views. His introduction to the general volume or the work on mental culture might have involved a methodological discussion akin to Malinowski's "mythmaking" in his *Argonauts*.[97] Similarly, Edgar Walden's two planned volumes could have assisted Stephan's agenda. Walden's work in northern New Ireland and its *malaggan* cultural complex (see next chapter) surely offered the opportunity for an extensive critique of earlier resident collectors and ethnographers, as demonstrated in his diary entries and letters. Together Stephan's and Walden's unwritten volumes represented in theory a significant shift in German anthropological activity.

Two interesting episodes corroborate these notions. The first derives from Augustin Krämer's intervention into the nature of the naval expedition's publications. Krämer was a great deal more traditional than his predecessor, Stephan. He immediately tackled the project geographically rather than methodologically. In his publication plans, three of the planned seven volumes were traditional ethnographic surveys of southern, central, and northern New Ireland. Two volumes were dedicated to Schlaginhaufen's physical anthropological observations, and only one (written by Walden) was dedicated to linguistics. Geographical concerns were primary and well fitted into what Krämer envisioned as monographic work, which he regarded as tied to material culture and its collection activity.[98] Even though Krämer's volumes were not published, his orchestration meant a curtailing of Stephan's methodological innovation.

The value of Walden's unpublished notes emerged during a brief controversy in 1916, when Elizabeth Krämer-Bannow published her observations regarding the German Naval Expedition.[99] Her musings, from a distinctive female perspective, were accompanied by a section written by her spouse, Augustin Krämer, who believed a male and therefore more scientific voice was needed to balance her account. August Eichhorn, assistant curator at the Oceanic division of the Berlin museum, employed Walden's notes to ridicule both their accounts. The book, he wrote to his superiors, represented little more than an amusing tale, and even the male-centered narrative by Augustin Krämer could not belie the fact that it was of little substance. Walden, by now a casualty of the Great War, in contrast, had spent considerable time and care to study the inner workings of the *malaggan* rituals. Eichhorn consequently argued that it was Walden's posthumous work, rather than those by the Krämers, that merited publication.[100] Although Walden's notes were never published, his notes were deemed important enough to discredit established ethnographers.[101] The methodological potential of Stephan's and Walden's work was apparent, yet following their deaths the results remained entombed in the archives of the Berlin Ethnological Museum.

The dialectic between a changing anthropological discipline in the German metropole and a maturing colonial administration located at the periphery of German New Guinea brought immediate results. While few museum officials advocated eliminating the collection of indigenous artifacts, their project was a far cry from Adolf Bastian's less-than-discriminating salvage agenda delineated in Chapter 1. Felix von Luschan, during his adamant defense of Berlin's monopoly over the German colonies, grew increasingly impatient with poor collecting practices by commercial agents (see Chapter 2). Similarly, beset on all sides by enterprising museum directors' ability to outstrip Berlin's collection efforts, Luschan chose to investigate qualitative collection activities put in practice by the German Naval Expedition under Emil Stephan's leadership. Such practices found the approval of Albert Hahl, who realized their potential in solving colonial predicaments. And while anthropologists actively resisted—much as they had done in the case of commercial companies—outsiders tinkering with their discipline, one would be hard-pressed to ignore the dialogues that emerged along the colonial periphery. Even Hahl's disgust at witnessing his "colonial ethnography" disintegrate among anthropological squabbles in the metropole cannot belie the methodological and ensuing theoretical implications developed by anthropologists operating along the periphery of German New Guinea. The ensuing Great War prevented German anthropologists from expanding in the direction of their Anglo-American counterparts. Recovering their efforts by means of a mild counterfactual analysis permits a global understanding of anthropology's history. However, understanding the crucial interplay between the colonial periphery and the national metropole requires that additional analytical attention be paid to the indigenous peoples residing in German New Guinea.

CHAPTER 6

Indigenous Reactions

Throughout the last five chapters I have examined the investigation of the ethnographic frontier in German New Guinea as a purely Western endeavor. While this is in no way inconsistent with the explicit aim of the present work, an investigation that seeks to uncover anthropology's global flavor should also take into account indigenous responses to the ethnographic frontier. In other words, while the preceding pages chronicle how ethnographic involvement in the Pacific shaped German anthropology at home and abroad, I now turn to indigenous reactions to the German appropriation of material culture.

This is easier said than done. Unlike the case of German anthropology, unitary indigenous influences along the ethnographic frontier are difficult to uncover. Indeed, investigations of Pacific contacts with Euro-American outsiders over the past forty years have generally oscillated between the extreme poles of tragedy and agency.[1] Most historical researchers now regard these extremes as unnecessary boundaries that may obscure more than they reveal. One prominent practitioner put it eloquently: "[There] is no simple story that is only about external efforts at domination and local means of resistance."[2] And yet, at the same time, historians have labored hard to expand our methodological arsenal over the past four decades. Bronwen Douglas, for instance, urges us to reexamine Western accounts of the Pacific Islands, to "read them against the grain" in an effort to reveal indigenous presences. Such presences, while incomplete, subvert the racial hierarchies stipulated in the imperial discourse and, at the same time, allow for a recognition of indigenous voices and forms of resistance and accommodation.[3] Similarly, researchers suggest an examination of new sources, some of which directly relate to the exercise at hand. Indigenous material culture, for instance, provides for a much needed "double vision."[4] Double visions also play an important role in what David Hanlon has recently coined "counterethnographies." These are studies "that constitute distinctive, particular inquiries into the colonizer's culture; that seek to know in order to cope; and that in playful, subversive ways reflect colonial anthropology back on itself."[5] Hanlon himself selected an example from the Hamburg South Sea Expedition to underscore his point. Expedition participant Paul Hambruch spent an extensive period of time on Pohnpei, an island now part of the Federated States of Micronesia, to investigate its indigenous society. Incidentally, Hambruch's lengthy stay of several months reflects the changing nature of German anthropology discussed in the last chapter, where participants in the Hamburg expedition opted to replace the extensive for more intensive research aims. In this fashion, Hambruch took great interest in the oral traditions of the island. Particularly attractive were accounts mentioning the prior existence of cannibals on Pohnpei. Hambruch's piercing and invasive questions about the whereabouts of these people received a prompt answer from his informant: "New Guinea, Sir." Hanlon understood this response to be a good example of counterethnography. Not only did this answer reflect a sense of mocking the colonial authorities, but it also revealed a local understanding of the extent and reach of German colonialism in the Pacific Islands.[6]

Such episodes of counterethnography mirror the findings of a growing body of literature generally labeled "histories of collecting." There histories emerged, not surprisingly, from museum-based scholars with an active interest in the acquisition histories of their collections. University-based anthropologists have frequently ignored or debased museums by labeling them "trophy houses" of a bygone "museum age" of anthropology.[7] Beset by postcolonial interpretations of museum arrangement and possible repatriation issues, responses from the museums appeared quickly.[8] Historians of collecting generally engage two lines of research. The first traces changes in meaning inherited in the transfer of artifacts from their original indigenous context to the hallways of Western museums.[9] The second reads indigenous agency inherited in the material artifacts displayed in museums. Rather than colonial trophies, the argument continues, artifacts reflect indigenous peoples' abilities to influence ethnographic collection activity.[10]

Traces of indigenous agency and "counterethnographies" also emerge through the fleeting but important Western accounts reporting the existence of institutions that resemble museums in the Pacific Ocean. One of the most famous examples of "indigenous museums" was located on the island of Tahiti in what is known today as French Polynesia. There, inside a *marae* (religious structure) located at Tarahoi, Captain William Bligh (returning to the Pacific following the ill-fated HMS *Bounty* episode) reported an odd collection of artifacts. They included mementos hailing from the *Bounty* mutineers (such as the red hair of the ship's barber), British symbols of power, and a portrait of James Cook. Tahitians usually transported this portrait to each arriving ship, asking its captain to add their signatures to the painting. Bligh did not make much of Tarahoi, but Pacific Island historian Greg Dening writing two hundred years later recognizes the place as an important Tahitian "museum" narrating the encounters between Oceanian and foreign societies. According to Dening, Tarahoi became a prominent "counterethnographic" institution where Tahitians took possession of European cultural artifacts.[11] Yet one hundred years following these encounters, German anthropologists consistently denied the possibility of such indigenous institutions. Deeply convinced of their "salvage" agenda, some anthropologists even went so far as to include the indigenous population in their projects. The argument that anthropologists were saving cultural relics not only for Western but also for indigenous society can be found in the writings of Richard Parkinson, an important resident collector who had established a sizable ethnographic collection in the Bismarck Archipelago of German New Guinea. Convinced of the need to extend the salvage to the indigenous peoples, he wrote: "Natives accompanied by their sons arrive at my doorstep to admire the old artifacts in my collection."[12]

The "salvage" agenda also provoked deep anthropological suspicions about changes occurring in material culture. While the Western appropriation ("salvage") of indigenous materials was accepted and strongly encouraged, the converse indigenous appropriation of Western materials resulted in the perceived corruption of the original intent behind artifact production and use. Anthropologists quickly attributed such corruptions to an emerging and thriving "tourist" market in New Guinea at the beginning of the twentieth century. Artifacts produced for consumption by untrained travelers were judged to be counterproductive to their original purposes.[13] Anthropologists deemed artifacts that incorporated Western materials, colors, and whose production involved Western iron tools as "suspect," "tainted," or in the worst case "inauthentic."[14]

Anthropological assessment of "inauthentic" artifacts indicates the existence of two divergent ethnographic imaginations in the Pacific Ocean. These dual imaginations are linked to earlier identified double visions. Greg Dening put it eloquently: "as many cultures of natives and strangers historicize their sea, they find their different cultural identities in the same process."[15] Allow me, for purposes of simplification, to deem these dual ethnographic constructs "Western" versus "Pacific" imaginations. The "Western" construction has been the major preoccupation of this work and will receive additional attention in the concluding section following this chapter. Briefly put, Western anthropological constructions imagined indigenous cultures as static entities and concentrated their efforts on the investigation of cultural (and racial) boundaries. According to the diffusionist variety of this imagination, change occurred as the consequence of the migration of people or their material cultures. Diffusionist anthropologists differed from their evolutionist counterparts in that they stipulated a stifled human inventiveness. Anthropologists could thus map cultures and their diffusion based on material culture since they deemed changes in artifacts to be a rare occurrence.[16] In the Pacific, their investigations involved an interrogation of the boundaries characterizing Melanesia, Micronesia, and Polynesia, or the ambiguous geographical legacies of the "Age of Discoveries." This age lasted well into the nineteenth century and brought important interconnections with ethnographic frontiers.

Investigations of "Pacific" anthropological constructs, in contrast, are only in their infancy. Over the past three decades, a general dissatisfaction with the tripartite division of the Pacific Islands (Melanesia, Micronesia, and Polynesia) has surfaced among anthropologists as well as historians. Archaeologists were among the first to raise concern, arguing that initial investigation of human diffusion into the watery expanse of the Pacific Ocean generally discounted adaptation to individual island environments.[17] Similarly, many scholars objected to the obvious racial connotations of the arbitrary divisions. The term Melanesia, for instance, derived from the Greek term *melas* referring to the skin color of the region's inhabitants. There followed increasing calls for alternative constructs reflecting indigenous rather than Western categories. Slowly, archaeological and historical investigations are identifying significant zones of cultural and economic interaction predating European arrival to the Pacific. The most prominent of these are located in the Caroline Islands, the Fiji-Samoa-Tonga triangle, and the island world surrounding New Guinea. Such investigations generally reject notions of "island paradises" and argue that island communities, in order to maximize their subsistence economy, reached beyond their cultural and linguistic horizons and developed powerful regional systems of trade interactions.[18] Investigations into how such trade circles interacted with the Euro-American expansion following the 1700s are currently under way.[19]

It is more than a distinct possibility that such regional systems also benefited from the expanding ethnographic frontier in German New Guinea. The interest in material culture from German New Guinea also provided for an increasing validation of indigenous culture and creative engagements. Artifacts themselves became much-welcomed trade items that allowed indigenous societies to engage the encroaching German colonial, commercial, and, most important, ethnographic frontiers. In this sense, the earlier "tainted" artifacts acquire new meaning when read against a "Pacific" rather than a "Western" tradition and are important components of Hanlon's counterethnographic project. Yet at the same time, they speak to a deeper historical tradition. Where Hanlon suggests that counterethnography emerges as the consequence of colonial encroachment, the artifacts under discussion below speak to a sense of continuity rather than rupture. More than just a product of colonial encounters, artifacts become crucial elements in solidifying social relationships and in the negotiation of fluid regional boundaries. These may include, but are not limited to, colonial interactions. One thing is certain, however; social interactions became more pronounced during German imperial times, and the power relationships were rarely on equal terms. But here again, the validation of indigenous material culture through the ethnographic frontier allowed for an extension of the artifacts' purpose to encompass German colonial society as well as neighboring indigenous communities.

ARRESTED COUNTERETHNOGRAPHY: WUVULU AND AUA

No single volume could ever do justice to the diversity of the hundreds of cultures and their counterethnographic reactions to the ethnographic frontier in New Guinea. Any such attempt would, by the very nature of the endeavor, remain piecemeal. What is needed then is a selection of representative regions whose inhabitants stood at the center of the ethnographic frontier. During the first decade of the twentieth century, two regions in particular qualify: the Western regions of the Bismarck Archipelago triggered ethnographic interest by suggesting cultural boundaries between Melanesia and Micronesia. The second prominent example is the island of New Ireland. Here the indigenous inhabitants produced seemingly surreal carvings that attracted widespread attention in Germany.

In Chapter 2 I discussed the implication of the "Matty" mystery for the interplay between commercial and ethnographic evaluations of indigenous artifacts. To recapitulate the main points: A failed labor recruiting trip of the New Guinea Company to the western regions of the Bismarck Archipelago had returned with artifacts from hitherto little contacted islands (Wuvulu and Aua).[20] Felix von Luschan in Berlin, while classifying the artifacts in his African and Oceanic division in 1895, noticed commonalities between the material culture of this region and a number of Micronesian islands lying to the north. Excited about the possibility of exploring a perceived cultural border between Micronesia and Melanesia, Luschan called for a systematic investigation of the region, known as Para-Micronesia in later anthropological literature. This call was answered with a vengeance by commercial companies, in particular Max Thiel's Hernsheim Company. Collections of material culture ultimately caused a major clash between Luschan and Thiel, with Luschan accusing the commercial agent of one of the greatest plunders in the history of ethnography. Thiel's response was to initiate an intensive ethnographic investigation of the region. He hired a collector who spent almost two years (1902 to 1904) in the Bismarck Archipelago, including a significant portion of time on Wuvulu and Aua. The purpose of this investigation was to enhance the value of the collected objects with ethnographic information. While the operation failed to yield the expected commercial success, it represented nevertheless the first recorded incident of fieldwork in German New Guinea. Conceived as a financial enterprise, this ethnographic investigation influenced successive anthropological studies in the German colony. The next pages explore how the tangle between ethnography and commercialism affected the indigenous societies residing on the islands of Wuvulu and Aua that stood at the center of attention from about 1896 to 1904. They represent a good example of arrested counterethnography.

Little is known about Wuvulu and Aua before the islands came into contact with the German anthropological gaze. The sparse ethnographic detail suggests that their societies maintained sustained contact that involved isles located in the western Bismarck Archipelago. Yet investigations into whether this region established elaborate trade networks must remain speculative.[21] One thing is certain, however: Luschan's assertion that Thiel's Hernsheim Company had cleaned the islands out of ethnographica in 1896 proved incorrect. When resident-collector Richard Parkinson visited the area on the survey vessel *Möwe* in 1899, he noted a thriving industry in ethnographic objects. Parkinson reported that no fewer than 110 canoes containing some 600 individuals greeted the ship roughly four miles (six kilometers) off the coast of Aua. Every canoe called out to trade ethnographica with the German vessel's crew. The majority of these objects contained the much coveted shark tooth weapons that had called Luschan's attention to material culture parallels with Micronesia and were therefore significantly featured in the 1896 ethnographic collection for the Hernsheim Company. The inhabitants of Aua, realizing the value of their material culture after the initial encounter with German commercial agents, were now offering a barter of these artifacts for glass beads, knives, and other steel implements. This encounter indicated that not only had earlier collection activity not exhausted the supply of artifacts, but it had rather stimulated the production of artifacts. When Parkinson arrived at Wuvulu only days later, he was greeted by a similar display. The sheer quantity of artifacts overwhelmed Parkinson, especially when he started to recognize among the traded items near perfect wooden imitations of iron hatchets traded by earlier Hernsheim representatives.[22] Luschan may have questioned the methods of the Hernsheim Company ethnographic romp in 1896 and admonished future collectors to be more careful, asking for more detailed ethnographic observations to accompany the acquired artifacts. The less than discriminating collection methods by Hernsheim's agents, however, initiated a possible "countereth-

Figure 4. Inhabitant of Wuvulu in one of Wuvulu's distinctive canoes (Courtesy Linden Museum Stuttgart)

nographic" moment in Wuvulu and Aua. Realizing the bartering potential of their material culture and the increasing demand for the artifacts by the arriving Westerners, they began to mass produce them. What Luschan and other German anthropological practitioners might have regarded as "tainted" artifacts, that is, devoid of indigenous meanings, were in fact "Para-Micronesian" attempts to incorporate the arriving German commercial and colonial frontier through ethnographic means.

The inhabitants of Wuvulu and Aua hardly could have foreseen the importance of such incorporation. Increasing demand for material culture and thriving ethnographic interest in the region triggered a second wave of trade settlements in the area. Wuvulu received a trading station in 1900, an event that was repeated on Aua two years later. The largest single impact for the islands was the arrival of Rudolph Heinrich Wahlen with seven European traders and one hundred laborers hailing from the malaria-ridden Aitape region located on the coast of New Guinea.[23] Although the main carrier of the disease, the female anopheles mosquito, seems to have been endemic to Wuvulu and Aua, the actual parasite provoking the disease was not. It was probably introduced into the bloodstream of infected laborers despite Wahlen's attempts at prevention; both laborers and traders took quinine regularly. Within a year, Wuvulu experienced a massive population decline. The original population, estimated to be between 2,000 and 2,500 people at the time of European contact in 1893, declined by late 1902 to about 1,000 inhabitants. Most people on Wuvulu perished not from malaria directly but from the ravages of the disease, which left them unable to withstand other respiratory infections introduced to the island. The massive decline was still ongoing when Thiel's ethnographer Hellwig reached the island in late 1902. A medical officer arriving with Hellwig, Otto Dempwolff, predicted that the deaths would continue.[24]

Aua also felt the impact, although there the population decline was less drastic than on Wuvulu. Yet Aua's population also declined, an event that immediately affected the production of ethnographic objects, greatly reducing Auan potential for counterethnography. Dempwolff, who had commented on the population decline on Wuvulu, noted his inability to purchase ethnographica in an area that had only three years earlier overwhelmed local collector Parkinson.[25] The search for ethnographica still continued unabated, partially because Wahlen was beset by different museum directors to provide artifacts and partially because Max Thiel, who had sent Hellwig to the island to collect what was left, expected a return on his commercial investment.[26] With the population decline influencing the production of further ethnographica, another source of revenue was targeted: grave sites. When Wahlen's traders busied themselves finding shell ornaments and other items among the deceased, their transgression triggered local retribution.[27] Shortly after Hellwig's departure from Aua in December of 1903, a group of armed warriors attacked the trader Otto Reimers. Reimers, who was engaged in trading copra with the people from the island on the verandah of his house, was suddenly grabbed from behind by a man. A second warrior jumped in front of the struggling Reimers and stabbed the trader several times in the abdomen with his spear. Soon after disposing of Reimers' body, the warriors spotted a trading schooner on the horizon. Fearing swift governmental punishment, a great number of people boarded their canoes in an attempt to flee across the water to the Ninigo group. Poor weather conditions and overcrowded canoes caused several vessels to capsize. An estimated 370 people perished in the incident, almost two out of every five inhabitants on Aua.[28]

The tragic incident on Aua did to that island what malaria had done to Wuvulu. By 1904 ethnographically aware travelers commented on the state of the island. "The Hernsheim Company," Richard Parkinson complained, "has completely depleted [Wuvulu and Aua] of artifacts, it is an ethnographic raid with no equal."[29] Augustin Krämer, on his brief visit to Wuvulu in 1906, witnessed what he called the disintegration of the island's social fabric. While approving of Hellwig's research efforts, Krämer condemned the excesses on the island. "The Trader," he was told, "is now king of the island."[30] Dempwolff put it more eloquently in 1904: "Eight years ago Luschan called upon [his fellow countrymen to explore the island of Wuvulu]. His call was not answered. Now I am afraid that missionaries may arrive just in time to administer the last rites to the dying few still remaining on Wuvulu."[31] Dempwolff was not entirely right because it was precisely the answer to Luschan's call that triggered the massive fatalities on Wuvulu and Aua. The lethal confluence of commercial and ethnographic interest in this region had arrested the efforts at counterethnography.

COUNTERETHNOGRAPHY AND HYBRID CARVINGS IN NEW IRELAND

The tragic aspects of the events on Wuvulu and Aua betray the agency inherited in the term "counterethnography." Such agency becomes more apparent when turning to the island of New Ireland. This second largest island in the Bismarck Archipelago covers roughly three thousand square miles and is home to some seventeen languages that complicate Western ethnographic classification. Since the arrival of German anthropologists to the area, the island has been classified into three distinct regions, each with its own distinct

Figure 5. Malaggan *masks (Courtesy Linden Museum Stuttgart)*

art styles. In the southeastern portion of the island are found small human representations made out of chalk, which ties the area to the material culture of the Gazelle Peninsula on New Britain. The central region of New Ireland is best known for its *uli* figures, whose emphasis on female breasts and male genitalia gives them an almost hermaphroditic appearance. Finally, the art of northern New Ireland is best characterized by the *malaggan*. This term denotes two different yet related things: the extensive funerary festivities honoring dead ancestors in northern New Ireland and the elaborate carvings produced for festive occasions. The appeal of the artifacts stems from the craftsmen's meticulous work and ability to carve surreal motives. Functioning simultaneously to strengthen clan ties, forge new alliances, and mark the transition between the living and the dead, *malaggan* permeated every aspect of New Ireland life.[32]

Although New Ireland was in close proximity to the Gazelle Peninsula on New Britain, the German administrative center, European settlement remained rare. Turnover among the first trading stores in the region was high, and many traders paid for their transgressions with their lives. Indigenous warfare and reprisals for abusive labor recruiting practices made permanent settlements a difficult venture. By the turn of the century, a colonial outpost was erected in northern New Ireland, thus speeding up the colonial pacification process.[33] This Kavieng station was later complemented by a second government station in Namatanai located in the central region of the island. The two officials overlooking colonial affairs were Franz Boluminski and Wilhelm Wostrack, who soon found themselves embroiled in the ethnographica trade that accompanied the pacification process. The opening of large regions of New Ireland to the outside world brought about the rapid transformation of the societies living on the island. The extension of Pax Germanica from the government stations was accompanied with large-scale road construction, the levy of head taxes, and massive labor recruiting for local and regional plantations throughout the Bismarck Archipelago and New Guinea. These measures fostered a decline in population, which greatly troubled Governor Albert Hahl. In investigating the possible causes behind this phenomenon, Hahl reviewed the concentration of major expeditions on this island. By 1910 most German residents agreed that the indigenous societies residing on New Ireland were greatly transformed. Colonial officials regarded New Ireland cultures, which had been "pacified" and integrated into German New Guinea's plantation economy, as close to extinction.[34] The postulated cultural and feared physical extinction of indigenous cultures nicely fit the salvage agenda of German anthropologists who had marveled at the extraordinary nature of New Ireland material culture ever since it arrived in Germany in the late 1870s (see Figure 5). Karl von Linden in Stuttgart, for instance, wrote: "I am almost ashamed to say that I am crazy about the extravagant carvings of Neu Mecklenburg [New Ireland]."[35]

Yet the German salvage agenda overlooked indigenous resilience and transformations inherited in their material cultures. An article by Louise Lincoln illustrates well the differing German and indigenous understandings of this particular type of ethnographica. Lincoln acknowledges a massive effect of the German colonial transformation on the indigenous population that ultimately also affected their material culture. She cautions us, however, against evaluating the carvings as mere material objects; a *malaggan* carving from northern New Ireland, for instance, stood not only for a particular mortuary ceremony but for all the economic and social functions that converged in its performance. Pigs, shell money, and taro, among other things, forged and maintained social relationships surrounding the festivities. Such events were severely disrupted by the influence of labor recruiting and mission efforts. At the same time (1885–1914), however, much as in the case of Wuvulu and Aua, massive amounts of artifacts found their way into museums around the world. Lincoln's estimate of 15,000 artifacts seems conservative, considering that the German Naval Expedition alone extracted 3,000 artifacts. Researchers noted that new forms of carvings started to appear as early as the 1880s; these new forms were aimed at satisfying European appetites more than ritual demands. Lincoln argues that such carvings were not part of the network of ritual and social entanglements, as "carvers may have produced hybridized carvings devoid of name, tradition, or ownership rights: A 'bizzare' or atypical piece, but one whose style might well closely resemble other pieces."[36]

Lincoln's choice of the word "hybridized" is interesting. Perhaps she meant to translate the generic metaphor of the "hybrid"—an offspring resulting from a mixture of two species with a marked tendency toward sterility—into the realm of art history. Incidentally, the same word has a different meaning for theorists of a more postmodern bent. For them "hybridity" refers to a mix of cultures that is characterized by novelty, dynamism, and cross-fertility, thus almost the opposite of Lincoln's usage.[37] For Lincoln, these artifacts were devoid of meaning and cultural baggage; they were pieces that looked nice on display but little more. I would maintain instead that these hallowed objects, these "hybrids," represent New Ireland's connection to a wider global context. Rather than being artifacts devoid of meaning, such "hybrids" incorporated foreign concepts into local understanding.

In constructing a new encompassing, rather than exclusive, definition of such hybrids, one needs to engage once again the "Pacific" constructs of ethnography and the expanded concept of counterethnography developed earlier in this chapter. Susanne Küchler's work on *malaggan* is helpful in this regard. Küchler argues for the existence of three major exchange systems in the area generally known as Melanesia. Exchange economies, best exemplified by the famed Kula ring explored by Bronislaw Malinowski, and cargo cults, millenarian movements aimed at explaining vast discrepancies in material culture between Melanesian and Western societies, are well known.[38] To these Küchler adds a third: sacrificial economy, which demands the destruction or removal of a ritual object. In Küchler's rendition, the *malaggan* figure is not devoid of meaning, but it has become "empty" once it has run its ritual cycle. She agrees with Lincoln that *malaggan* is more than just an object. Indeed it is a mnemonic device that provides visual cues for important names associated with clans. These names play a prominent role in the negotiation of political authority and land disputes. The object in this sense becomes a "skin" that is shed once the ritual has taken its course. It was through *malaggan* ceremonies that societies separated by linguistic and geological boundaries were united into homogeneous groups.[39] The ritual of *malaggan* then plays an important role in the fluidity of geographical boundaries in the "Pacific" ethnographic view. The salvage action of German ethnographers collected the "dead skins" of these rituals to fit them into clear-cut categories. It is from these divergent ethnographic imaginations that a counterethnography can successfully emerge. Küchler alludes to this when she speaks of the postcolonial possibilities inherited in the *malaggan*. During the first decade of the twentieth century on New Ireland, there was a forceful relocation of the indigenous population from the interior to the coastal areas in order to access their labor potential and to counter a perceived population decline. For the German administration this decline meant a major challenge to the plantation economy; to the indigenous peoples of the island, this decline, as in the case of Wuvulu and Aua, threatened their very social fabric. *Malaggan* exchanges aided in the integration of displaced individuals and the forging of novel clanic ties. What German ethnographers saw as an increase in *malaggan* production to meet Western demand for these carvings may have been a response to increasing social upheavals. Küchler noted that *malaggan* festivities expanded from northern to central regions of New Ireland during this time. In essence, this meant that there was probably significant overlap with *uli* ceremonies, involving hermaphrodite figures, whose function is less understood owing to the disappearance of these figures after missionary influence in the 1930s. Regardless of their initial usage, however, it is plausible that these figures came to embody similar functions to the *malaggan* rituals. There is even evidence that *malaggan* ceremonies were spreading beyond New Ireland. When a set of masks collected by the Norddeutscher Lloyd captain Karl Nauer on Nissan Island arrived in Leipzig, officials at this museum offered them for exchange to their counterparts at the Hamburg museum. A Hamburg Ethnological Museum official, after taking a close look at the photographs, responded:

I regard these masks as mere curiosities, as they are certainly not authentic. Otherwise local traders would have reported their existence to us earlier. Nissan Island after all has been in contact with the outside world for over twenty years. This means that [these masks] were either directly imported from [New Ireland] or imported by the numerous indentured laborers from this region. Indeed a great many masks bear a close resemblance with their [New Ireland] counterparts. Perhaps Capt. Nauer has done you a great favor by ordering the manufacture of these artifacts.[40]

There are many ways of interpreting this statement, but if Paul Hambruch's version is credible, then this is a clear episode of diffusion of *malaggan* ceremonies beyond New Ireland and an indication of shifting "Pacific" rather than static Western geographic and ethnographic constructs. In this sense, they also become counterethnographic in the wider sense defined above. *Malaggan*, a sacrificial economy aimed at integrating culturally and linguistically diverse groups, became more accentuated following the transformations triggered by German colonialism.[41] Küchler calls the expansion of *malaggan* ceremonies an expansive political economy of memory that mirrored an expansive German political economy based on the plantation society and indentured labor.[42] The question that remains to be answered is whether these two political economies interacted. In other words, one needs to explore whether these *malaggan* complexes were able to subsume German colonial actors and thereby subvert or counter the colonial as well as ethnographic frontiers.

COUNTERETHNOGRAPHY AND THE GERMAN ETHNOGRAPHIC
FRONTIER IN NEW IRELAND

Before the arrival of large-scale expeditions to German New Guinea, and in particular New Ireland, the main supply lines for anthropological museums were local collectors whose roles have received ample treatment in earlier chapters. Küchler's assertion that such collectors entered the *malaggan* unwittingly is only accurate insofar as they cared little to understand the cultural meanings behind the ceremonies. Their role was merely to collect the dead "skins" shed by the complex ceremonies.[43] These dead skins then are akin to Lincoln's "hybrids" but only in the sense that, after running their ritual cycle, the carvings had collectors. The lack of enthusiasm by local German collectors is best expressed by Emil Stephan's report to Felix von Luschan in Berlin: "Among 100 residents, 99 are pure opportunists. If they have any other interests than increasing their incomes, it is certainly not a keen interest in the life and practices of the dirty Kanaks."[44] Stephan maintained that such a state of affairs was counterproductive to ethnographic work, and he was particularly scandalized by the collection methods of some of the residents. Indeed, one ship captain informed Stephan that he would only ask native informants once because "if I ask [them] twice they always tell me something different."[45] Stephan's remark, aimed at discrediting the collection activity of local German residents, may reveal an additional counterethnographic pattern. Conflicting answers were perhaps a form of indigenous defense mechanism, as the informants had no intention of revealing the intents and purposes of their objects' ritual life. Shifting answers protected their ritual activity from colonial and evangelical intrusion.

I still have not answered the question of whether German colonial actors remained peripheral to the *malaggan* complexes or became deeply embroiled in them. In order to answer this question, I propose to approach it from the standpoint of aesthetics, economics, and ultimately culture. The first is firmly rooted in the Western ethnographic imagination, economics propose a transition to the indigenous side, while cultural aspects are concerned entirely with the indigenous *malaggan* complex. Aesthetics is very much connected to the salvage agenda. As local collectors returned acquired artifacts to anthropological centers throughout Germany, many officials began to doubt the "authenticity" of the objects. Production and technology were often regarded by early ethnographers as an indicator that older traditions were about to be abandoned. The introduction of steel and iron became tantamount to the "loss" of tradition. These new technologies were incorporated into the production of new ritual artifacts. However, using new technology did not necessarily entail corrupting "traditions." The production of an *uli* figure using traditional stone implements, German ethnographers were informed, took nearly two moons (months) to finish. Employing iron tools considerably shortened the production process. Augustin Krämer, for instance, observed an expert carver by the name of Lakam who was able to produce an *uli* in seven to eight hours with iron tools. *Malaggan* figures were carved in five to six hours.[46] Production material also illustrated transformations. Although ethnographers were advised to avoid "polluted" figures and to look for "authentic" figures reflecting ritual use, locally based collectors were less discriminating. There was a noticeable increase of Western products among the artifacts. Machine-produced *malaggan* masks were cloth decorated, while *uli* figures often sported "wash blue" (also known as Berlin blue), a commercially derived colorant.[47] Captain Karl Nauer again serves an important example. As a proud owner of fourteen *uli* figures, he sought to deliver them to Leipzig's museum in return for a Saxon decoration. On closer inspection, however, many of these *uli*s reflected a recent date and some even had the color blue. The anthropologists inspecting them doubted whether they had served a ritual purpose.[48] Faced with a possible rejection of the collection, Nauer strongly emphasized the importance of the *uli* figures, and if a museum was not willing to accept his artifacts, he threatened offering them to the next establishment: "With this shipment I hope to move closer to the gratitude of the Saxon kingdom [i.e., obtaining an official] state decoration. Should the deal fall through, I would not be terribly upset. Should this be the case, I would simply ask you to forward all crates of artifacts to the Linden Museum in Stuttgart."[49] The ability to play one museum against the other kept local collectors like Nauer in the game, even if their acquisition methods became increasingly suspect and ultimately triggered official expeditions to German New Guinea.

Another collector who played this game well was Franz Boluminski, who demonstrates the economic aspects of the current analysis. Boluminski staffed the first German colonial outpost at Nusa/Kavieng after the turn of the century. Governor Albert Hahl inspired the colonial official to collect *malaggan* carvings for German museums to secure state decorations. As a result, Boluminksi provided ethnographica for museums located in Berlin, Stuttgart, and Leipzig. Boluminksi, realizing the potential of these carvings, tried to monopolize their trade in much the same way he tried to control the indigenous people as a major labor reserve. In Boluminski's eyes the indigenous people of New Ireland were resources for colonial projects and personal aspirations. He constructed a highway that united northern and central New Ireland, a road informally known as "Boluminski highway" to this day. He was also instrumental in relocating the population from the interior of the island to coastal regions, where they could be easily counted and drawn into the German territory's developing plantation economy. Head taxes levied on the people integrated them into the colonial political economy, and they were ordered to produce the carvings destined to get Boluminksi his desired decorations.[50]

However, Boluminksi and others who benefited from this state of affairs had made calculations without considering the indigenous people. With the arrival of the German ethnographic expeditions following the year 1907, ethnographica prices spun out of control. Boluminski himself carried ample blame for this. Introducing a head tax a few years after establishing the colonial outpost in 1905, Boluminksi proudly proclaimed to have collected his first 20,000 marks from taxes in 1907.[51] He fully expected "his" indigenous subjects to be active in the plantation economy, writing: "Of course one has to give the natives the chance to make money."[52] Unfortunately for Boluminski, the plantation economy was not the only source of monetary support for indigenous peoples. Just a year after the introduction of the head tax, Boluminski complained about "his" subjects' greediness, as they were charging outrageous prices for their carvings.[53] This situation also affected Captain Karl Nauer, who reported bitterly:

> Imagine: the other day, a scoundrel of a competitor from the *Germania* [a postal steamer in the service of the Norddeutscher Lloyd] came to [New Ireland] and took for 700 marks—it is goddam true—an *uli* figure as old as the hills that I probably could have gotten for 200 marks. Should I encounter this hoarding animal I would probably have killed him. Not only did he take this precious object home for who knows whom, but he has increased with his shameless purchase the price of each *uli* by at least 150 marks. And now the guys here want 300 marks per piece. Krockenberger [a plantation owner] has three *uli* in his possession. I should have bought the figures half a year ago when he was charging 500 marks, but no, I had to laugh in his face for charging such an outrageous price. It is always the same story: He who laughs last. . . . [54]

Boluminski experienced similar developments in his colonial realm. While his tax was meant to stimulate New Ireland's plantation economy, Boluminski soon found that "his" artifacts were increasing in price. Whereas around 1900 *malaggan* carvings sold for 50 to 100 marks, by 1908 their price had increased to 400 to 800 marks.[55] When the Hamburg South Sea Expedition reached northern New Ireland, the colonial official offered them carvings at a price of 600 marks, which after long deliberation they decided to pay.[56] Boluminski's "liberal" colonial spending methods worried even Governor Hahl, who complained to a close associate that he had to spend much time "to keep Boluminski on a financial short leash."[57] While it is difficult to ascertain whether or not Boluminski's expenditures derived from spiraling ethnographica prices, it is apparent that Boluminski's own colonial policies, especially the head tax, complicated his ethnographic collection activity. While the German colonial official was stymied by his own colonial policies, increasing demand for ethnographica provided the indigenous peoples with an avenue to counter increasing financial demands from the German colony's political economy.

These developments sit well with either Lincoln's rendition of "hybrid" artifacts, meaning artifacts produced exclusively for sale, or Küchler's "sacrificial economy," where artifacts were sold to collectors because their ritual life had expired. Yet in both of these versions, the political economy of memory (*malaggan*) and that of the German colonial society (plantation economy) are relegated to separate realms that do not interact. Increasing demands for skins also provided a possibility to draw the German colonial society into the shifting cultural geography of the *malaggan* ceremonies.

We lack detailed insights into Boluminski's collection practices, and the information we do have is frequently colored by the critical attitude of anthropologists toward resident local collectors. Edgar Walden, of the German Naval Expedition, wrote to his superiors:

> Bol[uminski] has the pieces brought to him before purchase. He has no regard for exact classification of the objects. His purchased objects disappear in a shack in [Kavieng]. B. is a man of quick deeds and little patience. I am convinced that he wants to dispatch the collection immediately to Berlin. This does not concur with my attempt at a deeper understanding [of the objects]. Of course, we cannot prescribe what Boluminski should send to Berlin. As you know he is a very difficult man, who is soon upset if one does not say yes, amen, and bravo to each and every thing he says.[58]

Küchler's interpretation is once again relevant. While she theorizes that the *malaggan* ceremonies had little in common with colonial administration, she sees these ceremonies as important elements for repairing the social damage wrought by colonial penetration. What the Germans called "pacification," or Pax Germanica, was their attempt at solving Melanesian "chaos" and establishing what they perceived to be a better society.[59] Küchler argues that the *malaggan* figures were central to such pacification attempts, as they predated and ultimately survived the German colonial administration.[60] The *malaggan* ceremonies were vital to forging indigenous social alliances, and I believe that their function also extended to the German colonial administration. Another section of Walden's report to Berlin— while certainly written to discredit Boluminski's collection activity—also reveals indigenous agency and counterethnographic factors. Walden reports that Boluminski's acquisition of artifacts in his home at Kavieng was accompanied by a great deal of ritual activity. Boluminksi tried to impress indigenous visitors by having an orchestra play German marches, accompanied by a parade of indigenous police soldiers; the ceremony concluded with the raising of the imperial flag. The indigenous peoples in attendance brought with them artifacts and performed dances and speeches, activities not foreign to other *malaggan* exchanges on New Ireland. The ceremonies involved the exchange of goods, in Boluminski's case money for the desired carvings. Most of these festivities took place on a clearing outside Boluminski's complex that also served as an exercise ground for his police troops. While Boluminski clearly controlled the venue, the ceremonies may have carried different meanings for the participants. For Boluminski himself, the festivities reaffirmed German might and ultimately his own standing in the colonial society. Walden was more than happy to confirm this in his letter to Berlin.[61] For the indigenous people, Boluminski became incorporated into their society, though he was never completely informed about the clanic names that were involved in his acquisition of *malaggan* skins. Succumbing to a stroke in April of 1913, Boluminski never witnessed the end of the German colonial era, and his reign became immortalized in indigenous memory. His standing among the indigenous people in New Ireland is best exemplified by his posthumous fame. The indigenous people of northern New Ireland continued to hold festivities in his honor, and accounts describe how up to the 1930s Boluminski's grave site was frequently visited and said to contain magical powers. He may have acquired some of these supernatural powers not through his heavy administrative hand, but through his involvement in exchange ceremonies aimed at localizing global colonial forces.[62]

There are interesting parallels in the exploration and development of New Ireland and "Para-Micronesia." Both of these regions stood at the center of attention of the ethnographic frontier, and both regions were adversely affected by the German colonial administration. As well, both regions responded quickly to the challenges by restructuring material culture and providing means of exchanges that, at least in one case, in New Ireland, instigated and supported an already existing sacrificial economy. But there are also considerable differences between the two societies. While it is difficult to ascertain whether the inhabitants of Wuvulu and Aua had an exchange system similar to that on New Ireland, the "fatal" impact of their combined commercial and ethnographic frontiers prevented further development. In New Ireland widespread changes following the first decade of the twentieth century allowed for the growth of a *malaggan* network that was able to cope with population decline and forced relocations. The ethnographic frontier assisted these developments. The outside demand for artifacts by German and other ethnographic institutions was matched by an internal need to produce more artifacts, allowing integration of the plantation system and the *malaggan* political economy of memory. Local German collectors, such as Franz Boluminski and Karl Nauer, became instrumental in negotiating new social organizations in New Ireland. One cannot help but notice a sense of irony here. German anthropologists who set out to investigate stipulated static cultural boundaries separating the postulated areas of Melanesia, Micronesia, and Polynesia soon saw themselves enmeshed in the expansive exchange circles of indigenous people reshaping those very boundaries. There is more than counterethnography in this example. The above-discussed *malaggan* complexes speak to the more fluid ethnographic imaginations predating Europeans' arrival in the Bismarck Archipelago. These ceremonies illustrate not just another way of historicizing Oceanic encounters, but also how the global ethnographic frontier interacts with local indigenous concerns in the Pacific Ocean.

CHAPTER 7

The Ethnographic Frontier in German Postcolonial Visions

T he onset of Europe's Great War and the postwar era presented German anthropologists with a number of predicaments. Few practitioners doubted their nation's legitimate defensive struggle, which compelled them to accept the ensuing hardships. The initial optimism about further colonial annexations resulting from the conflict was quelled by the end of the hostilities. Not only was colonial expansion in Africa and Oceania halted, but the Treaty of Versailles eliminated the existing German colonial empire. This situation propelled German anthropologists to support a national attempt to regain lost territory. Colonial enthusiasts offered arguments for Germany's qualification to rule its territories. Likewise, anthropologists realized that the ethnographic descriptions and material culture collected along the ethnographic frontier in German New Guinea represented a didactic tool supporting postcolonial imaginations. Anthropologists thus worked in tandem with colonial apologists to illustrate German imperial accomplishments. The crafting of ethnographic monographs thus allowed anthropologists to whitewash potential German administrative wrongdoings, shifting potentially explosive issues to subsequent administrations of German New Guinea.

ETHNOGRAPHIC *BURGFRIEDEN* AND FAILED HOPES FOR ANNEXATION

The First World War deeply affected the German anthropological museum community. Most museum officials contended that their nation was fighting a just defensive war, for which they soon endured dire consequences. Museum personnel were drafted into uniform and sent to the military front, many never to return.[1] Museum officials endured the consequences of the "home front" following the British blockade of German ports. Official communications reflected increasing shortage of heating material, affecting both the personnel's health and the preservation of artifacts.[2] Moreover, selected museum buildings supported the war efforts. The Linden Museum in Stuttgart, for instance, was turned into a makeshift hospital because of its relative proximity to the Western Front.[3]

Despite such adverse circumstances, anthropologists remained cautiously optimistic about the future of their research. Those interested in physical anthropology turned to prisoner-of-war camps to update their studies on captured colonial and Eastern European troops.[4] By and large German museum anthropologists submitted to the doctrine of *Burgfrieden* (fortress under siege or civic truce) issued by Kaiser Wilhelm II. Michael Burleigh provides an apt definition of this term: "Domestic confessional, social, and political conflicts were to be put in suspended animation, to be miraculously resolved through a German victory, which was to preserve the authoritarian domestic social status quo from widespread demands for liberalization."[5] For museum anthropologists this meant a grudging acceptance of the distribution following the Sepik Expedition (1912–1913) according to Federal Council representation. Consequently the lion's share of the expedition reached the state museums located in Bavaria, Prussia, and Württemberg. Yet museum officials vowed to readdress this issue at the end of hostilities with an expected German victory.[6]

The hope for victory also resulted in the temporary illusion of German colonial expansion. Museum anthropology went so far as to demand the "annexation" of artifacts from European territory under German military occupation. Karl Weule in Leipzig, for instance, quickly appreciated that the German occupation of Belgium placed a number of important artifacts within the reach of his museum. The most important of these were the ethnographic collections housed in the Terveuren Museum located near the Belgian capital of Brussels. This museum's artifacts originated largely from the Belgian Congo, a colony with one of the most sinister imperial histories in Africa.[7] The importance of the Terveuren ethnographic treasures did not escape Weule's watchful eye. Still heading the German Ethnological Museum Association, he devised an ingenious plan. With the help of fellow museum officials belonging to his association, he appealed to the German military administration in Belgium in an attempt to secure the Terveuren collection as a rightful spoil of war. Deeply convinced of the ensuing German victory, Weule foresaw a logical expansion of the German empire in Africa and Oceania. Rather than patiently waiting for a favorable postwar settlement, however, he decided to be proactive. There was more at stake than artifacts from the Belgian Congo. Weule hoped that a diplomatic distribution of Terveuren ethnographica among German museums would provide a template for future artifact acquisition. In theory, the Terveuren distribution was to pave the way for future ethnographic exploration of colonial territory after peace negotiations. Weule's grand plan, however, failed to materialize. Although most museum directors agreed in principle to his acquisition, they quickly predicted opposition to its execution. Indeed, when Weule forwarded his proposal to the German occupation authorities, they quickly disapproved of the "deportation" of the Terveuren's artifacts to German museums.[8] The general mood against the German war effort, revealing the full extent of atrocities committed against the Belgian civilian population, did not support Weule's cause. Undoubtedly, German occupation authorities in Belgium were more concerned with overturning the negative image of Germanic "Huns" than with approving a few anthropologists' annexationist aims. Developments following the armistice made matters worse. The Versailles Conference stripped Germany of its empire in Africa and Oceania, formally ending all ethnographic research. From that moment on, any active German ethnographic endeavors were dependent on the goodwill of other European nations.[9] The postcolonial phase following Versailles greatly affected the nature of German anthropologists' research.

ESTABLISHING THE POSTCOLONIAL ETHNOGRAPHIC FRONTIER:
HEINRICH SCHNEE'S *KOLONIAL-LEXIKON*

The term "postcolonial" is a bit unorthodox when applied to the German context. Scholars generally employ this term to investigate how colonial legacy informs identity negotiations in former colonial dependencies.[10] At the same time historians following Edward Said's *Orientalism* examine the formation of "colonial discourse" that legitimized imperial takeover.[11] The German case is particularly intriguing in this regard. Germany was a relative latecomer to colonial annexation, a fact that in the words of Susanne Zantop allowed for a German colonial imagination without actual colonies.[12] Germans were also the first Europeans to lose their entire colonial empire, more than a generation before their British and French counterparts started to entertain the decolonization process in Africa, Asia, and Oceania. This unique situation deeply affected German museum anthropologists, who, devoid of colonial territory, had to negotiate their role in the mapping of postcolonial heritage. The argument that imperialism facilitated but did not bring about the formation of the anthropological discipline resonates with this situation. The development of anthropology as an academic discipline was well under way before the onset of the new imperialism. Likewise, the evaporation of colonial territory, as in the case of Germany, did not result in the demise of the discipline. Thus, the importance of Germany's postcolonial imagination as the main buttress of the anthropological endeavor needs to be highlighted.

Heinrch Schnee, former governor of German East Africa, championed the cause to regain German colonial territory. Arguing against the case of colonial German mismanagement (*koloniale Schuldlüge*), Schnee wrote copious treatises expounding the positive impact of German colonialism in Africa and Oceania.[13] His main monument to a Germanic "civilizing mission," however, was a colonial dictionary spanning three volumes.[14] These volumes included a number of prominent German anthropologists, such as Georg Thilenius, the driving force behind the Hamburg South Sea Expedition. Unlike Schnee's most inflammatory writings against the *koloniale Schuldlüge*, a detached scientific tone dominates the dictionary's entries. While the preface alludes to the unfair treatment of the German colonial cause in Versailles, the individual contributions ignore the loss of colonial territory. In fact, all the dictionary's entries appear to have been written as if time had stood still in August of 1914. In drafting this lasting monument to German colonialism, the contributors minimized conflicts among colonial agents and the indigenous peoples of Africa and Oceania. State colonial accomplishments shared equal space with positive ecclesiastical and ethnographic aims. Furthermore, by including leading German anthropologists, Schnee stressed the lasting contributions of this discipline to the German colonial vision.

Georg Thilenius was a natural candidate to oversee the integration of ethnography in Germany's postcolonial imagination. Chapter 4 has chronicled Thilenius' familiarity with Germany's attempt to restructure its colonial administration following Bernhard Dernburg's reform in 1907. In negotiating with Dernburg the development of a colonial institute in Hamburg, Thilenius became a member of the directorate and offered occasional courses in ethnography to budding colonial officials. His main connection to the German colonial secretaries in Berlin was Heinrich Schnee, who fondly remembered the Hamburg director when it came to compile the dictionary. Thilenius' familiarity with the colonial administration and contemporary ethnography in the former colonies came together in the anthropological contributions to the dictionary. Georg Thilenius assembled a team of able and willing anthropologists to enshrine the ethnographic frontier in Schnee's monument to German colonialism. Besides the Hamburg director, other ethnographers involved were Paul Hambruch and Ernst Sarfert, both veterans of the Hamburg South Sea Expedition. Hambruch was Thilenius' assistant responsible for the growth of the Oceanic division at Hamburg's museum. Ernst Sarfert was Hambruch's counterpart in Leipzig, where he tended to artifacts from Indonesia and Oceania. Of these individuals, Paul Hambruch was perhaps the most dedicated to the German colonial cause. Shortly before the conclusion of the First World War, Hambruch had published a number of articles about the future distribution of colonies in Oceania. Much like Weule, Hambruch was overconfident that a German victory was to result in annexation of French colonial territory in Oceania. When this did not materialize, Hambruch continued to agitate for the German cause, urging his compatriots to support colonial organizations in light of what he regarded to be an illegal stripping of Germany's colonies during the Versailles negotiations.[15] Where Thilenius was rather cautious about Schnee's arguments, it was Hambruch who swallowed the case for the restitution of the German colonies hook, line, and sinker. Thilenius' diplomatic opportunism and Hambruch's ideological commitment ultimately linked the ethnographic frontier in New Guinea with German emergent postcolonial imaginations. This transition materialized through Heinrich Schnee's colonial dictionary. Schnee's colonial dictionary presented an immense opportunity to popularize ethnographic findings beyond the confines of anthropological practitioners to attract colonial enthusiasts. In concrete terms this meant a strategic assortment of articles on the general, but popularized, notions of anthropology, broader contributions on the ethnographic exploration of Africa and Oceania, and entries on specific ethnographic puzzles.

Georg Thilenius' entry on ethnology (*Völkerkunde*) serves as a point of departure for the analysis of anthropology's integration in the colonial dictionary.[16] The article suggests that Thilenius had an awareness of colonial enthusiasts. He eschewed theoretical and methodological conflicts, and depicted a discipline that had reached maturity through embracing the allied fields of physical anthropology, geography, psychology, and linguistics. Rather than portraying obvious differences among ethnological approaches, Thilenius subsumed Bastian's psychological ideas and its diffusionist reaction. This was a strategic intervention that suggested cooperation rather than conflict among anthropological practitioners. Cooperation also emerged from Thilenius' delineation of ethnology as the study of human societies throughout the world and the ages. Suggesting ethnology's embrace of multiple intellectual endeavors also provided a natural connection to Germany's imperial, or more correctly postcolonial, imagination: "Ethnology is charged today with the task of charting European influences on the rest of the world. This allows for deeper insights into the process of acculturation among earlier societies, while, at the same time, affording more practical applications. By outlining laws governing cultural change, [ethnology] can contribute enormously to the colonial edifice." Thilenius painted a broad canvas for ethnology's relationship with colonialism. He left it to others to fill in the details. This task then fell to Ernst Sarfert, whose contribution regarding ethnographic collecting further delineated the roles of nontrained colonial enthusiasts in ethnographic research:

A careful evaluation of native cultures in our protectorates does not only contribute to scientific insights. . . . It also supports the more practical concerns of colonial policy. A proper evaluation of natives and their associated cultures provides an ideal point of departure to assist the acculturation process and allows them to reach a higher cultural outlook and purpose. Missed opportunities in this regard will posit a crucial delay to colonial goals. Furthermore, critical errors in colonial policies can lead, and have led in the past, to bitter repercussions. . . . Among the men who have contributed significantly to [ethnographic collection] the contributions of colonial officials and missionaries stand out. Missionaries, however, must free themselves of Christian prejudices that can adversely influence the results and scientific insights. I suggest therefore a close cooperation with local [ethnological] museums, whose officials delight in providing relevant information and literature. The present dictionary presents short entries about different ethnographic concerns.[17]

Thilenius and Sarfert carefully navigated a conceptual minefield. As outlined in earlier chapters, most anthropologists demonstrated concerns about colonial residents' input in ethnography. They favored instead the contributions of trained practitioners active in the field. Excluding missionaries and colonial officials from ethnographic work, however, was potentially offensive to colonial enthusiasts. Sarfert thus lauded their contributions, while cautioning nontrained German residents in the colonies to consult with local museum officials before venturing into the field. Integration rather than exclusion of colonial actors was the role of Germany's postcolonial ethnography, which suggested few rivalries affecting the anthropological discipline. Thilenius' and Sarfert's contributions to the colonial dictionary postulated ethnographic collaboration rather than conflict in Africa and Oceania. Such collaborations seemed enticing to colonial enthusiasts clamoring for a German postcolonial utopia, especially when they offered a contrast with competing British and French imperial regimes. Moreover, such postcolonial fictions triggered additional impetus for further articles on ethnographic exploration in the colonial dictionary.

Ethnographic articles in the German colonial dictionary followed a two-pronged approach. On a scientific level, anthropological research in the African and Oceanic colonies addressed specific ethnographic puzzles. The postcolonial context, in contrast, aimed at lessening the blame of German colonial agents. Schnee's political agenda was mostly concerned with the latter aspects. Anthropologists provided Schnee's vocal campaign to restore German imperial honor defiled by the "colonial lies" of the Versailles treaty negotiations with a mantle of scientific legitimacy.

Two entries in the colonial dictionary underscore this process. Thilenius coauthored with his assistant Paul Hambruch two articles on "Para-Micronesia" and "Polynesian Enclaves."[18] As stated at the beginning of these essays, these two regions bore a strategic scientific importance. For the entry on Polynesian enclaves, Hambruch and Thilenius wrote: "On the eastern borders of the Melanesian isles are located a number of small atolls whose population is not Melanesian but Polynesian." Similarly, they begin by defining Para-Micronesia as "the name applied by ethnologists to the western isles of the Bismarck Archipelago, whose population are culturally closer to Micronesia than to Melanesia." With a stroke of their pen Hambruch and Thilenius instantly illuminated an ethnographic issue: that within the colonial borders of German New Guinea there exist islands that are culturally, and by extension linguistically, more closely related to neighboring areas of Micronesia and Polynesia. In essence, the ethnographic frontier in this important German colony revealed islands whose indigenous inhabitants held vital answers to the investigation of ethnic borders between Melanesia and Polynesian, on one hand, and Melanesia and Micronesia, on the other. Furthermore, their articles also revealed an explosive concern: "[Para-Micronesia's] population is greatly declining. In some islands (for instance Kaniet) the indigenous inhabitants consciously brought about their demise; on others (e.g., on Ninigo and Wuvulu) the population declined because of diseases (malaria, etc.). Moreover, great accidents such as disasters on the sea have affected Luf and Aua." Hambruch and Thilenius encountered similar situations in the Polynesian enclaves: "Much like Para-Micronesia this region is also greatly affected by population decline: Niguria counts about 50, Tauu 20, and Nukumanu 100 individuals." While Hambruch and Thilenius were conspicuously silent about decline in the Polynesian enclaves, they forcefully commented on Para-Micronesia. Rather than faulting German agents, they indicted the indigenous inhabitants. Kaniet's population consciously stopped reproducing, while dangerous ocean voyages had taken a toll among the inhabitants of Aua and Luf. Diseases such as malaria (generally thought endemic to German New Guinea) affected the rest of the islands. The authors did not comment on the reasons for sudden outbreaks of malaria on Wuvulu following European contact. Nor did they expand on the reasons why Auans wanted to risk their lives on seemingly silly voyaging endeavors. Population decline, however, supported the immediate purpose of ethnography, namely, to record in the last hour the cultural heritage of "intriguing" populations. Both Para-Micronesia and the Polynesian enclaves were thus salvage operations in the classic sense of the term. Nevertheless, the remainder of Hambruch and Thilenius' contributions failed to live up to this promise. Their narrative abounds with almost random ethnographic information. A reader might be struck by the detailed information on tattooing or material culture and seemingly indiscriminate ethnographic information ranging from puberty rites to mortuary rituals. What is lacking, however, is a clear comparative section highlighting the ethnographic significance of Para-Micronesia and the Polynesian enclaves in the context of Oceanic ethnographic puzzles. Rather than a glaring omission, the absence of such a comparative framework is strategic. Hambruch and Thilenius regarded their task accomplished by just listing the information, leaving the comparative framework for future generations of anthropologists. Colonial enthusiasts reading over these articles might have justly wondered about the practicalities of this research, not realizing Hambruch and Thilenius' more crucial task. Besides salvaging the cultural heritage of Para-Micronesia or the Polynesian outliers, the two ethnographers expurgated German complicity in the population decline. They are silent about the German recruitment efforts in the Polynesian enclaves and the contribution of the ethnographic frontier to Aua and Wuvulu's population decline. As chronicled in Chapters 2 and 6, it was Felix von Luschan in Berlin who, on grasping the ethnographic potential of these islands, first commissioned commercial companies to collect artifacts. Commercial agents quickly complied. On the acquisition of artifacts they superimposed the establishment of trading stations. The importation of workers from the malaria-ridden areas of New Guinea quickly introduced the disease to Wuvulu, precipitating population decline. On Aua the ethnographer's complicity was even more apparent. There traders desecrated grave sites in search for precious artifacts coveted by anthropologists in Germany. When the enraged Auans killed one of them, the islanders quickly sought to flee German retaliation by leaving their island in overcrowded canoes. Rough seas capsized the indigenous canoes, which ultimately cost the lives of over half of the Auan population. What had by then become a potentially dangerous exploration threatened the legitimization of the ethnographic frontier through its humanitarian salvage action. By extension, the whole German colonial mission was questioned. Hambruch and Thilenius skillfully shifted the blame from anthropologists and commercial companies to preserve the German postcolonial fiction that ethnography furthered the imperial mission through thorough study of the indigenous peoples under its rule.

CRAFTING THE HAMBURG MONOGRAPHS

Georg Thilenius drew important lessons from his work on the colonial dictionary and quickly translated them into a series of monographs chronicling the exploits of the Hamburg South Sea Expedition. March 24, 1911, marked the official end of the expedition. A large festivity held in Hamburg honored the participants. Once the celebration subsided, each expedition member sought to produce ethnographic monographs. This was a daunting task that required digestion of personal observations, the diaries of other expedition members, and the ethnographic information available before the Hamburg expedition.[19] To provide rough guidelines, Thilenius evaluated the dictionary's postcolonial vision against the two existing traditions of field monographs and museum monographs developed before the First World War. Felix von Luschan and German Naval Expedition leader Emil Stephan espoused the first method of monographic research, which has received ample discussion in the preceding pages. This tradition, labeled "field monographs," argues for an intensive understanding of selected areas under research. While advocates of this method did not entirely reject the collection of material culture, they maintained that objects begged for a careful contextualization within local indigenous material culture. Such investigations demanded of the researcher long-term residence among a people to create an intimate familiarity with culture and language.[20] The development of this line of research grew from a confluence of two major forces: competition among ethnographic institutions and a general dissatisfaction with German residents' collecting methods. The final product underscored improvements in material culture collections. This transition, as described in Chapter 4, represented a watershed for ethnography because it ultimately viewed material culture collections as secondary to the development of sociocultural anthropology. The second tradition, called museum monographs, stemmed from similar conditions. However, rather than spending long periods of time in a particular location, its methodology emphasized comparative study of material culture.[21] The existence of a tremendous artifact backlog acquired before World War I suited Thilenius well. Furthermore, in connection with Germany's postcolonial realities, this second tradition looked for similarities in material culture in other German museums. Thilenius thus urged expedition participants to use collections in museums outside Hamburg to complement their own results. In short, Thilenius used Germany's colonial context to launch his expedition and manipulated his country's postcolonial situation to complete his monographs.

On the surface it is safe to say that his endeavor was a resounding success: the thirty-some volumes on the Hamburg South Sea Expedition were published over a period of over thirty years (1913–1954), representing not only the largest German ethnographic output in Oceania, but also one of the most extensive exercises in anthropological research in the area. The volumes mirror Hambruch and Thilenius' contributions to the German colonial dictionary. The monographs present few wide-sweeping generalizations and lack analytical focus, since their sole function was to record vanishing cultures. The volumes, guided by Adolf Bastian's spirit of inductive research and salvage operations, complemented the approximately 15,000 artifacts taken to Hamburg. They followed a standard topical organization. The first part was usually reserved for material on European contact with the particular island society, followed by a descriptive section on the demographic and geographical situation. The ethnographic section was divided into a large part on material culture with some space devoted to mental culture, generally complemented by fleeting observations recorded during the expedition. If space and material were available, the volumes generally closed with collections of stories and songs.

The crafting of the volumes proved difficult. The first monograph published in 1913, Otto Reche's work on the Sepik River ("Kaiserin-Augusta Fluss"), serves as a testimony.[22] Rushed to the printers to forestall the results of the mostly Berlin-sponsored Sepik Expedition in 1912–1913, the volume's introduction illustrates well the "museum monograph" genre of the Hamburg expedition. Owing to the lack of translators and the brevity of the expedition's stay in the region, Reche's main contribution was to provide an overview of Sepik artifacts, but here too he faced problems. He possessed many objects from the Hamburg expedition and gathered additional information from the Leipzig, Lübeck, and Stuttgart museums. However, when he inquired for assistance from the Berlin and Bremen museum officials, Reche found himself categorically rejected.[23] Undaunted by the competitive atmosphere among German institutions, Thilenius turned to the second monograph, edited by his assistant Paul Hambruch on the island of Nauru.[24] The outbreak of World War I hampered the publication process considerably. While some volumes achieved publication during the war, the end of the conflict proved to be fatal to the Hamburg Scientific Foundation's endowment. Rampant inflation reduced the once mighty foundation's fund to a trickle. Unable to cover all the costs for the monographs, Thilenius had to readjust his priorities while looking for additional funding sources.[25] He prioritized, for instance, the high islands over low-lying atolls in the Caroline Island chain. Similarly, the passing of prominent expedition participants before the project could be completed (Wilhelm Müller in 1917 and Paul Hambruch in 1933) meant additional delays. Thilenius was quick in hiring replacements, but Anneliese Eilers, Hans Damm, and Hans Nevermann, while trained in the area of Oceanic anthropology, sorely lacked the first-hand experience of the original expedition members. This state of affairs not only diluted the ethnographic expertise brought to the writing process but also engaged a generation of scholars whose formative years hardly coincided with the heyday of German colonialism. Their accounts were thus colored by interwar Germany's postcolonial realities.

To the untrained anthropological eye the assemblage of seemingly endless ethnographic data of the Hamburg monographs may seem odd. The volumes, however, followed the format of many ethnographic monographs in the early twentieth century.[26] Deeply rooted in the "salvage" tradition of recording rather than organizing, the peculiarity of the Hamburg volumes lies elsewhere. The German postcolonial context was a unique one for anthropologists since neither American, British, nor French practitioners operated in an imperial vacuum. It is thus not surprising for the German ethnographer's narrative to be partially tinged by Germany's postcolonial situation following the First World War. Thilenius' link to the vocal colonial circles of the colonial dictionary accentuated this context. The two significant examples I have selected highlight the postcolonial context lurking throughout the pages of the Hamburg monographs. The first one is the volume on Tobi, an island in the vicinity of the Palauan archipelago.[27] The second is drawn from Pohnpei, an island with a significant history of successful resistance against colonial rule.[28] Between 1910 and 1911, the island was shaken by a widespread indigenous uprising against German colonial rule, an event that tainted the pages of the Hamburg volumes.

The expedition members' sojourn on Tobi (from late August to early September 1909) was crucial in more ways than one. A negative portrayal by Horace Holden, who suffered greatly as a castaway among the Tobians, had popularized, or more appropriately demonized, the island and its inhabitants.[29] The preservation of Tobi's traditional society hinged on the island's relative remoteness from German or earlier Spanish colonial centers before the Hamburg expedition's arrival. Moreover, Tobi's society had little exposure to European diseases. In short, expedition members operated in a virtual "first contact" scenario, which distinguished the Tobi case from other Micronesian islands encountered by Hamburg expedition members.

The encounter between expedition members and Tobian society was marred by conflict. Two shamans on the island who claimed to have a direct connection to the local deity, Rugeiren, vehemently opposed the ethnographers' presence on the island. Predicting dire consequences for the local inhabitants, the shamans vociferously intervened in the daily routine of the German anthropologists. The expedition leader, Augustin Krämer, in return fetched two rifles from the expedition's steamer. Firing at random targets, Krämer sought to convince the inhabitants of the effectiveness of the German weapons. When he deemed this act to be less than convincing, Krämer resorted to the internment of selected shamans on the expedition steamer *Peiho*.[30]

Most significant, however, was the expedition's legacy of lethal diseases. Six months after the *Peiho*'s departure in 1909, a Dr. Buse arrived on the steamer *Delphin*. His mission figured as part of a general administrative inspection tour to investigate the health conditions in the southwest islands of Palau.[31] Interest in the inhabitants' welfare arose after the opening of phosphate mines on Angaur in 1909. This large economic undertaking demanded the German colonial administration's thorough exploration of the Carolinian human resources.[32] Tobi's large population, estimated by the Hamburg anthropologists at almost one thousand individuals, was particularly promising for future employment. Dr. Buse was disappointed because the familiar large number of canoes that had customarily greeted the occasionally visiting ships failed to materialize. When Buse stepped ashore, he encountered only a handful of Tobians, who quickly informed him that a respiratory disease (presumably influenza) had carried away no fewer than two hundred inhabitants. His informants claimed that the disease was introduced by the *Peiho*'s passengers. Tobian accounts involving Hamburg expedition members confronted Buse with a dilemma. His first impulse was to dismiss the account as "traditional South Sea lore."[33] After all, he argued, Tobians could easily blame outsiders for their misfortune just to distract attention from their own involvement. But Buse was willing to concede that foreign contact may have played a pivotal role in introducing the disease.

Buse's dilemma was hardly new. Disease had had an important place in the discourse of discovery since the eighteenth century. The introduction of infectious diseases, whether venereal or otherwise, undermined the "civilizing" aspects that were said to emerge from Western contact. This is perhaps best described in James Cook's own reflections. On his fourth visit to Tahiti in August of 1777, the indigenous inhabitants informed Cook that Spaniards had previously visited the island.[34] On the surface this meant little, since British voyages clearly precluded any Spanish claims to the island based on "first contact." As Cook kept inquiring into the Spanish visit, however, a more troublesome concern emerged. The Tahitians claimed that Spanish behavior radically differed from that of the British during their earlier visits. Indeed, the Spaniards maintained a clear distance from the Tahitians and even restrained from sexual contact. Furthermore, Cook realized that the Spaniards had introduced domesticated animals, in particular cattle, to the Tahitians. Nicholas Thomas describes how the British explorer saw himself anticipated by Spanish competitors in this "civilizing" act: "He would have been pained to learn that national enemies had somehow sustained a discipline he had been unable to sustain and had exempted themselves from violence [the introduction of venereal diseases] that Tahitians now associated particularly with the English. But most of all, he must have been appalled to gather that the Spanish had already brought cattle. . . . As in the business of discovery itself there was no prize for second place."[35]

Cook's dilemma was similar to Dr. Buse's following the visit to Tobi. There was one major difference: the British opted against annexation of the Society Islands, while Buse's report raised serious questions about the postulated principles of colonial rule, that is, the protection of indigenous peoples. Since metropolitan medical knowledge about contagion was inadequate, indigenous accounts about the introduction and spread of diseases were potentially explosive issues for the administration. Placed in the right context, such accounts offered useful arguments for further consolidation and expansion of colonial rule or in this case for postcolonial imagination. For instance, in 1907, three years before Buse's arrival, the government surgeon stationed in Yap, Dr. Born, wrote a detailed medical report on the Palauan population for Berlin's Colonial Office. One passage is particularly telling:

The most prominent Japanese influence [on Palau] is probably the introduction of venereal diseases. According to widespread beliefs among the Palauan natives, it was the arrival of the Japanese that first introduced syphilis to the islands. The people claim that prior to the Japanese arrival, noseless individuals were a rare occurrence. My own experiences seem to support the above statement because my periodic health inspections of Japanese ships often reveal several individuals with syphilis at a highly contagious stage.[36]

Born's report drew attention to an ominous Japanese presence in the Palauan islands. Only three German nationals were residing there at that time: a government official, a missionary, and a doctor; in contrast there were thirty Japanese residents who controlled the majority of the shipping and trade. Moreover, Born noticed that the Japanese presence was affecting Palauan songs and dances.[37] The increasing number of Japanese nationals in Palau and elsewhere in the Caroline Islands fueled a competitive economic atmosphere in which German companies were at a great disadvantage.[38] Disease could thus justify tighter control over Japanese individuals in the German colony before World War I. The issue became even more accentuated during the postcolonial context informing the writing of the Tobi monograph. Following 1914, the Japanese progressed from economic interlopers in the German territory to colonial administrators.

Anneliese Eilers, who did not participate in the original expedition, became the writer of the Tobi monograph. To reduce costs associated with this process, Tobi was treated together with the island of Ngulu. When Eilers wrote her book in the 1930s, German anthropologists were still editing the large number of reports gathered before 1914. Eilers thus faced a delicate interplay between salvaging a people's cultural heritage and witnessing their physical extermination by a disease introduced by the Hamburg expedition. While she did not deny the responsibility of the *Peiho*'s crew, she identified the Tobians rather than the ethnographers as culprits. Eilers revealed as the guilty party expedition translator Sisis and his wife, both of whom had been visibly ill at the time of the expedition. Similarly, the expedition leader's main interpreter, Pita, was so ill at times that Augustin Krämer's work was jeopardized. The last account available to Eilers, an obscure census published by the British government based on Japanese reports to the League of Nations, listed Tobi's population as fewer than two hundred individuals. She asserted that the decline represented a "sad testimony" to the Japanese administration.[39] The Japanese served as a readily available target to deflect responsibility for the mass deaths or exodus of the Tobian population.

What escaped Eilers' skilled editorial attention, or what she chose to omit, was the use of many Tobians in Angaur's phosphate mines by the German administration in the last years before World War I.[40] This event is well remembered in oral traditions on Tobi.[41] A last report on Tobi by Palauan station official Winkler in December 1913 mentioned that out of a total of 700 people, 388 inhabitants had succumbed to a recent outbreak of dysentery.[42] Thus, the population declined further after Tobians returning from Angaur or their German recruiters introduced additional diseases to the island. By 1914, the last year of the German administration in Micronesia, Tobi's population had receded to little over 300 individuals, close to the figures the Japanese provided. The Japanese authorities did not discontinue the exodus from the island, however, but followed the German model established in the first decade of the twentieth century.

Replicating the spirit of Thilenius and Hambruch's work on the colonial dictionary, Anneliese Eilers adeptly shifted blame away from the German colonial administration. Furthermore, her ethnographic text rooted the horror of depopulation in harsh Japanese measures. This explains expedition member Ernst Sarfert's glowing words introducing Eilers' volume: "It took all her love and devotion to craft the rather neglected material, collected from these unknown modest islets, into likewise modest building blocks, which, I am certain, will eventually find their proper place in a general cultural history of mankind. . . . Surely, [the] effort will be recognized as it contributes no end to Germany's colonial and scientific fame."[43] Indeed, Eilers' attempt to hold the Japanese administration responsible for Micronesia's ills has more recently been reiterated by Hermann Hiery, who compares the Japanese occupation of Micronesia to a steamroller:

Compared with the German colonial administration, the Japanese system was more totalitarian. The Japanese administration's attempt to force developments in a particular direction was more pressing, comprehensive, and direct. Japanese practice invites comparison with a steamroller, inexorably flatting everything in its path and compelling the front line of people fleeing before it to remove the rankest weeds. It may be that, to Micronesians, who had a strong sense of tradition, German methods also resembled the progress of a steamroller. But it was a different one; or at least, its drivers were different. Its progress slower, more careful, and less decisive. The driver took account of the changing landscape around him, often hesitating in his forward march, making a detour, or even changing direction. Occasional use of reverse gear was not unknown.[44]

Glenn Petersen recently scrutinized a similar episode of postcolonial sway in the Hamburg monographs. Petersen reflects on the long stay of Hamburg expedition participant, Paul Hambruch on the island of Pohnpei. Denouncing Hambruch's ethnographic errors and superficial interpretations, Petersen concludes that theoretical and colonial frameworks led Hambruch's research astray.[45] There is much truth to this, but the postcolonial context deserves equal consideration. Hambruch's ethnographic narratives saw the light of publication in three volumes published between 1932 and 1936.[46] While he provided the groundwork for these publications, his passing halfway through the project required once again the intervention of Anneliese Eilers, the author of the aforementioned Tobi volume. Although it is not clear to what extent she altered Hambruch's original manuscripts, the Pohnpei monographs posed yet another predicament to the German colonial administration's legacy in the Pacific. Merely a few weeks after Hambruch's departure from Pohnpei, the island was shaken by an uprising emerging from the district of Sokehs. The Sokehs rebellion had ample precedent, as the Pohnpeians had successfully resisted a Spanish occupation of their island following 1886. Fierce encounters between Pohnpeian and Iberian forces had limited Spanish influence to the island's capital of Colonia.[47] After a German administration took charge of the island in 1899, initial cooperation with indigenous leaders soon gave way to increasing tensions that ultimately resulted in the 1910–1911 rebellion. Determined to rule by example, German officials rushed in naval units and police soldiers from German New Guinea. Massive firepower and ruthless retaliations crushed the unrest. As a result, German authorities executed the main ringleaders and exiled their close associates to other islands in their colonial realm. Following the Versailles treaty, the Sokehs rebellion stood as a sad testimony against German colonial rule that underscored claims of imperial mismanagement. Petersen notes correctly that Hambruch in his ethnographic endeavors failed to appreciate the Sokehs rebellion in indigenous terms.[48] Hambruch's methodological blinders certainly obstructed his research on Pohnpei, yet the need to address the uprising's root causes in the crafting process of the monographs was a separate issue. Hambruch and subsequent editor Anneliese Eilers were caught in a bind. Accepting indigenous terms for the unrest was tantamount to an incrimination of the island's German administration. Despite ample evidence to the contrary, Eilers and Hambruch had to identify exogenous factors to Pohnpeian society. This left them with few alternatives. In fact, a single obvious choice remained: American missionaries. The American Board of Commissioners for Foreign Missions (ABCFM) had from one of their New England bases established a foothold in the Hawaiian Islands following 1820. After consolidating their Hawaiian presence, ABCFM missionaries extended their influence into Micronesia and by 1852 had settled on Pohnpei. Vying for Pohnpeian converts, the missionaries vehemently clashed with the Capuchin order introduced by the Spaniards following their arrival on the island. The Germans favored this order after purchasing the Caroline Island from Spain in 1899. It thus comes as little surprise that Hambruch and Eilers were partisans of Capuchin reports in their research since these sources frequently blamed American missionaries and their converts for instigating Pohnpeian indolence against Spanish or later German administrators.[49] The Pohnpei monographs of the Hamburg expedition identify American missionaries as the main seed of discord and the escalation of violence that ultimately erupted in the Sokehs rebellion of 1910. Eilers and Hambruch's ethnographic narrative thus included convenient postcolonial fictions that exonerated German colonial abuses in the Pacific Ocean.

Anthropologists labored hard to include the ethnographic frontier in Germany's postcolonial imaginary. They had little choice. The initial optimism that a German victory during the war would extend ethnographic treasures through additional colonial annexations soon dissipated at the end of the hostilities. To make matters worse, the Versailles treaty removed existing colonies from German control. While some anthropologists resigned themselves to their fate and shifted their attention elsewhere, a group centering on Georg Thilenius cooperated with Heinrich Schnee's initiative to assemble a legitimate claim for the return of the colonies. Schnee's colonial dictionary was initially intended as a monument to German colonial heritage, but Thilenius quickly realized anthropology's stakes. He spoke of anthropology's importance for effective colonial administration, yet, with no empire left to manage, such claims remained hollow. Indeed, a postcolonial contribution of the ethnographic frontier had to be found elsewhere, and

Thilenius drew extensively on changing concepts of the salvage idea. Bastian had initially linked salvage anthropology to an ethnographic frontier in the German Pacific colonies (see Chapter 1). This notion was further developed by Emil Stephan, who, in connection with the German Naval Expedition, proclaimed the salvage idea to be a German burden of honor (*nationale Ehrenschuld*) before the war. The immediate postwar era clearly fed such sentiments in Germany, and Thilenius quickly realized their usefulness. He drew lessons from the colonial dictionary through exploratory entries on Para-Micronesia and the Polynesian enclaves. Not only did Thilenius and his assistant Paul Hambruch skillfully investigate how German ethnographers salvaged the Oceanic cultural heritage for future generations of anthropologists, more important, their contributions also whitewashed any German complicity in the population decline affecting these islands.

Thilenius and Hambruch continued to explore the template provided by the colonial dictionary in the process of writing Hamburg expedition volumes. The editors thus readily placed a Tobian drastic population decline at the feet of the Japanese administration following the Germans into Micronesia. Similarly, they rejected indigenous terms in their interpretation of the Pohnpeian uprising against German control. In fact, Hambruch and Anneliese Eilers quickly identified American missionaries as culprits instigating hostilities over the course of two generations. Interpreted in this light, the Hamburg volumes are as much a tribute to the German ethnographic frontier in Oceania as they are attempts at exculpating the German colonial administration. Similarly, this process also exonerated anthropologists from any guilt by association. The politically informed salvage agenda thus secured an important space for Thilenius and his associates in Germany's postcolonial fictions.

Anthropology's Global Histories in Oceania

This conclusion proposes to return a global historical flavor to anthropology. To do so, I examine German tradition in light of other anthropological endeavors in the Pacific Ocean. I begin with a close glance at the academic and colonial settings of American and British anthropology in the Pacific Islands. I then explore general interbleeding ethnographic frontiers throughout the Pacific Islands. Finally, I seek to transcend German New Guinea to provide an outline of anthropological studies in the Pacific Ocean between 1760 and 1945.

THE OCEANIC PHASE OF BRITISH ANTHROPOLOGY: THE ACADEMIC SETTING

James Urry highlights the importance of the Pacific Islands for an "Oceanic phase" in British anthropology, lasting roughly from 1890 to 1930.[1] Contrasting British and German anthropology, it appears that British scholars moved faster from the "armchair" to the field. Famed British anthropologists such as W. H. R. Rivers, Alfred Haddon, and Charles Seligman all had considerable field experience, and the "expeditionary phase" of British anthropology predated Germany's by almost a decade. Much like their German counterparts, British anthropologists brought to bear a combination of evolutionary and diffusionist motives in trying to classify New Guinea's seemingly overwhelming linguistic and cultural diversity. In their attempts at linguistic classification, however, British anthropologists were less inimical to the idea of employing resident experts for their research.[2] Dr. R. H. Codrington, a missionary and leading authority on Austronesian languages, aided many anthropologists.[3] It was also through his assistance that Sydney Ray, a British school teacher, became involved in anthropological investigations. It was he who first classified non-Austronesian languages of New Guinea as "Papuan" and argued for a differential linguistic settlement of the region. According to Ray, Papuan languages indicated an earlier settlement of New Guinea, while Austronesian language groups of the region pointed to a more recent past.[4]

Investigations into the establishment of cultural and linguistic boundaries in the Pacific brought attention to the Torres Strait Islands. Located between Australia and New Guinea, this set of islands paralleled German investigations into Para-Micronesia (Wuvulu and Aua, see Chapters 2 and 6). Much like German anthropologists who sought to locate firm cultural boundaries between New Guinea and the islands of Micronesia to the north, their British counterparts inquired about similar boundaries between New Guinea and the Australian aboriginal population to the south. Unlike their German counterparts, however, British anthropologists did not engage resident commercial companies but sent their own venture, the Cambridge Torres Strait Expedition of 1898, to the region.[5] The success of this venture served as a major inspiration for Thilenius' own Hamburg South Sea Expedition (1908–1910). And much like Thilenius' later expedition, the Cambridge journey carried with it methodological innovation. The most prominent of these was W. H. R. Rivers' "genealogical method." Initially developed as a methodological shorthand for inadequate language training, the collection of genealogical data was soon performed by other British anthropologists. Of similar import was the emphasis on training a new generation of anthropologists to work in the intensive mode, urging them to live among individuals of a particular indigenous group to study their behavior and customs. Former Cambridge Expedition participants Rivers and Haddon at Cambridge and Seligman at the London School of Economics were leading proponents of this approach.[6]

Building on the experiences accumulated during the Torres Strait expedition, British anthropologists continued to explore Melanesia. With the support of the American W. Cooke-Daniels, Seligman launched another expedition that explored the southern coast of New Guinea in 1904. Similarly, in 1908, Rivers led an expedition funded by the Percy Sladen Trust to the Solomon Islands.[7] Seligman also realized that in order to accommodate the goals of the W. Cooke-Daniels expedition he needed to cross colonial boundaries. In 1903 he contacted Felix von Luschan in Berlin, soliciting his support with German colonial authorities. Luschan complied but also notified Governor Albert Hahl that, before long, he intended "to send our own scholars to your protectorate."[8] Not only was Luschan aware that the Berlin Ethnological Museum was lagging behind other German institutions, but now there were British expeditions to contend with. Seligman never made it to German New Guinea, but his American counterpart Dorsey would cause a major stir (see Chapter 4).

By the first decade of the twentieth century, British researchers were performing "intensive studies," a new concept for their German counterparts. On the Percy Sladen Trust Expedition, two researchers, Gerald Wheeler and A. M. Hocart, carried out intensive research. By 1910 there were researchers in the d'Entrecasteaux Islands, the Kiwai area of New Guinea, and Malekula in the New Hebrides. Similar to the German endeavors, many of these cases never saw much publication.[9] As Chapter 5 describes, death and the impact of the First World War prevented the flourishing of "intensive" studies in German anthropology.

At least one researcher survived his fieldwork to move on to an illustrious career in British academia: Bronislaw Malinowski. A student of Seligman at the University of London, Malinowski spent considerable time in the Trobriand Islands (1915, 1917–1918) and enthroned "intensive fieldwork" in one of his resulting monographs. Malinowski educated a whole new generation of anthropologists at the London School of Economics. While some of his students, for example, Raymond Firth, performed research in Oceania, most of them moved their research areas to the African continent following the 1930s.[10]

THE OCEANIC PHASE OF BRITISH ANTHROPOLOGY:
THE ADMINISTRATIVE SETTING

As in the German case, British colonial officials invested in anthropological study. Indeed, there were astonishing parallels between British governors and German administrators of the New Guinea Company. The main difference was that German New Guinea Company officials sought to make a handsome profit by uniting commercial and colonial interests in their anthropological endeavors (see Chapter 2). Large-scale commodification of ethnographic objects seems to have been absent from the British Pacific. However, the New Guinea Company's initial aims in their exhibition of collected artifacts at the Berlin Ethnological Museum were similar to those of British governors in Fiji and Papua. Before New Guinea Company administrators realized its commercial potential, they employed their ethnographic collection to present a cultural picture of the new colony and to promote German settlement. Likewise, in the British holdings of the Pacific Ocean, colonial officials brought together collections of material culture to depict their respective colonial territories and to illustrate the reach of British colonial rule. In Fiji, Governor Arthur Hamilton Gordon displayed artifacts to evoke and create "common denominators" underlying Fijian society. Gordon envisioned that commonalities in material culture could further the understanding of Fijian society, which in turn facilitated administrative practices.[11]

Lieutenant-Governor William MacGregor, after a brief tenure in Fiji, translated this idea to the British territory of Papua following 1888. MacGregor ventured to provide a collection representative of the commercial and cultural picture of British New Guinea and found a representative home for the collection in a newly opened museum in Brisbane. In his function of collector, MacGregor skillfully employed available means, especially government steamers. Yet despite such advantages, his collections remained piecemeal. They were composed of artifacts collected by government agents during first and subsequent encounters with indigenous peoples. MacGregor jealously guarded the ethnographic collection arriving in Brisbane and advised its curators to part only with occasional duplicates to avoid the splitting of this national collection.[12]

The idea of artifact centralization for colonial purposes also echoed in the British metropole. At almost the same time that German authorities were centralizing colonial collections in Berlin, an initiative emerged to create an Imperial Bureau of Ethnology. This institute, conceived of in the 1890s, was to collect information on the indigenous peoples living throughout the British empire. The proposal foresaw the creation of a central office in London destined to collect ethnographic information forwarded by colonial officers. Since colonial authorities failed to recognize the need for this endeavor, the enterprise met with little success.[13] Colonial authorities' failure to recognize the value of centralized colonial collections was also apparent in the German empire. However, Chapter 1 illustrates how Adolf Bastian and other scientific practitioners seized the opportunity for centralization. The need to store and evaluate botanical, ethnographic, and zoological specimens from the German colonies in Africa and Oceania ultimately saved the day. Berlin ethnological and natural historical museums became the central institutions to perform this task, reminding colonial officials of their duty to supply materials. Although the German centralization earned much praise in Britain, its background was frequently misunderstood. "Some politicians are anxious," British anthropologist Northcote Thomas told his colleagues, "that England should learn from the foreigner. Would that England could learn from [the Germans] that knowledge is power."[14] Museum directors in Britain generally had great respect for their German counterparts, as they generally regarded German museums to be better funded and supported. German centralization of ethnographic knowledge became something to be emulated.[15] The British admiration for German institutions represents a misreading of the situation. Institutional support for ethnology derived from local rather than national sources, and the much-hailed centralization of colonial artifacts in Berlin carried with it no federal monetary support. The relatively larger availability of funds attested to existing divisions among German museums rather than a direct federal policy toward ethnology.

If a dialogue between anthropologists and colonial administrators proved difficult in the imperial metropole, it was on the colonial periphery in Oceania that it bore fruit. Governor Albert Hahl's investment in German anthropology has received ample coverage in Chapter 5. New insights emerge, however, from reading his actions comparatively against the British academic setting. By the 1900s British anthropologists were making a successful transition from the museum to the university setting and were advocating an array of methodological innovations, including the "intensive study" of particular societies. Such transitions had considerable import for the administration of Papua. The Act of Confederation (1901) uniting the six Australian territories provided British officials with the possibility of transferring British Papua to the newly formed Australian government. By 1906 the formerly British territory passed into the hands of Australian administrators, who sought to emulate and even surpass British imperial models.

Hubert Murray, who arrived in Papua in 1904 as an imperial judge, had few positive comments on the anthropological engagement of his British predecessors. MacGregor's policy of artifact collecting to create a unified Papuan culture through a collection of indigenous artifacts smacked of antiquarianism. Murray commented on this seemingly outdated practice: "The members of what I have called the 'Colonial Office' party are strong adherents to the old regime, are imbued with horror, doubtless sincere, of Australian democracy, would inwardly rejoice if all white settlers—especially miners—could be removed from the country, and consider apparently that the destiny of British New Guinea would be fulfilled if it never became anything more than a glorified curiosity-shop and an extensive and very expensive ethnological museum."[16] A chance meeting with famed anthropologist Charles Seligman shortly after Murray's arrival in Papua in 1904 allowed him to recognize new possibilities for anthropological research. Seligman instilled in Murray a deeper appreciation of Papuan societies. At the same time, however, Murray remained suspicious of academic anthropologists: "[Anthropology] is a most fascinating study, though, as far as I can see, purely fantastic; the alleged facts being unsupported by evidence, and the inferences forced."[17] Murray's misgivings with trained anthropologists are best exemplified through his meeting with Bronislaw Malinowski. After conversing with this towering figure in British anthropology, he wrote: "He is a very clever man, I think, but I do not like him. It is not merely that he treats me with that strange mixture of patronage and intolerance which is the inseparable heritage of men of science. There is something wrong with him though I do not know what it is."[18] Malinowski returned the favor when he characterized the lieutenant governor as "a bit stiff, and [he] does not come out of his shell."[19] Murray's encounter with the Polish researcher partially contributed to his assessment that "most of [the anthropologists] are a little bit mad."[20] And Murray pushed Malinowski, technically an enemy alien, into the Trobriand Islands, partially contributing to the "Malinowskian moment" in British anthropology. Yet much like Hahl in German New Guinea, Murray had ambitious plans for a colonial anthropology.

Murray's engagement with anthropology resulted in two major outcomes. First, following the Great War, Murray's efforts yielded the appointment of a governmental anthropologist for Papua and New Guinea (Australia controlled the German territory following 1914). Second, to support the training of colonial officers destined for Papua and New Guinea, Australian authorities established a chair of anthropology at the University of Sydney. British social anthropologist Alfred Reginald Radcliffe-Brown held the chair until 1931. It was also in Sydney that Radcliffe-Brown established the well-known anthropological journal *Oceania*. Anthropologically trained administrators, especially F. E. Williams and E. W. P. Chinnery, took on prominent positions in the administration of Papua and New Guinea. Disagreements between administration and academic anthropologists soon ensued over ethnographic methods. Professional anthropologists under the guidance of Radcliffe-Brown and Malinowski frequently attacked Williams and Chinnery for their colonial anthropology, although their material was frequently consulted by academic anthropologists. The same anthropologists also resented their colonial counterparts acting as intermediaries and "gatekeepers" in the selection of field sites in the colonial territories. Although Murray was able to install a successful governmental anthropology, academic anthropologists now directed their attention away from Oceania toward the British colonies in Africa.[21]

The most obvious parallel between Murray's administration and that of Albert Hahl in German New Guinea is the recognition of anthropology's potential to address colonial predicaments. Similarly, both Hahl and Murray had considerable misgivings with artifact collection. There were, however, also considerable differences in how they employed anthropology and their practitioners. Murray was fortunate enough to encounter an already changing anthropological community on his arrival in Papua. Hahl, in contrast, had to deal with a German anthropological community whose discourse continued to be dictated by discussions on material culture emerging from the metropole. Lacking the benefits Murray experienced in changing British anthropological methods, Hahl actively steered anthropologists into new "intensive" investigations useful to his colonial realm. He consequently had direct influence on Emil Stephan and Richard Thurnwald and indirectly swayed Wilhelm Müller and Edgar Walden to pursue such studies. Only Thurnwald survived the Great War, thus minimizing a "Malinowskian moment" in German anthropology. Murray's actions created a colonial anthropology that answered colonial rather than academic dilemmas and determined the nature of ethnographic endeavors until the outbreak of the Second World War. Hahl's and Murray's investment in colonial anthropology found further application in the American administration of the Micronesian isles of the Trust Territory of the Pacific Islands following 1945.

THE OCEANIC PHASE OF AMERICAN ANTHROPOLOGY: THE ACADEMIC SETTING

Before the Second World War, American anthropological involvement in Oceania was slight.[22] Chapter 4 relates how the brief but eventful interlude of George Dorsey and the Field Museum affected German New Guinea. Dorsey's visit and Alfred Lewis' expedition to Oceania have recently been recovered from the margins of anthropological history.[23] On the whole, few museums followed Dorsey's lead, although many maintained lively exchange programs with European museums to further their African and Oceanic collections.[24]

The main exception to this lack of American investment in Oceania was the Bishop Museum located in Honolulu. Developed before the United States' annexation of the Hawaiian Islands in 1898, this institution soon moved from the classification of invaluable Hawaiian material to a general salvage operation in Polynesia. The start of this endeavor is generally tied to the First Pacific Science Congress, which took place in Honolulu in 1920. Herbert Gregory, acting director of the Bishop Museum since 1919, soon seized funding opportunities and sent scholars throughout the Polynesian triangle. Peter Buck (better known under his Maori name Te Rangi Hiroa), a leading contributor in this effort, replaced Gregory as director in 1936. As a result a large number of monographs appeared between 1920 and 1940. Their diffusionist bias and gridlock content have been widely criticized in the literature, yet they remain standard works for comparative purposes.[25] In this light, the scientific output of the Bishop Museum is not unlike that of the Hamburg South Sea Expedition. The Hamburg monographs, dealing mostly with the area of Micronesia, roughly coincide in date with those of the Bishop Museum.

Margaret Mead was a young scholar contributing to the Bishop Museum monographs, although she hailed from a different tradition. Her survey of Manua in the Samoan Island chain technically fits in the Bishop Museum framework, though it was a mere byproduct of her primary research on cultural differences in the development of adolescents.[26] Her mentor was none other than Franz Boas, educated in the German anthropological tradition only to settle at a young age in the United States.[27] Boas found initial employment in the United States' expanding museological landscape. He soon objected to unsound scientific practices and by 1895 settled at Columbia University, training a whole generation of American anthropologists. Before moving from a museum to a university setting, Boas engaged in research among the Native Americans of the Pacific Northwest. This field site alerted Boas to ethnographic possibilities beyond the American continent. Boas' own research never reached the intensive fashion of his British or even German counterparts, as most of his journeys to the field were surveys involving object collections. Yet these very endeavors on the Northwest Coast also led him to adopt a critical stance vis-à-vis museum practice. The American anthropological landscape changed dramatically when the generation of Boas' students incorporated such critiques into their writings.[28]

Although Boas looms large in the restructuring process of American anthropology, his involvement in Oceania remains minor. Two notable exceptions to America's lack of involvement in Oceania are the above-mentioned Margaret Mead and Laura Thompson, one of Alfred Kroeber's students at Berkeley, who carried out fieldwork on the island of Guam. Both Mead and Thompson had considerable assistance from the American presence in the Pacific Islands. This imperial presence became crucial for the furthering of American anthropology in the Pacific Islands.

THE OCEANIC PHASE OF AMERICAN ANTHROPOLOGY: THE ADMINISTRATIVE SETTING

The interconnection between administration and anthropology in the United States was closer than in Germany or in Great Britain. In fact, the interconnection between the ethnographic frontier and the expanding frontier of settlements made the American case unique, since neither British nor German anthropologists could claim the same immediacy for their own ethnographic research. The military campaigns against Native Americans in the United States (reaching its climax at Little Big Horn in 1876) brought conservationist and political concerns together. It was John Wesley Powell who convinced the American Congress that anthropology would yield useful insights for the peaceful transfer of American Indians into reservations. By 1879 Congress had developed the Bureau of American Ethnology to further such research. This institution's actual investigations, however, did not necessarily comply with the political goals proposed by Congress.[29] Localism was an important component in the formation of museums in the United States. Competitive spirit, which in Germany led to the proliferation of scientific institutions, also benefited from some government-sponsored institutions, although there never was the same type of monopoly as in Germany.[30] The Bureau of American Ethnology provided good examples to emulate. In Germany Bastian wanted to replicate the American effort in Berlin and proposed it to his museum administration.[31] Yet the results were minimal until a fortuitous windfall created an opportunity through the dreaded Federal Council Resolution chronicled in Chapters 1, 3, and 4.

American imperial expansion into the Pacific following the "Splendid Little War" brought about a greater anthropological interest in the Pacific. The Department of the Interior commissioned several anthropologists between 1906 and 1910, coinciding with the height of the expedition age in German New Guinea, to perform research in the Philippines. The results of the Philippine Ethnological Survey had little impact on the American administration of the archipelago, but it did provide a template for similar future projects. Similarly, the consciousness that Pacific Islanders could be regarded as something akin to Native Americans emerged. This point was emphasized when Franklin D. Roosevelt proposed a sweeping reorganization of the Bureau of Indian Affairs in 1934. Anthropologists were invited to address specific problems of Native American administration, and Laura Thompson, who was the wife of FDR's Bureau of Indian Affairs commissioner, John Collier, took such insights to the island of Guam, where she performed ethnographic investigations for the U.S. Navy in the late 1930s. While one could hardly speak of an Oceanic phase in American anthropology in that period, the arrival of World War II to the Pacific changed this state of affairs.[32]

The Japanese attack on Pearl Harbor created additional opportunities for American anthropologists. Peter Murdock, based at Yale University, immediately advised his associates and students to collect material about the Japanese occupied islands in the Pacific. While this initial survey was less useful for the actual fighting in the Pacific, it proved important information for subsequent administrative duties. In the interest of the defense of the United States, the islands of Micronesia became a testing ground for the marriage of anthropological research with administrative knowledge. Immediately following the occupation of the islands, the American administration created the Coordinated Investigation of Micronesian Anthropology (CIMA), which lasted until 1947. Out of the forty-one researchers who arrived in Micronesia, twenty-five were cultural anthropologists. CIMA and ensuing anthropological involvement did not represent the most extensive anthropological investigation of Oceania, but it triggered in earnest an Oceanic phase in American anthropology. While broadly conceived as an ethnographic survey, it was in fact more than that. Realizing that the German monographs dating to the Hamburg South Sea Expedition were neither sufficient in scope nor in method, most of the participants involved in the expedition undertook intensive field research partially inspired by a new American breed of cultural anthropology. Murdock's humble ethnographic moment following Pearl Harbor soon grew into a powerful anthropological force that rivaled established institutions in the Pacific Ocean. For instance, thanks to its expertise in Polynesian surveys, the Bishop Museum was involved in CIMA (especially through the survey of the Polynesian outlier Kapingamarangi). However, the vast majority of researchers who would dominate America's Oceanic phase following the Second World War came from universities located on the continental United States.[33]

Interbleeding Ethnographic Frontiers: 1760–1945

The comparative dimensions of German and Anglo-American anthropologies invite a wider world historical framework. Under the notion of interbleeding ethnographic frontiers emerges a sustained attempt to leave national histories behind and venture into Oceania's vast spaces. First, I seek to trace the global history of the anthropological endeavor as outlined in the introductory section. Second, and more broadly speaking, I wish to contribute to a world historical understanding of the Pacific Ocean. It is important to point out that the notion of interbleeding ethnographic frontiers is not entirely new. In his initial survey of "the European appropriation of indigenous things," Nicholas Thomas aptly explored collection motives behind anthropological, commercial, evangelical, and imperial endeavors.[34] His venture, however, was oriented around the location of novel theoretical horizons, not a chronology or better periodization of Oceania's anthropological endeavor.[35] Leaving behind the terra firma of national histories, I propose a brief chronology of anthropology in the Pacific between 1760 and 1945 or, better put, an attempt at a world history of the anthropological endeavor.

Anthropological endeavors clearly predate the year 1760. A history of Western anthropology has to begin with the arrival of the Spaniards to the Pacific Ocean. Despite emerging contributions to cartography and frequently violent first contacts, their descriptions of indigenous life were superficial and exemplified meager collection activity. Expeditions during the second half of the 1500s and the early 1600s (especially those performed by Mendaña and de Quiros) maintained a formal Spanish claim to the watery expanse of the Pacific that was little challenged by Dutch and British endeavors of the 1600s.[36]

British and French expeditions arriving in the Pacific during the second half of the 1700s were quite different in ambition and scope. Initially Spanish officials were unconcerned with scientific aims, perceiving them as a threat to their domains in the Americas and the Philippines. French and British excitement about Tahiti was quickly dismissed and Iberian sovereignty asserted through an incorporation of the islands into the Spanish discoveries of the 1600s. Some new forms of knowledge—especially material culture or, better, curiosities (*particularidades*)—raised Spanish interest. After realizing their minimal economic promise, the *particularidades* were soon downplayed. Spanish officials raised little doubt about the original ownership of all islands in the Pacific. Prince Masserano, Spanish ambassador to the Court of St. James, wrote: "I doubt that we can sit aside with indifference and watch these nationals travel frequently to [these islands] with the pretext of discovering new lands. . . . knowing very well that they ignore the Treaty of Utrecht under which no other nation than the Spanish should go to the Southern Sea."[37] When John Harrison developed a mechanical time measuring device, which allowed a relatively safe assertion of longitude, long elusive for Spanish, Dutch, and even early British mariners, more than a slight concern emerged among Spanish officials.[38] The ability for others to determine the exact location of islands in the Pacific and therefore encroach on existing Spanish claims caused concern and a change in attitude: "It is very much necessary to publish before long our travel relations and discoveries in the [Pacific]. We need to publish our maps, long promised, since for this [British] nation there exists no better act of possession than such publications. This will show clearly that we did arrive [in the Pacific] before any other nation."[39]

The notion of the ability to claim distant islands in the Pacific Ocean, a main concern of Spanish authorities, transformed the Spanish attitude toward learning about the widespread oceangoing peoples of the Pacific. Spanish attempts to outperform their French and British competitors led to the purchase of chronometers and other instruments in England. Many of these would find their way on the expeditions of Alejandro Malaspina (1789–1794), who, as the self-ascribed Columbus of the enlightened Spanish monarchy, tried to map and survey much of the northern Pacific. His results, however, became embroiled in European politics following the French Revolution.[40]

Indigenous ethnographic frontiers were constantly shifting, resting as they did on complex material exchanges. Europeans would only gradually understand the full extent of these frontiers as they frequently clashed with their attempts at fitting Oceanic cultural manifestations into ready-made categories. Harrison's chronometer made a cartographical apprehension of the area possible, whereupon categorization and nomenclature became a European fancy. The late-eighteenth-century voyages then provided a true starting point for a Euro-American imagination of the ethnographic frontiers in the Pacific Ocean.

Early categorization of Oceanic cultures rested on three pillars: casual and fleeting cultural observation, maturing concepts of race that were partially imported from Atlantic Ocean experiences, and a budding concern with material culture. Of these, as discussed in Chapter 2, material culture was the most problematic for the naturalists accompanying Cook on his voyages. Most of their collection activity was concerned with natural history, which, following the publication of Linneaus' *Systema Naturae* (1735), was equipped with a proper system of classification. Although no similar work existed for the classification of ethnographic objects, the naturalists traveling with Cook expressed interest in creating such a work, thus leading to an increase in collection activity involving curiosities. Interest in collecting material objects, other than as mementos, then started to increase. Because of this awareness, roughly two thousand artifacts can be traced to Cook's three voyages, with an increase in volume during his last two journeys.[41]

Fleeting cultural observations provided important additions to emergent ethnographic frontiers. The principle of attachment frequently guided European observations, which "translat[ed] varieties of experiences from an alien world into [familiar] practices."[42] This principle led to the validation of Polynesian chiefdoms in light of eighteenth-century European political systems. The search for an Oceanic indigenous nobility led to the establishment of exchanges with individuals the Europeans came to call kings.[43] The "nobler" societies in Polynesia contrasted sharply with those of Melanesia, which seemed to exhibit no resemblance to European models.

The emerging Polynesia/Melanesia divide gained additional momentum because it coincided with concepts of race emanating from the Atlantic context. By the time the exploration of the Pacific started in earnest, Europeans had realized that static categories of human taxonomy had begun to break down in the Atlantic world through migration, forceful or otherwise. The Spaniards, for instance, were the first to enshrine outward appearances in naming the Pacific Islands. By calling the large island located to the north of Australia New Guinea, they highlighted superficial affinities between the people of this island and west coast Africans. Such practices gained further inspiration through the work of Charles de Brosses. In his *Histoire des navigations aux terres australes* (a compendium of known voyages to the Pacific published in 1756), he first employed the term "Polynesia" for the far-flung islands in the eastern Pacific. Similarly, de Brosses was one of the first to speak of two races, one darker and one lighter colored, a tradition followed by later eighteenth-century writers.[44] Such suggested categories solidified with the publication of Dumont d'Urville's voyaging accounts in the 1830s. While d'Urville claimed to have authored the tripartite division of Melanesia, Micronesia, and Polynesia, many authors now regard him as popularizing the terms.[45] D'Urville's distinction professed a clear preference for Polynesian over Melanesia that soon became hegemonic.

The static Melanesia/Polynesia divide soon found critics. Nicholas Thomas, for instance, argued that "Polynesia came to seem of limited interest to anthropologists, presumably because the societies appeared heavily acculturated. In contrast, during the early decades of professional anthropology . . . many authentic and traditional tribal societies were seemingly found in Melanesia."[46] For the most part, the renewed interest in Melanesian societies did not stem from professional anthropologists but from resident traders and missionaries who, for different reasons, studied indigenous cultures. To be sure, missionaries approached Oceanic inhabitants with evangelical zeal and the clear goal to influence and change the cultures they were encountering. Missionaries frequently characterized Oceanic material culture as "idolatry," and, upon conversion of their subjects, commanded many objects to be burned, with only a few surviving objects to be kept as trophies celebrating the victorious path of Christianity.[47] However, not all missionaries were dismissive of the cultures they encountered. In fact, some provided vital ethnographic information for the burgeoning ethnographic institutions in European countries. While convinced of the need for their evangelical process, individual missionaries questioned the simple dichotomy of the Melanesia/Polynesia divide. George Brown, a Methodist missionary in the Bismarck Archipelago, for instance, noted that Melanesian societies used pottery, bows and arrows, and shell money—all items absent from the supposedly higher-ranking Polynesian societies.[48] Similarly, Robert Henry Codrington dedicated his Anglo-Catholic Mission work to understanding what he called the bedrock of the Melanesian mind. Codrington wrote extensively and sympathetically about his subjects and argued that in-depth linguistic and cultural study were required to enable Melanesian conversion. His writings informed leading British evolutionary anthropologists.[49]

The Melanesia/Polynesia hierarchy also caught the attention of an odd group of Pacific residents: traders and commercial agents. Nicholas Thomas rightly claims that the great majority of traders had little regard for indigenous cultures they deemed as an impediment to their commercial agenda.[50] Yet this was not universally the case, as Chapter 2 of the current work emphasizes. The growing German interest in ethnographica alerted traders to the marketability of indigenous objects. Some company representatives, especially the Godeffroy and Hernsheim ventures, invested considerable time and resources in designing what could be coined a "commercial ethnography." The experiment failed as a commercial scheme but generated some of the first intensive anthropological field studies in German New Guinea.

Trader and missionary activities coincided with an increasing imperial presence in the Pacific Islands.[51] Following the Napoleonic wars in Europe, a swelling number of expeditions proceeded to the Pacific, returning with an equally budding number of accounts, charts, and indigenous objects. The American Exploration Expedition (1838–1842), for instance, brought Oceanic artifacts that became the ground stock for the future Smithsonian Museum.[52] In the 1870s German naval expeditions did not bear the same significance, yet the artifacts collected by the SMS *Gazelle's* crew alerted Bastian and other German anthropologists to the importance of Melanesia as a "final" ethnographic frontier in the Pacific Ocean (see Chapter 1). These expeditions also provided road maps for colonial annexations. By the late nineteenth century these imperial frontiers reached New Guinea and Micronesia.

The establishment of colonial frontiers in Oceania both supported and contradicted the Western ethnographic project. The availability of an imperial infrastructure, such as naval vessels and imperial outposts, provided relatively easy access to artifacts and their producers. Yet at the same time, anthropologists frequently bemoaned the lack of synchronization between postulated ethnographic frontiers and imperial ones. While vigilant in voicing their critiques, anthropologists soon found respectable avenues in colonial publications. Georg Thilenius, the director of the Hamburg Ethnological Museum, for instance, accosted so-called colonial museums for their superficial ethnography. He noted that displays in colonial museums were severed from their neighboring areas by artificial colonial boundaries and had no comparative framework, hence no scientific purpose. Similarly, the German territories in Africa and the Pacific shared few common ethnographic features despite colonial displays suggesting the contrary.[53]

Despite the problematic interference of imperial boundaries with ethnographic frontiers, it was in the Pacific that the establishment of imperial territories assisted the development of ethnographic endeavors. The British and Germans were the two main imperial presences in the Pacific, with the French as a distant third. Both British and German imperial realms incorporated crucial ethnographic frontiers, especially territories that were identified as frontier regions between the stipulated static division of Melanesia, Micronesia, and Polynesia. The existence of such important ethnographic frontiers partially prompted Felix von Luschan to advocate a centralization of colonial artifacts in Berlin museums (see Chapters 1 and 3), even though his argument that other Germans museums did not have adequate scientific expertise became hotly contested. Two areas that most immediately spring to mind are the Torres Strait Islands, delineating a boundary between Melanesia and the inhabitants of Australia known as Aborigines, and the areas postulated as "Para-Micronesia" (see Chapters 2 and 6) that indicated a boundary between Melanesia and the islands composing Micronesia to the north. Because of to their location, both became central points of ethnographic attention: members of the Cambridge Expedition descended upon the Torres Strait Islands in 1898, while the German commercial/ethnographic engagement nearly obliterated the inhabitants of Para-Micronesia by 1904. In the long run, ethnographic investigations provided few concrete boundaries for capricious anthropological constructs. Methodologically, these studies were beneficial because of the creation of intensive participant observation.

A third important ethnographic boundary regarded Polynesian outliers. This set of about eighteen island populations was deemed culturally and linguistically closer to Polynesia than to either Melanesia or Micronesia. In this case imperial boundaries obstructed investigations since some of these Polynesian enclaves were located within German New Guinea, while others were within the British Solomon Islands. Ethnographically, the Polynesian outliers warranted extensive discussion in anthropological literature. William Churchill, for instance, claimed that such enclaves represented living proof of stepping stones into the island world of Polynesia.[54] Georg Thilenius, while traveling through the Pacific in the late nineteenth century, alleged the contrary, namely, that these enclaves represented an east to west migration—a "throwback" from already established Polynesian societies in the central and eastern Pacific.[55] The Hamburg South Sea Expedition (see Chapter 4) took this interest to German New Guinea in 1908. Many expedition members spent considerable time on the Polynesian enclaves. These contributed little to solving Thilenius' postulated puzzle but honed their intensive research skills. Concern about Polynesian outliers continued well into the interwar period, when Raymond Firth, trained by Bronislaw Malinowski, spent a year in Tikopia partially as a symbol of its significant standing along the ethnographic frontier.[56] Much as in the case of Para-Micronesia, recent studies suggest a much more complex settlement history than either Churchill or Thilenius envisioned. Archaeological studies have thoroughly discredited earlier models of "insular isolates," demonstrating that some of these islands stood at the center of important trade networks. The settlement history of Tikopia alone stretches back three thousand years, attesting to the outlier societies' inherent complexities.[57]

The implications of such methodological shifts for colonial administrations has received consideration earlier in this chapter. In comparing ethnographic frontiers, it is crucial to recall that Governor Albert Hahl became a main instigator for the "fieldwork" movement in Germany (Chapter 5). His Australian counterpart Hubert Murray, in contrast, could enjoy a cadre of already developed anthropological methodologies but at the same time contended with harsh critiques of his administrative studies from interwar academic anthropologists. Where Hahl failed to established a governmental anthropology, Murray managed to support two anthropologists in his administration. Yet, it was Hahl who kept ethnographic and imperial frontiers separate when German anthropologists reacted to a perceived American threat to German New Guinea. The looming American ethnographic "exploitation" became a major initiative for the creation of a pan-German effort to replace Berlin's monopoly over colonial artifacts. Exclusive ethnographic rights for individual nations were counterproductive in the long run, as other imperial powers, especially Great Britain and its dependencies, could consider closing their frontiers to German researchers. Hahl nipped such actions in the bud by emphasizing their negative implications. He thus prevented a subsuming of the ethnographic frontier by imperial and national concerns (see Chapter 4).

The last phase of the comparative ethnographic frontier in the Pacific emerged as a consequence of the Second World War. The 1930s witnessed the development of an important dialogue, albeit not always on amicable terms, between British social anthropologists and American cultural anthropologists. This dialogue gained additional momentum with Alfred Reginald Radcliffe-Brown's move from Sydney to the University of Chicago. Radcliffe-Brown's ethnographic imprint led to a number of important comparative projects stretching beyond the American continent to other regions of the world.[58] It was George Murdock at Yale University who, benefiting from the Pacific Theater of the Second World War, introduced similar considerations to the Pacific Ocean. By the end of the conflict, the CIMA project in Micronesia comprised both Boasian influences, in the form of cognitive and psychological concerns, and British social anthropological influences, in the form of kinship studies. CIMA and subsequent anthropological endeavors figured in the entrenchment of "fieldwork" at the dawn of the American Oceanic phase; it coincided with the ebbing of the British engagement in the Pacific Ocean.

This chronology presents a brief outline of a comparative global history of anthropology in the Pacific Ocean. On one hand, it illustrates the large contribution of German New Guinea to such a history. On the other hand, the narrative points out the need to expand these comparative concerns into a larger monograph. Such a task requires additional research into hitherto neglected ethnographic traditions. While much research is now available on American, British, French, and German traditions, little information is available on Spanish sources. Of equal weight is an understanding of indigenous ethnographic consciousnesses, either through counterethnography or other means (see Chapter 6). The bulk of such work remains tied to synecdoche, where individual Oceanic societies stand for the region as a whole.[59] It remains to be seen whether one can move beyond such literary devices to chronicle comparative indigenous ethnographic frontiers. This new paradigm is best exemplified by Epeli Hau'ofa in his influential "Our Sea of Islands," where he admonishes that new social scientific models are required in the postcolonial Pacific. Talking about a Tongan friend who frequently travels between the Pacific Basin and the Pacific Rim, he writes: "There are thousands like him, who are flying back and forth across national boundaries, the international dateline, and the equator, far above and completely undaunted by the deadly serious discourses below on the nature of the Pacific Century, the Asia-Pacific coprosperity sphere, and the dispositions of the post–cold war Pacific rim, cultivating their ever-growing universe in their own ways, which is as it should be, for therein lies their independence."[60] It is easy to substitute one of these discourses with anthropology. But far from setting stark dichotomies between indigenous and Western ethnographic frontiers, Hau'ofa suggests coexistence and continuity of indigenous and Western ethnographic frontiers. Following this line of thought, the present work finds its relevance in the investigation of those frontiers, while suggesting future research areas.

Notes

ABBREVIATIONS

AGS: Ministerio de Cultura, Archivo General de Simancas, Spain
AM: Außenministerium (Foreign Ministry), Dresden
BaHStA: Bayrisches Hauptstaatsarchiv, Munich
BArchF: Bundesarchiv Freiburg
BArchL: Bundesarchiv Lichterfelde, Berlin
BMH: Bishop Museum, Honolulu
BoP: Nachlaß Wilhelm von Bode (Bode Papers), Berlin
BrP: William T. Brigham papers, Honolulu
FMNH: Field Museum of Natural History, Chicago
FrP: Friederici papers, Hamburg
GStA-PK: Geheimes Staatsarchiv—Preußischer Kulturbesitz, Berlin
HAStK: Historisches Archiv der Stadt Köln, Cologne
HstAH: Hauptstaatsarchiv Hamburg
HStAS: Hauptstaatsarchiv Stuttgart
KB: Kopierbücher (Copies of Correspondence Sent), Leipzig
LiMSt: Linden Museum Stuttgart
LuP: Nachlaß Felix von Luschan (Luschan Papers), Berlin
MA Außenministerium, Munich
MfVD: Museum für Völkerkunde, Dresden
MfVH: Museum für Völkerkunde, Hamburg
MfVL: Museum für Völkerkunde, Leipzig_
MfVM: Museum für Völkerkunde, Munich
MK: Kultusministerium (Cultural Ministry), Munich
MNZHUB: Museum für Naturkunde Zentralinstitut der Humboldt-Universität zu Berlin
MV: Minsterium für Volksbildung (Cultural Ministry), Dresden
R 1001: Reichskolonialamt (German Colonial Office File), Berlin
RJMfV: Rautenstrauch-Joest Museum für Völkerkunde, Cologne
RM: Reichsmarine (Imperial Naval Files), Freiburg
SächHStAD: Sächsisches Hauptstaatsarchiv, Dresden
SB-PK: Staatsbibliothek zu Berlin—Preußischer Kulturbesitz (Berlin State Library)
SchP: Nachlaß Heinrich Schnee (Schnee Papers), Berlin
SMB-PK, MV: Staatliche Museen zu Berlin—Preußischer Kulturbesitz, Museum für Völkerkunde (Berlin Ethnological Museum)
SMB-PK, ZA: Staatliche Museen zu Berlin—Preußischer Kulturbesitz, Zentralarchiv (Central Archive), Berlin
SSE: Südsee Expedition, Hamburg
ÜMB: Übersee Museum Bremen

1. The literature on the increasing dialogue between anthropology and history is growing quickly. One of the pioneers of this endeavor is Bernard S. Cohn, whose most influential essays are collected in *An Anthropologist among the Historians and Other Essays* (Oxford: Oxford University Press, 1987). For a political economy standpoint consult Eric Wolf, *Europe and the People without History* (Berkeley: University of California Press, 1982), and William Roseberry, *Anthropologies and Histories: Essays in Culture, History, and Political Economy* (New Brunswick: Rutgers University Press, 1989). Works that incorporate recent postmodern perspectives are David W. Cohen, *The Combing of History* (Chicago: University of Chicago Press, 1994); John and Jean Comaroff, *Ethnography and the Historical Imagination* (Boulder: Westview Press, 1992); Bronwen Douglas, *Across the Great Divide: Journeys in History and Anthropology* (Amsterdam: Harwood Academic Publishers, 1998). James D. Fabion provides an interesting starting point in his "History in Anthropology," *Annual Review of Anthropology* 22 (1993): 35–54.

2. Jerry H. Bentley, *Shapes of World History in Twentieth-Century Scholarship* (Washington, DC: American Historical Association, 1996), 22.

3. Alex Calder, Jonathan Lamb, and Bridget Orr, "Introduction: Postcoloniality and the Pacific," in *Voyages and Beaches: Pacific Encounters: 1769–1840*, ed. Alex Calder, Jonathan Lamb, and Bridget Orr (Honolulu: University of Hawai'i Press, 1999), 7.

4. Some examples of this approach are Marshall Sahlins, *Anahulu: The Anthropology of History in the Kingdom of Hawaii*, vol. 1: *Historical Ethnography* (Chicago: University of Chicago Press, 1992). Sahlins argues that Hawaiian chiefs' conspicuous consumptions exasperated the arrival of Western economic forces. Nicholas Thomas, *Entangled Objects: Exchange, Material Culture and Colonialism in the Pacific* (Cambridge, MA: Harvard University Press, 1991), argues for a localizing understanding of exchange between Oceanic and Euro-American players. For a general overview of cultural history and the role of anthropology in the same, see Patrick Manning, *Navigating World History: Historians Create a Global Past* (New York: Palgrave, 2003), chapter 13. Although Manning intends the concept in a somewhat different manner, the above authors would fit in his microcultural analytical scheme.

5. Wolf, *Europe*, 13.

6. On a general theoretical treatment of fieldwork, see Akhil Gupta and James Ferguson, eds., *Anthropological Locations: Boundaries and Grounds of a Field Science* (Los Angeles: University of California Press, 1997). For the development of fieldwork in British anthropology, see George Stocking, *After Tylor: British Social Anthropology* (Madison: University of Wisconsin Press, 1995); on the shift in funding priorities, see George Stocking, "Philanthropoids and Vanishing Cultures: Rockefeller Funding and the End of the Museum Era in Anglo-American Anthropology," in *The Ethnographer's Magic and Other Essays in Anthropology*, ed. George Stocking (Madison: University of Wisconsin Press, 1992), 178–211.

7. See, for instance, Peter Pels and Oscar Salemink, "Introduction: Locating Colonial Subjects of Anthropology," in *Colonial Subjects: Essays on the Practical History of Anthropology*, ed. Peter Pels and Oscar Salemink (Ann Arbor: University of Michigan Press, 1999), 1–52.

8. Marvin Harris, *The Rise of Anthropological Theory* (New York: Thomas Crowell, 1968). Harris' work privileges cultural materialism over other approaches to anthropological work. George Stocking, "On the Limits of 'Presentism' and 'Historicism' in the Historiography of the Behavioral Science," *The Journal of the History of Behavioral Science* 1 (1965): 211–218, provides important insights into such approaches.

9. The output of this field is best illustrated by its History of Anthropology series issued by the University of Wisconsin Press. There are ten volumes to date, most of them edited by George Stocking.

10. See George Stocking, *Victorian Anthropology* (New York: Basic Books, 1987).

11. See, for instance, George Stocking, ed., *Colonial Situations: Essays on the Contextualization of Ethnographic Knowledge* (Madison: University of Wisconsin Press, 1993).

12. Kenneth Pommeranz, *The Great Divergence* (Princeton: Princeton University Press, 2000); see also Andre Gunder Frank, *ReOrient: Global Economy in the Asian Age* (Berkeley: University of California Press, 1998).

13. See, for instance, Peter Pels and Oscar Salemink, eds., *Colonial Subjects: Essays on the Practical History of Anthropology.*

14. Some of important works in this regard are Martin Lewis and Kären Wigen, *The Myth of Continents: A Critique of Metageography* (Berkeley: University of California Press, 1997). The same authors propose an alternative "ocean-centered" view of the world in a collection of essays titled "Oceans Connect" in *The Geographical Review* 89 (1999). Consult here in particular the essay by Jerry H. Bentley, "Sea and Ocean Basins as Framework for Historical Analysis," 215–224. Another contribution is Rainer F. Buschmann's "Oceans of World History: Delineating Aquacentric Views in the Global Past," *History Compass* 2 (2004), WD 68: 1–9. Three important collections on world history and the explorations of oceans are Daniel Finamore, ed., *Maritime History as World History* (Gainesville: University Press of Florida, 2004); Bernhard Klein and Gesa Mackenthun, eds., *Sea Changes: Historicizing the Ocean* (New York: Routledge, 2004); and Jerry H. Bentley, Renate Bridenthal, and Kären Wigen, eds., *Seascapes: Maritime Histories, Littoral Cultures, and Transoceanic Exchanges* (Honolulu: University of Hawai'i Press, 2007).

15. Bronislaw Malinowski, *Argonauts of the Western Pacific: An Account of Native Enterprise and Adventure in the Archipelagoes of Melanesian New Guinea* (New York: E. P. Dutton, 1961). Malinowski's exercise of self-fashioning is skillfully unpacked by George Stocking in his "The Ethnographer's Magic: British Anthropology from Tylor to Malinowski," in George Stocking, *The Ethnographer's Magic and Other Essays in the History of Anthropology* (Madison: University of Wisconsin Press, 1995). See also Margaret Mead, *Coming of Age in Samoa: A Psychological Study of Primitive Youth for Western Civilization* (New York: Morrow, 1928); for an in-depth analysis of the impact of Mead's work, consult Lenora Foerstel and Angela Gilliam, eds., *Confronting the Margaret Mead Legacy: Scholarship, Empire, and the South Pacific* (Philadelphia: Temple University Press, 1992).

16. Bruce M. Knauff, *From Primitive to Postcolonial in Melanesian Anthropology* (Ann Arbor: University of Michigan Press, 1999), 12; see also Doug Dalton, "Melanesian Can(n)ons: Paradoxes and Prospects in Melanesian Ethnography," in *Excluded Ancestors, Inventible Traditions: Essays towards a More Inclusive History of Anthropology*, ed. Richard Handler (Madison: University of Wisconsin Press, 2000), 284–305.

17. Bronwen Douglas, "Seaborne Ethnography and the Natural History of Man," *Journal of Pacific History* 38 (2003): 3–27.

18. See, for instance, Chris Gosden and C. Pavlides, "Are Islands Insular? Landscape vs. Seascape in the Case of the Arawe Islands, PNG," *Archaeology in Oceania* 29 (1994): 162–171; Paul D'Arcy, "Cultural Divisions and Island Environments since the Time of Dumount d'Urville." *Journal of Pacific History* 38 (2003): 217–235; Paul D'Arcy, *People of the Sea: Environment, Identity, and History* (Honolulu: University of Hawai'i Press, 2006); Epeli Hau'ofa, "Our Sea of Islands," *The Contemporary Pacific* 6 (1994): 147–161; and his "The Ocean in Us," *The Contemporary Pacific* 10 (1998): 391–411; see also Klaus Dodds and Stephen A. Royle,

"The Historical Geography of Islands: Introduction: Rethinking Islands," *Journal of Historical Geography* 29 (2003): 487–498.

19. Richard Sorrensen, "The Ship as Scientific Instrument in the Eighteenth Century," *Osiris* 11 (1996): 221–236.

20. The implications of James Cook's voyages are currently explored in Brian Richardson, *Longitude and Empire: How Captain Cook's Voyages Changed the World* (Vancouver: University of British Columbia Press, 2005). Consult especially chapter 5 for changes in anthropological thinking.

21. Tom Ryan, "'Le Président des Terres Australes' Charles de Brosses and the French Enlightenment Beginnings of Oceanic Anthropology," *Journal of Pacific History* 37 (2002): 157–186.

22. On the problematic designations of these areas, see David Hanlon, "Micronesia: Writing and Rewriting the Histories of a Non-Entity," *Pacific Studies* 12 (1989): 1–21; Nicholas Thomas, "The Force of Ethnology: Origins and Significance of the Melanesia/Polynesia Division," *Current Anthropology* 30 (1989): 27–34. This important division will be discussed in subsequent chapters.

23. A recent issue of the *Journal of Pacific History* is dedicated to d'Urville's legacy. The most prominent essay is Serge Tcherkézoff's "A Long and Unfortunate Voyage towards the 'Invention' of the Melanesia/Polynesia Distinction 1595–1832," *Journal of Pacific History* 38 (2003): 175–196.

24. Richard White, *The Middle Ground: Indians, Empires, and Republics in the Great Lakes Region, 1650–1815* (New York: Cambridge University Press, 1991); Jeremy Adelman and Stephen Aron, "From Borderlands to Borders: Empires, Nation-States, and the Peoples in between in North American History," *American Historical Review* 104 (1999): 814–841.

25. For a view of frontiers in the Chinese context, consult Thomas J. Barfield, *The Perilous Frontier: Nomadic Empires and China, 221 BCE to AD 1757* (Cambridge, MA: Blackwell, 1989); for the Roman context see Steven K. Drummond and Lynn Nelson, *The Western Frontier of Imperial Rome* (Armonk, NY: M. E. Sharpe, 1994).

26. David Chappell, "Ethnogenesis and Frontiers," *Journal of World History* 4 (1993): 267–275.

27. Mary Louise Pratt, *Imperial Eyes: Travel Writing and Transculturation* (New York: Routledge, 1992).

28. Greg Dening, *Islands and Beaches: Discourse on a Silent Land: Marquesas, 1774–1880* (Honolulu: University of Hawai'i Press, 1980).

29. James Clifford, "On Ethnographic Allegory," in *Writing Culture: The Poetics and Politics of Ethnography,* ed. James Clifford and George Marcus (Berkeley: University of California Press, 1986), 98–121.

30. Renato Rosaldo, *Culture and Truth: The Remaking of Social Analysis* (Boston: Beacon Press, 1989).

31. H. Glenn Penny, *Objects of Culture: Ethnology and Ethnographic Museums in Imperial Germany* (Chapel Hill: University of North Carolina Press, 2002), 30–34.

32. See, for instance, Pels and Salemink, eds., *Colonial Subjects;* and Nicholas Thomas, *Colonialism's Culture: Anthropology, Travel, and Government* (Princeton, NJ: Princeton University Press, 1994).

33. The *Deutsches Kolonial-Lexikon,* edited by Heinrich Schnee (Leipzig: Quelle und Meyer, 1920), estimated the total land surface of German New Guinea at about 241,231 square kilometers. German Samoa, the other possession in the Pacific Ocean, amounted to about 2,572 square kilometers or a little over 1 percent of the size of German New Guinea.

34. Susanne Zantop, *Colonial Fantasies: Conquest, Family, and Nation in Precolonial Germany, 1770–1870* (Durham: Duke University Press, 1997).

35. Harry Liebersohn, "Coming of Age in the Pacific: German Ethnography from Chamisso to Krämer," in *Worldly Provincialism: German Anthropology in the Age of Empire*, ed. H. Glenn Penny and Matti Bunzl (Ann Arbor: University of Michigan Press, 2003), 31–46.

36. See, for instance, Stewart Firth, "German Firms in the Pacific Islands, 1857–1914," in *Germany in the Pacific and the Far East, 1870–1914*, ed. John Moses and Paul Kennedy (St. Lucia: University of Queensland Press, 1977), 3–27.

37. Stewart Firth, *New Guinea under the Germans* (Melbourne: University of Melbourne Press, 1982).

38. Ibid., 174.

39. Hermann Hiery, *The Neglected War: The German South Pacific and the Influence of World War I* (Honolulu: University of Hawai'i Press, 1995), 3; see also his *Das Deutsche Reich in der Südsee (1900–1921): Eine Annäherung an die Erfahrungen verschiedener Kulturen* (Göttingen: Vandenhoeck & Ruprecht, 1995).

40. Ibid., 7.

41. Klaus Neumann, "The Stench of the Past: Revisionism in Pacific Islands and Australian History," *The Contemporary Pacific* 10 (1998): 31–35. Neumann stresses the importance of knowing one's place in the production of history. He is in line with a number of recent historians who argue for a reflexive account of one's historical narrative.

CHAPTER 1: BERLIN'S MONOPOLY

1. The most concise treatment of Prussian museum policy is Karl Hammer, "Preußische Museumspolitik im 19. Jahrhundert," in *Bildungspolitik in Preußen zur Zeit des Kaiserreichs*, ed. Peter Baumgart (Stuttgart: Klett-Cotta, 1980), 268–275.

2. Even if official Prussian state contributions were to remain rather limited during the Second Reich, they still vastly surpassed the contributions of other states within the German union. See, for instance, Sebastian Müller, "Official Support and Bourgeois Opposition in Wilhelminian Culture," in *The Divided Heritage: Themes and Problems in German Modernism*, ed. Irit Rogoff (Cambridge: Cambridge University Press, 1990), 168–169.

3. Hammer, "Preußische Museumspolitik," 268–269; Werner Knopp, "Blick auf Bode," in *Wilhelm von Bode: Museumsdirektor und Mäzen*, ed. Kaiser-Friedrich-Museums-Verein (Berlin: Staatliche Museen zu Berlin, 1995), 13–16; Sigrid Otto, "Wilhelm Bode—Journal eines tätigen Lebens," in *Wilhelm von Bode: Museumsdirektor und Mäzen*, ed. Kaiser-Friedrich-Museums-Verein (Berlin: Staatliche Museen zu Berlin, 1995), 29. Ludwig Pallat wrote an extensive work on Schöne's tenure in Berlin using unpublished material lost during the Second World War: *Richard Schöne, Generaldirektor der königlichen Museen zu Berlin: Ein Beitrag zur Geschichte der preußischen Kulturverwaltung* (Berlin: W. de Gruyter, 1952).

4. This topic will receive extensive treatment in the introduction to Chapter 2.

5. Following its emergence, the commission was further subdivided to accommodate regional variations, such as Oceania and Africa. Felix von Luschan to William Brigham, 18 February 1898, BrP, box 2, folder 9, item 3, BMH; Sigrid Westphal-Hellbusch, "Hundert Jahre Museum für Völkerkunde Berlin: Zur Geschichte des Museums," *Baessler Archiv* 21 (1973): 9.

6. For an alternative view of the Berlin museum, see H. Glenn Penny, *Objects of Culture*, chapter 5; see also his "Bastian's Museum: On the Limits of Empiricism and the Transformation of German Ethnology," in *Worldly Provincialism: German Anthropology in the Age*

of Empire, ed. H. Glenn Penny and Matti Bunzl (Ann Arbor: University of Michigan Press, 2003), 86–126.

7. Anonymous, "Die Einweihung des neuen Museums für Völkerkunde in Berlin," *Correspondenz-Blatt der deutschen Gesellschaft für Anthropologie, Ethnologie, und Urgeschichte* 18 (1887): 3.

8. Civilian Cabinet to von Goessler, 5 November 1886, GStA-PK, I HA, rep. 89, no. 20489.

9. Wilhelm von Bode's reflections *Mein Leben* (Berlin: Reckendorf, 1930) provide a number of interesting anecdotes concerning the business of museum administration during the Wilhelmine period. For his observation of Friedrich Wilhelm's behavior at the opening ceremony, see vol. 2, 64.

10. Anonymous, "Einweihung," 4.

11. It was George Stocking who first emphazised the important link between material culture and wealthy benefactors. See his "Philanthropoids and Vanishing Cultures: Rockefeller Funding and the End of the Museum Era in Anglo-American Anthropology," in *The Ethnographer's Magic*.

12. Bode, *Mein Leben*, vol. 1, 164–170; Thomas Gaehtgens, *Die Berliner Museumsinsel im deutschen Kaiserreich: Zur Kulturpolitik der Museen in der wilhelminischen Epoche* (Munich: Deutscher Kunstverlag, 1992), 14–18, 77–78; Werner Knopp, "Blick auf Bode," 13.

13. Westphal-Hellbusch, "Hundert Jahre," 65–68.

14. Minister Goessler did not fail to mention their important services to the museum in his speech; see Anonymous, "Einweihung," 2.

15. Fritz Kramer's description of Bastian as a traveler without shadow seems appropriate, although his characterization of Bastian's collection as "irrational" seems exaggerated. See his *Verkehrte Welten: Zur imaginären Ethnographie des 19. Jahrhunderts*, 2nd ed. (Frankfurt: Syndikat, 1981), 74–81.

16. Max Buchner, conservator of the ethnographic collections in Munich, commented: "To read Bastian? Impossible! He is best revered undigested." Wolfgang Smolka, *Völkerkunde in München: Voraussetzungen, Möglichkeiten und Entwicklungslinien ihrer Institutionalisierung (ca. 1850–1933)* (Berlin: Duncker & Humblot, 1994), 162. For an intriguing argument supporting Bastian's linguistic experimentation, see Andrew Zimmerman, *Anthropology and Antihumanism in Imperial Germany* (Chicago: University of Chicago Press, 2001), 55–57.

17. Westphal-Hellbusch, "Hundert Jahre," 5–8.

18. The literature on Adolf Bastian is vast. Some of the most prominent works include Matti Bunzl, "Franz Boas and the Humboldian Tradition: From *Volksgeist* and *Nationalcharakter* to and Anthropological Concept of Culture," in *Volksgeist as Method and Ethic: Essays on Boasian Ethnography and the German Anthropological Tradition*, ed. George Stocking (Madison: University of Wisconsin Press, 1996), 48–52; Manfred Gothsch, *Die deutsche Völkerkunde und ihr Verhältnis zum Kolonialismus: Ein Beitrag zur kolonialideologischen und kolonialpraktischen Bedeutung der deutschen Völkerkunde in der Zeit von 1870 bis 1975* (Baden Baden: Nomus, 1983), 7–23; Klaus Peter Koepping, *Adolf Bastian and The Psychic Unity of Mankind* (St. Lucia: University of Queensland Press, 1983); Woodruff Smith, *Politics and The Sciences of Culture in Germany, 1840–1920* (Oxford: Oxford University Press, 1991). 103–104, 116–120; Westphal-Hellbusch, "Hundert Jahre," 2–6. For two prominent recent interpretations on Bastian, see Penny, *Objects of Culture*, 18–23, and Zimmerman, *Anthropology and Antihumanism*, 45–48.

19. On the salvage agenda emerging out of Bastian's thought, see also Penny on the doctrine of scarcity, *Objects of Culture*, 30–34, 52–53, 79–94.

20. An excellent discussion on the term "authenticity" in Western contexts can be found in Christopher Steiner, *African Art in Transit* (Cambridge: Cambridge University Press, 1994), chapter 5. Steiner locates many of the views on "authenticity" as emerging after the First World War. The common denominator of such views, however, emerged earlier than that. Bastian's own view on material culture underscores this point.

21. Rosaldo, *Culture and Truth*, chapter 3; see also Clifford, "On Ethnographic Allegory," 113–117.

22. The ambigious relationship between ethnography and colonial agents in the Pacific Ocean receives attention in the next chapter.

23. There is a growing body of literature on the Polynesia-Melanesia divide. For some important milestones, see Nicholas Thomas, "Force of Ethnology," and his *In Oceania: Visions, Artifacts, Histories* (Durham: Duke University Press, 1997), chapter 5; see also Douglas, *Across the Great Divide*, 35–67. There is also an important set of articles on d'Urville's distinction in a 2003 issue of the *Journal of Pacific History* (vol. 38, no. 2).

24. This information is drawn from the following letter: Adolf Bastian to General Prussian Museum Administration, 8 May 1880, SMB-PK, MV, IB Bastian/E 1285/80, as well as Adolf Bastian, *Zur Kenntniss Hawaii's: Nachträge und Ergänzungen in Oceanien* (Berlin: Dümmlers, 1883), vii–xi, 112; see also Koepping, *Adolf Bastian*, 22.

25. Adolf Bastian to General Prussian Museum Administration, 16 December 1884, GStA-PK, I HA, rep. 76 Kultusministerium, sect. 15, abt. XI, bd. 4, my emphasis.

26. Adolf Bastian to General Prussian Museum Administration, 1 June 1881, GStA-PK, I HA, rep. 76 Kultusministerium, sect. 15, abt. XI, bd. 2; see also Adolf Bastian, *Der Papua des dunklen Inselreiches im Lichte psychologischer Forschung* (Berlin: Weidmannsche Buchhandlung, 1885), 325–328.

27. Records of negotiations are contained in file SMB-PK, MV, IB 48.

28. *Malaggan* carvings and ceremonies of New Ireland will receive additional attention in Chapter 6.

29. Adolf Bastian, *Inselgruppen in Oceanien: Reiseerlebnisse und Studien* (Berlin: Dümmlers, 1883), iv.

30. Bastian, *Inselgruppen in Oceanien*, v–vi; and his *Der Papua*, 325–331.

31. Arnold Jacobi, *Fünfzig Jahre Museum für Völkerkunde zu Dresden* (Berlin: Julius Bard, 1925), 24–26.

32. SächHStAD, Ministerium für Volksbildung, no. 19306.

33. A. B. Meyer, "Denkschrift über Desiderate des kgl. Ethnographischen Museums zu Dresden in Bezug auf Gegenden welche die Schiffe der Kaiserlichen Deutschen Marine berühren" (Dresden, 1883), SB-PK, LuP, case 6. Meyer's booklet amounted more to a list of artifacts than to a systematic attempt to coordinate the ethnographic efforts of the German navy. The location of this document among Luschan's papers indicates, however, that Luschan was at least partially influenced by Meyer's pamphlet as he attempted to set up his own questionnaires at the turn of the century.

34. On the German annexations in the Pacific Islands, see Stewart Firth, *New Guinea under the Germans*, 7–20.

35. Adolf Bastian to General Museum Administration, 16 December 1884, GStA-PK, I HA, rep. 76 Ve, sect. 15, abt. XI, bd. 6.

36. The prominent work suporting Bismarck's social imperialistic mind-set continues to be Hans-Ulrich Wehler, *Bismarck und der Imperialismus* (Cologne: Kiepenheuer & Witsch, 1969).

37. See, for instance, Woodruff Smith, *Politics*, 164–167.

38. Consult the correspondence contained in GStA-PK, I HA, rep. 76 Kultusministerium, sect. 15, abt. XI, especially bd. 6–7.

39. Kurt Krieger, "Hundert Jahre Museum für Völkerkunde Berlin: Abteilung Afrika," *Baessler Archiv* 21 (1973): 101–140.

40. The negotiations are contained in the following file: GStA-PK, I HA, rep. 76 Ve, sect. 15, abt. XI, bd. 6.

41. Wolfgang Lustig, "'Außer ein paar zerbrochenen Pfeilen nichts zu verteilen . . . ': Ethnographische Sammlungen aus den deutschen Kolonien und ihre Verteilungen an Museen 1889 bis 1914," *Mitteilungen des Museums für Völkerkunde Hamburg n.f.* 18 (1988): 157; Thilenius to Carl Ebermaier, 27 January 1908, MfVH, D 2, 23; compare this view, however, to Cornelia Essner, "Berlins Völkerkunde-Museum in der Kolonialära: Anmerkungen zum Verhältnis von Ethnologie und Kolonialismus in Deutschland," in *Berlin in Geschichte und Gegenwart: Jahrbuch des Landesarchivs Berlin,* ed. Hans Reichhardt (Berlin: Siedler, 1986), 65–94.

42. Schöne to von Goessler, 13 January 1888, GStA-PK, I HA, rep. 76 Ve, sect. 15, abt. XI, bd. 7.

43. See Essner, "Berlins Völkerkunde-Museum," 72–76.

44. Foreign Ministry to Cultural Ministry, 15 January 1888 and 23 March 1888, GStA-PK, I HA, rep. 76 Ve, sect. 15, abt. XI, bd. 7.

45. Between 1889 and 1909 German colonial officers provided 20,521 (1,667 from the German colonies located in the Pacific) artifacts for the Berlin museum. SMB-PK, MV, IB 46/E 1806/09. Considering that this figure did not include artifacts obtained through official expeditions sponsored by the Reich, the extent of the monopoly becomes obvious. This number, for instance, is larger than the entire inventory of some other German medium-sized museums. The museums located in Cologne had roughly 18,500 artifacts in 1906 and Lübeck roughly 15,000 artifacts in 1910.

46. von Goessler to Richard Schöne, 3 August 1889, SMB-PK, MV, IB 46/E 763/90.

47. The committee issued registers in 1889, 1892, 1897, 1899, 1901, and 1903. See BArchL, R 1001/6130. Advertisement of the registers occurred in the major colonial periodicals. See, for instance, "verschiedene Mitteilungen" in *Deutsches Kolonialblatt* 8 (1902): 77, and 10 (1904): 99.

48. See *Deutsches Kolonialblatt* 1891 (2): x, and 1896 (7): 669.

49. Adolf Bastian to Prussian General Museum Administration, 24 September 1894, SMB-PK, MV, IB 46/E 1208/94.

50. Schnee, *Deutsches Kolonial-Lexikon,* s.v. "Botanische Sammlungen," by George Volkens; s.v. "Zoologische Sammlungen," by Matsche.

51. See Michael O'Hanlon, "Introduction," in *Hunting the Gatherers: Collectors, Agents, and Agency in Melanesia, 1870s–1930s,* ed. Michael O'Hanlon and Robert L. Welsch (New York: Berghahn Books, 2000), 27–28.

52. Karl Möbius, in *Drittes Verzeichniss der abgebbaren Doubletten der aus den deutschen Schutzgebieten eingegangenen wissenschaftlichen Sendungen* (Berlin: General Museum Administration, 1897), BarchL, R 1001/6130.

53. Unlike Bastian's case, there is little information available on Felix von Luschan in print. Fritz Graebner, "Adolf Bastian 100. Geburtstag," *Ethnologica* 3 (1926): ix–xii, tried to claim Bastian's work for the diffusionist camp in German ethnology, while commenting negatively on Luschan's abilities as an ethnological curator. According to Graebner, Bastian made a mistake by selecting Luschan for the African and Oceanic collection, since

Luschan had no clear expertise in this regard. Graebner's attacks on Luschan were more personal than intellectual in nature, but given Graebner's intellectual standing in the history of German ethnology, his statement has become somewhat paradigmatic in the English-speaking literature. Koepping, *Bastian*, 23, and Woodruff Smith, *Politics*, 104, 112, are just two examples of the unquestioning adoption of Graebner's assessment. For a more positive assessment of Luschan, see Benoit Massin's fascinating article "From Virchow to Fischer: Physical Anthropology and 'Modern Race Theories' in Wilhelmine Germany," in *Volksgeist as Method and Ethic: Essays on Boasian Ethnography and the German Anthropological Tradition*, ed. George Stocking (Madison: University of Wisconsin Press, 1996), 79–154. Biographical accounts of Luschan's life in German have, unfortunately, remained piecemeal. Fritz Kiffner's attempt to write a biography of Luschan was cut short by Kiffner's passing in 1969. For an all-too-brief overview of his ethnographic legacy, see Walter Rusch, "Der Beitrag Felix von Luschans für die Ethnographie," *Ethnographische und Archäologische Zeitschrift* 27 (1986): 439–453. John David Smith is currently working on an intellectual biography of Luschan and his role in defining issues of "race." For a stimulating preview consult his article "W. E. B. Du Bois, Felix von Luschan, and Racial Reform at the *Fin de Siècle*," *Amerikastudien* 47 (2002): 23–38.

54. Felix von Luschan's curriculum vitae, 15 November 1888, SB-PK, LuP, case 18; Felix von Luschan to General Museum Administration, (date not legible) 1891, SB-PK, LuP, case 21.

55. Robert Proctor, "From *Anthropologie to Rassenkunde* in the German Anthropological Tradition," in *Bones, Bodies, Behavior: Essays on Biological Anthropology*, ed. George Stocking (Madison: University of Wisconsin Press, 1988), 141.

56. See Graebner, "Adolf Bastian," ix–xii.

57. See, for instance, the correspondence housed in SMB-PK, MV, IB Australien.

CHAPTER 2: COMMERCIALIZING THE ETHNOGRAPHIC FRONTIER

1. Mary Helms, *Ulysses' Sail: An Ethnographic Odyssey of Power, Knowledge, and Geographical Distance* (Princeton: Princeton University Press, 1988).

2. Michel Foucault, *The Order of Things: An Archaeology of the Human Sciences* (New York: Vintage, 1970). See also Susan Pearce, *On Collecting: An Investigation into Collecting in the European Tradition* (New York: Routledge, 1995), 111.

3. Bernard Smith, *European Vision and the South Pacific, 1780–1850* (Oxford: Oxford University Press, 1960), 88.

4. Stephen Greenblatt, *Marvelous Possessions: The Wonder of the New World* (Chicago: University of Chicago Press, 1991).

5. Nicholas Thomas, *In Oceania*, 106–119.

6. Pearce, *On Collecting*, 114–119.

7. Werner Muensterberger, *Collecting: An Unruly Passion* (Princeton: Princeton University Press, 1994), 183–184.

8. Pratt, *Imperial Eyes*, chapter 2.

9. Adrienne Kaeppler, *"Artificial Curiosities": Being an Exposition of Native Manufacture Collected on Three Pacific Voyages of Captain James Cook, R. N.* (Honolulu: Bishop Museum Press, 1975), 37–38.

10. Nicholas Thomas, *In Oceania*, 116. See also his "Licensed Curiosity: Cook's Pacific Voyages," in *The Cultures of Collecting*, ed. John Elsner and Roger Cardinal (Cambridge: Harvard University Press, 1994), 116–136.

11. Kaeppler, *"Artificial Curiosities,"* 37–39; Bernard Smith, *European Vision*, 87–92; Nicholas Thomas, *Entangled Objects*, 128.

12. Ruth P. Dawson, "Collecting with Cook: The Forsters and Their Artifact Sale," *Hawaiian Journal of History* 8 (1979): 5–16.

13. Hilke Thode-Aurora, "Die Famile Umlauff und ihre Firmen—Ethnographika-Händler in Hamburg," *Mitteilungen aus dem Museum für Völkerkunde Hamburg* 22 (1992), 143–158. The inventory books of the Umlauff company are available at the Museum für Völkerkunde Hamburg. They all carry the same last entry: "Destroyed through enemy fire 24/25 July 1943." On the shifting value of ethnographica on the international market, consult Penny, *Objects of Culture*, chapter 2.

14. For an overview of German commercial activity in the Pacific, consult Stewart Firth, "German Firms," 3–25; Peter Hempenstall, "Survey of German Commercial Activities in the South Pacific from 1880 to 1914, with Special Reference to Samoa and New Guinea" (B.A. hon. thesis, University of Queensland, 1969).

15. Bastian's attempts are best exposed in the correspondence files of the Berlin Ethnological Museum (SMB-PK, MV, IB Australien).

16. Nicholas Thomas, *Entangled Objects*, 162–167.

17. See, for instance, Jacobi, *Fünfzig Jahre*, 27.

18. Emil Stephan to Felix von Luschan, 14 November 1907, SB-PK, LuP, Stephan file.

19. There is a vast literature on the commercial activity of the Godeffroy Company. For details of the ethnographic activity of this company, consult Susanne Fülleborn, "Die ethnographischen Unternehmungen des Hamburger Handelshauses Godeffroy" (M.A. thesis, University of Hamburg, 1985); H. Glenn Penny "Science and the Marketplace: The Creation and Contentious Sale of the Museum Godeffroy," *Journal of the Pacific Arts Association* 21/22 (2000): 7–22 and his *Objects of Culture*, 54–58.

20. Johann Kubary to Adolf Bastian, 3 January 1884, SMB-PK, MV, IB 11/n.n.

21. Obituaries for Godeffroy are very telling; see, for instance, Rudolf Virchow in *Zeitschrift für Ethnologie* 17 (1885): 53–54.

22. Fülleborn, "Die ethnographischen Unternehmungen," 169–172.

23. The Umlauff Company introduced earlier in this chapter serves as an example.

24. The many Godeffroy duplicates acquired by other German museums illustrate that the response was good, however.

25. J. D. E. Schmeltz and Rudolf Krause, *Die ethnographisch-anthropologische Abteilung des Museum Godeffroy in Hamburg: Ein Beitrag zur Kunde der Südsee-Völker* (Hamburg: Friedrichsen & Co., 1880).

26. See, for instance, Richard Andree, "Zur Ethnographie der Südsee," *Globus* 39 (1881): 60–63.

27. J. D. E. Schmeltz, "Rudolf Virchow, in Memoriam," *Internationales Archiv für Ethnographie* 16 (1904): xii.

28. Godeffroy expected one million marks for the collection. The great majority of it, however, went to Leipzig for 95,000 marks. Hamburg acquired about seven hundred ethnological objects along with all the natural specimens for about 50,000 marks. See Jürgen Zwernemann, *Hundert Jahre Hamburgisches Museum für Völkerkunde* (Hamburg: Museum für Völkerkunde, 1980), 18.

29. The lengthy diplomatic and financial struggle over the Godeffroy heritage is best delineated in Penny, "Science and the Marketplace."

30. This is particularly evident in a report on the Godeffroy collection forwarded by

Adolf Bastian to his Prussian Museum Administration, 20 November 1882, SMB-PK, MV, IB 5/E 2229/82.

31. von Goessler to Richard Schöne, 16 October 1885, SMB-PK, MV, IB Litt C/E 216/85.

32. Adolf von Hansemann to Richard Schöne, 3 January 1886, SMB-PK, MV, IB Litt C/E 13/86.

33. Records of the negotiations between the Prussian Museum Administration and Hansemann's New Guinea Company are housed in the Berlin Ethnological Museum, SMB-PK, MV, IB Litt C. The final agreement is filed under "Agreement New Guinea Company and General Museum Administration," 3 August 1886, SMB-PK, MV, IB Litt C/E 179/86.

34. Otto Finsch, *Systematische Uebersicht der Ergebnisse seiner Reisen und schriftstellerischen Thätigkeit (1859–1899)* (Berlin: R. Friedländer & Sohn, 1899), 27–28.

35. The financial disaster of the Godeffroy Company left both of these individuals scrambling for new employers. Kubary tried, unsuccessfully, to start a career as an ethnologist in Germany. Parkinson, affiliated himself with his sister-in-law, the famed "Queen" Emma, to start a new commercial venture. On Kubary's troubled life see, for instance, George W. Stocking Jr., "Maclay, Kubary, Malinowski: Archetypes from a Dreamtime of Anthropology," in *Colonial Situations*, ed. George Stocking, 25–32. Parkinson's ethnographic career has received increased attention in recent years; see Jim Specht, "Traders and Collectors: Richard Parkinson and Family in the Bismarck Archipelago, P.N.G.," *Journal of the Pacific Arts Association* 21/22 (2000): 23–38. His main ethnographic contribution, *Dreißig Jahre in der Südsee: Land und Leute, Sitten und Gebräuche im Bismarckarchipel und auf den deutschen Salomoninseln* (Stuttgart: Stecker & Schröder, 1907), is now available in translation as *Thirty Years in the South Seas: Land and People, Customs and Traditions in the Bismarck Archipelago and on the German Solomon Islands* (Honolulu: University of Hawai'i Press, 2000).

36. Richard Parkinson to Felix von Luschan, 25 April 1893, SB-PK, LuP, Parkinson file.

37. See paragraph five of the "Allgemeine Bestimmungen über die Satzung der Beamten im Schutzgebiet der Neu Guinea Compagnie," Adolf von Hansemann, 10 May 1891, BArchL, R 1001, file 2410.

38. Bernard Hagen, *Unter den Papua: Über Land und Leute, Thier und Pflanzenwelt in Kaiser-Wilhelmsland* (Wiesbaden: C. W. Kreidel, 1899), 79–80.

39. A search of the New Guinea Company files at the Museum for Natural History in Berlin (MNZHUB, SII—Neu Guinea Compagnie) neither confirmed nor disproved the account supplied in Stephan von Kotze, *Südsee-Erinnerungen* (Berlin: Dom Verlag, 1925), 22–26. There is some evidence to support Kotze's version in Bernard Hagen, *Unter den Papua*, 80, as well as in Richard Neuhauss, *Deutsch Neuguinea*, vol. 1 (Berlin: Reimer, 1911), 467, although the perpetrator is never mentioned by name. On a more personal note, I wonder if similar processes also occurred in the realm of ethnography. Besides numerous complaints against the company's collection restrictions, my inquiry into German museum files did not reveal a comparable case of obvious forgery.

40. Records of the planning of the Kaiser Wilhelmsland and Ramu expeditions are contained in BArchL, R 1001, files 2367–2369.

41. Albert Hahl to Wilhelm Solf (Secretary for Colonial Affairs), 4 July 1913, BArchL, R 1001, file 2369.

42. See file IB Litt C, vol. 2, in SMB-PK, MV.

43. Felix von Luschan to Karl von Linden (ethnographic collector in Stuttgart), 18 April 1899, LiMSt, Luschan file.

44. Felix von Luschan, *Beiträge zur Völkerkunde der deutschen Schutzgebiete* (Berlin: Reimer, 1897), 65.

45. See, for instance, Maximilian Krieger, "Das Kolonial-Museum zu Berlin," *Deutsche Kolonialzeitung* 12 (1899): 390–391; BArchL R 1001/6360.

46. Felix von Luschan to Admiral Strauch, 29 November 1897, SMB-PK, MV, IB 46/E 1427/97.

47. Luschan, *Beiträge,* i.

48. Felix von Luschan to Regent of Mecklenburg Duke Johann Albrecht, 10 November 1897, SMB-PK, MV, IB 46/E 1340/97; J. F. G. Umlauff to Felix von Luschan, 17 August 1899, SB-PK, LuP, J. F. G. Umlauff file.

49. Patricia Seed explores the role of naming in her *Ceremonies of Possession in Europe's Conquest of the New World, 1492–1640* (Cambridge: Cambridge University Press, 1995). Colonial naming during the so-called New Imperialism awaits similar treatment.

50. Felix von Luschan, "Zur geographischen Nomenclatur der Südsee," *Zeitschrift für Ethnologie* 30 (1898): 390–397; C. H. Read "Confusion in Geographical Names," *Journal of the Anthropological Institute of Great Britain and Ireland* n.s. 1 (1899): 330; Hans Seidel, Review of Luschan's *Beiträge zur Völkerkunde der deutschen Schutzgebiete, Deutsches Kolonialblatt* 11 (1898): 150; Felix von Luschan to Karl von Linden, 29 April 1901, LiMSt, Luschan file.

51. Peter Sack, *Land between Two Laws: Early European Land Acquisition in New Guinea* (Canberra: Australian National University Press, 1973), 65–66, 74–75.

52. Max Buchner to Felix von Luschan, 29 November 1894, SB-PK, LuP, Buchner file. Max Buchner was the custodian of the ethnographic collections in Munich. Fellow ethnologists labeled him "difficult."

53. Arthur Baessler, *Südsee-Bilder* (Berlin: A. Asher & Co., 1895), 45–106; *Neue Südsee-Bilder* (Berlin: Reimer, 1900), 279–286, 358–362; Parkinson to A. B. Meyer, 20 December 1897, MfVD, accession file Richard Parkinson.

54. The expert was none other than Georg Thilenius (to Karl von Linden, 3 March 1899, LiMSt, Thilenius file), who later became director of the Hamburg Ethnological Museum.

55. The *Deutsche Handel- und Plantagengesellschaft* was a consortium of German commercial and financial companies. Its aim was to prevent the sale of the landholdings of the Godeffroy company after its financial collapse in 1879.

56. Felix von Luschan wanted to select some artifacts from the collection for the Berlin museum. However, a rich patron bought the whole collection and donated it to Hellwig's native city of Halle. See the exchange between Luschan and Hellwig in SMB-PK, MV, IB Australien/E 202/99.

57. The British captain Carteret christened the islets "Maty" (Wuvulu) and "Durour" (Aua). John Hawkesworth, while compiling Carteret's travels for the British Admiralty, misspelled one of them, named after the secretary of the Royal Society, as "Matty." The early literature on these islands continued to carry this name until more detailed study of the eighteenth-century literature discovered the mistake. See Paul Hambruch, "Wuvulu und Aua (Maty- und Durour-Inseln) auf Grund der Sammlung F. E. Hellwig aus den Jahren 1902 bis 1904," *Mitteilungen aus dem Museum für Völkerkunde zu Hamburg* 2 (1908): 7; an abbreviated version of this section can be found in Rainer Buschmann," Exploring Tensions in Material Culture: Commercialising Ethnography in German New Guinea, 1870–1904," in *Hunting the Gatherers: Ethnographic Collectors, Agents and Agency in Melanesia, 1870s–1930s,* ed. Michael O'Hanlon and Robert L. Welch (New York: Berghahn Books, 2000), 67–68.

58. Hambruch, "Wuvulu und Aua," 8.

59. Felix von Luschan, "Zur Ethnographie der Matty-Insel," *Internationales Archiv für Ethnographie* 8 (1895): 41–56.

60. On the contemporary debate over the Melanesia, Micronesia, Polynesia division, see, for instance, Nicholas Thomas, "Force of Ethnography," for a more compromising position see Donald Denoon et al., eds. *The Cambridge History of the Pacific Islanders* (Cambridge: Cambridge University Press, 1997), 6–9.

61. Augustin Krämer, "Vuvulu und Aua (Maty und Durour Insel)," *Globus* 93 (1908): 254–257, argued for the term "Para-Micronesia" to designate what he called Micronesian outliers in Melanesia. Another term seems to be "Western Islands" (of the Bismarck Archipelago), which include besides Wuvulu and Aua the island of Manu; the Ninigo group; as well as the Kaniet, Sae, and Luf islands. The term "Para-Micronesia" is still very much in usage for these islands, although recent research suggests that earlier literature overemphasized Micronesian affinity. Henning Hohnschopp, "Untersuchung zum Para-Mikronesien-Problem unter besonderer Berücksichtigung der Wuvulu- und Aua-Kultur," *Arbeiten aus dem Institut für Völkerkunde der Universität zu Göttingen* 7 (1973), argues against the term "Para-Micronesia," suggesting instead a "Wuvulu-Aua cultural complex."

62. Felix von Luschan, "Zur Ethnographie"; and his "Über die Matty-Insel," *Verhandlungen der Gesellschaft für Erdkunde zu Berlin* 22 (1895): 442–449.

63. Richard Parkinson to Felix von Luschan, 8 March 1898, SMB-PK, MV, IB Australien/E 224/98.

64. Andersen's report as recorded by F. E. Hellwig can be found in Hambruch, "Wuvulu und Aua," 9–10.

65. Hambruch, "Wuvulu und Aua," 8–9; Stewart Firth, *New Guinea under the Germans,* 114; Felix von Luschan, "R. Parkinsons Beobachtungen auf Bóbolo und Hún (Matty und Durour)," *Globus* 78 (1900): 72.

66. Eduard Hernsheim to Felix von Luschan, 26 August 1896, SMB-PK, MV, IB Australien/E 1018/96; Felix von Luschan note to file, 3 October 1896, SMB-PK, MV, IB Australien/E 1131/96.

67. Felix von Luschan to Naval Admiral Knorr, 7 August 1897, SMB-PK, MV, IB 48/E 1009/97.

68. J. F. G. Umlauff to Felix von Luschan, 19 February 1897, SMB-PK, MV, IB Australien/E 181/97.

69. Luschan, *Beiträge,* 71.

70. Emil Stephan to Felix von Luschan, 14 November 1907, SB-PK, LuP, Stephan file.

71. On Hellwig's collection see SMB-PK, MV, IB Australien/E 1056/98 and E 202/99.

72. Hellwig spent the months of November and December 1902 on Wuvulu, returning for an extended stay in 1904. Between August and December 1903 Hellwig stayed on Aua. See Hambruch, "Wuvulu and Aua," 10–11. Hellwig's diaries, often mentioned in Hambruch's publication, could not be located in the Hamburg Ethnological Museum.

73. Henrika Kuklick, "After Ishmael: The Fieldwork Tradition and Its Future," in *Anthropological Locations: Boundaries and Grounds of a Field Science,* ed. Akhil Gupta and James Ferguson (Berkeley: University of California Press, 1997), 49.

74. James Clifford, *Routes: Travel and Translation in the Late Twentieth Century* (Cambridge: Harvard University Press, 1997), 64–72.

75. Akhil Gupta and James Ferguson, "Discipline and Practice: 'The Field' as Site, Method, and Location in Anthropology," in *Anthropological Locations: Boundaries and Grounds*

of a Field Science, ed. Akhil Gupta and James Ferguson (Berkeley: University of California Press, 1997), 1–46.

76. Stocking, "Philanthropoids and Vanishing Cultures," 178–211.

77. A deal between Thiel and Wahlen guaranteed Hellwig unlimited access to Wuvulu and Aua as well as all ethnographic objects collected by Wahlen's traders. Although extensive research did not uncover any official document between Thiel and Wahlen, the conditions are reproduced in an undated excerpt from a letter of Heinrich Richard Wahlen to Captain Jaspers (HMS *Möwe*), SMB-PK, MV, IB 48/E 1289/03.

78. F. E. Hellwig to Albert Hahl, 17 November 1903, BArchL, R 1001/2990; excerpt reprinted in *Deutsches Kolonialblatt* 15 (1903): 242–243.

79. The Imperial Navy, for instance, notified Luschan in Berlin (SMB-PK, MV, IB 48/E 1534/02); Cologne received word through Küppers-Loosen, who collected for its museum in German New Guinea (RJMfV, 1905/21); Governor Hahl notified the Colonial Division within the German Foreign Office (2 January 1904, BArchL, R1001/2990); Hahl also communicated the importance of the collection to Karl von Linden in Stuttgart (23 June 1904, LiMSt, Hahl file).

80. See, for instance, RJMfV, 1905/21; HAStK, bst. 614, no. 449; SMB-PK, MV, IB Australien/E 1536/04.

81. Georg Thilenius to Richard Parkinson, 6 February 1906, MfVH, SS 1, vol. 1. Thilenius claimed to have convinced the directors of the Hernsheim Company to sell this collection during an extensive dinner; see Georg Thilenius to Felix von Luschan, 26 November 1904, SMB-PK, MV, IB Australien/E 1724/04. On Hamburg's financing of the purchase of Hellwig's collection see Zwernemann, *Hundert Jahre,* 37–38.

82. Georg Küppers-Loosen to Willi Foy, undated letter, RJMfV, 1904/27.

83. Luschan's proposal, dated 15 December 1903, is held in BArchL, R 1001/2372. An additional file housed at the Berlin Ethnological Museum on the planning of this expedition was among personal files that I could not access.

84. Luschan's proposal, 15 December 1903.

85. Wilhelm Waldeyer to Felix von Luschan, 25 February 1904, SB-PK, LuP, Waldeyer file.

86. Felix von Luschan to Prussian Museum Administration, 8 May 1906, BArchL, R 1001/2372.

CHAPTER 3: LOSING THE MONOPOLY

1. Britain's punitive expedition into the heart of the Benin empire returned with many examples of that society's elaborate bronze works. International collectors scrambled to acquire the bronzes, preventing their centralization in England. On the significance of these collections for British museums, see Annie Coombes, *Reinventing Africa: Museums, Material Culture, and Popular Imagination in Late Victorian and Edwardian England* (New Haven: Yale University Press, 1994); for German museums see Penny, *Objects of Culture,* 71–79, and Stefan Eisenhofer, "Felix von Luschan and Early German Language Studies of Benin," *African Arts* 30 (1997): 62–67.

2. Felix von Luschan, *Anleitung für ethnographische Beobachtungen und Sammlungen in Afrika und Ozeanien,* 3rd ed. (Berlin: Museum für Völkerkunde, 1904), 5–6.

3. This practice was hardly Luschan's original idea. By 1874 the British Association of the Advancement of Science had published its *Notes and Queries on Anthropology, for the Use of Travelers and Residents in Uncivilized Lands.* As the title suggests, the evolutionary schemes of

Edward Burnett Tylor heavily influenced it. See George Stocking, *After Tylor*, 15–16; on the publication's impact on the development of British anthropology, see James Urry, "Notes and Queries on Anthropology and the Development of Field Methods in British Anthropology 1870–1920," *Proceedings of the Royal Anthropological Institute for 1972*, 45–57.

4. Felix von Luschan to Albert Hahl, 19 June 1897, SMB-PK, MV, IB 46/E 760/97.

5. Felix von Luschan, *Anleitungen für ethnographische Beobachtungen und Sammlungen* (Berlin: Museum für Völkerkunde, 1899).

6. Luschan, *Anleitungen;* translation by Markus Schindlbeck in "The Art of Collecting: Interactions between Collectors and the People They Visit," *Zeitschrift für Ethnologie* 118 (1993): 61. Unfortunately for Luschan, other museum directors advised their client collectors in the German colonies simply to follow Luschan's instructions when assembling collections for Stuttgart. See Karl Möbius to Prussian Ministry of Culture, 23 December 1904, SMB-PK, MV, IB 46/E 1977/04.

7. Kurt Krieger, "Hundert Jahre," 109.

8. Westphal-Hellbusch, "Zur Geschichte," 29; on the Berlin museum chaos see also Penny, *Objects of Culture,* chapter 5.

9. H. Glenn Penny, "Bastian's Museum," 102–110.

10. Kurt Krieger, "Hundert Jahre," 110.

11. Martin Heydrich, "Ethnologica—Neue Folge," *Ethnologica* n.f. 1 (1959): iii–v, provides a helpful and concise overview of the publications emerging from German museums between 1875 and 1919.

12. Ibid., iii.

13. Felix von Luschan, "Ziele und Wege der Völkerkunde in den deutschen Schutzgebieten," in *Verhandlungen des Deutschen Kolonialkongresses 1902 zu Berlin am 10. und 11. Oktober 1902* (Berlin: Reimer, 1903), 163–171. Luschan's article touches upon the need for monographs on individual societies to allow for comparative studies among the German colonies but fails to provide a clear explanation of the cooperation between ethnology and colonial praxis.

14. Jürgen Hagel and Wolfgang Meckelein, *Hundert Jahre Gesellschaft für Erd- und Völkerkunde zu Stuttgart e. V. (Württembergischer Verein für Handelsgeographie)* (Stuttgart: Gesellschaft für Erd- und Völkerkunde, 1982), 8–35; Friedrich Kussmaul, "Linden-Museum Stuttgart, Staatliches Museum für Völkerkunde Rückblick–Umschau–Ausblick," *Tribus* 24 (1975), 18–27.

15. Felix von Luschan to Karl von Linden, 2 November 1892, LiMSt, Luschan file; Felix von Luschan to General Museum Administration, 21 September 1892, SMB-PK, MV, IB 46/E 880/92.

16. Linden to Luschan, 16 July 1895, LiMSt, Luschan file. Linden alludes to the situation in Germany before the unification of 1871 where each small state was protective of its own interests with little regard for larger German issues. The situation of the southern German states is particularly telling. While they supported the Prussian campaign against France in 1870–1871, most southern states (Württemberg included) had opposed Prussia in the war of 1866, fighting instead on the Austrian side. The Bundesrat Resolution of 1889 also intensified fault lines among German museums and fueled localism within the German empire. There is a growing body of literature on localism in the German empire. See, for instance, Alon Corfino, *The Nation as Local Metaphor: Württemberg, Imperial Germany, and National Memory, 1871–1918* (Chapel Hill: University of North Carolina Press, 1997); Celia Applegate, *A Nation of Provincials: The German Idea of Heimat* (Berkeley: University of California Press, 1990); H. Glenn Penny, "Fashioning Local Identities in the Age of Nation-

Building: Museums, Cosmopolitan Traditions, and Intra-German Competition," *German History* 17 (1999): 488–504, and also his "Municipal Displays: Civic Self-Promotion and the Development of German Ethnographic Museums, 1870–1914," *Social Anthropology* 6 (1998): 157–168.

17. Karl von Linden to Karl Weule, 25 July 1903, LiMSt, Leipzig Museum file.

18. A few examples from German New Guinea illustrate the point. Resident trader Max Thiel felt that an order would highlight his important standing in the Bismarck Archipelago's colonial community. Colonial administrator Franz Boluminski argued that, unlike his counterparts in Africa, colonial authorities and family members alike often overlooked his accomplishments. For Boluminski, orders derived from collecting activity could raise awareness. Franz Hefele, an officer for the Hamburg-America Line, reported to Linden that only decorated officers could greet high-ranking European dignitaries. See LiMSt, Boluminski, Thiel, and Hefele files.

19. Alastair Thompson, "Honours Uneven: Decorations, the State and Bourgeois Society in Imperial Germany," *Past and Present* 144 (1994): 171–173; see also Zimmerman, *Anthropology and Antihumanism*, 168–169.

20. Gustav Ackermann, *Ordensbuch sämtlicher in Europa blühender und erloschener Orden und Ehrenzeichen* (Annaberg: Rudolph & Dieterici, 1855; reprint, Leipzig: Reprint Verlag, not dated), 56–57 (page reference is to reprint edition); Maximilian Gritzner, *Handbuch der Ritter und Verdienstorden aller Kulturstaaten der Welt innerhalb des XIX. Jahrhunderts* (Leipzig: Weber, 1893), 596–599.

21. On the Prussian nomination system see Thompson, "Honours Uneven," 174–184.

22. Emil Stephan to Felix von Luschan, 14 November 1907, SB-PK, LuP, Stephan papers; see also Edgar Walden expedition diary entry, 3 December 1907; SMB-PK, MV, IB 71/E 888/08. Max Thiel, resident administrator of the Hernsheim Company, was featured in Chapter 2.

23. Felix von Luschan to Karl von Linden, 29 April 1901, LiMSt, Luschan file.

24. The following exchange between Felix von Luschan and Karl von Linden derives from LiMSt, Luschan file.

25. Felix von Luschan to Willi Foy, 25 January 1906, HAStK, bstd. 614, no. 356.

26. Georg Thilenius, *Das Hamburgische Museum für Völkerkunde* (Berlin: Reimer, 1916), 5–12; Jürgen Zwernemann, *Hundert Jahre*, 3–28.

27. Werner von Melle, *Dreißig Jahre Hamburger Wissenschaft, 1891–1921*, vol. 2 (Hamburg: Broschek & Co., 1923), 504–510.

28. Frank Spencer, ed., *History of Physical Anthropology* (New York: Garland, 1997), s.v. "Archiv für Anthropologie," by Ursula Zängl-Kumpf.

29. MfVH, D 4, 4.

30. Chapter 2 highlighted the importance of this collection in establishing alleged boundaries between Melanesia and Micronesia.

31. Georg Thilenius to Willi Foy, 19 November 1906, original in HAStK, bstd. 614, no. 347; copy in MfVH, MC, 2.

32. Thilenius' *Das Hamburgische Museum* (pp. 16–72) best illustrates his program.

33. Felix von Luschan to Georg Thilenius, 21 June 1906; Thilenius to Luschan, 24 June 1906, SB-PK, LuP, Thilenius file.

34. Georg Thilenius, "Bodes Denkschrift über die Museen in Berlin," *Korrespondenz-Blatt der Deutschen Gesellschaft für Anthropologie, Ethnologie und Urgeschichte* 38 (1907): 38.

35. Georg Thilenius, "Die Hamburger Südsee-Expedition," *Globus* 93 (1908): 337.

36. Hambruch, "Wuvulu und Aua," preface.

37. Thilenius, "Bodes Denkschrift," 38–39. Georg Thilenius to Wilhelm Bode, 13 March 1907, SMB-PK, ZA, BoP, Thilenius file; Georg Thilenius to Wilhelm Bode, 18 March 1907, MfVH, MB 10.

38. Woodruff Smith, *Politics and the Sciences of Culture*, chapter 8; Penny, "Bastian's Museum," 110–124.

39. See, for instance, Friedrich Ratzel, *Völkerkunde*, 3 vols. (Leipzig: Bibliographisches Institut, 1885–1888), and *Anthropo-Geographie, oder Grundzüge der Anwendung der Erdkunde auf die Geschichte* (Stuttgart: Engelhorn, 1882).

40. Bernard Ankermann, "Kulturkreise und Kulturschichten in Afrika," *Zeitschrift für Ethnologie* 37 (1905): 54–84; Fritz Graebner, "Kulturkreise und Kulturschichten in Ozeanien," *Zeitschrift für Ethnologie* 37 (1905): 23–53.

41. Leo Frobenius, "Kulturformen Oceaniens," *Petermanns Geographische Mitteilungen* 46 (1900): 204–215, 234–238, 262–271.

42. The new approach was not without its problems, but this is not the place to critique the *Kulturkreis* paradigm since others have taken this up in some detail. For instance, see Robert Lowie, *The History of Ethnological Theory* (New York: Farrar & Rinehart, 1937), 177–195; Woodruff Smith, *Politics and the Sciences of Culture*, 156–161; Zimmerman, *Anthropology and Antihumanism*, chapter 9.

43. Fritz Graebner to General Museum Administration, 30 November 1906, SB-PK, LuP, Graebner file.

44. Felix von Luschan to General Museum Administration, 9 December 1906, SB-PK, LuP, Graebner file.

45. Lothar Pützstück, *"Symphonie in Moll": Julius Lips und die Kölner Völkerkunde* (Pfaffenweiler: Centaurus, 1995), 29–36.

46. Closer to home, Foy critiqued Weule's attempt to arrange artifacts in evolutionary sequences as a subjective endeavor, which did not follow careful cultural historical study. Consult Foy's response to Karl Weule's "Die praktischen Aufgaben der Völkermuseen auf Grund Leipziger Erfahrungen," *Korrespondenzblatt Archiv für Anthropologie* 41 (1910): 78.

47. William Foy, "Das städtische Rautenstrauch-Joest-Museum für Völkerkunde in Cöln," *Ethnologica* 1 (1909): 28.

48. Ibid., 25–68; Georg Thilenius, "Die Eröffnung des Rautenstrauch-Joest-Museums in Köln," *Korrespondenz-Blatt der Deutschen Gesellschaft für Anthropologie, Ethnologie und Urgeschichte* 37 (1907): 6–10.

49. Foy, "Das städtische Museum," 50.

50. Fritz Graebner, "Der Neubau des Berliner Museums für Völkerkunde und andere praktische Zeitfragen der Ethnologie," *Globus* 94 (1908): 213.

51. More entrenched criticism of Luschan's administration of the African and Oceanic division can be found in a number of letters directed at the Prussian Museum Administration: Fritz Graebner to General Prussian Museum Adminstration, 30 November 1906, SB-PK, LuP, Graebner file; Fritz Graebner to Wilhelm Bode, 8 October and 21 November 1908, SMB-PK, ZA, BoP, Graebner file.

52. See, for instance, LiMSt, Leipzig file.

53. Karl Weule, "Die nächsten Aufgaben und Ziele des Leipziger Völkermuseums," *Jahrbuch des Städtischen Museums für Völkerkunde zu Leipzig* 3 (1910): 151–174; a shorter version is reproduced in Weule, "Die praktischen Aufgaben."

54. Karl Weule to Felix von Luschan, 30 December 1904, SB-PK, LuP, Weule file.

55. Giselher Blesse, "Internationale Beziehungen des Museums für Völkerkunde

Leipzig, 1869–1945," *Mitteilungen aus dem Museum für Völkerkunde Leipzig* 50 (1985): 42–43; Völkerkunde Museum, "Die Entwicklung des Museums für Völkerkunde 1901 bis 1905," *Jahrbuch des Städtischen Museums für Völkerkunde* 1 (1907): 17–18; Weule's correspondence with collectors residing in the German colonies is housed in the Leipzig museum, MfVL, KB 1903/04. On Weule's colonial connections see also Fritz Krause, "Dem Andenken Karl Weules," *Jahrbuch des Städtischen Museums für Völkerkunde* 9 (1922–1925): 13–17. On the history of the Leipzig museum, see H. Glenn Penny, " 'Beati possedentes:' Die Aneignung materieller Kultur und die Anschaffungspolitik des Leipziger Völkerkundemuseums," *Comparativ: Leiziger Beiträge zur Universalgeschichte und vergleichender Gesellschaftsforschung* 10 (2000): 68–103.

56. Felix von Luschan to Colonial Division of the German Foreign Office, 3 January 1903, SMB-PK, MV, IB 46/E 6/03; The Federal Council's Resolution was reprinted in the April edition of the *Deutsches Kolonialblatt* 14 (1903): 169–170; see Kurt Krieger, "Hundert Jahre," 114.

57. Karl von Linden to Albert Hahl, 21 July 1903, LiMSt, Hahl file.

58. Karl von Linden to Albert Hahl, 21 July 1903, 14 October 1903, LiMSt, Hahl file; Karl von Linden to Arno Senfft, 27 February 1905, LiMSt, Senfft file.

59. Weule's outgoing letters to the collectors illustrate this state of affairs, MfVL, KB 1903/04.

60. Two copies of this letter (Karl Weule to Karl Hagen 1 February 1904, MfVH, D 2, 23, and Karl Weule to Hugo Schauinsland, 1 February 1904, ÜMB, Kopierbuch, 1904) prove that Weule's appeal reached Hamburg and Bremen. Weule's letters to Brunswick, Munich, and Stuttgart can be found in MfVL, KB 1904.

61. Karl Weule to Karl von Linden, 17 February 1904, MfVL, KB 1903/04.

62. Giselher Blesse, "Hans Meyer und Leipzig: Vom Wirken einer Familie und 'Ihrer' Stadt," in Museum für Völkerkunde Leipzig, *Kunst aus Benin: Afrikanische Meisterwerke aus der Sammlung Hans Meier* (Leipzig: Museum für Völkerkunde, 1994), 109–134.

63. Felix von Luschan to Karl Möbius, 25 July 1904, SMB-PK, MV, IB 46/E 1064/04.

64. Georg Thilenius to Carl Ebermeier, 27 January 1908, MfVH, D 2, 23.

65. Bode, *Mein Leben*, vol. 2, 175.

66. Felix von Luschan to Wilhelm Bode, 16 November 1906, SB-PK, LuP, Bode file. Realizing the forcefulness of his response, Luschan asked Bode to exclude this letter from the official museum correspondence files. See also Felix von Luschan, "Ziele und Wege eines modernen Museums für Völkerkunde," *Globus* 88 (1905): 238–240.

67. Wilhelm Bode, "Denkschrift betreffend Erweiterungs- und Neubauten bei den Königlichen Museen in Berlin," February 1907, reprinted in Bode, *Mein Leben*, vol. 2, 244–248.

68. Thilenius, "Bodes Denkschrift," 38–39.

69. Georg Thilenius to Wilhelm Bode, 13 March 1907, SMB-PK, ZA, BoP, Thilenius file; 18 March 1907, MfVH, MB 10; Felix von Luschan to Georg Thilenius, 17 May 1907, MfVH, MB 10.

70. See, for instance, Herbert Abel, *Vom Raritätenkabinet zum Bremer Überseemuseum: Die Geschichte einer hanseatischen Sammlung aus Übersee* (Bremen: Röver, 1970), 121–125; Hugo H. Schauinsland, *Unterwegs in Übersee: Aus den Reisetagebüchern und Dokumenten des früheren Direktors des Bremer Übersee-Museums*, ed. Anne Dünzelmann (Bremen: H. M. Hauschild, 1999), 39, 151, 154; on German New Guinea consult 170–187.

71. Georg Küppers-Loosen to Willi Foy, undated letter (1904), RStJMV, 1904/27.

72. Peter Sack and Dymphna Clark, eds., *German New Guinea: The Annual Reports* (Canberra: Australian National University Press, 1979), 84.

73. Between 1898 and 1905 the Berlin museum forwarded one or two thousand marks to support the navy's collection effort. See SMB-PK, MV, IB 48; see also, Emil Stephan, *Südseekunst: Beiträge zur Kunst des Bismarckarchipels und zur Urgeschichte der Kunst überhaupt* (Berlin: Reimer, 1907), iv.

74. This included the spoils of the second Ramu expedition, which amounted to one thousand objects. SMB-PK, MV, IB 46/E 888/00.

75. As Figure 2 indicates, in 1902 Georg Fritz sent 472 artifacts to Berlin, or 61 percent of the total volume (742 artifacts) from the German Pacific. SMB-PK, MV, IB 46/E 1390/03.

76. In 1904 the *Möwe*'s collection amounted to 69 percent (six hundred artifacts) of the entire volume from the German Pacific. SMB-PK, MV, IB 46/E 1861/05.

77. See the listing of artifacts supplied by colonial officials to the museum, SMB-PK, MV, IB 46/E1806/09.

78. See, SMB-PK, MV, IB 46/ E 1870/06, and E 1858/07. See the flow of decorations from Stuttgart to the territory in Table 1 to gain an idea where most of the artifacts were heading.

79. Karl von Linden to Albert Hahl, 21 July 1903, LiMSt, Hahl file.

80. Felix von Luschan, commentary, 10 December 1904, SMB-PK, MV, IB 46/E 1977/04.

81. While this correspondence is missing from the Stuttgart files, Luschan's and Linden's exchange is kept in the colonial files of the Berlin museum, SMB-PK, MV, IB 46/E 161/05. Linden went to great lengths to attest his innocence in connection with Meyer's initiative. Luschan would have none of it. He even wrote in the margin of one of Linden's letters: "Professor Hans Meyer has communicated to me that it was Count Linden who initiated the motion. Ergo!!!" Karl von Linden to Felix von Luschan, 17 February 1905, SMB-PK, MV, IB 46/E 161/05.

82. Luschan's proposal borrowed heavily from the dictum *cuius regio, eius religio* issued by the Diet of Augsburg (1555). This Diet tried to settle the differences between adherents to the Roman Catholic and Protestant faiths by allowing each ruler to determine the religious confession of his realm. See, for instance, Steven Ozment, *Protestants: The Birth of a Revolution* (New York: Image Books, 1991), 71.

83. Luschan to Thilenius, 27 March 1905, MfVH, MB 10; Luschan to Foy, 25 January and 11 October 1906, HAStK, bstd. 614, no. 356.

84. Michael O'Hanlon, "Introduction," 12–15.

85. Felix von Luschan to Prussian Museum Administration, 15 and 18 August 1909, SMB-PK, MV, IB 46/E 1806/09; Felix von Luschan to Prussian Museum Administration, 8 October 1909, SMB-PK, MV, IB 46/E 2120/09.

86. See Arthur Baessler, 6 May 1903 in GStA-PK, I HA, rep. 89, no. 20489, bd 3.

87. Marion Melk-Koch, *Auf der Suche nach der menschlichen Gesellschaft: Richard Thurnwald* (Berlin: Reimer, 1989), 52–54.

CHAPTER 4: RESTRUCTURING ETHNOLOGY AND IMPERIALISM

1. The Term "Expedition Age" is borrowed from Robert Welsch, ed., *An American Anthropologist in Melanesia: A. B. Lewis and the Joseph N. Field South Pacific Expedition 1909–1913*, vol. 1 (Honolulu: University of Hawai'i Press, 1998).

2. The Herero-Nama War and the Maji-Maji uprising have received ample consideration in the historical literature. For Southwest Africa see, for instance; Helmut Bley, *South-West Africa under German Rule, 1894–1914* (Evanston: Northwestern University Press, 1971), 149–169. The wider African context of these uprisings is explored in Lewis Gann and Peter Duignan, *The Rulers of German Africa, 1884–1914* (Stanford: Stanford University Press, 1977), 118–125. Woodruff Smith, *The German Colonial Empire* (Chapel Hill: University of North Carolina Press, 1978), chapters 4 and 7, relates these crises to the context of German colonialism; for the anthropological context, see Andrew Zimmerman, *Anthropology and Antihumanism*, 244–245.

3. The tenure of the New Guinea Company (1885–1899) serves as a case in point.

4. Jake Spidle, "The German Colonial Civil Service: Organization, Selection, Training," Ph.D. dissertation, Stanford University, 1972, chapter 2; Werner Schiefel, *Bernhard Dernburg 1865–1937: Kolonialpolitiker und Bankier im wilhelminischen Deutschland* (Zürich: Atlantis, 1981), 30–37.

5. Schiefel, *Dernburg*, 37–45; Woodruff Smith, *Colonial Empire*, chapter 12; Spidle, "Colonial Civil Service," chapter 5.

6. Woodruff Smith, *Politics and the Sciences of Culture*, 170–171.

7. Bernhard Dernburg, quoted in Winfred Baumgart, "German Imperialism in Historical Perspective," in *Germans in the Tropics: Essays on German Colonial History*, ed. Arthur Knoll and Lewis Gann (New York: Greenwood Press, 1987), 159.

8. Schiefel, *Bernhard Dernburg*, remains the most detailed study of Dernburg's colonial legacy to date.

9. The relationship between Dernburg and Luschan was cool at best, and no extensive correspondence between the two is recorded in Luschan's papers. The Bode file, SB-PK, LuP, contains Dernburg's card. Written on the back is a short note dated 23 October 1906: "Will gladly entertain Professor von Luschan."

10. Karl von Linden to Franz Boluminski, 7 August 1907, LiMSt, Boluminski file. Count Linden complained that Dernburg cared little about the colonial distribution issue.

11. An in-depth political study of the Colonial Council can be found in Pogge von Strandmann, "The Kolonialrat, Its Significance and Influence on German Politics," Ph.D. dissertation, Oxford University, 1970.

12. Hans Meyer, "Die geographischen Grundlagen und Aufgaben in der wirtschaftlichen Erforschung unserer Schutzgebiete," in *Verhandlungen des Deutschen Kolonialkongresses 1902 zu Berlin am 10. und 11. Oktober 1902* (Berlin: Reimer, 1903), 73.

13. Hans Meyer, "Übersicht über die Ergebnisse der Expeditionen der Landeskundlichen Kommission des Reichskolonialamt," in *Verhandlungen des Deutschen Kolonialkongresses 1910 zu Berlin am 6., 7. und 8. Oktober 1910* (Berlin: Reimer, 1910), 5–10.

14. Karl Weule, "Der Stand der ethnographischen Forschung in unseren Kolonien," in *Verhandlungen des Deutschen Kolonialkongresses 1905 zu Berlin am 5., 6. und 7. Oktober 1905* (Berlin: Reimer, 1906), 17–25.

15. By 1908 Hans Meyer had strengthened his ties to the Leipzig Ethnological Museum after assuming chairperson responsibilities of the newly founded Society for Ethnology in Leipzig. "Die Entwicklung des Museums 1908," *Jahrbuch des Städtischen Museums für Völkerkunde zu Leipzig* 3 (1910): 11.

16. Weule, "Stand der ethnographischen Forschung," 20–21.

17. On the negotiations following this expedition, see BArchL, R 1001, 2373.

18. Felix von Luschan to General Museum Administration, 12 April 1907, SMB-PK, MV, IB 46/E 691/07.

19. Melle, *Dreißig Jahre,* vol. 1, 362–406.

20. Hans Fischer, *Die Hamburger Südsee-Expedition: Über Ethnographie und Kolonialismus* (Frankfurt: Syndikat, 1981); chapters 2 and 3 provide in-depth analysis of the colonial and scientific aims of Thilenius' expedition.

21. The information is condensed from Melle's memoirs, *Dreißig Jahre,* vol 2, chapter 4.

22. Georg Thilenius, in a proposal dated from 1904, cited in Fischer, *Hamburger Südsee-Expedition,* 38; Thilenius, who had traveled extensively in the Pacific around the turn of the century, was quite familiar with the labor questions in German New Guinea. An article he had written served as the basis for his proposal: Georg Thilenius, "Die Arbeiterfrage in der Südsee," *Globus* 77 (1900): 69–72.

23. Albert Hahl to Georg Thilenius, 6 December 1904, MfVH, SSE 1.

24. See the correspondence in BArchL, R 1001, 2372.

25. Letter containing proposal from Georg Thilenius to Max Warburg and Adolph Woermann, 4 March 1905, BArchL, R 1001, 2372.

26. Georg Thilenius to Max Warburg and Adolph Woermann, 4 March 1905; see also Fischer, *Hamburger Südsee-Expedition,* 49; Melle, *Dreißig Jahre,* 511–517.

27. See, for instance, Anita Herle and Sandra Rouse, eds., *Cambridge and the Torres Strait: Centenary Essays on the 1898 Anthropological Expedition* (New York: Cambridge University Press, 1998).

28. Unfortunately, Thilenius forgot to extend the same provisions to the crew of the chartered steamer *Peiho.* This brought about a competition over artifacts between scientists and crew members, some of them collecting specifically for Karl von Linden to cure their "chest pains" for Württemberg decorations. Intensive negotiations with officials of Hamburg-America Line, the original owners of the *Peiho* finally solved this impasse. See, for instance, LiMSt, Heferle file and MfVH, SSE 3.

29. See, for instance, Georg Thilenius to Wilhelm Müller, 21 December 1908, MfVH, SSE 6.6.

30. The scientific aims of Thilenius' expedition are described in his "Die Hamburger Schiffsexpedition," vol. 1, 21–40. See also Fischer, *Hamburger Südsee-Expedition,* chapters 2 and 3.

31. Alfred Beit to Wilhelm Bode, 19 May 1906, SMB-PK, ZA, BoP, Beit file.

32. Georg Thilenius to Felix von Luschan, 20 September 1906, SB-PK, LuP, Thilenius file.

33. See BArchL, R 1001, 2372.

34. Felix von Luschan to Wilhelm Bode, undated letter 1908, SB-PK, LuP, Bode file.

35. For instance, see Walter Hubatch, *Die Ära Tirpitz: Studien zur deutschen Marinepolitik, 1890–1918* (Göttingen: Musterschmidt, 1955); also Ivo Nikolai Lambi, *The Navy and German Power Politics, 1862–1914* (Boston: Allen & Unwin, 1984).

36. Harding Ganz, "The German Navy in the Far East and the Pacific: The Seizure of Kiautschou and After," in *Germany in the Pacific and the Far East, 1870–1914,* ed. John Moses and Paul Kennedy (St. Lucia: University of Queensland Press, 1977), 115–136.

37. Felix von Luschan to Admiral Alfred von Tirpitz, 5 November 1898, SMB-PK, MV, IB 48/E 1223; see also "Kleine Nachrichten," *Globus* 75 (1899): 18.

38. SMB-PK, MV, IB 48.

39. SMB-PK, MV, IB 48/E 1289/03; Stephan to Luschan, 7 December 1903, SB-PK, LuP, Stephan file.

40. Emil Stephan, "Beiträge zur Psychologie der Bewohner von Neupommern: Nebst

ethnographischen Mitteilungen über die Barriai und über die Insel Hunt (Duror)," *Globus* 88 (1905): 209.

41. See Andrew Zimmerman, *Anthropology and Antihumanism,* chapter 10.

42. Emil Stephan to Felix von Luschan, 14 October 1904, SMB-PK, MV, IB 48/E 17/05.

43. Emil Stephan, *Südseekunst;* Emil Stephan and Fritz Graebner, *Neu Mecklenburg (Bismarck Archipel): Die Küste von Umuddu bis Kap St. Georg: Forschungsergebnisse bei den Vermessungsfahrten von S.M.S. Möwe im Jahre 1904* (Berlin: Reimer, 1907).

44. Fritz Graebner, "Neubau," 215–216; see also his *Methode der Ethnology* (Heidelberg: Carl Winters, 1911), 7–11.

45. Graebner, *Methode,* 9

46. Fritz Graebner, "Vorwort," in Stephan and Graebner, *Neu Mecklenburg.*

47. Felix von Luschan's review of Stephan's *Südseekunst* and Stephan and Graebner's *Neu Mecklenburg* appears in *Zeitschrift für Ethnologie* 39 (1907): 1005. This review also illustrates Luschan's investment in the German navy. Instead of focusing on a thorough review of the works, Luschan emphasizes the supposedly active role of the German navy in the development of the ethnographic frontier in an effort to flatter naval officials into supporting future endeavors of the Berlin museum. Stephan assisted in this task by dedicating his works to the German Admiralty.

48. Fritz Graebner to Felix von Luschan, 29 July 1908, SB-PK, LuP, Stephan file.

49. Graebner, "Neubau," 215.

50. Felix von Luschan to Prussian General Museum Administration, 17 August 1909, SMB-PK, MV, IB Australien, E 1648/09.

51. Felix von Luschan to Otto Schlaginhaufen, 12 August 1908, SMB-PK, MV, IB 71/E 2265/08.

52. Penny, "Bastian's Museum," 102–110.

53. Stephan, *Südseekunst,* 119–132.

54. Straub's review of Stephan's *Südseekunst* highlighted the importance of a German *"Nationalschuld."* See *Deutsche Kolonialzeitung* 16 (1907): 160–161.

55. The negotiations between the Naval Office and German colonial authorities can be found in BArchL, R 1001, 2370.

56. Felix von Luschan to Albert Hahl, 28 January 1908, SMB-PK, MV, IB 71/E 2408/07.

57. Felix von Luschan to Emil Stephan, 28 June 1906; Emil Stephan to Felix von Luschan, 4 July 1906, SMB-PK, MV, IB 71/E 1180/06; Luschan instructed Stephan to insert an additional 40,000 marks to cover publication costs into the Naval Office's budget at a later date. Emil Stephan expedition diary entry, 28 January 1908, SMB-PK, MV, IB 71/E 888/08. Luschan had trouble finding participants for his expedition, eventually settling for Otto Schlaginhaufen from Dresden's museum. Dresden director Arnold Jacobi had been eclipsed by the collection activity of Karl Weule in Leipzig and was all too happy to accept Luschan's offer for participation. For the duration of the expedition, Schlaginhaufen was not able to collect for Dresden, yet he made up for it during his subsequent stay in German New Guinea. This included an important trip up the Sepik River. See SMB-PK, MV, IB 71, and Otto Schlaginhaufen's account, *Muliama: Zwei Jahre unter Südsee-Insulanern* (Zürich: Orell Füssli, 1959).

58. Alfred von Tirpitz to Felix von Luschan 19 March 1907, SMB-PK, MV, IB 71/E 511/07.

59. The research vessel *Planet* replaced the aging *Möwe* in 1906.

60. Bavarian Ministry of Cultural Affairs to Bavarian Ministry for Foreign Affairs, 15 January 1913, BaHStA, Kultusministerium (MK), 19455.

61. Friedrich von Lindequist (Undersecretary of Colonial Affairs) to Saxon Foreign Ministry, 23 July 1909, 11 February 1910, SächHStAD, Außenministerium, 8960.

62. The minutes of this meeting were forwarded to the individual participants; see Bernhard Dernburg to Georg Thilenius, 12 May 1910, MfVH, D 2, 23; see also SMB-PK, MV, IB 46/E 536/10.

63. Among these "second-rate" museums were the institutions located in Bremen and Stuttgart that were actively involved in the ethnographic frontier in German New Guinea.

64. Georg Thilenius' strategies received special attention in Lustig, "Ethnographische Sammlungen," 157–178. Lustig's vantage point remains glued to a specific crucial file (D 2, 23) in the Hamburg museum. I attempt to read Thilenius' plan against the wider backdrop of German ethnological museums in general and Felix von Luschan's alternate plan in particular.

65. Felix von Luschan to Prussian Museum Administration, 15 and 18 August 1909, SMB-PK, MV, IB 46/E 1806/09; Felix von Luschan to Prussian Museum Administration, 8 October 1909, SMB-PK, MV, IB 46/E 2120/09.

66. Felix von Luschan to Lucius Scherman, 10 August 1909, SMB-PK, MV, IB 46/E 1806/09.

67. The fifty-page-long notes on this meeting can be found in both Hamburg and Berlin. An extended summary of these proceedings can be found in Lustig, "Ethnographische Sammlungen," 170–173.

68. Circular issued by Friedrich von Lindequist (German Colonial Office), 25 August 1911, MfVH, D 2.23.

69. Augustin Krämer, "Gouvernmentale Übergriffe in ethnographische Arbeitsgebiete und Mittel zur Abhilfe," *Globus* 96 (1909): 264–266.

70. On the development of the Field Museum and the collection activities of George Amos Dorsey, see Douglas Cole, *Captured Heritage: The Scramble for Northwest Coast Artifacts,* 2nd edition (Norman: University of Oklahoma Press, 1995), 165–176, 212–215; on Dorsey in German New Guinea, see Robert Welsch, *An American Anthropologist,* 21, and his "One Time, One Place, Three Collections: Colonial Processes and the Shaping of Some Museum Collections from German New Guinea," in *Hunting the Gatherers: Ethnographic Collectors, Agents, and Agency in Melanesia,* ed. Michael O'Hanlon and Robert L. Welsch (London: Berghahn Books, 2000), 161–164.

71. See, for instance, George A. Dorsey, "Notes on Museums in Central Europe," *American Anthropologist* 1 (1899): 462–474.

72. See Chapter 2 and also Penny, *Objects of Culture,* 102–106.

73. George Dorsey to F. J. V. Skiff (Director), 22 July 1905, FMNH, Director's file.

74. Dorsey wrote about his adventures in German New Guinea in installments that ran between 18 September and 6 October of 1909 in the *Chicago Daily Tribune.* See also Welsch, *An American Anthropologist,* 21, and his "One Time, One Place, Three Collections," 161–164.

75. The Sepik River is best known for its exuberant examples of Oceanic art. On the early ethnographic exploration of the Sepik River, see Markus Schindlbeck, "The Art of Headhunters: Collection Activity and Recruitment in New Guinea at the Beginning of the Twentieth Century," in *European Impact and Pacific Influence: British and German Colonial Policy in the Pacific Islands and the Indigenous Response,* ed. Hermann Hiery and John MacKenzie (London: Tauris Academic Studies, 1997), 31–43.

76. Albert Hahl to German Colonial Office, 17 January 1909, BArchL, R 1001, 6107.

77. Welsch, "One Time," 165–167.

78. George Dorsey to Fred. Skiff, 8 August 1908, FMNH, Director's file. Dorsey also made arrangements to hire resident collectors Heinrich Voogdt and Richard Parkinson for the Field Museum.

79. Richard Neuhauss to Felix von Luschan, 20 September 1909, SMB-PK, MV, IB 79/E 2592/08; Wilhelm Müller to Georg Thilenius, 9 October 1908, MfVH, SSE 6.6.

80. Unsigned letter excerpt (presumably authored by Hamburg South Sea Expedition participant Wilhelm Müller) to Albert von LeCoq, 14 June 1909, SMB-PK, MV, IB Australien/E 1684/09.

81. Richard Neuhauss to Felix von Luschan, 20 September 1909, SMB-PK, MV, IB 79/E 2591/09; see also Neuhauss, "Brief des Hrn. R. Neuhauss aus Neu-Guinea—Sissanu (nahe der holländischen Grenze) 1 September 1909," *Zeitschrift für Ethnologie* 41 (1909): 962–963.

82. Felix von Luschan to Richard Neuhauss, 7 January 1910, SMB-PK, MV, IB 79/E 2591/09.

83. Albert Hahl to Felix von Luschan, 9 November 1909, SB-PK, LuP, Hahl file. Luschan and others overestimated the capabilities of the Field Museum of Natural History. The museum never organized a large-scale expedition to German New Guinea but dispatched a lone researcher to the area. Despite operating alone, the museum's representative Albert B. Lewis assembled an astonishing, well-determined collection from German New Guinea. Lewis' diary is expertly analyzed in Welsch, *An American Anthropologist,* vol. 1.

84. Georg Thilenius to Carl Ebermaier (German Colonial Office), 27 January 1908, MfVH, D 2, 23.

85. The best illustration of Bode's involvement against Luschan can be found in a letter from Alexander von Danckelman to Felix von Luschan, 14 January 1917, SB-PK, LuP, Danckelman file.

86. Gerd Koch, "Hundert Jahre Museum für Völkerkunde: Abteilung Südsee," *Baessler Archiv* 21 (1973): 146–147.

87. August Eichhorn to Wilhelm Bode, 25 March 1914, SMB-PK, ZA, BoP, Eichhorn file.

88. Wilhelm Bode to Cultural Ministry, 13 March 1913, SMB-PK, MV, IB 48/E 302/12.

89. Woodruff Smith, *German Colonial Empire.*

90. Friedrich von Lindequist to Wilhelm Bode, 23 January 1911, SMB-PK, ZA, BoP, Lindequist file.

91. Friedrich von Lindequist's proposal dated 22 April 1911. Two copies of this document are available in BaHStA, Außenministerium (MA), 76227; SächHStAD, Außenministerium, 8960.

92. Bavarian Cultural Ministry to Bavarian Foreign Ministry, 6 May 1911, BaHStA, Außenministerium (MA), 76227; Saxon General Museum Administration to Saxon Foreign Ministry, 13 May 1911, SächHStAD, Außenministerium, 8960.

93. Hugo Schauinsland to Mayor Barkhausen, 28 April 1911, ÜMB/D 1911.

94. The correspondence is housed in MfVH, D 2, 32, vol. XIII.

95. Wilhelm Solf to Wilhelm Bode, 8 March 1915, SMB-PK, MV, IB 79a/E 224/15.

96. See SMB-PK, MV, IB 79a. The First World War prevented any large-scale publi-

cation of the expedition's results. On the planning of the expedition and Richard Thurnwald's participation in the same, see Melk-Koch, *Richard Thurnwald*, 161–165.

97. Woodruff Smith, *German Colonial Empire*, 215–219.

98. German Colonial Office to Prussian Foreign Office, 7 February 1912, SMB-PK, IB 46/E 302/12.

99. Bavarian Ministry of Culture to Bavarian Foreign Ministry, 15 January 1913, BaHStA, Kultusministerium, 19455.

100. Augustin Krämer diary entry, 20 January 1913, LiMSt, vol. 21; Augustin Krämer to German Museums, 27 January 1913, MfVL, file Verein deutscher Museen für Völkerkunde.

101. Augustin Krämer, "Museumsverbände und ihre Zwecke," *Korrespondenzblatt der Deutschen Gesellschaft für Anthropologie, Ethnologie und Urgeschichte* 44 (1913): 33–35.

102. Detailed information is housed in Hamburg: MfVH, D 6, 1; Leipzig: MfVL, file Verein deutscher Museen für Völkerkunde; Berlin: SMB-PK, ZA, XVII; and Bremen: ÜMB/A/V 3.

103. Solf's proposal dated 23 December 1913 and the reactions to this letter are housed in SMB-PK, MV, IB 46/E 54/14.

104. Wilhelm Solf to Karl Weule (Chairperson of the Society for German Ethnological Museums), 9 April 1914, MfVH, D 2, 23.

105. Karl Weule to Museum Society Members, 18 May 1914, file Verein deutscher Museen für Völkerkunde; Georg Thilenius to Karl Weule, 19 May 1914, MfVH, D 2, 23.

106. Karl Weule to Willi Foy, 18 July 1914, MfVL, file Verein deutscher Museen für Völkerkunde.

107. Augustin Krämer to Felix von Luschan, 22 October 1914, SB-PK, LuP, Krämer file.

108. A lone testimony to the attempts to settle the distribution issue is a file in the German Colonial Archive (BArchL, R 1001) numbered 6130: Compilation of Catalogs of the Scientific Collections Arriving from the German Colonies. A folder with this designation exists, but it contains no documents.

CHAPTER 5: ALBERT HAHL AND THE COLONIZATION OF THE ETHNOGRAPHIC FRONTIER

1. Peter Biskup, "Dr. Albert Hahl—Sketch of a German Colonial Official," *Australian Journal of Politics and History* 14 (1968): 343–344; and Sack, *Land between Two Laws*, 93–95.

2. See, for instance, Helmut Cristmann, Peter Hempenstall, and Dirk Ballendorf, *Die Karolinen-Inseln in deutscher Zeit: Eine kolonialgeschichtliche Fallstudie* (Münster: Lit Verlag, 1991), 9–13; the diplomatic tangles are best illustrated in Richard Brown, "The German Acquisition of the Caroline Islands, 1898–1899," in *Germany in the Pacific and Far East, 1870–1914*, ed. John Moses and Paul Kennedy (St. Lucia: University of Queensland Press, 1977), 137–155.

3. The diplomatic negotiations surrounding the partition of the Samoan Islands are best explained in Paul Kennedy's *The Samoan Tangle: A Study in Anglo-German-American Relations, 1878–1900* (St. Lucia: University of Queensland Press, 1974), chapter 5.

4. On Bruno Mencke, the fate of his collections, and the wider German museological context, see Rainer Buschmann, "The Ethnographic Frontier in German New Guinea (1870–1914) (Ph.D. dissertation, University of Hawaiʻi , 1999), 157–162.

5. Krämer, "Gouvernmentale Übergriffe," 264–266.

6. Refer, for instance, to Karl von Linden to Albert Hahl, 13 May, 21 July, and 14 October 1903, LiMSt, Hahl file.

7. Hahl, cited in Emil Stephan to Felix von Luschan, 14 November 1907, SB-PK, LuP, Stephan file.

8. Almost five hundred artifacts arrived at the Stuttgart museum via Albert Hahl; see LiMSt, Hahl file. Civic pride again played a crucial role. Although a native of Bavaria, Linden appealed to Hahl's Württemberg ancestry on his father's side in order to gain the governor's patronage.

9. Albert Hahl to Karl von Linden, 7 June 1905, LiMSt, Hahl file.

10. Albert Hahl to Karl Weule, 1 March 1910, MfVL, accession file 1909, no. 104.

11. On Hahl's financial troubles see Stewart Firth, *New Guinea under the Germans*, 72–73.

12. Albert Hahl to Heinrich Schnee, 2 October 1901, GStA-PK, I HA, SchP. Schnee was a high-ranking colonial official in German New Guinea and Samoa before becoming a main advisor to Bernhard Dernburg in the newly created Colonial Office.

13. Albert Hahl to Heinrich Schnee, 13 May 1908, GStA-PK, I HA, SchP.

14. Quote from Albert Hahl to Karl von Linden, 20 January 1903, LiMSt, Hahl file; see also Franz Boluminski to Karl von Linden, 16 April 1903, LiMSt, Boluminski file.

15. Karl von Linden to Wilhelm Wostrack, 25 November 1904, LiMSt, Wostrack file.

16. Emil Stephan to Felix von Luschan, 29 February 1908, SMB-PK, MV, IB 71/E 1136/08.

17. Edgar Walden, expedition diary entry, 3 December 1907, SMB-PK, MV, IB 71/E 888/08.

18. Albert Hahl to Karl von Linden, 18 November 1907, LiMSt, Hahl file.

19. Karl von Linden to Albert Hahl, 8 January 1908, LiMSt, Hahl file.

20. Karl von Linden to Albert Hahl, 31 March 1908, LiMSt, Hahl file.

21. Albert Hahl to Heinrich Schnee, 13 March 1908, GStA-PK I HA, SchP.

22. Two important biographies dealing with Albert Hahl's impact on German New Guinea are Peter Biskup, "Dr. Albert Hahl," 342–357; and Stewart Firth, "Albert Hahl: Governor of New Guinea," in *Papua New Guinea Portraits: The Expatriate Experience*, ed. James Griffin, 28–47 (Canberra: Australian National University Press, 1978).

23. Albert Hahl, "Über die Rechtsanschauungen der Eingeborenen eines Theils der Blanchebucht und des Inneren der Gazellenhalbinsel," *Nachrichten über Kaiser Wilhelmsland* 13 (1897): 68–85; see also Biskup, "Dr. Albert Hahl," 350–351.

24. For a review of Hahl's ideas on establishing local authority figures, see Stewart Firth, *New Guinea under the Germans*, 74–75; contrast that with Hiery, *Das Deutsche Reich*, 115–120.

25. Stewart Firth, "Albert Hahl," 32, and Hempenstall, "The Neglected Empire: The Superstructure of the German Colonial State in German Melanesia," in *Germans in the Tropics: Essays in German Colonial History*, ed. A. Knoll and L. Gann (New York: Greenwood Press, 1987), 100–102, illustrate some failed examples of Hahl's system.

26. Albert Hahl, "Mitteilungen über Sitte und rechtliche Verhältnisse auf Ponape," *Ethnologisches Notizblatt* 2 (1901): 1–13; and "Feste und Tänze der Eingeborenen von Ponape," *Ethnologisches Notizblatt* 3 (1902): 95–102.

27. Quote from Albert Hahl to German Colonial Office, 27 October 1911, BArchL, R 1001, 2994. Hahl was referring to the renditions of early ethnographer Otto Finsch and local resident ethnographer Richard Parkinson.

28. On the controversies concerning German rule in New Guinea, see the introduction to this work and Hiery, *Das deutsche Reich* as well as his *Neglected War.*

29. On the German anthropologists' bias toward material culture, see, for instance, Suzanne Marchand, "The Rhetoric of Artifacts and the Decline of Classical Humanism: The Case of Josef Strzygowski," *History and Theory* 33 (1994): 106–130.

30. Albert Hahl to Karl von Linden, 9 September 1900, LiMSt, Albert Hahl file.

31. Albert Hahl to Felix von Luschan, 10 March 1900, SB-PK, LuP, Albert Hahl file; Albert Hahl to Karl Weule, 1 November 1907, MfVL, acquisition file 1907/113.

32. Albert Hahl to Karl Weule, 1 November 1907, MfVL, acquisition file 1907/113.

33. The literature on "fieldwork" in the Anglo-American tradition is vast. See, for instance, the collection by Gupta and Ferguson, *Anthropological Locations;* Stocking, *After Tylor,* especially chapter 6; also his *The Ethnographer's Magic,* 12–59. For a good introduction to the German status of fieldwork, see Andrew Zimmerman, *Anthropology and Antihumanism,* chapter 10.

34. Malinowski, *Argonauts of the Western Pacific,* 11.

35. Stewart Firth, "Colonial Administration and the Invention of the Native," in *The Cambridge History of Pacific Islanders,* ed. Donald Denoon et al. (Cambridge: Cambridge University Press, 1997), 262.

36. The term "investigative modality" is borrowed from Bernard Cohn, *Colonialism and Its Forms of Knowledge: The British in India* (Cambridge: Cambridge University Press, 1996), 3–15. The Foucauldian marriage between anthropological science and colonial execution of power is best described by Ernst Sarfert, directorial assistant and curator of the Oceanic and Indonesian division of the Leipzig museum: "To collect [vital ethnographic information] a trained gaze is needed to penetrate the most remote corners of the natives' bags and living-quarters and to understand native life in all its facets." Schnee, *Deutsches Kolonial-Lexikon,* vol. 3, s.v. "Sammeln, ethnographisches."

37. Stewart Firth, "Labour in German New Guinea," in *Papua New Guinea: A Century of Colonial Impact (1884–1984),* ed. Sione Latukefu (Port Moresby: National Research Institute, 1989), 179–202.

38. See for instance Doug Munro and Stewart Firth, "Company Strategies—Colonial Policies," in *Labour in the South Pacific,* ed. Clive Moore, Jacqueline Leckie, and Doug Munro (Townsville: James Cook University Press, 1990), 5–7.

39. Albert Hahl to Georg Thilenius, 6 December 1904, MfVH, SSE 1.

40. Melk-Koch, *Richard Thurnwald,* 89.

41. Ibid., 30–34, 44–49.

42. Ibid., 76–80.

43. For an ethnographic summary of his research, see Richard Thurnwald, "Im Bismarckarchipel und auf den Salomoneninseln, 1906–1909," *Zeitschrift für Ethnologie* 42 (1910): 98–147.

44. Melk-Koch, *Richard Thurnwald,* 80–87.

45. Albert Hahl to Felix von Luschan, 30 October 1908, SB-PK, LuP, Albert Hahl file.

46. Thurnwald's reluctant ethnographic collection policy was tied to his changing outlook on anthropology. For a recent analysis of his collection practices in German New Guinea, see Marion Melk-Koch, "Melanesian Art—or Just Stones and Junk? Richard Thurnwald and the Question of Art in Melanesia," *Pacific Arts* 21/22 (2000): 53–68.

47. Melk-Koch, *Richard Thurnwald,* 131–132.

48. Ibid., 133–143.

49. Richard Thurnwald, "Das Rechtsleben der Eingeborenen der deutschen Südsee-inseln, seine geistigen und wirtschaftlichen Grundlagen: Auf Grund einer im Auftrage des Berliner Museums für Völkerkunde unternommenen Forschungsreise 1906–1909," *Blätter für vergleichende Rechtswissenschaft und Volkswirtschaftslehre* 6 (1910): 3–46.

50. Thurnwald nicknamed this language "Bitchin-English," underscoring the limited applicability of this form of communication. Melk-Koch, *Richard Thurnwald*, 88.

51. Thurnwald, "Das Rechtsleben," 46.

52. See Vicki Lugere, "The Native Mother," in *The Cambridge History of Pacific Islanders*, ed. Donald Denoon et al., 280–287; Margaret Jolly, "Other Mothers: Maternal 'Insouciance' and the depopulation debate in Fiji and Vanuatu, 1890–1930," in *Maternities and Modernities*, ed. K. Ram and M. Jolly (Cambridge: Cambridge University Press, 1998), 183–215.

53. Richard Thurnwald, "Die eingeborenen Arbeitskräfte in Südseeschutzgebiet," *Kolomale Rundschau* 10 (1910): 627.

54. Albert Hahl to Richard Thurnwald, 9 July 1910, cited in Melk-Koch, *Richard Thurnwald*, 135.

55. Melk-Koch, *Richard Thurnwald*, 134–135.

56. Ibid., 162–165.

57. These include the American ventures described in Chapter 4, a researcher sent out by the Bremen museum, supported by the Norddeutscher Lloyd shipping company, and a number of private and semiprivate sponsored endeavors. In other words, the German territory was bristling with researchers. For a good overview of these expeditions, consult Markus Schindlbeck, "Deutsche wissenschaftliche Expeditionen und Forschungen in der Südsee bis 1914," in *Die deutsche Südsee 1884–1914: Ein Handbuch*, ed. Hermann Hiery (Paderborn: F. Schöningh, 2000), 132–155.

58. The transformation of New Ireland during the first decade of the twentieth century is discussed in Rainer Buschmann, "Franz Boluminski and the Wonderland of Carvings: Towards an Ethnography of Collection Activity," *Baessler Archiv* n.f. 44 (1996): 185–210; Louise Lincoln, "Art and Money in New Ireland: History, Economy, and Cultural Production," in *Assemblage of Spirits: Idea and Image in New Ireland*, ed. Louise Lincoln (New York: Georg Braziller Publishing, 1987); and Peter Lomas, "The Early Contact Period in Northern New Ireland (Papua New Guinea): From Wild Frontier to Plantation Economy," *Ethnohistory* 28 (1981): 1–21.

59. Albert Hahl to German Colonial Office (RKA), 23 April 1908, BArchL, R 1001, 2373; Albert Hahl to Felix von Luschan, August 9, 1908, SMB-PK, IB 71/E 2092/08.

60. See, for instance, Cohn, *Colonialism*, chapter 2: "The Command of Language and the Language of Control."

61. See the previous chapter on the planning stages of this expedition.

62. Hahl's opinion is contained in a letter from Emil Stephan to Felix von Luschan, 14 November 1907, SB-PK, LuP, Stephan file.

63. Albert Hahl to Emil Stephan, 26 January 1908, SB-PK, LuP, Hahl file.

64. Felix von Luschan to General Museum Administration, 7 March 1907, SMB-PK, MV, IB 71/E 435/07.

65. Emil Stephan expedition diary entry, 4 September 1907, SMB-PK, MV, IB 71/E 31/08.

66. Emil Stephan to Felix von Luschan, 29 February 1908, SMB-PK, MV, IB 71/E 1136/08.

67. Hans Meyer (Chairman of the Geographical Commission) to German Colonial Office, 16 August 1907, BArchL, R 1001, 2373.

68. Albert Hahl to Karl von Linden, 20 April 1908, LiMSt, Hahl file.

69. Albert Hahl to Heinrich Schnee, 13 March 1908, GStA-PK, SchP.

70. Georg Friederici to Hans Meyer, 18 October and 9 November 1908, BArchL, R 1001, 2373; draft for a presentation on his travels in German New Guinea, 1908–1910, MfVH, Friederici papers.

71. Hermann Singer, "Die Verwendung des Afrikafonds," *Globus* 97 (1910): 110–111.

72. See Emil Stephan expedition diary entry, 28 January 1908, SMB-PK, MV, IB 71/E 888/08; and Georg Friederici, "Das Pidgin-Englisch in Deutsch Neuguinea," *Koloniale Rundschau* 1911 (11): 92–102.

73. Emil Stephan, "Ursachen des Volksrückganges und Vorschläge zu seiner Erhaltung auf Grund von Untersuchungen über die Bevölkerung von Muliama," original in SMB-PK, MV, IB 71/E 995/08.

74. On the competitive aspects of German expeditions, see the previous chapter.

75. Meyer was obviously referring to the centralization of artifacts in Berlin following the Federal Council's resolution of 1889. Felix von Luschan to General Prussian Museum Administration, 19 June 1908, SMB-PK, MV, IB 71/E 1258/08.

76. Felix von Luschan to General Prussian Museum Administration, 26 June 1908, SMB-PK, MV, IB 71/E 1258/08.

77. Their letters are contained in BArchL, R 1001, 2370.

78. Augustin Krämer to Karl von Linden, 17 June 1909, LiMSt, Krämer file. In Krämer's defense, one should point out, however, that he had already agreed to lead the Hamburg expedition's second year through the Micronesian portions of the German colony. There was thus considerable time pressure to bring the venture to a positive conclusion. The naval expedition convinced Krämer, much like Stephan, to terminate his employment with the German navy and to embark on a full-time anthropological career. See Dietrich Schleip, "Ozeanistische Ethnologie und Koloniale Praxis: Das Beispiel Augustin Krämer," M.A. thesis, Tübingen University, 1989.

79. Albert Hahl to Felix von Luschan, 9 November 1909, SB-PK, LuP, Hahl file.

80. Albert Hahl to Felix von Luschan, 9 August 1908, SMB-PK, MV, IB 71/E 2092/08. To guard against criticism from his own administration, Luschan wrote in the margins of the letter: "Without Stephan I would never have sent them to the territory." Luschan actually removed Hahl's most scourging indictments against the naval expedition from the official museum files. The letters can be found in the Hahl file among the Luschan papers in SB-PK. Hahl was even more direct when he shared his opinions of the naval expedition personnel with Krämer, who faithfully recorded Hahl's outburst in his diary. Recalling a conversation with Schlaginhaufen, Hahl repeated his assertion that "what you are researching is common knowledge. You just don't believe us so you send the researchers so they can publish about it." About Edgar Walden, Hahl condescendingly remarked that "he tried to conquer the world, but nothing came of it." August Krämer personal diary, undated entry "Hahlia," LiMSt, vol. 19.

81. Melk-Koch, *Richard Thurnwald*, 162–163.

82. The term "Malinowskian moment" is inspired by James Clifford, *Routes*, 64–69.

83. Edgar Walden to Felix von Luschan, 16 January 1908, SMB-PK, MV, IB 71/E 888/08.

84. Edgar Walden to Felix von Luschan, 18 July 1908, SMB-PK, MV, IB 71/E 1908/08. Walden refers in this passage to Richard Parkinson's classic *Dreißig Jahre in der Südsee*.

85. Wilhelm Müller to Georg Thilenius, 9 October 1908, MfVH, SSE 6, 6.

86. Ibid.

87. See, for instance, Alice L. Conklin, "Civil Society, Science, and Empire in Late Republican France: Foundation of Paris's Museum of Man," *Osiris* 17 (2002): 260, for a general view on the impact of the war on anthropological museological practice.

88. The publication history of the naval expedition will be discussed below.

89. On Edgar Walden's death see SMB-PK, MV, IB 71/E 82/15.

90. Thilenius' keen editorial hand may have eliminated compromising comments in Müller's monograph on Yap.

91. See Melk-Koch, *Richard Thurnwald*, 245–251.

92. Consult, for instance, Rainer F. Buschmann, "Tobi Captured: Converging Ethnographic and Colonial Visions on a Caroline Island," *Isla: A Journal of Micronesia Studies* 4 (1996): 332–336.

93. Counterfactual history is currently fashionable among many prominent practitioners. See, for instance, J. H. Elliott, "*Afterword*, Atlantic History: A Circumnavigation," in *The British Atlantic World: 1500–1800*, ed. David Amitage and M. J. Braddick (New York: Palgrave, 2002), 241–243; Johannes Bullhof, "What If? Modality and History," *History and Theory* 38 (1999): 145–168.

94. Alfred von Tirpitz to Prussian Cultural Ministry, 23 September 1908, SM-PK, MV, IB 71/E 2143/08.

95. SM-PK, MV, IB 71/E 1109/11.

96. Emil Stephan expedition diary entry, 28 January 1908, SM-PK, MV, IB/E 888/08.

97. Malinowki's *Argonauts* is prefaced by an extensive introduction that takes issue with anthropological methodologies.

98. Augustin Krämer, "Über Museums- und Feldmonographen," *Korrespondenz-Blatt der Deutschen Gesellschaft für Anthropologie, Ethnologie und Urgeschichte* 43 (1912): 22–24.

99. Elisabeth Krämer-Bannow, *Bei kunstsinnigen Kannibalen der Südsee: Wanderungen auf Neu-Mecklenburg 1908–1909* (Berlin: Reimer, 1916).

100. Adolf Eichhorn to General Museum Director, 12 December 1916, SMB-PK, MV, IB 71/E 1032/16.

101. A small article based on Walden's notes appeared more than three decades after the conclusion of the expedition: Hans Nevermann, "Totenfeiern und Malagane von Nord-Neumecklenburg: Nach Aufzeichnungen von E. Walden," *Zeitschrift für Ethnologie* 72 (1940): 11–38.

CHAPTER 6: INDIGENOUS REACTIONS

1. See, for instance, David Chappell, "Active Agents vs. Passive Victims: Decolonized Historiography or Problematic Paradigm?" *The Contemporary Pacific* 7 (1995): 303–326.

2. David Hanlon, *Remaking Micronesia: Discourses over Development in a Pacific Territory, 1944–1982* (Honolulu: University of Hawai'i Press, 1998), 13.

3. Douglas, *Across the Great Divide.*

4. Thomas and Losche, *Double Vision,* see also Thomas' *In Oceania.*

5. David Hanlon, "Magellan's Chroniclers? American Anthropology's History in Micronesia," in *American Anthropology in Micronesia: An Assessment,* ed. Robert Kiste and Mac Marshall (Honolulu: University of Hawai'i Press, 1999), 72.

6. Ibid., 72–73.

7. A frequently cited article is William Sturtevant's "Does Anthropology Need Museums?" *Proceedings of the Biological Society of Washington* 82 (1969): 619–650.

8. See Nicholas Thomas, *Entangled Objects;* O'Hanlon and Welsch, *Hunting the Gatherers;* Enid Schildkrout and Curtis Keim, eds., *The Scramble for Art in Central Africa* (New York: Cambridge University Press, 1998); Chris Gosden and Chantal Knowles, *Collecting Colonialism: Material Culture and Colonial Change* (New York: Berg, 2001); Chris Gosden and Chantal Knowles, *Possessing Culture: Museums, Anthropology and German New Guinea* (New York: Berg Publishers, 2006); an interesting starting point is provided by Anna Laura Jones, "Exploding Canons: The Anthropology of Museums," *Annual Review of Anthropology* 22 (1993): 201–220.

9. This line of research is greatly influenced by postcolonial theories; see, for instance, James Clifford, *The Predicament of Culture: Twentieth-Century Ethnography, Literature, and Art* (Cambridge: Harvard University Press, 1988); Sally Price, *Primitive Art in Civilized Places* (Chicago: University of Chicago Press, 1989).

10. See Welsch, "One Time, One Place"; for an extended example of this approach, see also his *American Anthropologist in Melanesia.*

11. Greg Dening, "Possessing Tahiti," *Archaeology in Oceania* 21 (1986): 103–118.

12. Parkinson, *Dreißig Jahre,* xvi.

13. Felix von Luschan's insistence, for instance, that careless collecting, including that of his competitors, would just yield "curiosities" but not "ethnographica" serves as an important case in point. See, for instance, Chapter 4 of this work.

14. Mention of such artifacts can be found throughout museum correspondence and occasionally in publication. The best example of this is Otto Finsch's *Südseearbeiten: Gewerbe- und Kunstfleiss, Tauschmittel und "Geld" der Eingeborenen, auf Grundlag der Rohstoffe und der geographischen Verbreitung* (Hamburg : L. Friedrichsen & Co., 1914).

15. Greg Dening, "Deep Times, Deep Spaces: Civilizing the Sea," in *Sea Changes: Historicizing the Ocean,* ed. Bernhard Klein and Gesa Mackenthun (New York: Routledge, 2004), 13–35.

16. These arguments were elaborated on in Chapter 4.

17. See, for instance, Patrick Vinton Kirch, *The Evolution of Polynesian Chieftainships* (New York: Cambridge University Press, 1984).

18. Epeli Hau'ofa, "Our Sea of Islands," *The Contemporary Pacific* 6 (1994): 148–161; D'Arcy, "Cultural Divisions"; K. R. Howe, *Nature, Culture, and History: The Knowing of Oceania* (Honolulu: University of Hawai'i Press, 2000).

19. Important contributions are Paul D'Arcy, "Connected by the Sea: Towards a Regional History of the Western Caroline Islands," *Journal of Pacific History* 36 (2001): 163–182; Mark L. Berg, "Yapese Politics, Yapese Money, and the *Sewei* Tributary Network before World War I," *Journal of Pacific History* 27 (1992): 150–165.

20. British cartographic designation assigned Wuvulu and Aua the names Matty and Durour, names they carried until they became the subject of an intense ethnographic observation.

21. Hohnschopp, "Untersuchungen zum Para-Mikronesien-Problem" argues, for instance, for the existence of a "Wuvulu and Aua cultural complex" that includes other islands.

22. Luschan, "R. Parkinsons Beobachtungen."

23. Hambruch, "Wuvulu und Aua"; Otto Dempwolff, "Über aussterbende Völker (Die Eingeborenen der 'westlichen Inseln' in Deutsch-Neu-Guinea)" *Zeitschrift für Ethnologie* 36 (1904): 384–415.

24. Hambruch, "Wuvulu und Aua," 23–24; Dempwolff, "Über aussterbende Völker," 411–413.

25. Dempwolff, "Über aussterbende Völker," 408.

26. See, for instance, the correspondence in the Wahlen file, LiMSt; Wahlen's appointment as Norwegian consul was partially attributable to extensive donations to museums in this country.

27. Albert Hahl, *Governor in New Guinea*, ed. and trans. Peter Sack and Dymphna Clark (Canberra: Australian University Press, 1980), 105; Wahlen to Karl von Linden, 15 April 1904, LiMSt, Wahlen file.

28. Stewart Firth, *New Guinea under the Germans*, 114–115; Hambruch, "Wuvulu und Aua," 10–12.

29. Richard Parkison to Felix von Luschan, 6 February 1904, SB-PK, LuP, Parkinson file.

30. Krämer, "Vuvulu und Aua."

31. Dempwolff, "Über aussterbende Völker," 413.

32. Louise Lincoln, "Introduction," 13, and Tibor Bodrogi, "New Ireland Art in Cultural Context," 18, in *Assemblage of the Spirit*, ed. Louise Lincoln.

33. On New Ireland's significance for the colonial economy, see also Chapter 5. Lomas, "Early Contact Period"; Brigitte Derlon, *De mémoire et d'oubli: Anthropologie des objets malaggan de Nouvelle-Irlande* (Paris: CRNS Éditions, 1997), 24–29.

34. See, for instance, Franz Boluminski to Karl Weule, 23 September 1908, MfVL, acquisition file 1913, no. 92; Georg Thilenius to Karl Sapper, 25 June 1908, MfVH, D 2, 27, vol. 3.

35. Karl von Linden to Max Thiel, 27 June 1907, LiMSt, Thiel file.

36. Lincoln, "Art and Money in New Ireland, 41.

37. On the misnomer of "hybridity" see Robin Cohen, *Global Diasporas: An Introduction* (Seattle: University of Washington Press, 1997), 130–131.

38. Malinowski, *Argonauts;* Lamont Lindstrom, *Cargo Cult: Strange Stories of Desire from Melanesia and Beyond* (Honolulu: University of Hawai'i Press, 1993).

39. Susanne Küchler, *Malanggan: Art, Memory, and Sacrifice* (New York: Berg, 2002); see also her influential "Sacrificial Economy and Its Objects: Rethinking Colonial Collecting in Oceania," *Journal of Material Culture* 2 (1997): 39–60; and her "Malangan: Art and Memory in a Melanesian Society," *Man* 22 (1987): 238–255.

40. Paul Hambruch to Ernst Sarfert, 11 October 1913, MfVH, ML 2, vol. iv.

41. Küchler, "Malangan," 239–241.

42. Küchler, *Malanggan,* 1–10.

43. Küchler, "Sacrificial Economy."

44. Emil Stephan to Felix von Luschan, 14 November 1907, SB-PK, LuP.

45. Emil Stephan, *Südseekunst,* 3.

46. Augustin Krämer, *Die Málangane von Tombára* (Munich: Georg Müller, 1925), 77.

47. Klaus Helfrich, *Malaggan 1: Bildwerke von Neuirland* (Berlin: Museum für Völkerkunde, 1973), 19.

48. Ernst Sarfert to Karl Nauer, 25 September 1911, MfVL, KB 1911; on Nauer's role in the ethnographica trade of German New Guinea, see also Rainer Buschmann, "Karl Nauer and the Politics of Collecting Ethnographic Objects in German New Guinea," *Pacific Arts* 21/22 (2000): 93–102.

49. Karl Nauer to Ernst Sarfert, 19 November 1912, MfVL, acquisition file 1913,

no. 19. Nauer was well aware of the liberal decoration bestowal policy of the Stuttgart institution and used this threat to expedite a Saxon decoration.

50. I have explored Boluminski's impact on New Ireland and his role as a collector in detail in Buschmann, "Franz Boluminski and the Wonderland of Carvings."

51. Franz Boluminski to Karl von Linden, 12 June 1907, LiMSt, Boluminksi file.

52. Franz Boluminski to Karl von Linden, 24 November 1906, LiMSt, Boluminski file.

53. Franz Boluminski to Karl Weule, 31 January 1908, MfVL, acquisition file 1908, no. 43.

54. Karl Nauer to Ernst Sarfert, 2 May 1911, MfVL, acquisition file 1911.

55. Albert Hahl to Karl von Linden, 18 January 1902, LiMSt, Hahl file; Max Thiel to Karl von Linden, 4 April 1908, LiMSt, Thiel file.

56. Fülleborn expedition diary entry, 4–10 October 1908, MfVH.

57. Albert Hahl to Heinrich Schnee, 13 March 1908, GStA-PK, SchP.

58. Edgar Walden to Felix von Luschan, 16 January 1908, SMB-PK, MV, IB 71/E 1136/08.

59. This notion is perpetuated in recent literature. Hiery argues in *The Neglected War* that the Germans employed "Melanesian" methods in their pacification of the region (pp. 4–7).

60. Küchler, "Sacrificial Economy," 49–50.

61. Edgar Walden to Felix von Luschan, 16 January 1908, SMB-PK, MV, IB 71/E 1136/08.

62. Hempenstall, "The Neglected Empire," 99; Hiery, *The Neglected War,* 257–258.

CHAPTER 7: THE ETHNOGRAPHIC FRONTIER IN GERMAN POSTCOLONIAL VISIONS

1. As discussed in Chapter 5, among the casualties of the Great War were a number of anthropologists who were leaning toward an intensive exploration of indigenous society.

2. See, for instance, Georg Thilenius to Karl Weule, 29 November 1916, MfVH, D 6, 1.

3. Friedrich Kussmaul, "Linden-Museum Stuttgart, Staatliches Museum für Völkerkunde Rückblick–Umschau–Ausblick," *Tribus* 24 (1975): 18–27.

4. Andrew Evans, "Anthropology at War: Racial Studies of POWs during World War I," in *Worldly Provincialism: German Anthropology in the Age of Empire,* ed. H. Glenn Penny and Matti Bunzl (Ann Arbor: University of Michigan Press, 2003), 198–229. Evans locates in these studies of enemies as "racial others" an important foundation for later Nazi *Rassenkunde.*

5. Michael Burleigh, *The Third Reich: A New History* (New York: Hill and Wang, 2000), 28.

6. Chapter 4 has addressed the artifact distribution issue in detail.

7. For a recent popular history of this colony, consult Adam Hochschild, *King Leopold's Ghost: A Story of Greed, Terror, and Heroism in Colonial Africa* (Boston: Mariner Books, 1999).

8. Karl Weule to Bernard Ankermann, 28 June 1914; Georg Thilenius to Karl Weule, 29 June 1915; Ankermann to Weule, 29 June 1915, MfVL, Verein deutscher Museen für Völkerkunde.

9. Richard Thurnwald, for instance, returned to New Guinea in the 1930s supported by the Rockefeller Foundation; see Melk-Koch, *Richard Thurnwald,* 271.

10. See, for instance, Carol A. Breckenridge and Peter van der Veer, eds., *Oriental-ism and the Postcolonial Predicament: Perspectives on South Asia* (Philadelphia: University of Pennsylvania Press, 1993), and Gyan Prakash, ed., *After Colonialism: Imperial Histories and Postcolonial Displacements* (Princeton: Princeton University Press, 1995).

11. Edward Said, *Orientalism* (New York: Vintage Books, 1978); see also his *Culture and Imperialism* (New York: Vintage Books, 1994).

12. Zantop, *Colonial Fantasies*.

13. Heinrich Schnee, *Die koloniale Schuldlüge* (Munich: Buchverlag der Süddeutschen Monatshefte, 1927), and his English translation, *German Colonization, Past and Future: The Truth about the German Colonies* (London: Allen & Unwin, 1926).

14. Schnee, *Deutsches Kolonial-Lexikon* (Leipzig, 1920), now available at http://www.stub.bildarchiv-dkg.uni-frankfurt.de/Bildprojekt/Lexikon/lexikon.htm.

15. Paul Hambruch, "Neukaledonien," *Südsee-Bote* 2 (1918): 32–33, 52–55; and his "Europa und die Aufteilung der Südsee: Ein geschichtlicher Rückblick," *Südsee-Bote* 2 (1918): 2–6. See also Hans Fischer, *Völkerkunde im Nationalsozialismus: Aspekte der Anpas-sung, Affinität und Behauptung einer wissenschaftlichen Disziplin* (Berlin: Reimer Verlag, 1990), 110.

16. Schnee, *Kolonial-Lexikon*, s.v. "Völkerkunde."

17. Ibid., s.v. "Sammeln von wissenschaftlich wichtigen Gegenständen."

18. Ibid., s.v. "Paramikronesien" and "Polynesische Exklaven."

19. Georg Thilenius, "Plan der Expedition," in *Ergebnisse der Südsee-Expedition 1908–1910*, I, ed. G. Thilenius (Hamburg: Friedrichsen, 1927).

20. The distinction between "field monographs" and "museum monographs" is bor-rowed from Augustin Krämer's "Über Museums- und Feldmonographen."

21. Zimmerman, *Anthropology and Antihumanism*, 235–238.

22. Otto Reche, "Kaiserin Augusta Fluss," in *Ergebnisse der Südsee-Expedition 1908–1910*, II.A, vol. 1, ed. G. Thilenius (Hamburg: Friedrichsen, 1913).

23. Ibid., 2–4.

24. Paul Hambruch, "Nauru," in *Ergebnisse der Südsee-Expedition 1908–1910*, II.B, vol. 1, ed. G. Thilenius (Hamburg: Friedrichsen, 1914).

25. A brief history of the publication process is chronicled in Otto Reche, "Nova Bri-tannia" in *Ergebnisse der Südsee-Expedition 1908–1910*, II.A, vol. 4, ed. G. Thilenius (Ham-burg: Friedrichsen, 1954). This last volume was issued three decades after the first and written by the last surviving expedition member.

26. Indeed, Franz Boas' ethnographies of the Northwest Coast Indians display similar topical organizations. See Ira Jacknis, "The Ethnographic Object and the Object of Ethnog-raphy in the early Career of Franz Boas," in *Volksgeist as Method and Ethic: Essays on Boasian Ethnography and the German Anthropological Tradition*, ed. George Stocking (Madison: Uni-versity of Wisconsin Press, 1996), 185–214.

27. Information from this section is drawn from Buschmann, "Tobi Captured."

28. Peter Hempenstall and Noel Rutherford, *Protest and Dissent in the Colonial Pacific* (Suva: University of the South Pacific Press, 1984), 98–118; see also Hempenstall's, *Pacific Is-landers under German Rule: A Study in the Meaning of Colonial Resistance* (Canberra: Australian National University Press, 1978).

29. Horace Holden, *A Narrative of the Shipwreck, Captivity and Suffering of Horace Holden and Benjamin H. Nute; Who Were Cast Away in the American Ship Mentor, on the Pelew Islands, in the Year 1832* (Boston: Russel, Shattuk, 1836).

30. Buschmann, "Tobi Captured," 325–331.

31. Buse, "Eine Reise nach den südlich von Palau gelegenen Inseln," *Deutsches Kolonialblatt* 21 (1910): 937–938.

32. Stewart Firth,"German Labour Policy in Nauru and Angaur, 1906–1914," *Journal of Pacific History* 13 (1978): 36–52.

33. Buse, "Palau," 937.

34. The best rendition of the Spanish visits to Tahiti remains Bolton Glanvill Corney, *The Quest and Occupation of Tahiti by Emissaries of Spain during the Years 1772–1776*, 3 vols. (London: Hakluyt Society, 1913–1919).

35. Nicholas Thomas, *Cook: The Extraordinary Voyages of Captain James Cook* (New York: Walker & Co., 2003), 334.

36. Ludwig Born, "Ärztlicher Bericht über die Palau-Inseln," BArchL, R 1001, 3004.

37. Ibid.

38. Mark Peattie, *Nan'yo: The Rise and Fall of the Japanese in Micronesia, 1884–1945* (Honolulu: University of Hawaiʻi, 1988), 24–26.

39. Anneliese Eilers,"Westkarolinen: Tobi und Ngulu," in G. Thilenius, ed., *Ergebnisse der Südsee-Expedition 1908–1910*, II.B, vol. 9 (Hamburg: Friedrichsen, 1936), 86–87.

40. Stewart Firth, "German Labour Policy."

41. Peter Black, "The Teachings of Father Marino: Christianity on Tobi Atoll, in *Mission, Church and Sect in Oceania*, ed. J. Boutilier, D. Hughes, and S. Tiffany (Ann Arbor: University of Michigan Press, 1978), 307–354.

42. Wilhelm Winkler, "Eine Reise nach den Inseln Sonsorol, Pur, Melier, und Tobi," *Amtsblatt für das Schutzgebiet Deutsch Neuguineas* 6 (1914): 68–69.

43. Ernst Sarfert,"Vorwort zu Anneliese Eilers Westkarolinen," in *Ergebnisse der Südsee-Expedition 1908–1910*, II.B, vol. 9, ed. G. Thilenius (Hamburg: Friedrichsen, 1936).

44. Hiery, *The Neglected War,* 134.

45. Glenn Peterson, "Hambruch's Colonial Narrative: Pohnpei, German Cultural Theory, and the Hamburg Expedition Ethnography of 1908–1910," *Journal of Pacific History* 42 (2007): 317–330.

46. Paul Hambruch, "Ponape," in *Ergebnisse der Südsee-Expedition 1908–1910*, II.B, vol. 7, ed. G. Thilenius (Hamburg: Friedrichsen, 1932); Paul Hambruch and Anneliese Eilers, "Ponape," in *Ergebnisse der Südsee-Expedition 1908–1910*, II.B, vol. 7, ed. G. Thilenius (Hamburg: Friedrichsen, 1936).

47. David Hanlon, *Upon a Stone Altar: A History of the Island of Pohnpei to 1890* (Honolulu: University of Hawaiʻi Press, 1988), chapters 6 and 7.

48. Petersen, "Hambruch's Colonial Narrative," 327–329.

49. Ibid., 324–326.

CONCLUSION: ANTHROPOLOGY'S GLOBAL HISTORIES IN OCEANIA

1. James Urry, "Making Sense of Diversity and Complexity: The Ethnological Context and Consequences of the Torres Strait Expedition and the Oceanic Phase in British Anthropology, 1890–1935," in *Cambridge and the Torres Strait: Centenary Essays on the 1898 Anthropological Expedition*, ed. Anita Herle and Sandra Rouse (Cambridge: Cambridge University Press, 1998), 201–233. Urry argues that British anthropology started to shift its emphasis to Africa in the fourth decade of the twentieth century. See also Jack Goody, *The Expansive Moment: The Rise of Social Anthropology in Britain and Africa* (New York: Cambridge University Press, 1995).

2. On the interrelationship between British anthropologists and missionaries, con-

sult Diane Langmore, *Missionary Lives: Papua, 1874–1914* (Honolulu: University of Hawai'i Press, 1989), 111–126.

3. Stocking, *After Tylor,* 34–46.

4. Urry, "Making Sense," 202–206.

5. The importance of this expedition is best highlighted in Anita Herle and Sandra Rouse, eds., *Cambridge and the Torres Strait;* see also Stocking, *After Tylor,* 98–115.

6. Stocking, *After Tylor,* 115–123; and his "Ethnographer's Magic," 27–40.

7. Urry, "Making Sense," 210 and 222.

8. Felix von Luschan to Albert Hahl, 8 June 1903, SMB-PK, MV, IB Australien/E 725/03.

9. Stocking, "Ethnographer's Magic," 29–32.

10. Michael W. Young, "The Careless Collector: Malinowski and the Antiquarians," in *Hunting the Gatherers: Ethnographic Collectors, Agents, and Agency in Melanesia, 1870s–1930s,* ed. Michael O' Hanlon and Robert Welsch (New York: Berghahn Books, 2000), 181–202.

11. Nicholas Thomas, "Material Culture and Colonial Power: Ethnographic Collecting and the Establishment of Colonial Rule in Fiji," *Man* 24 (1989): 41–56; and his *Entangled Objects,* 167–175.

12. Michael Quinnell, " 'Before It Has Become Too Late': The Making and Repatriation of Sir William MacGregor's Official Collection from British New Guinea," in *Hunting the Gatherers: Ethnographic Collectors, Agents, and Agency in Melanesia, 1870s–1930s,* ed. Michael O'Hanlon and Robert L. Welsch (New York: Berghahn Books, 2000), 81–102.

13. Henrika Kuklick, *The Savage Within: The Social History of British Anthropology, 1885–1945* (New York: Cambridge University Press, 1991), 44–47; Stocking, *After Tylor,* 372–373, 376–377.

14. Northcote Thomas, "Review of Luschan's *Anleitungen für ethnographische Beobachtungen und Sammlungen in Afrika und Ozeanien,*" *Man* 5 (1905): 47–48. Thomas looms large in the history of British anthropology as one of the first governmental anthropologists working in the African colonies. See Kuklick, *The Savage Within,* 199–201; Stocking, *After Tylor,* 377–378.

15. Coombes, *Reinventing Africa,* 59–60, 110.

16. Hubert Murray to Deakin, 26 March 1906, in Francis West, ed., *Selected Letters of Hubert Murray* (New York: Oxford University Press, 1970), 37.

17. Murray to his brother George, 19 February 1909, in West, *Selected Letters,* 53.

18. Murray to George, 5 October 1914, in West, *Selected Letters,* 83.

19. Bronislaw Malinowski, *A Diary in the Strict Sense of the Term* (Stanford: Stanford University Press, 1967), entry 13 September 1914, 8.

20. Murray to his son Patrick, 2 November 1930, in West, *Selected Letters,* 123.

21. Ian Campbell, "Anthropology and the Professionalization of Colonial Administration in Papua and New Guinea," *Journal of Pacific History* 33 (1998): 69–90; Geoffrey Gray, " 'There Are Many Difficult Problems': Ernst William Pearson Chinnery—Government Anthropologist," *Journal of Pacific History* 38 (2003): 313–330; George Stocking, "Gatekeeper to the Field: E. W. P. Chinnery and Ethnography of the New Guinea Mandate," *History of Anthropology Newsletter* 9 (1982): 3–12; Geoffrey Gray, "Being Honest to My Science: Reo Fortune and J. H. P. Murray, 1927–1930," *Australian Journal of Anthropology* 10 (1999): 56–76. Murray's dealings with British anthropologists also enter the pages of general histories of anthropology; see, for instance, Kuklick, *The Savage Within,* 49; Stocking, *After Tylor,* 385.

22. See, for instance, Robert C. Kiste and Mac Marshall, "American Anthropology in Micronesia, 1941–1997," *Pacific Science* 54 (2000): 265–274, and their edited volume

American Anthropology in Micronesia: An Assessment (Honolulu: University of Hawai'i Press, 1999).

23. See Welsch, *An American Anthropologist in Melanesia,* and his "One Time, One Place."

24. Frequent exchanges between American and German museums are documented in acquisition files. German museums sought to extend their holdings of Native American artifacts, while American museums generally expected African or Pacific artifacts in return.

25. The monographs served as a major source for Irvin Goldman's *Ancient Polynesian Society* (Chicago: University of Chicago Press, 1970). For a celebratory overview of the Bishop Museum's survey of Polynesian cultures, consult Peter H. Buck (Te Rangi Hiroa), *An Introduction to Polynesian Anthropology* (Honolulu: Bishop Museum, 1945). For a far more critical view, see Nicholas Thomas, *Out of Time: History and Evolution in Anthropological Discourse* (New York: Cambridge University Press, 1989), 32–33, 43–49, and 53–55.

26. Margaret Mead, *The Social Organization of Manua* (Honolulu: Bishop Museum Press, 1930).

27. On the German roots of Franz Boas' thought, consult George Stocking, ed., *Volksgeist as Method and Ethic: Essays on Boasian Ethnography and the German Anthropological Tradition* (Madison: University of Wisconsin Press, 1996).

28. On Boas' fieldwork see Ira Jacknis, "The Ethnographic Object." Boas' influence on American anthropology has been chronicled countless times and need not be reiterated here. Some highlights are George Stocking's *Race, Culture, and Evolution: Essays in the History of Anthropology* (New York, 1968); *The Ethnographer's Magic and Other Essays in the History of Anthropology,* especially chapters 2, 3, and 4; and *Delimiting Anthropology: Occasional Essays and Reflections* (Madison: University of Wisconsin Press, 2001), especially chapters 1–4.

29. On the history of the bureau, consult Regna Darnell, "The Development of American Anthropology, 1879–1920: From the Bureau of American Ethnology to Franz Boas" (Ph.D dissertation, University of Pennsylvania, 1969).

30. Regna Darnell, *And Along Came Boas: Continuity and Revolution in Americanist Anthropology* (Philadelphia: John Benjamins, 1998), chapters 1 and 2.

31. Adolf Bastian to General Museum Administration, 16 December 1884, GStA-PK, I HA, rep. 76, Kultusministerium, sect. 15, abt. XI, bd. 5.

32. Robert C. Kiste and Suzanne Falgout, "Anthropology and Micronesia: The Context," in *American Anthropology in Micronesia: An Assessment,* ed. Robert C. Kiste and Mac Marshall (Honolulu: University of Hawai'i Press, 1999), 15–16.

33. Ira Bashkow, "The Dynamics of Rapport in a Colonial Situation: David Schneider's Fieldwork on the Island of Yap," in *Colonial Situations: Essays on the Contextualization of Ethnographic Knowledge,* ed. George Stocking (Madison: University of Wisconsin Press, 1991), 170–242; see also Kiste and Marshall, *American Anthropology.*

34. Nicholas Thomas, *Entangled Objects,* chapter 4.

35. On the importance of periodization in world history research and instruction, see Jerry H. Bentley, "Cross-Cultural Interaction and Periodization in World History," *American Historical Review* 101 (1996): 749–770.

36. O. H. K. Spate, *The Spanish Lake* (Minneapolis: University of Minnesota Press, 1979).

37. Correspondence of the Spanish Ambassador De Masserano, 21 August 1771, AGS, Estado, Legajo 6981. The Treaty of Utrecht ended the war of the Spanish Succession (1713). While Spain and its ally France had important territorial losses (especially Gibraltar for the Spanish), the treaty conceded Spain political and economic hegemony over the Pacific Ocean.

38. Ibid., 11 June 1765, AGS, Legajo 6959.

39. Ibid., 14 June 1776, AGS, Legajo 6994.

40. See, for instance, John Kendrick, *Alejandro Malaspina: Portrait of a Visionary* (Ithaca: McGill-Queen's University Press, 1999).

41. The most complete account of collections on material culture resulting from Cook's voyages is Adrienne L. Kaeppler's *"Artificial Curiosities."*

42. Anthony Pagden, *European Encounters with the New World* (New Haven: Yale University Press, 1993), 21.

43. Harry Liebersohn, "Images of Monarchy: Kamehameha I and the Art of Louis Choris," in *Double Vision: Art Histories and Colonial Histories in the Pacific,* ed. Nicholas Thomas and Diane Losche (New York: Cambridge University Press, 1999), 44–64; and his "Discovering Indigenous Nobility: Tocqueville, Chamisso, and Romantic Travel Writing," *American Historical Review* 99 (1994): 746–766.

44. Ryan, " 'Le Président des Terres Australes.' "

45. Tcherkézoff, "A Long and Unfortunate Voyage"; for broader insights on the development of "race" in the nascent Oceanic ethnography, consult Douglas, "Seaborne Ethnography."

46. Nicholas Thomas, "The Force of Ethnography," 31.

47. Nicholas Thomas, *Entangled Objects,* 151–162.

48. Helen Gardner, "Gathering for God: George Brown and the Christian Economy in the Collection of Artifacts," in *Hunting the Gatherers: Ethnographic Collectors, Agents and Agency in Melanesia, 1870s–1930s,* ed. Michael O' Hanlon and Robert L. Welsch (New York: Berghahn Books, 2000), 35–54.

49. Stocking, *After Tylor,* 34–44.

50. Nicholas Thomas, *Entangled Objects,* 162–167.

51. Nicholas Thomas, *Colonialism's Culture: Anthropology, Travel, and Government* (Princeton: Princeton University Press, 1994), reminds us not to merge missionary and commercial agendas into a frequently postulated imperial monolith.

52. A recent popular account of this expedition is Nathaniel Philbrick, *Sea of Glory: America's Voyage of Discovery, the U.S. Exploring Expedition, 1838–1842* (New York: Viking, 2003).

53. Schnee, *Deutsches Kolonial-Lexikon,* s.v. "Kolonialmuseen."

54. William Churchill, *The Polynesian Wanderings,* Carnegie Institution of Washington Publication 134 (Washington, D.C., 1911).

55. Georg Thilenius, *Ethnologische Ergebnisse aus Melanesien,* vol. 1 (Halle: E. Karras 1902).

56. Stocking, After Tylor, 341. Raymond Firth, *We the Tikopia: A Sociological Study of Kinship in Primitive Polynesia* (London: Allen and Unwin, 1957 [orig. 1936]), remains an anthropological classic. Less concerned about delineating boundaries, Firth provides a sympathetic account of a society whose members take on individual rather than abstract traits.

57. Patrick Kirch, "The Polynesian Outliers," *Journal of Pacific History* 19 (1984): 224–238.

58. Stocking, *After Tylor,* 352–360.

59. A good example, besides Chapter 6, is Douglas, "Seaborn Ethnography," which employs Aboriginal Australians as a synecdoche in her exploration of the formation of European "natural history" (p. 4).

60. Hau'ofa, "Our Sea of Islands," 160.

Bibliography

ARCHIVAL SOURCES

Berlin
Bundesarchiv Lichterfelde (BArchL)
Reichskolonialamt (German Colonial Office File) (R 1001)
Geheimes Staatsarchiv—Preussischer Kulturbesitz (GStA-PK)
Nachlaß Heinrich Schnee (Schnee Papers) (SchP)
Museum für Naturkunde Zentralinstitut der Humboldt-Universität zu Berlin (MNZHUB)
Staatliche Museen zu Berlin—Preussischer Kulturbesitz, Museum für Völkerkunde
        (Berlin Ethnological Museum) (SMB-PK, MV)
Staatliche Museen zu Berlin—Preussischer Kulturbesitz, Zentralarchiv (Central Archive)
        (SMB-PK, ZA)
Nachlaß Wilhelm von Bode (Bode Papers) (BoP)
Staatsbibliothek zu Berlin—Preussischer Kulturbesitz (Berlin State Library) (SB-PK)
Nachlaß Felix von Luschan (Luschan Papers) (LuP)

Bremen
Übersee Museum Bremen (ÜMB)

Chicago
Field Museum of Natural History (FMNH)

Cologne
Historisches Archiv der Stadt Köln (HAStK)
Rautenstrauch-Joest Museum für Völkerkunde (RJMfV)

Dresden
Museum für Völkerkunde (MfVD)
Sächsisches Hauptstaatsarchiv (SächHStAD)

Freiburg
Bundesarchiv Freiburg (BArchF)
Reichsmarine (Imperial Naval Files) (RM)

Hamburg
Hauptstaatsarchiv Hamburg (HstAH)
Museum für Völkerkunde Hamburg (MfVH)

Honolulu
Bishop Museum (BMH)
William T. Brigham papers (BrP)

Leipzig
Museum für Völkerkunde (MfVL)
Kopierbücher (Copies of Correspondence Sent) (KB)
Acquisition files

Munich
Bayrisches Hauptstaatsarchiv (BaHStA)
Museum für Völkerkunde (MfVM)

Simancas (Spain)
Ministerio de Cultura, Archivo General de Simancas (AGS)

Stuttgart
Hauptstaatsarchiv Stuttgart (HStAS)
Linden Museum Stuttgart (LiMSt)

PRINTED SOURCES

Abel, Herbert. *Vom Raritätenkabinet zum Bremer Überseemuseum: Die Geschichte einer hanseatischen Sammlung aus Übersee.* Bremen: Röver, 1970.
Ackermann, Gustav. *Ordensbuch sämtlicher in Europa blühender und erloschner Orden und Ehrenzeichen.* Annaberg: Rudolph & Dieterici Verlag, 1855; reprint, Leipzig: Reprint, not dated.
Adelman, Jeremy, and Stephen Aron. "From Borderlands to Borders: Empires, Nation-States, and the Peoples in Between in North American History." *American Historical Review* 104 (1999): 814–841.
Andree, Richard. "R. Parkinson." *Globus* 79 (1901): 239–240.
———. "Zur Ethnographie der Südsee." *Globus* 39 (1881): 60–63.
Ankermann, Bernard. "Kulturkreise und Kulturschichten in Afrika." *Zeitschrift für Ethnologie* 37 (1905): 54–84.
Appadurai, Arjun. "Introduction: Commodities and the Politics of Value." In *The Social Life of Things,* edited by Arjun Appadurai, 3–63. Cambridge: Cambridge University Press, 1986.
Applegate, Celia. *A Nation of Provincials: The German Idea of Heimat.* Berkeley: University of California Press, 1990.
Asad, Talal, ed. *Anthropology and the Colonial Encounter.* Atlantic Highlands: Humanities Press, 1973.
Baessler, Arthur. *Neue Südsee-Bilder.* Berlin: Reimer, 1900.
———. *Südsee-Bilder.* Berlin: A. Asher & Co., 1895.
Barfield, Thomas J. *The Perilous Frontier: Nomadic Empires and China, 221 BCE to AD 1757.* Cambridge, MA: Blackwell, 1989.
Bashkow, Ira. "The Dynamics of Rapport in a Colonial Situation: David Schneider's Fieldwork on the Island of Yap." In *Colonial Situations: Essays on the Contextualization of*

Ethnographic Knowledge, edited by George Stocking, 170–242. Madison: University of Wisconsin Press, 1991.

Bastian, Adolf. *Inselgruppen in Oceanien: Reiseerlebnisse und Studien*. Berlin: Dümmlers, 1883.

———. *Der Papua des dunklen Inselreiches im Lichte psychologischer Forschung*. Berlin: Weidmannsche Buchhandlung, 1885.

———. *Zur Kentniss Hawaii's: Nachträge und Ergänzungen zu Oceanien*. Berlin: Dümmlers, 1883.

Baumgart, Winfred. "German Imperialism in Historical Perspective." In *Germans in the Tropics: Essays on German Colonial History*, edited by Arthur Knoll and Lewis Gann, 151–164. New York: Greenwood Press, 1987.

Bentley, Jerry H. "Cross-Cultural Interaction and Periodization in World History," *American Historical Review* 101 (1996): 749–770.

———. "Sea and Ocean Basins as Framework for Historical Analysis." *The Geographical Review* 89 (1999): 215–224.

———. *Shapes of World History in Twentieth-Century Scholarship*. Washington, DC: American Historical Association, 1996.

Bentley, Jerry H., Renate Bridenthal, and Kären Wigen, eds. *Seascapes: Maritime Histories, Littoral Cultures, and Transoceanic Exchanges*. Honolulu: University of Hawai'i Press, 2007.

Berg, Mark. "Yapese Politics, Yapese Money, and the *Sewei* Tributary Network before World War I." *Journal of Pacific History* 27 (1992): 150–165.

Bergner, Felicitas. "Ethnographisches Sammeln in Afrika während der deutschen Kolonialzeit. Ein Beitrag zur Sammlungsgeschichte der deutschen Völkerkundemuseen." *Paideuma* 42 (1996): 225–235.

Biskup, Peter. "Dr. Albert Hahl—Sketch of a German Colonial Official." *The Australian Journal of Politics and History* 14 (1968): 342–357.

Black, Peter. "The Teachings of Father Marino: Christianity on Tobi Atoll. In *Mission, Church and Sect in Oceania*, edited by J. Boutilier, D. Hughes, and S. Tiffany, 307–354. Ann Arbor: University of Michigan Press, 1978.

Blesse, Giselher. "Hans Meyer und Leipzig: Vom Wirken einer Familie und 'Ihrer' Stadt." In Museum für Völkerkunde Leipzig, *Kunst aus Benin: Afrikanische Meisterwerke aus der Sammlung Hans Meier*, 109–134. Leipzig: Museum für Völkerkunde, 1994.

———. "Internationale Beziehungen des Museums für Völkerkunde Leipzig, 1869–1945." *Mitteilungen aus dem Museum für Völkerkunde Leipzig* 50 (1985): 41–46.

Bley, Helmut. *South-West Africa under German Rule, 1894–1914*. Evanston: Northwestern University Press, 1971.

Bode, Wilhelm von. *Mein Leben*. 2 vols. Berlin: Reckendorf, 1930.

Breckenridge, Carol, and Peter van der Veer, eds. *Orientalism and Postcolonial Predicament*. Philadelphia: University of Pennsylvania Press, 1993.

Brown, Richard. "The German Acquisition of the Caroline Islands, 1898–1899." In *Germany in the Pacific and Far East, 1870–1914*, edited by John Moses and Paul Kennedy, 137–155. St. Lucia: University of Queensland Press, 1977.

Buck, Peter H. (Te Rangi Hiroa). *An Introduction to Polynesian Anthropology*. Honolulu: Bishop Museum, 1945.

Bullhof, Johannes. "What If? Modality and History." *History and Theory* 38 (1999): 145–168.

Bunzl, Mattie. "Franz Boas and the Humboldian Tradition: From *Volksgeist* and *Nationalcharakter* to an Anthropological Concept of Culture." In *Volksgeist as Method and Ethic:*

Essays on Boasian Ethnography and the German Anthropological Tradition, edited by George Stocking, 17–78. Madison: University of Wisconsin Press, 1996.

Burleigh, Michael. *The Third Reich: A New History.* New York: Hill and Wang, 2000.

Buschmann, Rainer. "Colonizing Anthropology: Albert Hahl and the Ethnographic Frontier in German New Guinea." In *Worldly Provincialism: German Anthropology in the Age of Empire,* edited by H. Glenn Penny and Matti Bunzl, 230–255. Ann Arbor: University of Michigan Press, 2003.

———. "Exploring Tensions in Material Culture: Commercialising Ethnography in German New Guinea, 1870–1904." In *Hunting the Gatherers: Ethnographic Collectors, Agents and Agency in Melanesia, 1870s–1930s,* edited by Michael O'Hanlon and Robert L. Welch, 55–79. New York: Berghahn Books, 2000.

———. "Franz Boluminski and the Wonderland of Carvings: Towards an Ethnography of Collection Activity." *Baessler Archiv* n.f. 44 (1996): 185–210.

———. "The Ethnographic Frontier in German New Guinea (1870–1914)" Ph.D. dissertation, University of Hawai'i, 1999.

———. "Karl Nauer and the Politics of Collecting Ethnographic Objects in German New Guinea," *Pacific Arts* 21/22 (2000): 93–102.

———. "Oceans of World History: Delineating Aquacentric Views in the Global Past." *History Compass* 2 (2004), WD 68: 1–9.

———. "Tobi Captured: Converging Ethnographic and Colonial Visions on a Caroline Island." *Isla: A Journal of Micronesia Studies* 4 (1996): 317–340.

Buse. "Eine Reise nach den südlich von Palau gelegenen Inseln." *Deutsches Kolonialblatt* 21 (1910): 937–938.

Calder, Alex, Jonathan Lamb, and Bridget Orr. "Introduction: Postcoloniality and the Pacific." In *Voyages and Beaches: Pacific Encounters: 1769–1840,* edited by Alex Calder, Jonathan Lamb, and Bridget Orr, 1–24. Honolulu: University of Hawai'i Press, 1999.

Campbell, Ian. "Anthropology and the Professionalization of Colonial Administration in Papua and New Guinea." *Journal of Pacific History* 33 (1998): 69–90.

Chappell, David. "Active Agents vs. Passive Victims: Decolonized Historiography or Problematic Paradigm?" *The Contemporary Pacific* 7 (1995): 303–326.

———. "Ethnogenesis and Frontiers." *Journal of World History* 4 (1993): 267–275.

Christmann, Helmut, Peter Hempenstall, and Dirk Ballendorf. *Die Karolinen-Inseln in deutscher Zeit: Eine kolonialgeschichtliche Fallstudie.* Münster: Lit, 1991.

Churchill, William. *The Polynesian Wanderings.* The Carnegie Institute of Washington Publication 134. Washington, DC, 1911.

Clifford, James. "Introduction: Partial Truths." In *Writing Culture: The Politics and Poetics of Ethnography,* edited by James Clifford and George Marcus, 1–26. Berkeley: University of California Press, 1986.

———. "On Ethnographic Allegory." In *Writing Culture: The Poetics and Politics of Ethnography,* edited by James Clifford and George Marcus, 98–121. Berkeley: University of California Press, 1986.

———. *The Predicament of Culture: Twentieth-Century Ethnography, Literature, and Art.* Cambridge: Harvard University Press, 1988.

———. *Routes: Travel and Translation in the Late Twentieth Century.* Cambridge: Harvard University Press, 1997.

Cohen, David W. *The Combing of History.* Chicago: University of Chicago Press, 1994.

Cohen, Robin. *Global Diasporas: An Introduction.* Seattle: University of Washington Press, 1997.

Cohn, Bernard. *An Anthropologist among the Historians and Other Essays.* Oxford: Oxford University Press, 1987.

———. *Colonialism and Its Forms of Knowledge: The British in India.* Cambridge: Cambridge University Press, 1996.

Cole, Douglas. *Captured Heritage: The Scramble for Northwest Coast Artifacts.* 2nd edition. Norman: University of Oklahoma Press, 1995.

Comaroff, John, and Jean Comaroff. *Ethnography and the Historical Imagination.* Boulder: Westview Press, 1992.

Conklin, Alice L. "Civil Society, Science, and Empire in Late Republican France: Foundation of Paris's Museum of Man." *Osiris* 17 (2002): 255–290.

Coombes, Annie. *Reinventing Africa: Museums, Material Culture and Popular Imagination in Late Victorian and Edwardian England.* New Haven: Yale University Press, 1994.

Cooper, Frederick, and Ann Stoler. "Introduction: Tensions of Empire: Colonial Control and Visions of Rule." *American Ethnologist* 16 (1989): 609–621.

Corfino, Alon. *The Nation as Local Metaphor: Württemberg, Imperial Germany, and National Memory, 1871–1918.* Chapel Hill: University of North Carolina Press, 1997.

Corney, Bolton Glanvill. *The Quest and Occupation of Tahiti by Emissaries of Spain During the Years 1772–1775.* 3 vols. London: Hakluyt Society, 1913–1919.

Dalton, Doug. "Melanesian Can(n)ons: Paradoxes and Prospects in Melanesian Ethnography." In *Excluded Ancestors, Inventible Traditions: Essays towards a More Inclusive History of Anthropology,* edited by Richard Handler, 284–305. Madison: University of Wisconsin Press, 2000.

D'Arcy, Paul. "Connected by the Sea: Towards a Regional History of the Western Caroline Islands." *Journal of Pacific History* 36 (2001): 163–182.

———. "Cultural Divisions and Island Environments since the Time of Dumont d'Urville." *Journal of Pacific History* 38 (2003): 217–235.

———. *People of the Sea: Environment, Identity, and History.* Honolulu: University of Hawai'i Press, 2006.

Darnell, Regna. *And Along Came Boas: Continuity and Revolution in Americanist Anthropology.* Philadelphia: John Benjamins, 1998.

———. "The Development of American Anthropology, 1879–1920: From the Bureau of American Ethnology to Franz Boas." Ph.D. dissertation, University of Pennsylvania, 1969.

Dawson, Ruth. "Collecting with Cook: The Forsters and Their Artifact Sale." *The Hawaiian Journal of History* 8 (1979): 5–16.

Dempwolff, Otto. "Über aussterbende Völker (Die Eingeborenen der 'westlichen Inseln' in Deutsch-Neu-Guinea)." *Zeitschrift für Ethnologie* 36 (1904): 384–415.

Dening, Greg. "Deep Times, Deep Spaces: Civilizing the Sea." In *Sea Changes: Historicizing the Ocean,* edited by Bernhard Klein and Gesa Mackenthun, 13–35. New York: Routledge, 2004.

———. *Islands and Beaches: Discourse on a Silent Land: Marquesas 1774–1880.* Honolulu: University of Hawai'i Press, 1980.

———. "Possessing Tahiti." *Archaeology in Oceania* 21 (1986): 103–118.

Denoon, Donald, et al., eds. *The Cambridge History of the Pacific Islanders* (Cambridge: Cambridge University Press, 1997).

Derlon, Brigitte. *De mémoire et d'oubli: Anthropologie des objets malanggan de Nouvelle-Irlande.* Paris: CNRS Édition, 1997.

"Das Deutsche Kolonialmuseum." *Deutsche Kolonialzeitung* 10 (1897): 402–403.

Dodds, Klaus, and Stephen A. Royle. "The Historical Geography of Islands: Introduction: Rethinking Islands." *Journal of Historical Geography* 29 (2003): 487–498.

Dorsey, George Amos. "Notes on Museums in Central Europe." *American Anthropologist* 1 (1899): 462–474.

Douglas, Bronwen. *Across the Great Divide: Journeys in Anthropology and History.* Amsterdam: Harwood Publishers, 1998.

———. "Seaborne Ethnography and the Natural History of Man." *Journal of Pacific History* 38 (2003): 3–27.

Drummond, Steven K., and Lynn Nelson. *The Western Frontier of Imperial Rome.* Armonk, NY: M. E. Sharpe, 1994.

Eilers, Anneliese. "Westkarolinen: Tobi und Ngulu." In *Ergebnisse der Südsee-Expedition 1908–1910,* II, B, vol. 9, edited by G. Thilenius. Hamburg: Friedrichsen, 1936.

"Die Einweihung des neuen Museums für Völkerkunde in Berlin." *Correspondenz-Blatt der deutschen Gesellschaft für Anthropologie, Ethnologie, und Urgeschichte* 18 (1887): 1–8.

Eisenhofer, Stefan. "Felix von Luschan and Early German Language Studies of Benin." *African Arts* 30 (1997): 62–67.

Elliott, J. H. "*Afterword,* Atlantic History: A Circumnavigation." In *The British Atlantic World: 1500–1800,* edited by David Armitage and M. J. Braddick, 233–249. New York: Palgrave, 2002.

"Die Entwicklung des Museums 1908." *Jahrbuch des Städtischen Museums für Völkerkunde zu Leipzig* 3 (1910).

Essner, Cornelia. "Berlins Völkerkunde-Museum in der Kolonialära: Anmerkungen zum Verhältnis von Ethnologie und Kolonialismus in Deutschland." In *Berlin in Geschichte und Gegenwart: Jahrbuch des Landesarchivs Berlin,* edited by Hans Reichhardt, 65–94. Berlin: Siedler, 1986.

———. *Deutsche Afrikareisende im neunzehnten Jahrhundert: Zur Sozialgeschichte des Reisens.* Stuttgart: Steiner, 1985.

Evans, Andrew. "Anthropology at War: Racial Studies of POWs during World War I." In *Worldly Provincialism: German Anthropology in the Age of Empire,* edited by H. Glenn Penny and Matti Bunzl, 198–229. Ann Arbor: University of Michigan Press, 2003.

Fabion, James D. "History in Anthropology" *Annual Review of Anthropology* 22 (1993): 35–54.

Finamore, Daniel, ed. *Maritime History as World History.* Gainesville: University Press of Florida, 2004.

Finsch, Otto. *Südseearbeiten: Gewerbe- und Kunstfleiss, Tauschmittel und "Geld" der Eingeborenen, auf Grundlage der Rohstoffe und der geographischen Verbreitung.* Hamburg: Friedrichsen, 1914.

———. *Systematische Übersicht der Ergebnisse seiner Reisen und schriftstellerischen Thätigkeit (1859–1899).* Berlin: Friedländer & Sohn, 1899.

Firth, Raymond. *We the Tikopia: A Sociological Study of Kinship in Primitive Polynesia.* London: Allen and Unwin, 1957 [orig. 1936].

Firth, Stewart. "Albert Hahl: Governor of New Guinea." In *Papua New Guinea Portraits: The Expatriate Experience,* edited by James Griffin, 28–47. Canberra: Australian National University Press, 1978.

———. "Colonial Administration and the Invention of the Native." In *The Cambridge History of Pacific Islanders,* edited by Donald Denoon et al., 253–280. Cambridge: Cambridge University Press, 1997.

———. "German Firms in the Pacific Islands, 1857–1914." In *Germany in the Pacific and the Far East, 1870–1914,* edited by John Moses and Paul Kennedy, 3–27. St. Lucia: University of Queensland Press, 1977.

———."German Labour Policy in Nauru and Angaur, 1906–1914." *Journal of Pacific History* 13 (1978): 36–52.

———. "Labour in German New Guinea." In *Papua New Guinea: A Century of Colonial Impact (1884–1984),* edited by Sione Latukefu, 179–202. Port Moresby: National Research Institute, 1989.

———. *New Guinea under the Germans.* Melbourne: University of Melbourne Press, 1982.

Fischer, Hans. *Die Hamburger Südsee-Expedition: Über Ethnographie und Kolonialismus.* Frankfurt: Syndikat, 1981.

———. *Völkerkunde im Nationalsozialismus: Aspekte der Anpassung, Affinität und Behauptung einer wissenschaftlichen Disziplin.* Berlin: Reimer, 1990.

Foerstel, Lenora, and Angela Gilliam, eds. *Confronting the Margaret Mead Legacy: Scholarship, Empire, and the South Pacific.* Philadelphia: Temple University Press, 1992.

Foucault, Michel. *The Order of Things: An Archaeology of the Human Sciences.* New York: Vintage, 1970.

Frank, Andre Gunder. *ReOrient: Global Economy in the Asian Age.* Berkeley: University of California Press, 1998.

Friederici, Georg. "Das Pidgin-Englisch in Deutsch Neuguinea." *Koloniale Rundschau* 1911 (11): 92–102.

Frobenius, Leo. "Kulturformen Ozeaniens." *Petermanns Geographische Mitteilungen* 46 (1900): 204–271.

Fülleborn, Susanne. "Die ethnographischen Unternehmungen des Hamburger Handelshauses Godeffroy." M.A. thesis, University of Hamburg, 1985.

Gaehtgens, Thomas. *Die Berliner Museumsinsel im deutschen Kaiserreich: Zur Kulturpolitik der Museen in der wilhelminischen Epoche.* Munich: Deutscher Kunstverlag, 1992.

Gann, Lewis, and Peter Duignan. *The Rulers of German Africa, 1884–1914.* Stanford: Stanford University Press, 1977.

Ganz, Harding. "The German Navy in the Far East and the Pacific: The Seizure of Kiautschou and After." In *Germany in the Pacific and the Far East, 1870–1914,* edited by John Moses and Paul Kennedy, 115–137. St. Lucia: University of Queensland Press, 1977.

Gardner, Helen. "Gathering for God: George Brown and the Christian Economy in the Collection of Artifacts." In *Hunting the Gatherers: Ethnographic Collectors, Agents and Agency in Melanesia, 1870s–1930s,* edited by Michael O' Hanlon and Robert L. Welsch, 35–54. New York: Berghahn Books, 2000.

Gareis, Sigrid. *Exotik in München: Museumsethnologische Konzeptionen im historischen Wandel am Beispiel des Staatlichen Museums für Völkerkunde München.* Munich: Anacon Verlag, 1990.

Goldman, Irvin. *Ancient Polynesian Society.* Chicago: University of Chicago Press, 1970.

Goody, Jack. *The Expansive Moment: The Rise of Social Anthropology in Britain and Africa.* Cambridge: Cambridge University Press, 1995.

Gosden, Chris, and Chantal Knowles. *Collecting Colonialism: Material Culture and Colonial Change.* New York: Berg, 2001.

———. *Possessing Culture: Museums, Anthropology and German New Guinea.* New York: Berg, 2006.

Gosden, Chris, and C. Pavlides. "Are Islands Insular? Landscape vs. Seascape in the Case of the Arawe Islands, PNG." *Archaeology in Oceania* 29 (1994): 162–171.

Gothsch, Manfred. *Die deutsche Völkerkunde und ihr Verhältnis zum Kolonialismus: Ein Beitrag zur kolonialideologischen und kolonialpraktischen Bedeutung der deutschen Völkerkunde in der Zeit von 1870 bis 1975.* Baden-Baden: Nomos Verlag, 1983.

Graebner, Fritz. "Adolf Bastian 100. Geburtstag." *Ethnologica* 3 (1926): ix–xii.

———. "Kulturkreise und Kulturschichten in Ozeanien." *Zeitschrift für Ethnologie* 37 (1905): 23–53.

———. *Methode der Ethnologie.* Heidelberg: Carl Winters, 1911.

———. "Der Neubau des Berliner Museums für Völkerkunde und andere praktische Zeitfragen der Ethnologie." *Globus* 94 (1908): 213–216.

Gray, Geoffrey. "Being Honest to my Science: Reo Fortune and J. H. P. Murray, 1927–1930," *Australian Journal of Anthropology* 10 (1999): 56–76.

———. "'There Are Many Difficult Problems:' Ernst William Pearson Chinnery—Government Anthropologist." *Journal of Pacific History* 38 (2003): 313–330.

Greenblatt, Stephen. *Marvelous Possessions: The Wonder of the New World.* Chicago: University of Chicago Press, 1991.

Gritzner, Maximilian. *Handbuch der Ritter- und Verdienstorden aller Kulturstaaten der Welt innerhalb des XIX. Jahrhunderts.* Leipzig: Weber, 1893.

Gruber, J. W. "Ethnographic Salvage and the Shaping of Anthropology." *American Anthropologist* 72 (1970): 1289–1299.

Gupta, Akhil, and James Ferguson, eds. *Anthropological Locations: Boundaries and Grounds for a Field Science.* Berkeley: University of California Press, 1997.

———. "Discipline and Practice: 'The Field' as Site, Method, and Location in Anthropology." In *Anthropological Locations: Boundaries and Grounds of a Field Science,* edited by Akhil Gupta and James Ferguson, 1–46. Berkeley: University of California Press, 1997.

Hagel, Jürgen, and Wolfgang Meckelein. *Hundert Jahre Gesellschaft für Erd- und Völkerkunde zu Stuttgart e. V. (Württembergischer Verein für Handelsgeographie).* Stuttgart: Gesellschaft für Erd- und Völkerkunde, 1982.

Hagen, Bernard. *Unter den Papua: Über Land und Leute, Thier und Pflanzenwelt in Kaiser-Wilhelmsland.* Wiesbaden: C. W. Kreidel, 1899.

Hahl, Albert. "Feste und Tänze der Eingeborenen von Ponape." *Ethnologisches Notizblatt* 3 (1902): 95–102.

———. *Governor in New Guinea.* Edited and translated by Peter Sack and Dymphna Clark. Canberra: Australian National University, 1980.

———. "Mitteilungen über Sitten und rechtliche Verhältnisse auf Ponape." *Ethnologisches Notizblatt* 2 (1901): 1–13.

———. "Über die Rechtsanschauungen der Eingeborenen eines Theils der Blanchebucht und des Inneren der Gazellenhalbinsel." *Nachrichten über Kaiser Wilhelmsland* 13 (1897): 68–85.

Hambruch, Paul. "Europa und die Aufteilung der Südsee: Ein geschichtlicher Rückblick," *Südsee-Bote* 2 (1918): 2–6.

———. "Nauru." In *Ergebnisse der Südsee-Expedition 1908–1910,* II.B, vol. 1, edited by G. Thilenius. Hamburg: Friedrichsen, 1914.

———. "Neukaledonien." *Südsee-Bote* 2 (1918): 32–33, 52–55.

———. "Wuvulu und Aua (Maty- und Durour-Inseln) auf Gund der Sammlung F. E. Hellwig aus den Jahren 1902 bis 1904. *Mitteilungen aus dem Museum für Völkerkunde zu Hamburg* 2 (1908): 1–154.

Hammer, Karl. "Preußische Museumspolitik im 19. Jahrhundert." In *Bildungspolitik in*

Preußen zur Zeit des Kaiserreichs, edited by Peter Baumgart, 256–277. Stuttgart: Klett-Cotta, 1980.

Hanlon, David. "Magellan's Chroniclers? American Anthropology's History in Micronesia." In *American Anthropology in Micronesia: An Assessment,* edited by Robert Kiste and Mac Marshall, 53–79. Honolulu: University of Hawai'i Press, 1999.

———. "Micronesia: Writing and Rewriting the Histories of a Non-Entity." *Pacific Studies* 12 (1989): 1–21.

———. *Remaking Micronesia: Discourses over Development in a Pacific Territory, 1944–1982.* Honolulu: University of Hawai'i Press, 1998.

———. *Upon a Stone Altar: A History of the Island of Pohnpei to 1890.* Honolulu: University of Hawai'i Press, 1988.

Harris, Marvin. *The Rise of Anthropological Theory.* New York: Thomas Crowell, 1968.

Hau'ofa, Epeli. "Our Sea of Islands." *The Contemporary Pacific* 6 (1994): 148–161.

———. "The Ocean in Us." *The Contemporary Pacific* 10 (1998): 391–411.

Helfrich, Klaus. *Malanggan 1: Bildwerke von Neuirland.* Berlin: Museum für Völkerkunde, 1973.

Helms, Mary. *Ulysses' Sail: An Ethnographic Odyssey of Power, Knowledge, and Geographical Distance.* Princeton: Princeton University Press, 1988.

Hempenstall, Peter. "The Neglected Empire: The Superstructure of the German Colonial State in German Melanesia." In *Germans in the Tropics: Essays in German Colonial History,* edited by Arthur Knoll and Lewis Gann, 93–117. New York: Greenwood Press, 1987.

———. *Pacific Islanders under German Rule: A Study in The Meaning of Colonial Resistance.* Canberra: Australian National University Press, 1978.

———. "Survey of German Commercial Activities in the South Pacific from 1880 to 1914, with Special References to Samoa and New Guinea." B.A. honors thesis, University of Queensland, 1969.

Hempenstall, Peter, and Noel Rutherford. *Protest and Dissent in the Colonial Pacific.* Suva: University of the South Pacific Press.

Herle, Anita, and Sandra Rouse, eds. *Cambridge and the Torres Strait: Centenary Essays on the 1898 Anthropological Expedition.* Cambridge: Cambridge University Press, 1998.

Heydrich, Martin. "Ethnologica—Neue Folge." *Ethnologica* n.f. 1 (1959): iii–viii.

Hiery, Hermann. *Das Deutsche Reich in der Südsee (1900-1921): Eine Annäherung an die Erfahrungen verschiedener Kulturen.* Göttingen: Vandenhoeck & Ruprecht, 1995.

———. *The Neglected War: The German South Pacific and the Impact of World War I.* Honolulu: University of Hawai'i Press, 1995.

Hinsley, Curtis. *Savages and Scientists: The Smithsonian Institution and the Development of American Anthropology, 1846–1910* (Washington, DC: Smithsonian Institution, 1981).

Hochschild, Adam. *King Leopold's Ghost: A Story of Greed, Terror, and Heroism in Colonial Africa.* Boston: Mariner Books, 1999.

Hohnschopp, Henning. "Untersuchungen zum Para-Mikronesien-Problem unter besonderer Berücksichtigung der Wuvulu- und Aua-Kultur." *Arbeiten aus dem Institut für Völkerkunde der Universität Göttingen* 7 (1973): 1–170.

Holden, Horace. *A Narrative of the Shipwreck, Captivity and Suffering of Horace Holden and Benjamin H. Nute; Who Were Cast Away in the American Ship Mentor, on the Pelew Islands, in the Year 1832.* Boston: Russel, Shattuk, 1836.

Howe, Kerry. *Nature, Culture, and History: The Knowing of Oceania.* Honolulu: University of Hawai'i Press, 2000.

Hubatch, Walter. *Die Ära Tirpitz: Studien zur deutschen Marinepolitik, 1890–1918.* Göttingen: Musterschmidt, 1955.

Jacknis, Ira. "The Ethnographic Object and the Object of Ethnography." In *Volksgeist as Method and Ethic: Essays on Boasian Ethnography and the German Anthropological Tradition,* edited by George Stocking, 185–214. Madison: University of Wisconsin Press, 1996.

Jacobi, Arnold. *Fünfzig Jahre Museum für Völkerkunde zu Dresden.* Berlin: Julius Bard, 1925.

Jolly, Margaret. "Other Mothers: Maternal 'Insouciance' and the Depopulation Debate in Fiji and Vanuatu, 1890–1930." In *Maternities and Modernities,* edited by K. Ram and M. Jolly, 183–215. Cambridge: Cambridge University Press, 1998.

Jones, Anna Laura. "Exploding Canons: The Anthropology of Museums." *Annual Review of Anthropology* 22 (1993): 201–220.

Kaeppler, Adrienne. *"Artificial Curiosities": Being an Exposition of Native Manufacture Collected on Three Pacific Voyages of Captain James Cook, R.N.* Honolulu: Bishop Museum Press, 1975.

Kendrick, John. *Alejandro Malaspina: Portrait of a Visionary.* Ithaca: McGill-Queen's University Press, 1999.

Kennedy, Paul. *The Samoan Tangle: A Study in Anglo-German-American Relations, 1878–1900.* St. Lucia: University of Queensland Press, 1974.

Kirch, Patrick Vinton. *The Evolution of Polynesian Chieftainships.* Cambridge: Cambridge University Press, 1984.

———. "The Polynesian Outliers." *Journal of Pacific History* 19 (1984): 224–238.

Kiste, Robert C., and Suzanne Falgout. "Anthropology and Micronesia: The Context." In *American Anthropology in Micronesia: An Assessment,* edited by Robert C. Kiste and Mac Marshall, 11–51. Honolulu: University of Hawai'i Press, 1999.

Kiste, Robert C., and Mac Marshall, eds. *American Anthropology in Micronesia: An Assessment.* Honolulu: University of Hawai'i Press, 1999.

———. "American Anthropology in Micronesia, 1941–1997." *Pacific Science* 54 (2000): 265–274.

Klein, Bernhard, and Gesa Mackenthun, eds. *Sea Changes: Historicizing the Ocean.* New York: Routledge, 2004.

"Kleine Nachrichten." *Globus* 75 (1899).

Knauff, Bruce. *From Primitive to Postcolonial in Melanesian Anthropology.* Ann Arbor: University of Michigan Press, 1999.

Knopp, Werner. "Blick auf Bode." In *Wilhelm von Bode: Museumsdirektor und Mäzen,* edited by Kaiser-Friedrich-Museums-Verein, 7-20. Berlin: Staatliche Museen zu Berlin, 1995.

Koch, Gerd. "Hundert Jahre Museum für Völkerkunde: Abteilung Südsee." *Baessler Archiv* n.f. 21 (1973): 141–174.

Koepping, Klaus Peter. *Adolf Bastian and the Psychic Unity of Mankind.* St. Lucia: University of Queensland Press, 1983.

Kotze, Stephan von. *Südsee-Erinnerungen.* Berlin: Dom, 1925.

Krämer, Augustin. "Gouvernmentale Übergriffe in ethnographische Arbeitsgebiete und Mittel zur Abhilfe." *Globus* 96 (1909): 264–266.

———. *Die Málangane von Tombára.* Munich: Georg Müller, 1925.

———. "Museumsverbände und ihre Zwecke." *Korrespondenz-Blatt der Deutschen Gesellschaft für Anthropologie, Ethnologie und Urgeschichte* 44 (1913): 33–35.

———. "Der Neubau des Berliner Museums für Völkerkunde im Lichte der ethnographisch-en Forschung." *Globus* 86 (1904): 21–24.

———. *Die Samoa-Inseln, Entwurf einer Monographie mit besonderer Berücksichtigung Deutsch Samoas.* 2 vols. Stuttgart: Schweizerbart, 1902/1903.

———. *The Samoan Islands: An Outline of a Monograph with Particular Consideration of German Samoa.* Translated by Theodore Verhaaren. 2 vols. Honolulu: University of Hawai'i Press, 1994.

———. "Über Museums- und Feldmonographen." *Korrespondenz-Blatt der Deutschen Gesell-schaft für Anthropologie, Ethnologie und Urgeschichte* 43 (1912): 22–24.

———. "Vuvulu und Aua (Maty und Durour Insel)." *Globus* 93 (1908): 254–257.

Kramer, Fritz. *Verkehrte Welten: Zur imaginären Ethnographie des 19. Jahrhunderts.* 2nd ed. Frankfurt: Syndikat, 1981.

Krämer-Bannow, Elisabeth. *Bei kunstsinningen Kannibalen in der Südsee: Wanderungen auf Neu-Mecklenburg 1908–1909.* Berlin: Reimer, 1916.

Krause, Fritz. "Dem Andenken Karl Weules." *Jahrbuch des Städtischen Museums für Völkerkunde zu Leipzig* 9 (1922–1925): 13–28.

Krickeberg, Walter. "Zum Geleit." *Baessler Archiv* n.f. 1 (1952): 1–7.

Krieger, Kurt. "Hundert Jahre Museum für Völkerkunde Berlin: Abteilung Afrika." *Baessler Archiv* n.f. 21 (1973): 101–140.

Krieger, Maximilian. "Das Kolonialmuseum zu Berlin." *Deutsche Kolonialzeitung* 12 (1899): 390–391.

Küchler, Susanne. "Malangan: Art and Memory in a Melanesian Society." *Man* 22 (1987): 238–255.

———. *Malanggan: Art, Memory, and Sacrifice.* New York: Berg, 2002.

———. "Sacrificial Economy and Its Objects: Rethinking Colonial Collecting in Oceania." *Journal of Material Culture* 2 (1997): 39–60.

Kuklick, Henrika. "After Ishmael: The Fieldwork Tradition and Its Future." In *Anthropo-logical Locations: Boundaries and Grounds of a Field Science,* edited by Akhil Gupta and James Ferguson, 47–65. Berkeley: University of California Press, 1997.

———. *The Savage Within: The Social History of British Anthropology, 1885–1945.* Cambridge: Cambridge University Press, 1991.

Kussmaul, Friedrich. "Linden-Museum Stuttgart: Staatliches Museum für Völkerkunde Rückblick–Umschau–Ausblick." *Tribus* 24 (1975): 17–66.

Lambi, Ivo Nikolai. *The Navy and German Power Politics, 1862–1914.* Boston: Allen & Unwin, 1984.

Langmore, Diane. *Missionary Lives: Papua, 1874–1914.* Honolulu: University of Hawai'i Press, 1989.

Lewis, Martin, and Kären Wigen. *The Myth of Continents: A Critique of Metageography.* Berkeley: University of California Press, 1997.

Lewis, Philip "The Social Context of Art in Northern New Ireland." *Fieldiana: Anthropology* 58 (1969).

Liebersohn, Harry. "Coming of Age in the Pacific: German Ethnography from Chamisso to Krämer." In *Worldly Provincialism: German Anthropology in the Age of Empire,* edited by H. Glenn Penny and Matti Bunzl, 31–46. Ann Arbor: University of Michigan Press, 2003.

———. "Discovering Indigenous Nobility: Tocqueville, Chamisso, and Romantic Travel Writing." *American Historical Review* 99 (1994): 746–766.

———. "Images of Monarchy: Kamehameha I and the Art of Louis Choris." In *Double*

Vision: Art Histories and Colonial Histories in the Pacific, edited by Nicholas Thomas and Diane Losche, 44–64. Cambridge: Cambridge University Press, 1999.

Lincoln, Louise. "Art and Money in New Ireland: History, Economy, and Cultural Production." In *Assemblage of Spirits: Idea and Image in New Ireland*, edited by Louise Lincoln. New York: George Braziller, 1987.

————, ed. *Assemblage of Spirits: Idea and Image in New Ireland*. New York: Georg Braziller, 1987.

Lindstrom, Lamont. *Cargo Cult: Strange Stories of Desire from Melanesia and Beyond*. Honolulu: University of Hawai'i Press, 1993.

Lomas, Peter. "The Early Contact Period in Northern New Ireland (Papua New Guinea): From Wild Frontier to Plantation Economy." *Ethnohistory* 28 (1981): 1–21.

Lowie, Robert. *The History of Ethnological Thought*. New York: Farrar & Rinehart, 1937.

Lugere, Vicki. "The Native Mother." In *The Cambridge History of Pacific Islanders*, edited by Donald Denoon et al., 280–287. Cambridge: Cambridge University Press, 1997.

Luschan, Felix von. *Anleitungen für ethnographische Beobachtungen und Sammlungen*. Berlin: Museum für Völkerkunde, 1899.

————. *Anleitungen für ethnographische Beobachtungen und Sammlungen in Afrika und Ozeanien*. 3rd ed. Berlin: Museum für Völkerkunde, 1904.

————. *Beiträge zur Völkerkunde der deutschen Schutzgebiete*. Berlin: Reimer, 1897.

————. "R. Parkinsons Beobachtungen auf Bóbolo und Hún (Matty und Durour)." *Globus* 78 (1900): 69–78.

————. "Über die Matty-Insel." *Verhandlungen der Gesellschaft für Erdkunde zu Berlin* 22 (1895): 443–449.

————. "Ziele und Wege der Völkerkunde in den deutschen Schutzgebieten." In *Verhandlungen des Deutschen Kolonialkongresses 1902 zu Berlin am 10. und 11. Oktober 1902*, 163–171. Berlin: Reimer, 1903.

————. "Ziele und Wege eines modernen Museums für Völkerkunde." *Globus* 88 (1905): 238–240.

————. "Zur Ethnographie der Matty-Insel." *Internationales Archiv für Ethnographie* 8 (1895): 41–56.

————. "Zur Ethnographie des Kaiserin-Augusta-Flusses." *Baessler Archiv* 1 (1911): 104–117.

————. "Zur geographischen Nomenclatur der Südsee." *Zeitschrift für Ethnologie* 30 (1898): 390–397.

Lustig, Wolfgang. "'Außer ein paar zerbrochenen Pfeilen nichts zu verteilen . . . ': Ethnographische Sammlungen aus den deutschen Kolonien und ihre Verteilung an Museen 1889 bis 1914." *Mitteilungen aus dem Museum für Völkerkunde Hamburg* n.f. 18 (1988): 157–178.

Malinowski, Bronislaw. *Argonauts of the Western Pacific*. New York: E. P. Dutton, 1961 [1922].

————. *A Diary in the Strict Sense of the Term*. Stanford: Stanford University Press, 1967.

Manning, Patrick. *Navigating World History: Historians Create a Global Past*. New York: Palgrave, 2003.

Marchand, Suzanne. "The Rhetoric of Artifacts and the Decline of Classical Humanism: The Case of Josef Strzygowski." *History and Theory* 33 (1994): 106–130.

Marcus, George, and Michael Fischer. *Anthropology as Cultural Critique: An Experimental Moment in the Human Sciences*. Chicago: University of Chicago Press, 1986.

Massin, Benoit. "From Virchow to Fischer: Physical Anthropology and 'Modern Race Theories' in Wilhelmine Germany." In *Volksgeist as Method and Ethic: Essays on Boasian*

Anthropology and the German Anthropological Tradition, edited by George Stocking, 79–154. Madison: University of Wisconsin Press.

Mead, Margaret. *Coming of Age in Samoa: A Psychological Study of Primitive Youth for Western Civilization.* New York: Morrow, 1928.

———. *The Social Organization of Manua.* Honolulu: Bishop Museum Press, 1930.

Melk-Koch, Marion. *Auf der Suche nach der menschlichen Gesellschaft: Richard Thurnwald.* Berlin: Reimer, 1989.

———. "Melanesian Art—or Just Stones and Junk? Richard Thurnwald and the Question of Art in Melanesia." *Pacific Arts* 21/22 (2000): 53–68.

Melle, Werner von. *Dreißig Jahre Hamburger Wissenschaft, 1891–1921.* 2 vols. Hamburg: Broschek & Co., 1923.

Meyer, Hans. "Die geographischen Grundlagen und Aufgaben in der wirtschaftlichen Erforschung unserer Schutzgebiete." In *Verhandlungen des Deutschen Kolonialkongresses 1902 zu Berlin am 10. und 11. Oktober 1902,* 72–83. Berlin: Reimer, 1903.

———. "Übersicht über die Ergebnisse der Expeditionen der Landeskundlichen Kommission des Reichskolonialamt." In *Verhandlungen des Deutschen Kolonialkongresses 1910 zu Berlin am 6., 7. und 8. Oktober 1910,* 5–15. Berlin: Reimer, 1910.

Moore, Clive. "Workers in Colonial Papua New Guinea: 1884–1975." In *Labour in the South Pacific,* edited by Clive Moore, Jacquelin Leckie, and Doug Munro, 30–46. Townsville: James Cook University Press, 1990.

Muensterberger, Werner. *Collecting: An Unruly Passion.* Princeton: Princeton University Press, 1994.

Müller, Andrea. "Der Lloyd-Kapitän Karl Nauer als Sammler in der Südsee für das Übersee-museum." *Arbeiterbewegung und Sozialgeschichte* 10 (2002): 32–56.

Müller, Sebastian. "Official Support and Bourgeois Opposition in Wilhelminian Culture." In *The Divided Heritage: Themes and Problems in German Modernism,* edited by Irit Rogoff, 163–190. Cambridge: Cambridge University Press, 1994.

Munro, Doug, and Stewart Firth. "Company Strategies—Colonial Policies." In *Labour in the South Pacific,* edited by Clive Moore, Jacquelin Leckie, and Doug Munro, 3–29. Townsville: James Cook University Press, 1990.

Neuhauss, Richard. "Brief des Hrn. R. Neuhauss aus Neu-Guinea—Sissanu (nahe der holländischen Grenze) 1 September 1909." *Zeitschrift für Ethnologie* 41 (1909): 962–963.

———. *Deutsch Neuguinea.* 3 vols. Berlin: Reimer Verlag, 1911.

Neumann, Klaus. "The Stench of the Past: Revisionism in Pacific Islands and Australian History." *The Contemporary Pacific* 10 (1998): 31–64.

Nevermann, Hans. "Totenfeiern und Malagane von Nord-Neumecklenburg: Nach Aufzeichnungen von E. Walden. *Zeitschrift für Ethnologie* 72 (1940): 11–38.

O'Hanlon, Michael. "Introduction." In *Hunting the Gatherers: Collectors, Agents, and Agency in Melanesia, 1870s–1930s,* edited by Michael O'Hanlon and Robert Welsch, 1–34. New York: Berghahn Books, 2000.

O'Hanlon, Michael, and Robert Welsch, eds. *Hunting the Gatherers: Ethnographic Collectors, Agents and Agency in Melanesia.* New York: Berghahn Books, 2000.

Otto, Sigrid. "Wilhelm von Bode—Journal eines tätigen Lebens." In *Wilhelm von Bode. Museumsdirektor und Mäzen,* edited by Kaiser-Friedrich-Museums-Verein, 23–50. Berlin: Staatliche Museen zu Berlin.

Ozment Steven. *Protestants: The Birth of a Revolution.* New York: Image Books, 1991.

Pagden, Anthony. *European Encounters with the New World.* New Haven: Yale University Press, 1993.

Pallat, Ludwig. *Richard Schöne, Generaldirektor der königlichen Museen zu Berlin: Ein Beitrag zur Geschichte der preußischen Kulturverwaltung.* Berlin: W. de Gruyter, 1952.

Parkinson, Richard. *Dreißig Jahre in der Südsee: Land und Leute, Sitten und Gebräuche im Bismarckarchipel und auf den deutschen Salomoninseln.* Stuttgart: Strecker & Schröder, 1907.

———. *Thirty Years in the South Seas: Land and People, Customs and Traditions in the Bismarck Archipelago and on the German Solomon Islands.* Honolulu: University of Hawai'i Press, 2000.

Pearce, Susan. *On Collecting: An Investigation into Collecting in the European Tradition.* London: Routledge, 1995.

Peattie, Mark. *Nan'yo: The Rise and Fall of the Japanese in Micronesia, 1884–1945.* Honolulu: University of Hawai'i Press, 1988.

Pels, Peter, and Oscar Salemink. "Introduction: Locating Colonial Subjects of Anthropology." In *Colonial Subjects: Essays on the Practical History of Anthropology,* edited by Peter Pels and Oscar Salemink, 1–52. Ann Arbor: University of Michigan Press, 1999.

Penny, H. Glenn. "Bastian's Museum: On the Limits of Empiricism and the Transformation of German Ethnology." In *Worldly Provincialism: German Anthropology in the Age of Empire,* edited by H. Glenn Penny and Matti Bunzl, 86–126. Ann Arbor: University of Michigan Press, 2003.

———. "'Beati possedentes:' Die Aneignung materieller Kultur und die Anschaffungspolitik des Leipziger Völkerkundemuseums." *Comparativ: Leipziger Beiträge zur Universalgeschichte und vergleichender Gesellschaftsforschung* 10 (2000): 68–103.

———. "Fashioning Local Identities in the Age of Nation-Building: Museums, Cosmopolitan Traditions, and Intra-German Competition." *German History* 17 (1999): 488–504.

———. "Municipal Displays: Civic Self-Promotion and the Development of German Ethnographic Museums, 1870–1914." *Social Anthropology* 6 (1998): 157–168.

———. *Objects of Culture: Ethnology and Ethnographic Museums in Imperial Germany.* Chapel Hill: University of North Carolina Press, 2002.

———. "Science and the Marketplace: The Creation and Contentious Sale of the Museum Godeffroy." *Journal of the Pacific Arts Association* 21/22 (2000): 7–22.

Penny, H. Glenn, and Matti Bunzl, eds. *Worldly Provincialism: German Anthropology in the Age of Empire.* Ann Arbor: University of Michigan Press, 2003.

Petersen, Glenn. "Hambruch's Colonial Narrative: Pohnpei, German Cultural Theory, and the Hamburg Expedition Ethnography of 1908–1910." *Journal of Pacific History* 42 (2007): 317–330.

Philbrick, Nathaniel. *Sea of Glory: America's Voyage of Discovery, the U.S. Exploring Expedition, 1838–1842.* New York: Viking, 2003.

Pommeranz, Kenneth. *The Great Divergence.* Princeton: Princeton University Press, 2000.

Prakash, Gyan, ed. *After Colonialism: Imperial Histories and Postcolonial Displacements.* Princeton: Princeton University Press, 1995.

Pratt, Mary Louise. *Imperial Eyes: Travel Writing and Transculturation.* New York: Routledge, 1992.

Price, Sally. *Primitive Art in Civilized Places.* Chicago: University of Chicago Press, 1989.

Proctor, Robert. "From *Anthropologie* to *Rassenkunde* in the German Anthropological Tradition." In *Bones, Bodies, Behavior: Essays on Biological Anthropology,* edited by George Stocking, 138–179. Madison: University of Wisconsin Press, 1988.

Pützstück, Lothar. *"Symphonie in Moll": Julius Lips und die Kölner Völkerkunde.* Pfaffenweiler: Centaurus, 1995.

Quinnell, Michael. "'Before It Has Become Too Late': The Making and Repatriation of Sir

William MacGregor's Official Collection from British New Guinea." In *Hunting the Gatherers: Ethnographic Collectors, Agents and Agency in Melanesia, 1870s–1930s*, edited by Michael O'Hanlon and Robert L. Welsch, 81–102. New York: Berghahn Books, 2000.

Ratzel, Friedrich. *Anthropo-Geographie, oder Grundzüge der Anwendung der Erdkunde auf die Geschichte.* Stuttgart: Engelhorn, 1882.

———. *Völkerkunde.* 3 vols. Leipzig: Bibliographisches Institut, 1885–1888.

Read, C. "Confusion in Geographical Names." *Journal of the Anthropological Institute of Great Britain* n.s. 1 (1899): 330.

Reche, Otto. "Kaiserin Augusta Fluss." In *Ergebnisse der Südsee-Expedition 1908-1910*, II.A, vol. 1, edited by G. Thilenius. Hamburg: Friedrichsen, 1913.

———, "Nova Britannia." In *Ergebnisse der Südsee-Expedition 1908–1910*, II.A, vol. 4, edited by G. Thilenius. Hamburg: Friedrichsen, 1954.

Richardson, Brian. *Longitude and Empire: How Captain Cook's Voyages Changed the World.* Vancouver: University of British Columbia Press, 2005.

Rosaldo, Renato. *Culture and Truth: The Remaking of Social Analysis.* Boston: Beacon Press, 1989.

Roseberry, William. *Anthropologies and Histories: Essays in Culture, History, and Political Economy.* New Brunswick: Rutgers University Press, 1989.

Rusch, Walter. "Der Beitrag Felix von Luschans für die Ethnographie." *Ethnographische und Archäologische Zeitschrift* 27 (1986): 439–453.

Ryan, Tom. "'Le Président des Terres Australes' Charles de Brosses and the French Enlightenment Beginnings of Oceanic Anthropology." *Journal of Pacific History* 37 (2002): 157–186.

Sack, Peter. *Land between Two Laws: Early European Land Acquisition in New Guinea.* Canberra: Australian National University Press, 1973.

Sack, Peter, and Dymphna Clark, eds. *German New Guinea: The Annual Reports.* Canberra: Australian University Press, 1979.

Said, Edward. *Culture and Imperialism.* New York: Vintage, 1994.

———. *Orientalism.* New York: Vintage, 1978.

Sahlins, Marshall. *Anahulu: The Anthropology of History in the Kingdom of Hawaii*, vol. 1: *Historical Ethnography.* Chicago: University of Chicago Press, 1992.

Schauinsland, Hugo H. *Unterwegs in Übersee: Aus den Reisetagebüchern und Dokumenten des früheren Direktors des Bremer Übersee-Museums*, edited by Anne Dünzelmann. Bremen: H. M. Hauschild, 1999.

Schiefel, Werner. *Bernard Dernburg 1865–1937: Kolonialpolitiker und Bankier im wilhelminischen Deutschland.* Zürich: Atlantis, 1981.

Schildkrout, Enid, and Curtis Keim, eds. *The Scramble for Art in Central Africa.* New York: Cambridge University Press, 1998.

Schindlbeck, Markus. "The Art of Collecting: Interactions between Collectors and the People They Visit." *Zeitschrift für Ethnologie* 118 (1993): 57–67.

———. "The Art of Headhunters: Collecting Activity and Recruitment in New Guinea at the Beginning of the Twentieth Century." In *European Impact and Pacific Influence: British and German Policy in the Pacific Islands and the Indigenous Response*, edited by Hermann Hiery and John MacKenzie, 31–43. London: Tauris Academic Studies, 1997.

———. "Deutsche wissenschaftliche Expeditionen und Forschungen in der Südsee bis 1914." In *Die deutsche Südsee 1884–1914: Ein Handbuch*, edited by Hermann Hiery, 132–155. Paderborn: F. Schöningh, 2000.

Schlaginhaufen, Otto. *Muliama: Zwei Jahre unter Südsee-Insulanern*. Zürich: Orell Füssli, 1959.

Schleip, Dietrich. "Ozeanistische Ethnologie und Koloniale Praxis: Das Beispiel Augustin Krämer." M.A. thesis, Tübingen University, 1989.

Schmeltz, J. D. E. "Johann Stanislaus Kubary." *Internationales Archiv für Ethnographie* 10 (1897): 132–136.

———. Review of Otto Finsch's "Ethnographische Belegstücke aus der Südsee." *Internationales Archiv für Ethnographie* 7 (1894): 265–269.

———. "Rudolf Virchow, in Memoriam." *Internationales Archiv für Ethnographie* 16 (1904): vii–xiii.

Schmeltz, J. D. E., and Rudolf Krause. *Die ethnographisch-anthropologische Abteilung des Museum Godeffroy in Hamburg: Ein Beitrag zur Kunde der Südsee-Völker*. Hamburg: Friedrichsen, 1880.

Schnee, Heinrich. *Deutsches Kolonial-Lexikon*. 3 vols. Leipzig: Quelle und Meyer, 1920.

———. *Die koloniale Schuldlüge*. Munich: Buchverlag der Süddeutschen Monatshefte, 1927.

Seed, Particia. *Ceremonies of Possession in Europe's Conquest of the New World, 1492–1640*. Cambridge: Cambridge University Press, 1995.

Seidel, Hans. Review of Luschan's *Beiträge zur Ethnographie der deutschen Schutzgebiete*. *Deutsches Kolonialblatt* 11 (1898): 149–150.

Singer, Hermann. "Kleine Nachrichten," *Globus* 98 (1910): 385.

———. "Das neue deutsche Kolonialprogramm und die Eingeborenenfrage." *Globus* 93 (1908): 203–205.

———. "Reichskolonialamt und Reichsetat für die Schutzgebiete." *Globus* 89 (1906): 16–17.

———. "Die Verwendung des Afrikafonds." *Globus* 97 (1910): 110–111.

Smith, Bernard. *European Vision and the South Pacific*. Oxford: Oxford University Press, 1960.

Smith, John David. "W. E. B. Du Bois, Felix von Luschan and Racial Reform at the *Fin de Siècle*." *Amerikastudien* 47 (2002): 23–38.

Smith, Woodruff. *The German Colonial Empire*. Chapel Hill: University of North Carolina Press, 1978.

———. *Politics and the Sciences of Culture in Germany, 1840–1920*. Oxford: Oxford University Press, 1991.

Smolka, Wolfgang. *Völkerkunde in München: Voraussetzungen, Möglichkeiten und Entwicklungslinien ihrer Insititutionalisierung (ca. 1850–1933)*. Berlin: Dunker & Humblot, 1994.

Sorrensen, Richard. "The Ship as Scientific Instrument in the Eighteenth Century." *Osiris* 11 (1996): 221–236.

Spate, O. H. K. *The Spanish Lake*. Minneapolis: University of Minnesota Press, 1979.

Specht, Jim. "Traders and Collectors: Richard Parkinson and Family in the Bismarck Archipelago, P.N.G." *Journal of the Pacific Arts Association* 21/22 (2000): 23–38.

Spencer, Frank, ed. *History of Physical Anthropology* 2 vols. New York: Garland, 1997.

Spidle, Jake. "The German Colonial Civil Service: Organization, Selection, Training." Ph.D. dissertation, Stanford University, 1972.

Steiner, Christopher. *African Art in Transit*. Cambridge: Cambridge University Press, 1994.

Stephan, Emil. "Beiträge zur Psychologie der Bewohner von Neupommern: Nebst ethnographischen Mitteilungen über die Barriai und über die Insel Hunt (Duror)." *Globus* 88 (1905): 205–210, 216–221.

———. *Südseekunst: Beiträge zur Kunst des Bismarckarchipels und zur Urgeschichte der Kunst überhaupt.* Berlin: Reimer, 1907.

Stephan, Emil, and Fritz Graebner. *Neu Mecklenburg (Bismarck Archipel): Die Küste von Umuddu bis Kap St. Georg: Forschungsergebnisse bei den Vermessungsfahrten von S.M.S. Möwe im Jahre 1904.* Berlin: Reimer, 1907.

Stocking, George. *After Tylor: British Social Anthropology, 1888–1951* Madison: University of Wisconsin Press, 1995.

———, ed. *Colonial Situations: Essays on the Contextualization of Ethnographic Knowledge.* Madison: University of Wisconsin Press, 1993.

———. *Delimiting Anthropology: Occasional Essays and Reflections.* Madison: University of Wisconsin Press, 2001.

———. *The Ethnographer's Magic and Other Essays in the History of Anthropology.* Madison: University of Wisconsin Press, 1995.

———. "Gatekeeper to the Field: E. W. P. Chinnery and Ethnography of the New Guinea Mandate." *History of Anthropology Newsletter* 9 (1982): 3–12.

———. "Maclay, Kubary, Malinowski: Archetypes from a Dreamtime of Anthropology." In *Colonial Situations: Essays on the Contextualization of Ethnographic Knowledge,* edited by George Stocking. Madison: University of Wisconsin Press, 1993.

———. "On the Limits of 'Presentism' and 'Historicism' in the Historiography of the Behavioral Science." *The Journal of the History of Behavioral Science* 1 (1965): 211–218.

———. *Race, Culture, and Evolution: Essays in the History of Anthropology.* New York, 1968.

———. *Victorian Anthropology.* New York: Basic Books, 1987.

———, ed. *Volksgeist as Method and Ethic: Essays on Boasian Ethnography and the German Anthropological Tradition.* Madison: University of Wisconsin Press, 1996.

Strandmann, Pogge von. "The Kolonialrat, Its Significance and Influence on German Politics." Ph.D. dissertation, Oxford University, 1970.

Sturtevant, William. "Does Anthropology Need Museums?" *Proceedings of the Biological Society of Washington* 182 (1969): 619–650.

Tcherkézoff, Serge. "A Long and Unfortunate Voyage towards the 'Invention' of the Melanesia/Polynesia Distinction 1595–1832." *Journal of Pacific History* 38 (2003): 175–196.

Thilenius, Georg. "Die Arbeiterfrage in der Südsee." *Globus* 77 (1900): 69–72.

———. "Bodes Denkschrift über die Museen in Berlin." *Korrespondenz-Blatt der Deutschen Gesellschaft für Anthropologie, Ethnologie und Urgeschichte* 38 (1907): 37–39.

———. "Die Eröffnung des Rautenstrauch-Joest-Museums in Köln." *Korrespondenz-Blatt der Deutschen Gesellschaft für Anthropologie, Ethnologie und Urgeschichte* 37 (1907): 6–10.

———, ed. *Ergebnisse der Südsee-Expedition, 1908–1910.* Hamburg: Friedrichsen, 1927.

———. "Ethnographische Pseudomorphosen in der Südsee." *Globus* 81 (1902): 118–122.

———. *Ethnologische Ergebnisse aus Melanesien.* 2 vols. Halle: E. Karras, 1902–1903.

———. *Das Hamburgische Museum für Völkerkunde.* Berlin: Reimer Verlag, 1916.

———. "Die Hamburger Schiffexpedition." In *Ergebnisse der Südsee-Expedition, 1908–1910,* edited by Georg Thilenius, I, 21–40. Hamburg: Friedrichsen, 1927.

———. "Die Hamburger Südsee-Expedition." *Globus* 93 (1908): 336–337.

Thode-Arora, Hilke. "Die Familie Umlauff und ihre Firmen—Ethnographica-Händler in Hamburg." *Mitteilungen aus dem Museum für Völkerkunde Hamburg* n.f. 22 (1992): 143–158.

Thomas, Nicholas. *Colonialism's Culture: Anthropology, Travel, and Government.* Princeton: Princeton University Press, 1994.

————. *Cook: The Extraordinary Voyages of Captain James Cook.* New York: Walker & Co., 2003.

————. *Entangled Objects: Exchange, Material Culture, and Colonialism in the Pacific.* Cambridge: Harvard University Press, 1991

————. "The Force of Ethnology: Origins and Significance of the Melanesia/Polynesia Divide." *Current Anthropology* 30 (1989): 27–34.

————. *In Oceania: Visions, Artifacts, Histories.* Durham: Duke University Press, 1997.

————. "Licensed Curiosity: Cook's Pacific Voyages." In *The Cultures of Collecting*, edited by John Elsner and Roger Cardinal, 116–136. Cambridge, MA: Harvard University Press, 1994.

————. "Material Culture and Colonial Power: Ethnographic Collecting and the Establishment of Colonial Rule in Fiji." *Man* 24 (1989): 41–56.

————. *Oceanic Art.* London: Thames & Hudson, 1995.

————. *Out of Time: History and Evolution in Anthropological Discourse.* New York: Cambridge University Press, 1989.

Thomas, Nicholas, and Diane Losche, eds. *Double Vision: Re-Imagining Art and Colonialism in the Pacific.* New York: Cambridge University Press, 1999.

Thomas, Northcote. "Review of Luschan's *Anleitung für ethnographische Beobachtungen und Sammlungen in Africa und Ozeanien.*" *Man* 5 (1905): 47–48.

Thompson, Alastair. "Honours Uneven: Decorations, the State and Bourgeois Society in Imperial Germany." *Past and Present* 144 (1994): 171–204.

Thurnwald, Richard. "Die eingeborenen Arbeitskräfte im Südseeschutzgebiet." *Koloniale Rundschau* 10 (1910): 607–632.

————. "Im Bismarckarchipel und auf den Salomoneninseln, 1906–1909." *Zeitschrift für Ethnologie* 42 (1910): 98–147.

————. "Das Rechtsleben der Eingeborenen der deutschen Südseeinseln, seine geistigen und wirtschaftlichen Grundlagen: Auf Grund einer im Auftrag des Berliner Museums für Völkerkunde unternommenen Forschungsreise 1906–1909." *Blätter für vergleichende Rechtswissenschaft und Volkswirtschaftslehre* 6 (1910): 3–46.

Urry, James. "Making Sense of Diversity and Complexity: The Ethnological Context and Consequences of the Torres Strait Expedition and the Oceanic Phase in British Anthropology, 1890–1935." In *Cambridge and the Torres Strait: Centenary Essays on the 1898 Anthropological Expedition*, edited by Anita Herle and Sandra Rouse, 201–233. New York: Cambridge University Press, 1998.

————. "Notes and Queries on Anthropology and the Development of Field Methods in British Anthropology 1870–1920." *Proceedings of the Royal Anthropological Institute for 1972*, 45–57.

Virchow, Rudolf. "Caesar Godeffroy." *Zeitschrift für Ethnographie* 17 (1885): 53–54.

Völkerkunde Museum. "Die Entwicklung des Museums für Völkerkunde 1901 bis 1905." *Jahrbuch des Städtischen Museums für Völkerkunde* 1 (1907).

Wehler, Hans-Ulrich. *Bismarck und der Imperialismus.* Cologne: Kiepenheuer & Witsch, 1969.

Welsch, Robert, ed. *An American Anthropologists in Melanesia: A. B. Lewis and the Joseph N. Field South Pacific Expedition 1909–1913.* 2 vols. Honolulu: University of Hawai'i Press, 1998.

————. "One Time, One Place, Three Collections: Colonial Processes and the Shaping of Some Museum Collections from German New Guinea." In *Hunting the Gatherers: Ethnographic Collectors, Agents and Agency in Melanesia, 1870s–1930s*, edited by Michael O'Hanlon and Robert L. Welsch, 155–179. London: Berghahn Books, 2000.

West, Francis, ed. *Selected Letters of Hubert Murray.* Oxford: Oxford University Press, 1970.

Westphal-Hellbusch, Sigrid. "Hundert Jahre Museum für Völkerkunde Berlin: Zur Geschichte des Museums." *Baessler Archiv* 21 (1973): 1–99.

Weule, Karl. "Die nächsten Aufgaben und Ziele des Leipziger Völkermuseums." *Jahrbuch des Städtischen Museums für Völkerkunde zu Leipzig* 3 (1910): 151–174.

———. "Die praktischen Aufgaben der Völkermuseen auf Grund Leipziger Erfahrungen." *Korrespondenzblatt Archiv für Anthropologie* 41 (1910): 70–78.

———. "Der Stand der ethnographischen Forschung in unseren Kolonien." In *Verhandlungen des Deutschen Kolonialkongresses 1905 zu Berlin am 5. 6. und 7. Oktober 1905*, 17–30. Berlin: Reimer, 1906.

White, Richard. *The Middle Ground: Indians, Empires, and the Republics in the Great Lakes Region, 1650–1815.* New York: Cambridge University Press, 1991.

Winkler, Wilhelm. "Eine Reise nach den Inseln Sonsorol, Pur, Melier, und Tobi." *Amtsblatt für das Schutzgebiet Deutsch Neuguineas* 6 (1914): 68–69.

Wolf, Eric. *Europe and the People without History.* Berkeley: University of California Press, 1982.

Young, Michael W. "The Careless Collector: Malinowski and the Antiquarians." In *Hunting the Gatherers: Ethnographic Collectors, Agents, and Agency in Melanesia, 1870s–1930s*, edited by Michael O' Hanlon and Robert Welsch, 181–202. New York: Berghahn Books, 2000.

Zantop, Susanne. *Colonial Fantasies: Conquest, Family, and Nation in Precolonial Germany, 1770–1870.* Durham: Duke University Press, 1997.

Zimmerman, Andrew. *Anthropology and Antihumanism in Imperial Germany.* Chicago: University of Chicago Press, 2001.

———. "Selin, Pore, and Emil Stephan in the Bismarck Archipelago: A 'Fresh and Joyful Tale' of the Origin of Fieldwork." *Journal of the Pacific Arts Association* 21/22 (2000): 69–84.

Zwernemann, Jürgen. *Hundert Jahre Hamburgisches Museum für Völkerkunde.* Hamburg: Museum für Völkerkunde, 1980.

Index

Africa, 8–9, 10, 12, 23, 24, 48, 65, 72, 86, 97, 101, 138, 139, 140, 141, 142, 156, 165
Africa fund, 75
African and Oceanic Division of the Berlin Ethological Museum, 9–10, 24, 26, 29, 50–51, 57, 65, 69–70, 86, 91
American Board of Commissioners for Foreign Missions, 152
American Exploration Expedition, 167
Andersen, A. F. V., 43
Angaur, 148, 150
Ankermann, Bernard, 60, 91
Anthropology: comparative, 154–170; and economics, 107; and ethnology, 141; and genealogical method, 155; history of, 1–4; legal issues and, 103, 106–108; and missionaries, 45–46, 80–81, 142, 154, 166; multiple contextualization of, 2; museums and, 119; and Native Americans, 161–162; Oceanic constructions of, 121–122; and prisoner of war research, 138; and traders, 29–49, 81, 166–167; Western Constructions of, 120
Aristotle, 16
Artifacts (indigenous), 10–11, 29–32; annexation of, 138–139; and authenticity, 19, 120, 131–132, 171n. 20; collecting of, 68–70, 79–80, 184n. 3; collection histories, 119; as commodities, 30–32; as curiosities, 30–32; distribution among German museums, 91–96; as "ethnographica," 30–32; as hybrids, 128; as national property, 93–95; price increase of, 110, 133; Primary Collecting, 68–70, 71, 80, 82–84, 85, 110; Secondary Collecting, 69, 85

Atlantic Ocean, 4, 5, 165
Aua (Durour), 41–47, 58, 59, 99, 122–126, 135, 143–144
Australia, 158–159, 169; Act of Confederation, 158
Australian Aborigines, 155

Baessler, Arthur, 52, 69–70
Barriai, 81, 84
Bastian, Adolf, 9–10, 12, 16–25, 28, 32, 42, 50, 53, 56, 58, 59–60, 63, 86, 141, 146, 157, 162, 167, 176nn. 16, 18
Beit, Alfred, 76, 80
Belgian Congo, 138–139
Benin, 51, 184n. 1
Benningsen, Rudolf von, 54, 99
Bentley, Jerry H., 1
Bismarck, Otto von, 23–24, 72
Bismarck Archipelago, 8, 39, 41, 46, 75–76, 82, 86, 99, 105, 122, 136
Bligh, William, 119
Boas, Franz, 161, 169, 204n. 26
Bode, Wilhelm, 59, 65–66, 80, 90–91, 93
Boluminski, Franz, 54, 101–102, 127, 132–135, 186n. 18
Born, Ludwig, 149
Bosnia-Herzegovina, 106
Bougainville, 88, 106
Boundaries, 5, 8, 43, 79, 165–166
Brosses, Charles de, 165–166
Brown, George, 166
Buchner, Max, 40, 176n. 16, 182n. 52
Buck, Peter (Te Rangi Hiroa), 160
Bühlow, Bernard von, 73
Bukans, 43–44
Bureau of American Anthropology, 161–162

Munich, 14, 85, 93; Oxford (Pitt-Rivers), 61; Stuttgart, 10, 53–57, 64, 66, 69, 80, 93, 94, 100, 132, 137–138, 146, 196n. 8; Terveuren, 138–139; Umlauff, 32, 38, 88; Vienna, 66, 79; Washington (Smithsonian), 79, 167
Evolutionism, 2, 18, 120–121; critique of, 61
Expedition Age, 189n. 1
Extensive studies, 3, 17, 69, 80, 84, 92, 145

Federal Council's Resolution of 1889, 25, 50–51, 53, 63, 64, 67–68, 78, 85, 162
Fieldwork, 1, 3, 45–46, 81, 104–105, 110, 113–117, 156, 159–160, 168–169
Fiji, 33, 89, 121, 156–157
Finsch, Otto, 35–36, 37, 196n. 27
Firth, Raymond, 156, 168, 208n. 56
Firth, Stewart, 8–9
Folk ideas, 18–19, 21–22; critique of, 62
Forster, Georg, 31–32
Foucault, Michel, 30–31
Foy, Willi, 58, 63, 68
France, 8, 11, 21, 139, 142, 147, 164, 167
Friederici, Georg, 76, 111
Friedrich Wilhelm. See Wilhelm I
Frontiers, 5–6; and borderlands, 5; Jackson Turner and, 5
Fülleborn, Friedrich, 79

Geographical Commission, 74–76, 91, 93–96; expedition to German New Guinea, 75–76, 108, 111–112
German Colonial Council, 65, 74
German Colonial Division, 24–26, 63, 73
German Colonial Exhibition, 37–38
German Colonial Office, 73–74, 84–86, 90, 91, 94, 99, 101
German colonialism, 8–9; restructuring of, 72–74
German East Africa, 63, 74, 75, 140; Maji-Maji uprising in, 72
German Foreign Office, 16, 24, 25, 73
German Imperial Navy, 16, 21–23, 24, 67–68, 81, 83–84, 115, 192n. 47
German Nationalisms, 185n. 16
German Naval Expedition, 83–84, 102–103, 106, 107, 110–113, 114–116, 128, 145, 192n. 57

German Naval League, 81
German South Sea Expedition, 47–49; as inspiration for the Hamburg South Sea Expedition, 76–77
German Southwest Africa, 72, 74, 91, 99; Herero uprising in, 72
Gordon, Arthur Hamilton, 156
Graebner, Fritz, 60–63, 82, 110
Great Britain, 3, 8, 11, 21, 39, 51, 99, 107–108, 137, 139, 142, 147, 148–149, 150, 163–164; Oceanic phase of British anthropology, 154–160
Greek Mythology, 21
Greenblatt, Stephen, 30
Gregory, Herbert, 160
Guam, 8, 99, 161–162

Haddon, Alfred, 154, 155
Hahl, Albert, 10–11, 37, 54, 67, 78, 88, 90, 95, 97, 99–113, 116–117, 133, 155, 158, 159, 160–161, 168–169, 196n. 8, 199n. 80
Hambruch, Paul, 119, 130, 140, 143–144, 146, 150, 151–152
Hamburg Scientific Foundation, 76–79, 114, 146
Hamburg South Sea Expedition, 76–80, 81, 108, 109–110, 112, 113–114, 119, 133, 140, 150, 155, 160, 168, 199n. 78; monographs of, 144–153, 163
Hanlon, David, 118–121
Hansemann, Adolf von, 35–36, 37
Harrison, John, 164
Hau'ofa, Epeli, 170
Hawai'i, 20–21, 29, 47, 152, 160
Heferle, Franz, 186n. 18
Hellwig, Franz, 41, 45–47, 58, 59, 125
Helms, Mary, 29
Hiery, Hermann, 9, 150–151
Hocart, A. M., 156
"Hottentot" elections, 73
Humboldt, Alexander von, 59

Imperial Bureau of Ethnology, 157
Imperialist nostalgia, 6, 20
Indian Ocean, 4, 5
Intensive research, 80, 83–84, 97, 156, 159–160

pacification of, 127–128, 132, 134; head tax in, 127, 132–133

Niguria, 143

Ninigo, 42, 125, 143, 183n. 61

Nissan Island, 129–130

Norddeutscher Lloyd, 55, 67, 106, 129, 133, 198n. 57

Nugulu, 149

Nukumano, 143

O'Hanlon, Michael, 69

Orders. *See* Decorations

Pacific Northwest, 161

Pacific Ocean, 3–9; ethnographic frontier in, 19–21, 163–170

Palau, 99, 147, 148, 149, 150

Papua, 156–157, 158–160

Papuan Languages, 154–155

Para-Micronesia, 41–47, 59, 99, 122–126, 135, 143–144, 155, 168, 183n. 61

Parkinson, Richard, 36, 43, 55, 123, 125, 181n. 35, 194n. 78; critique of, 113, 196n. 27

Participant observation. *See* Fieldwork

Particularizing anthropology (localism), 1–2

Penny, Glenn, 6

Peoples of culture, 18

Peoples of nature, 18–19; critique of concept, 81–82

Percy Sladen Trust, 155–156

Philippines, 89, 162, 164; ethological survey of, 162

Pidgin English, 107, 109, 110, 198n. 50

Pita, 150

Pohnpei, 54, 119, 147; ethnography of, 103; uprising on, 151–152

Polynesia, 5, 8, 20–21, 42, 47, 65, 79, 121, 135, 143, 165–166; outliers of, 143–144, 168

Population decline, 105–106, 108, 109, 111–112, 124–125; and postcolonial studies, 143–144

Postcolonial studies, 7, 11; and German colonies, 139

Postmodern, 128

Powell, John Wesley, 161

Pratt, Mary Louise, 6, 31

Race, 120, 165–166, 179n. 53

Radcliffe-Brown, Alfred Reginald, 159, 169

Ratzel, Friedrich, 59–60

Ray, Sydney, 154–155

Reche, Otto, 92–93, 146

Reimers, Otto, 125

Rhodes, Cecil, 76

Rivers, W. H. R., 154, 155

Rome, 6

Roosevelt, Franklin D., 162

Rosaldo, Renato, 6, 20

Rugeiren, 147

Russo-Japanese War, 48

Sae, 183n. 61

Salvage anthropology, 6, 19–21, 53, 83; colonialism and, 104; commercial possibilities of, 30–32; and indigenous appropriation of western artifacts, 120; national agenda and, 83–84, 91; Post-colonialism and, 153

Samoa, 9, 21, 48, 72, 99, 105, 121

Sapper, Karl, 75–76, 111

Sarfert, Ernst, 140–142, 197n. 36

Schlaginhaufen, Otto, 113, 115, 192n. 57, 199n. 80

Schmeltz, Johann Dietrich Eduard, 33–35

Schnee, Heinrich, 78, 140, 152, 196n. 12

Schöne, Richard, 13–14, 175n. 3

Scientific collection, 27, 66

Scientific publications, 33, 34–35, 36, 44–45, 52, 57–59, 62, 63, 75, 78, 79, 82–83, 110, 114–116, 144–153, 159, 164

Seligman, Charles, 154, 155, 156, 158

Senfft, Arno, 55

Sepik River (Kaiserin Augusta Fluss), 86–88, 91, 94, 96, 99; expedition to, 91–93, 108, 113, 138, 146, 193n. 75

Ships: *Bounty*, 119; *Delphin*, 148; *Gazelle*, 21–22, 167; *Germania*, 133; *Hyäne*, 22; *Möwe*, 44, 67–68, 81, 84, 123, 192n. 59; *Peiho*, 147–150, 191n. 28; *Planet*, 84, 192n. 59; *Seestern*, 106; *Siar*, 89; *Sumatra*, 55; *Welcome*, 43; *Ysabel*, 41

Singapore, 89

Singer, Hermann, 111

Smith, Bernard, 30

About the Author

RAINER F. BUSCHMANN is an associate professor of history and founding faculty member at the California State University Channel Islands, where he was instrumental in the establishment of the world history component of the history major. He is the author of a recently published textbook, *Oceans in World History* (2006).

Production Notes for Buschmann | *Anthropology's Global Histories*

Jacket design by Julie Matsuo-Chun, based on the series design by April Leidig-Higgins

Text design by Elsa Carl of Clarence Lee Design, in Adobe Caslon with display type in Tiepolo

Text composition by Santos Barbasa Jr.

Printing and binding by The Maple-Vail Book Manufacturing Group

Printed on 60 lb. Text White Opaque, 426 ppi.